HIGH-PERFORMANCE Cams & Valvetrains

Theory, Technology, and Selection

Billy Godbold

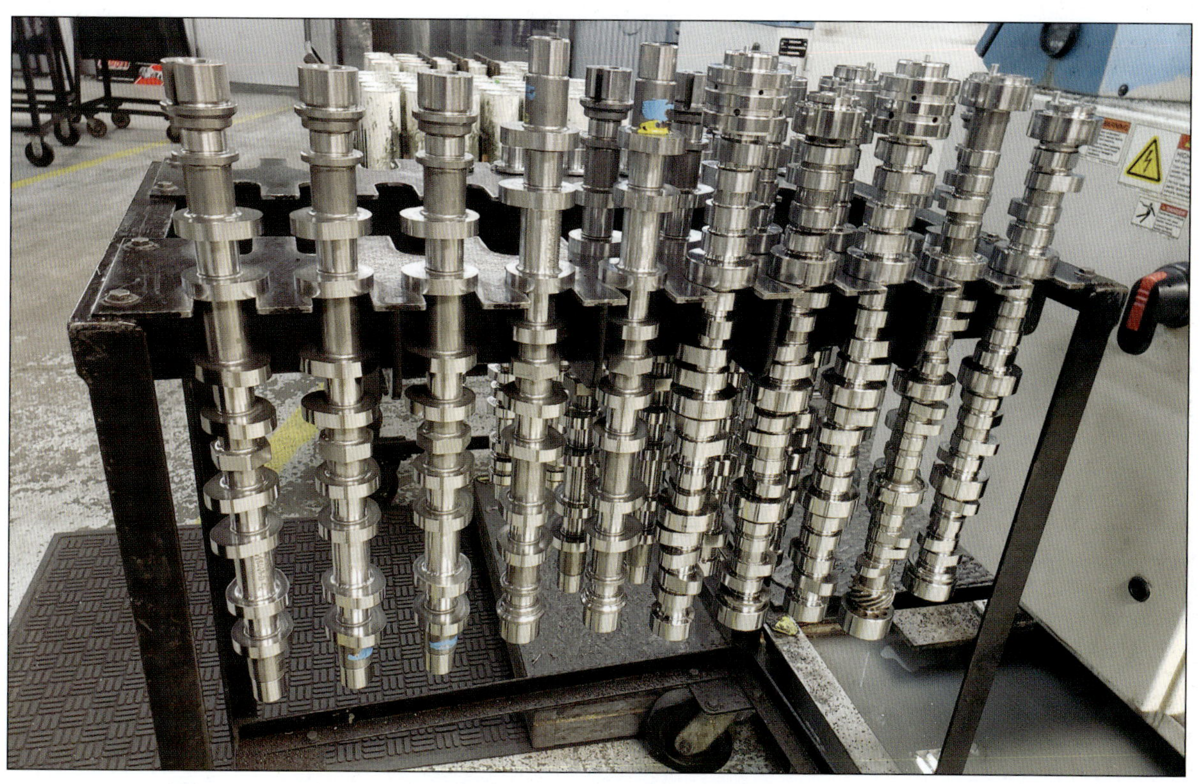

CarTech®

CarTech®

CarTech®, Inc.
6118 Main Street
North Branch, MN 55056
Phone: 651-277-1200 or 800-551-4754
Fax: 651-277-1203
www.cartechbooks.com

Edit by Wes Eisenschenk
Layout by Monica Seiberlich

ISBN 978-1-61325-754-8
Item No. SA533

Library of Congress Cataloging-in-Publication Data Available

Written, edited, and designed in the U.S.A.
Printed in China
10 9 8 7 6 5 4 3 2

All photos are courtesy of Billy Godbold unless otherwise noted.

DISTRIBUTION BY:

Europe
PGUK
63 Hatton Garden
London EC1N 8LE, England
Phone: 020 7061 1980 • Fax: 020 7242 3725
www.pguk.co.uk

Australia
Renniks Publications Ltd.
3/37-39 Green Street
Banksmeadow, NSW 2109, Australia
Phone: 2 9695 7055 • Fax: 2 9695 7355
www.renniks.com

Canada
Login Canada
300 Saulteaux Crescent
Winnipeg, MB, R3J 3T2 Canada
Phone: 800 665 1148 • Fax: 800 665 0103
www.lb.ca

CONTENTS

CHAPTER 1

THE LANGUAGE OF CAMSHAFTS

Have you ever been in a place were almost no one spoke your language? I had that opportunity several times, and when expected, there is an enjoyable challenge to the experience.

I grew up around engines and machinery on a family farm in rural Mississippi and worked in a machine shop over the summer while attending college. I accepted a job at Competition Cams right out of graduate school in January 1995. I loved engines and had been reading *Hot Rod* for as long as I could remember, taken the core engineering classes, and built a small-block Chevy and swapped it into a Jeep CJ7. With my background, I probably walked in thinking, "This is going to be easy." I was in for a wonderful surprise.

In the camshaft industry, there is a common language that is used without any thought about how well someone outside might understand. Most people have seen or heard these terms a few times, so they politely nod and everything continues. Unfortunately, this can lead to a minimal transfer of information. It would be like me listening to someone speaking in a language I did not understand. I might catch a few words but wouldn't grasp the main point of what was communicated. That was my experience for several months after I started training for my new job on the tech line at Competition Cams.

Image 1-1: You can fill a small binder with all the prints, tables, specifications, inspection reports, and other information about a single camshaft. Even with all that in hand, much of the jargon used might be confusing. The beginning of this book dives into the language of performance camshafts.

As I wrote this book, it became clear that I was also guilty of what had unintentionally been done to me. It is far easier to speak about performance camshafts in jargon and acronyms that are well understood by the few people who deal with camshafts every day. However, these terms are not taught in school or through the normal course of

Image 1-2: I saved my own money to purchase camshafts much like these three. My goal in this chapter is to help you understand camshaft terms so that you can make better decisions when selecting the best camshaft for your engine. I was fortunate to make a few good decisions for my own cars over the years—but not without some great assistance.

Reader's Tip

Acronyms in this book are spelled out on first reference. However, subsequent references use only the acronym. Due to the large number of acronyms in this book, it's easy to forget what each acronym stands for. The glossary in the back of this book serves as a quick reference to help you find what they mean.

learning how to build performance engines. While the engine I built for my Jeep had a 268 high-energy camshaft, I simply trusted the person who told me it was the best choice for my application.

What is a Camshaft?

The engineering definition of a camshaft is any device that converts rotational motion into translational motion. Cams are used in

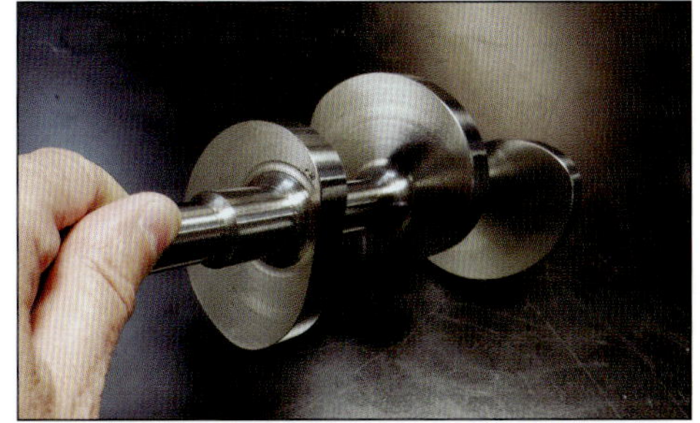

Image 1-3: Occasionally, I get to use what I have learned in racing to help the larger world. Using the same design techniques used in 10,000-plus-rpm valvetrain systems to make a smoother and longer-lasting oxygen pump for US fighter aircraft was a really cool application of our unique resources.

Image 1-4: Camshafts don't have to be large or move valves in four-stroke internal-combustion engines to be a "real" cam. However, for the remainder of the book, I will try to keep the discussion to performance engines and racing.

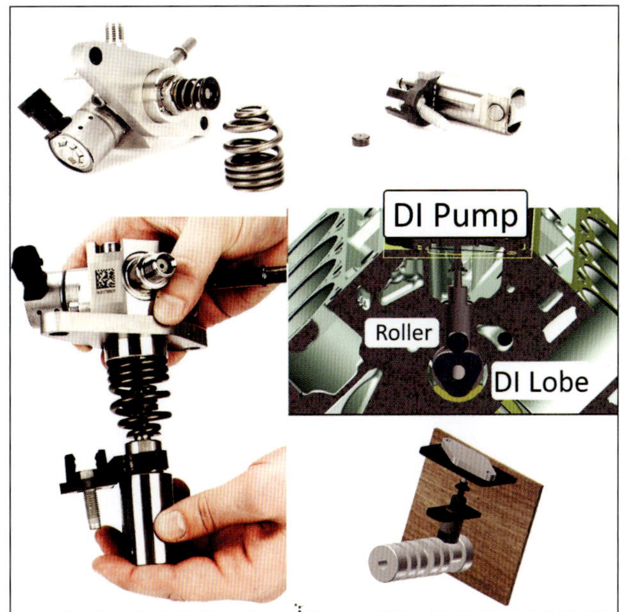

Image 1-6: This image shows the layout and components regarding how the direct-injection pump fits on the back of a GM LT-1 engine. The spring acts just like a valve spring, so careful profile development here can limit engine speed just as much as it can on the other 16 cam lobes of this engine.

Image 1-5: This direct-injection pump tri-lobe is closer to what is found throughout the rest of the book than the compressor pump lobes, but it may not be quite what you might have in mind. Increasing the stroke of the direct-injection pump while also increasing the dynamic stability at high RPM has given Comp a huge advantage in direct-injection racing applications.

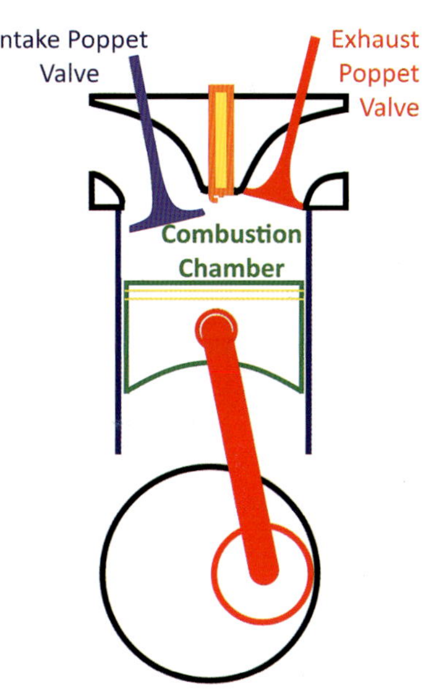

Image 1-7: There are a few options regarding engine valves. Poppet valves are dominant over rotary valves and other options because they can open to the high-flow position quickly and seal the chamber effectively. They can do so while requiring minimal intrusion into the combustion chamber. If they did not spend so much time fighting with the piston for real estate in the chamber, they might be considered perfect for internal-combustion engines.

everything from rifle scopes to most machines from the industrial revolution. We had the opportunity to use our high-speed race-engine development tools to improve the cam lobes for the oxygen generator pumps of a fighter aircraft.

These same design techniques are quite useful for direct-injection fuel-pump lobes as well. However, for the scope of this book, I am focused on camshafts for performance and racing, thus, dealing with the camshafts that move the valves of a four-stroke engine.

Camshafts open and close poppet valves to allow airflow out of and into a combustion chamber. Then, the valves seal for optimum combustion and power. What first shocked me as I learned about cam design was how few of the modern techniques involve designing the physical camshaft. If you went back to the 1920s, engine designers designed a camshaft lobe geometrically. The standard profiles were initially drawn by hand as a circle for the nose, a circle for the base circle, and two arcs that linked the two (as shown in Image 1-8).

These three-arc designs were improved by moving from the profile to a tappet motion-centric design approach. Each of the black tangent lines in Image 1-9 represent the flat-tappet face position at every 10 degrees from the nose. In this graphical format, the lobe is static and rotates the tappet bore and engine around the camshaft. This relative motion is a common way to develop the cam surface today and is generally known as the theory of envelopes.

We made Image 1-11 more than a decade ago as a tool to help customers think about camshaft terms, and we never knew it would become such a popular internet meme. It is certainly worth studying. However, when designing camshafts, the lobes surfaces are the final piece to the puzzle but not our focus. This is rather unique to camshafts. When engineers design a connecting rod, they start by drawing a rod shape. When one starts designing a cylinder head, they typically start with a port shape or valve and chamber. Even when designing a crankshaft, the designer

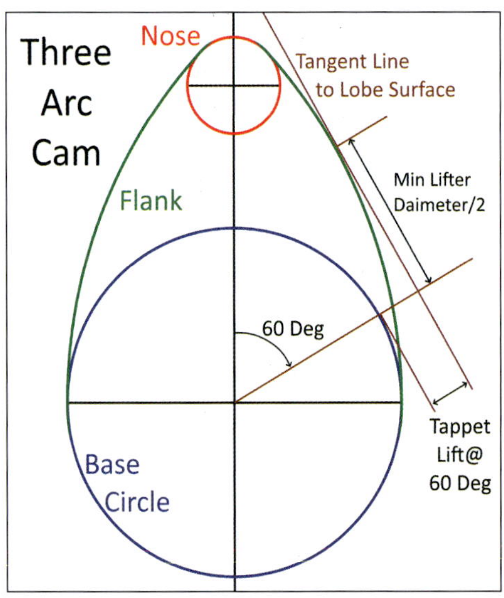

Image 1-8: The first engine cam designs were constructed from three tangent circles. The blue arc is the base circle. The green arc (mirrored on the closing) is called the flank arc. The red arc is the nose. These were typically constructed as a model lobe on a bench grinder that was polished and used to create a master. The brown line tangent to the flank is both the lifter face at 60 degrees and the model grinder setting when this was created.

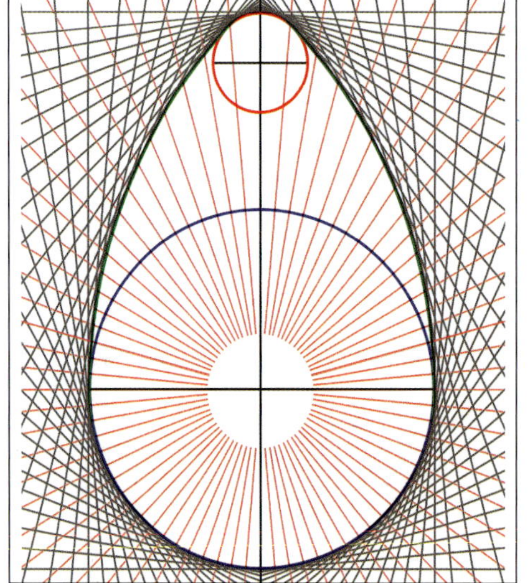

Image 1-9: More detail is shown regarding how that lobe was created. In this view, the lobe is stationary and the tappet rotated around the camshaft. Each gray line represents both the tappet face and the model grinder tool path. That 1:1 relationship between tappet lift and model grinder setting certainly helped the early cam designers. With modern valvetrain systems, these designers would need a lifetime spent without computers to hand-calculate all the conversions.

Image 1-10: If you want to know about the math of valve-to-lobe motion conversions and the theory of envelopes, all of these books are good references. Cam Design Handbook *by Harold Rothbart one is probably my favorite. While the math is fascinating, I doubt it can help anyone choose the right cam for racing.*

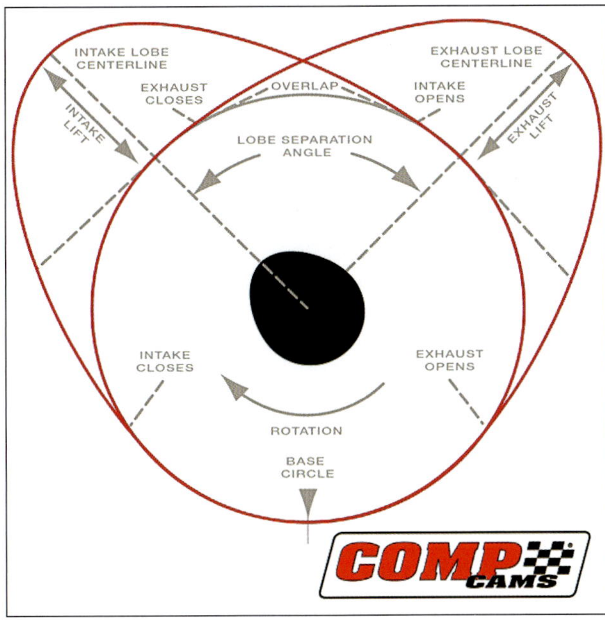

Image 1-11: I made this graphic with the marketing department for our NHRA trailer with the idea that it could help customers with questions at an event. In the middle, the black shape is a section of a camshaft. This helps, but it shows the endpoint of a cam design and not where we start.

starts with the throws and mains and then starts adding and shaping the counterweights.

Unlike these other parts, when I start designing a camshaft, I always start with the motion of the valve that I am trying to control. I probably look at plots like Image 1-12 20 or more times every day and typically place one camshaft valve motion over another to think about how one might perform better than the other in a given application. We will begin by defining the acronyms and terms on this plot and build upon that foundation.

Basic Terms

There are words that I have used hundreds of times, thinking that I understood them well. Then, I wound up embarrassed when I tried to write a strict definition. This is not just a struggle for our day, but C.S. Lewis wrote a wonderful essay titled "The Death of Words" (published in *The Spectator* on September 22, 1944) that points out how any word is only useful when everyone understands its exclusive meaning. When I describe how long a camshaft lobe keeps a valve open, I often specify its duration at a given tappet lift to give far more information than saying something general like, "It is pretty big," "3/4 race," or "Stage 2."

Slogging through definitions may be a bit burdensome, but a few are rather tricky (lobe separation). Even the simple ones (lift) need qualifiers added (tappet or valve). Going through these terms in detail will increase understanding and hopefully provide useful perspective.

Tappet or Follower

Every cam lobe has a follower (lifter or tappet) that rides along the

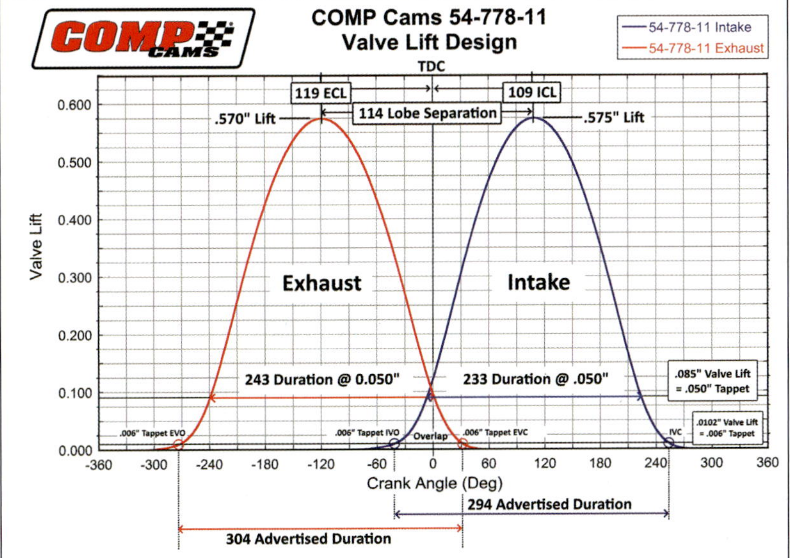

Image 1-12: This format is more useful for looking at a cam design than the lobe surface. We always start with the valve motion desired and work our way backward through the valvetrain to the lobe profile. Sometimes, the system limits what you can do, so the lobe limits can force you to change your design ideas. This was common with 0.842-inch flat-tappet lifters and small journals, but most newer engines have very few design limits.

Image 1-13: Several 0.842-inch flat-lifter designs are shown. All have a 50- to 60-inch-radius face (not flat). Most have very small edge chamfers, and the three on the left have diamond-like carbon (DLC)-coated faces. The third lifter from the right has a chilled iron foot insert. When we design a camshaft, we often move quickly from the valve motion to designing how we want this lifter to move up and down the lifter bore relative to the resting position on the base circle.

Image 1-14: Roller lifters (followers or tappets) have a number of advantages over flat-tappet lifters, especially when trying to maximize lift and area. These are Comp Cams Sportsman solid-roller lifters for a big-block Chevy. Just like designing for a flat tappet, we design the lifter motion and not the lobe shape. With a roller, we don't have to worry about going off the edge, but the flank region can become too concave (inverted) to grind.

Image 1-16: The wrong approach is to take an earlier design, maybe something from the 1980s that was developed for a small-block Chevy (1.868-inch journal), and grind that same lobe surface just 0.200 inch larger on either this 2.165 LS or even larger for the 2.244-inch Hemi journal sizes. Doing so greatly increases the valve quickness and will most likely result in failure. Some companies may try this approach, but it is the wrong method.

surface to convert the cam rotation into valve translation. Most people are familiar with flat and roller tappets. Instead of designing around a lobe shape, the actual design is either focused on valve motion (best) or tappet motion, especially in applications that might run any of several various rocker-arm geometries. The lobe shape is simply what is required to achieve that motion.

Tappet Lift and Valve Lift

Lift should be easy, right? Tappet lift is defined as the rise of the tappet (follower or lifter) from its position on the camshaft base circle.

Likewise, valve lift is defined as the distance the valve moves from its resting position on the seat. Maximum lift for any profile will be the highest tappet rise above the base circle achieved at any crank angle.

TDC

Top dead center (TDC) is the crank angle where the piston stops rising in the bore, changes directions, and begins to drop. The piston stops

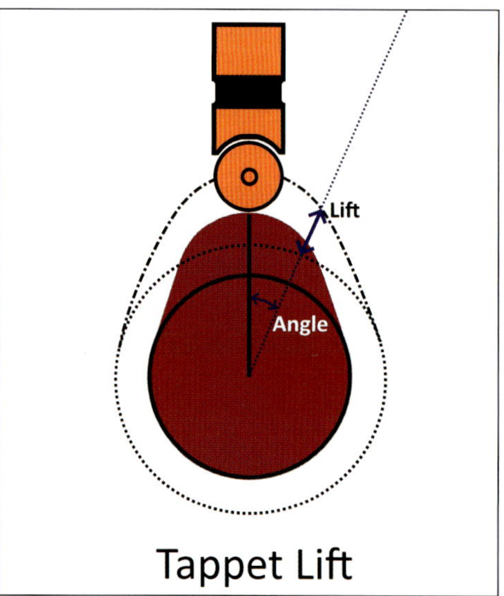

Image 1-17: When we talk about tappet lift, think about the dotted path of the center of the wheel axle around the lobe surface. That is not the same as the wheel radius plus the lobe surface, as the wheel contacts the lobe farther out as velocity increases to create a different path.

Image 1-15: This shows the valve back though the rocker and pushrod to the lifter and camshaft for a modern LS solid-roller design. Thinking about this as a system is the preferred way to design any camshaft. Note that we are designing how we want the valve to move and convert it back through this system to the required profile.

Image 1-18: Moving from tappet lift to valve lift, it is easiest to put a dial indicator on the retainer. This shows the dial indicator lined up parallel to the valve to measure valve lift accurately. (Photo Courtesy Jeff Smith)

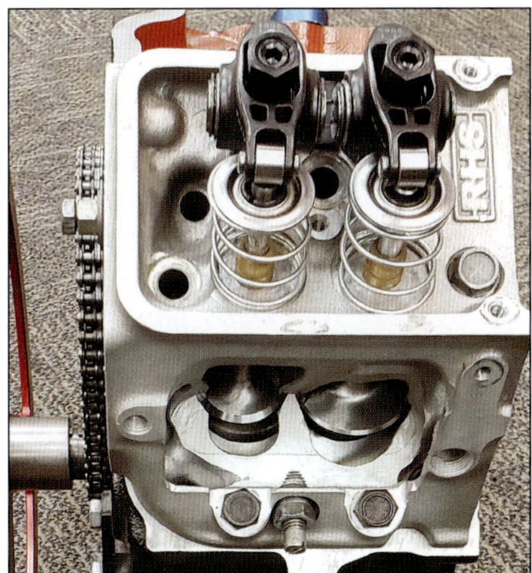

Image 1-19: Chris Brown, the manager who initially hired me into the Comp Cams tech office, made this small-block Chevy inspection stand so that we could practice degreeing camshafts and watch the valves with a dial indicator and see how it opens the ports as they move. It is helpful to have a sectioned engine like this to play with when thinking about camshafts and engines.

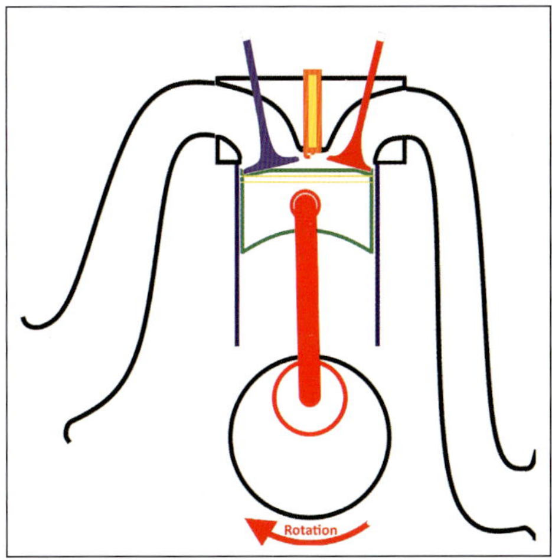

Image 1-20: At TDC, the crank throw and rod line up with the cylinder bore to force the piston to the top of the stroke. At TDC overlap, both valves are open and snuggled very close to the piston. About 330 degrees later, the spark plug ignites and combustion begins as the piston approaches TDC firing.

Image 1-21: Even with the drastically different valve angles of the Gen III Hemi, the engineers at Dodge did a great job setting up the rocker system for rather straight pushrod angles with a single lifter bore angle on each cylinder bank. Keeping pushrods straight while reducing machine setup is very important on production engines.

at the top twice every four strokes: once near the plug-firing event that begins combustion and a second time as the exhaust valve is closing and the intake valve is opening between the exhaust and intake strokes. We will discuss finding top dead center (TDC) in detail in Chapter 2.

ICL

The intake centerline (ICL) is the angle in crank degrees from the piston reaching TDC (overlap) to the intake valve reaching maximum lift. Looking back at Image 1-12, the intake reaches peak lift 109 crank degrees after TDC, hence a 109 ICL or intake centerline. The engine's performance and intake valve to piston clearance are highly dependent on the intake centerline.

ECL

The exhaust centerline (ECL) is the angle in crank degrees from the exhaust valve reaching peak lift and the piston reaching TDC. Again, in Image 1-12, the exhaust reaches peak lift 119 crank degrees before TDC, hence a 119 ECL or exhaust centerline. As with the ICL, this ECL is very important to performance and the exhaust valve-to-piston clearance.

Lobe Separation

The term "lobe separation" traces itself back to a time when all intake and exhaust lifters for each bank were always in a line. This is the arrangement on the flathead Ford, small-block Chevy, and continues in most production V-8 engines, including the GM LS, LT, Ford Godzilla, and Chrysler Hemi.

While inline lifter bores are the most common arrangement, applications like the big-block Chevy, as well as most NASCAR and NHRA Pro Stock engines, have the exhaust lifters rotated out to a different angle than the intake for straighter pushrod angles. Pushrods are very stiff in pure compression but not in bending, so you want a very straight load path. Hence, on applications like Dan Jesel's Equal 8, where every possible advantage has been investigated, the exhaust lifter bores are rotated considerably compared to the intakes.

Looking at Image 1-23, if the physical angle between the intake

Image 1-22: The GM LS is built around a single lifter-bore angle, but it is much easier with an inline-valve Wedge head. The LS angle is 45 degrees from vertical, which makes the camshaft math really easy.

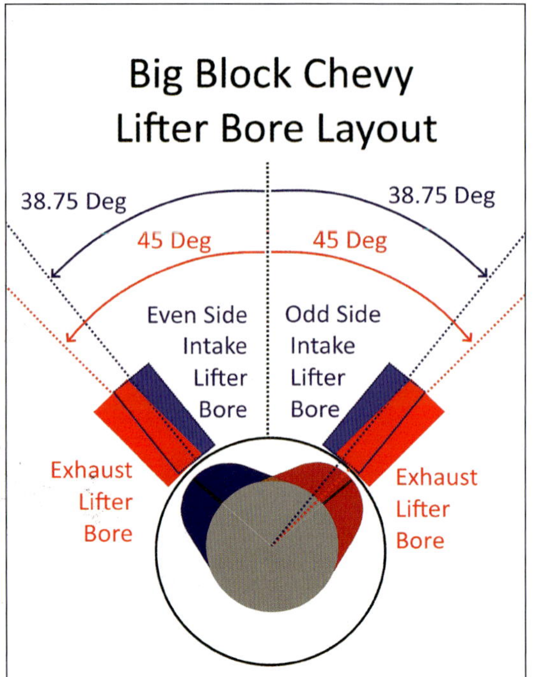

Image 1-23: The big-block Chevy stock 38.75-degree intake and 45-degree exhaust lifter-bore angles help keep the lifters and pushrods aligned with its canted valve arrangement and the same rocker design on intake and exhaust. However, having splayed lifter-bore angles lead to a turning point in the definition of lobe separation. The engine would not perform properly with the same camshaft-lobe angles on the two banks. To keep things less confusing for the aftermarket, people began using the term lobe separation as the average of the intake and exhaust centerlines and not the camshaft angle.

and exhaust lobes was 110 degrees on the odd side of a big-block Chevy, the exhaust lift would reach max later (later ECL) by 6.25 cam degrees, or 12.5 crank degrees. Hence, it would act like a 97.5 lobe separation in terms of the crank angle between max exhaust and max intake lift. On the even side, this 110-degree cam lobe angle acts like a 122.5-degree lobe separation on straight lifer bores.

Because lobe separation is a key idea for engine builders, the industry changed the definition of this term. Instead of the physical angle between lobes that is implied, industry-wide lobe separation is

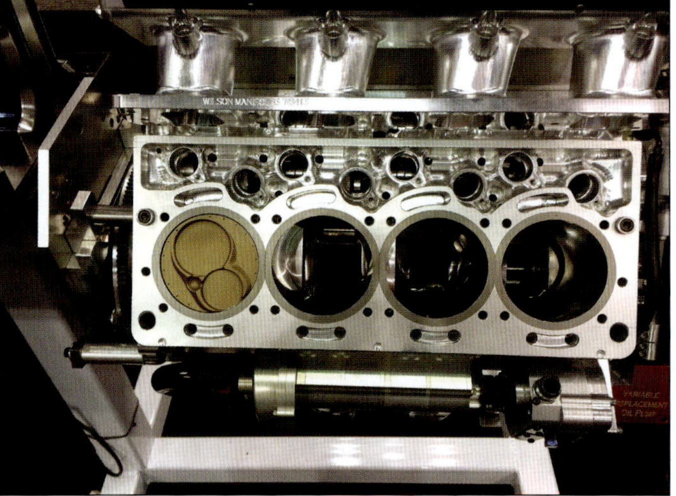

Image 1-24: On a modern race engine, such as Dan Jesel's Equal 8, the lifters can be rotated significantly. Hence, to use the lobe-separation term on something like this to mean what it means on a normal engine, the average centerline definition is extremely helpful.

Image 1-25: Using the new definition of lobe separation, we can incorporate this term even with overhead camshafts where there are no lifter bores. We simply design the valve motion and index the lobes so that the max valve lift centerlines are apart by the required average centerline.

defined as the average of the intake and exhaust max lift centerlines or (ICL + ECL) ÷ 2. With this definition, we can talk about lobe separation for overhead-cam applications, such as the Toyota 22RE in Image 1-25, even when there are no real lifter bores.

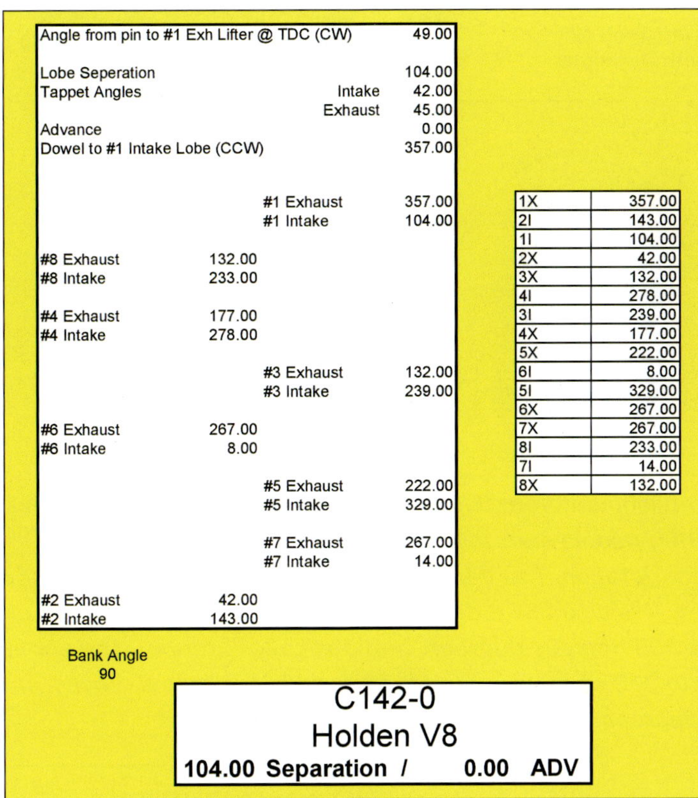

Angle from pin to #1 Exh Lifter @ TDC (CW)			49.00
Lobe Seperation			104.00
Tappet Angles		Intake	42.00
		Exhaust	45.00
Advance			0.00
Dowel to #1 Intake Lobe (CCW)			357.00
		#1 Exhaust	357.00
		#1 Intake	104.00
#8 Exhaust	132.00		
#8 Intake	233.00		
#4 Exhaust	177.00		
#4 Intake	278.00		
		#3 Exhaust	132.00
		#3 Intake	239.00
#6 Exhaust	267.00		
#6 Intake	8.00		
		#5 Exhaust	222.00
		#5 Intake	329.00
		#7 Exhaust	267.00
		#7 Intake	14.00
#2 Exhaust	42.00		
#2 Intake	143.00		

1X	357.00
2I	143.00
1I	104.00
2X	42.00
3X	132.00
4I	278.00
3I	239.00
4X	177.00
5X	222.00
6I	8.00
5I	329.00
6X	267.00
7X	267.00
8I	233.00
7I	14.00
8X	132.00

Bank Angle
90

C142-0
Holden V8
104.00 Separation / 0.00 ADV

Image 1-26:* *These are the Excel calculation sheets we used based on the timing set pin or keyway angle at TDC, lifter bore angles, lobe separation, and advance to calculate the lobe angles down any camshaft. Some overheads are a little more complicated, as the effective lifter-bore angles can change with lift or base-circle size.

Advance

If we went back to the early flathead automotive days, engine builders installed their camshaft with the number-1 piston at TDC and then rotated the camshaft with a level on the exhaust and intake valve faces until they had the same lift and were level. This was called "splitting overlap" and was a common way to install a race camshaft, which typically resulted in a nearly equal ECL and ICL. Going back to the 110 LSA example, this represented a 110 ECL and ICL. However, it did not take long for people to see that if the ICL was moved a few degrees closer to TDC, the engine typically responded well, especially at lower RPM.

The term "advance," often abbreviated as "ADV," was coined as the difference between the lobe-separation angle (LSA) and ICL. If you rotate the camshaft 2 cam degrees, which equals 4 crank degrees forward (4-stroke camshafts typically rotate at half crank speed), the ICL is 4 degrees less than the lobe separation.

Looking again at Image 1-12, this camshaft has a 109-degree ICL and 119-degree ECL. The average of these numbers [(109 + 119) ÷ 2] is the 112-degree LSA. Calculating the advance is simply the 112 LSA minus a 109 ICL (or 5 degrees). Using lobe separation and advance is a more common way to describe camshafts in the American pushrod V-8 world because there are so many easy ways to change the advance by rotating the camshaft with respect to the crank using adjustable timing sets. If a camshaft was ground for 109 ICL and 119 ECL but installed with a four-degree retard timing setting, the centerlines will move to 113 ICL and 115 ECL.

Note that we move both the ICL and ECL when we advance or retard a camshaft, but the average of these centerlines (lobe separation) will not change. However, in applications with independent intake and exhaust camshafts, it is easier to talk about the ECL and ICL settings, as they are not forced to move together.

The relationship among LSA, advance, ICL, and ECL is as follows:

- Advance = (exhaust centerline – intake centerline) ÷ 2
- Lobe separation = (exhaust centerline + intake centerline) ÷ 2
- Exhaust centerline = lobe separation + advance
- Intake centerline = lobe separation – advance
- Retard = opposite of advance

Duration

If I have a pet peeve, it is when someone specifies a duration without specifying the lift. If you want to see me squirm, ask me, "What is the best 280-duration camshaft?"

Duration is defined as how many crankshaft degrees a camshaft profile maintains more than a given lift. For most cam-in-block, overhead-valve applications, durations are given with respect to lifter or tappet lift. Duration is only meaningful if the lift at which it is measured is given. Any advertised duration without the specified lift (which is unfortunately very common) is an arbitrary and meaningless number. Almost every profile will be 300 degrees of duration at some tappet lift, but it is also 200 degrees of duration at another lift.

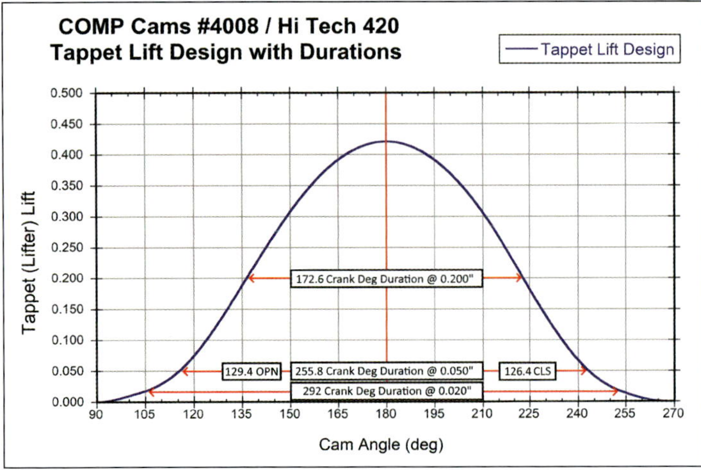

Image 1-27: No accomplishment from this book would be much better than hearing people start to include the rated lift when they mention a duration. The #4008 profile is 176.2 degrees duration. It is also 255.8 degrees duration, 292 degrees duration, 300 degrees duration, and basically every duration from 0 to 330 at some given lift. How difficult is it to say 255.8 degrees at 0.050-inch lift?

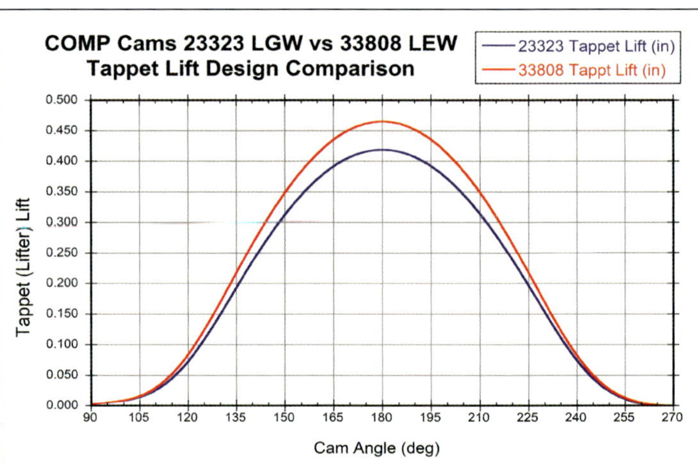

Image 1-28: These two profiles are very different at 0.020-, 0.050- and 0.200-inch duration. Looking at the tappet lift, we believe the red curve is much faster than the blue. However, this only accounts for what is going on at the tappet. The engine does not really know or care how the tappet moves when it comes to performance.

You can ignore any duration number that is given without a corresponding lift value. At Comp Cams, all overhead cams are rated at the valve, so these duration numbers do not seem to correlate well to how those same camshafts check outside the engine with a cam doctor–style gauge.

The way many engine builders compare race profiles is to compare the durations at 0.020 inch, 0.050 inch, and 0.200 inch for a given lobe lift (as shown in Image 1-27). The assumption is that for a given 0.050-inch duration, the smaller the 0.020-inch duration and largest 0.200-inch duration, the squarer and better performance a lobe can produce if stable. The problem with this point of view is that air demand and flow are never constant through either the intake or exhaust port. We now know that fast opening/slow closing lobes run differently than slow opening/fast closing lobes, even when all the durations are the same.

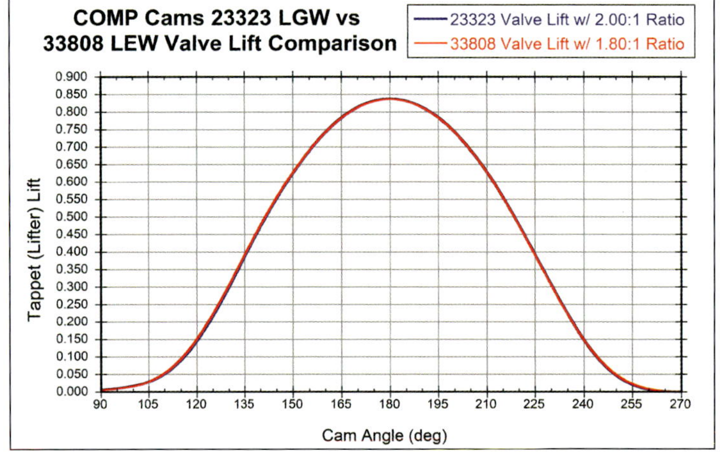

Image 1-29: The engine cares a great deal about how the valves move, and these two different tappet-lift profiles were designed to achieve similar valve motion. They are not exactly the same, as the red curve still gets a few thousandths ahead at 120 degrees, but almost no one would look at those tappet lift specs in a lobe catalog and guess how close these are at the valve.

People often confuse tappet durations and valve durations. A 256 at 0.050-inch tappet lift design (such as the Comp part number 23323) with a 2.0:1 ratio is extremely close to the same duration at the valve as a 261 at 0.050-inch tappet lift design (Comp part number 33808) when it is coupled with a 1.8:1 ratio. Note the specs for the 33808 seem more aggressive when looking at the 0.020-, 0.050- and 0.200-inch tappet durations compared to the 23323.

However, with the rocker speeding up the motion on the 23323, the resulting valve motion is extremely close to that of the faster 33808 with less rocker ratio. Both these lobe families are extremely successful but only when coupled with the correct ratios. This was only a 0.2 change in rocker ratio, but it corresponded to a 5-degree change in valve duration, which is a nice growth reference to remember. When someone makes an extreme ratio change (for example: 1.6:1 to 2.2:1) to properly select a camshaft, I need to overlay the valve motion plots between the systems. Otherwise, I risk being lost on the new tappet duration.

Image 1-32: At Comp Cams, we set up the four Adcole gauges in a room adjacent to the grinders. Note the Landis right outside the lab window. We had Adcole develop special software to make the programing and setup easy among various engine families and custom grinds.

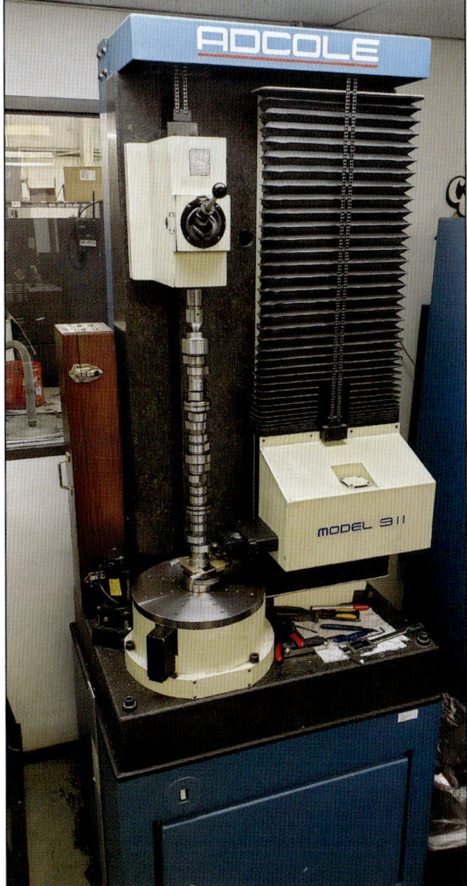

Image 1-30: My longtime boss and mentor, Scooter Brothers, used to tell me that quality ball bearings can't be made while trying to measure them with a wooden ruler. Our first Adcole vertical rotary CMM basically shut Comp Cams down for the first three days after it came online in 1999. It was like looking at something under a microscope for the first time, and I was a little scared. However, as we learned to use the gauge, every cam we produced got tremendously better.

Image 1-33: The same bench centers that are useful for checking runout also make great inspection stands. Here, the quality-control personnel looks for any chatter under great lighting and then runs a straightedge across adjacent journals to see if any lobe noses peak above the journals, which makes installation impossible in most cam-in-block V-8 applications.

Image 1-31: The probe arm on each Adcole has a diffraction grating encoder to measure down in the wavelength of light range. The probe is a carbide disk or rod that matches the engine-follower geometry. We take data every tenth of a degree for three complete rotations on each lobe. The first is 0.150 inch below center, then one on center, then one 0.150 inch above center to measure crown and taper.

Cam Degrees versus Crank Degrees

If you have looked at most cam drives (chain, belt, or gear), you probably noticed the cam side has twice as many teeth as the crank. For a four-stroke engine, the crank must make two complete rotations equal to 720 degrees between TDC firing events before everything on the valvetrain side repeats as the cam turns 360 degrees.

The 2:1 crank-degree to cam-degree ratio can add some confusion. Camshafts are generally designed, manufactured, and

Image 1-34: Speaking of making ball bearings, once you have great measurement devices, you can invest in the best grinders available. This new 1,200-mm Landis LT1e is probably my favorite grinder, as the heavy base of the larger machine makes it more rigid than the smaller grinders. All of the eight Okuma grinders, two Landis grinders, and the Adcole gauges use cam-degree encoders and files. However, converting to crank degrees is as easy as multiplying by 2.

Image 1-35: The tappet-lift files of every degree must be converted to wheel position of the CNC as it turns. This 350-mm OD wheel runs about 3,500 rpm. This photo was taken with the coolant off to show the carbon-fiber hub wheel that reduces vibration and chatter. (Photo Courtesy Dan Freeman)

Image 1-36: We still have a handful of older Berco manual grinders for odd jobs. These are amazing machines, especially with a CNC-produced master. That degree head is in camshaft degrees, and everything is basically controlled by hand. Some of the most amazing craftsmen I have met ran these machines. Having that level of craftsmanship move over to the CNCs (where you can do everything even more repeatably and do so with 20 times more coolant) has been a huge blessing.

Image 1-37: We have two offices filled almost floor to ceiling with about 20,000 Berco masters. I remember when we had two pieces of pegboard that held every master.

Image 1-38: Even with all the manufacturing tools in camshaft degrees, what really matters is what the valve does with respect to the camshaft. When Ben Strader set up this engine at EFI University, he wanted to know how the valves were going to move relative to the red wheel on the crankshaft.

inspected outside the engine in cam-degree increments, which makes some sense because the grinder or inspection angular encoder is attached to the camshaft. However, camshafts run and are checked in the engine in crank degrees with a degree wheel on the crank.

Overall, this is not difficult, except occasionally, when there is a cam design plot centered with the max lift at 180 degrees. Remember to multiply all the durations measured in this format by 2 to go from cam to crank degrees.

Intensity

Harvey Crane wanted a number to express how quickly a profile moved the tappet from near the seat to 0.050-inch lift and then back from 0.050 inch to the seat. He came up with the following set of intensity terms to rate how quick designs were compared to one another.

Intensity numbers are like golf scores, elapsed times, and lap times. Low numbers are generally better and always quicker. Remember that a very high intensity number is not ideal, and a small number is more aggressive.

Major Intensity

Typically used for solid profiles but always useful, major intensity (MI) is defined as the duration at 0.020 inch minus the duration at 0.050 inch. This is typically the best measure of how responsive any profile will be at low RPM. However, because the opening and closing sides of a valve's movement do something very different in terms of flow, we found it is important to look at the opening and closing splits as well as the overall intensity.

One needs to understand that lash and major intensity are intertwined. A 36-degree MI run with 0.028-inch lash can be quicker than a 33-degree MI with 0.018-inch lash.

Intensity Splits

When we look at intensity, showing both the opening side and closing side contributions separately is very useful information. In the Comp Cams lobe catalogs, we specify the MI and opening and closing contributions as follows: MI 36.2 (18.6/17.6).

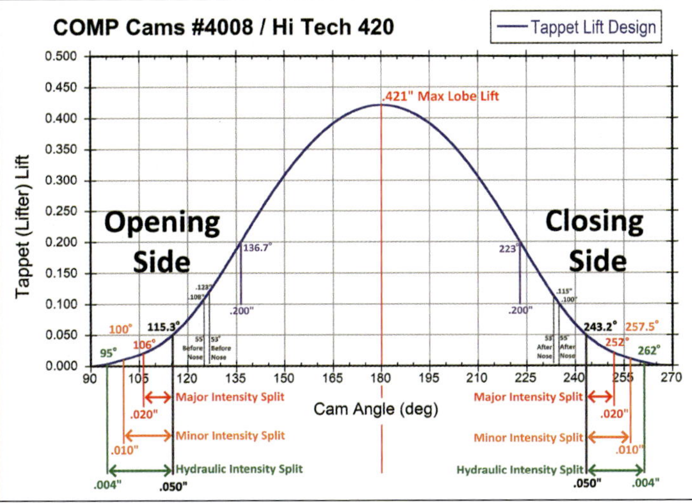

Image 1-39: With numbers in red, gold, green, black, purple, and gray, you might think that we have everything imaginable to describe this #4008 profile listed. That is only half true. We are going to use these numbers to describe how quickly the lifter goes between points. Harvey Crane came up with the term "intensity" to quantify this quickness.

Here, the profile takes 18.6 crank degrees (9.3 cam degrees) from 0.020-inch to 0.050-inch tappet lift on the opening side and then 17.6 crank degrees (8.8 cam degrees) going back down from 0.050-inch to 0.020-inch tappet lift on the closing side.

This is important because there could be five different profiles that all have the same 36.2-degree major intensity. A design with a 14.0-degree opening split and 22.2 closing split performs very differently both in terms of the power curve and the dynamic stability than one with a 18.6/17.6 split. Typically, the faster-closing design acts smaller on the intake due to the earlier intake-valve-seating event.

Minor Intensity

Minor intensity is the 0.010-inch duration minus the 0.050-inch duration. This intensity is most often important when comparing the tappet durations for either tight lash or overhead-cam solid designs. In applications where 0.020 inch is relatively high compared to the actual seat contact points, minor intensity can be more useful than major intensity.

However, these always tend to trend together, so you can compare two overhead cams based on major intensity if you keep in mind that a 27-degree major intensity with a tight lash design might not have any quicker motion at the valve than a 36-degree design run with looser lash.

Hydraulic Intensity

Some believe that hydraulic cam designs are fundamentally different than solid designs. From a cam designer's point of view, how I design hydraulic and solid designs are only different because of the difference in effective lash.

The standard for hydraulic seat timing for the Society of Automotive Engineers (SAE) is 0.006-inch valve lift. Comparing dynamic data from many systems, most hydraulic systems act like a solid with about 0.004-inch lash at low RPM. However, this effective lash typically grows to about 0.010 inch to 0.014 inch at high speed due to deflection in the lifter and system. Modern light and stiff valvetrains, such as the LS, tend to have the effective lash grow a little less and allow them to be more stable at high speed. Some of the older Harley-Davidson systems with long pushrods and rocker arms tend to grow considerably more past 6,000 rpm. Most hydraulic systems fall somewhere between these extremes.

To compare hydraulic designs, Harvey Crane came up with the term "hydraulic intensity," which is the duration at 0.004-inch tappet lift minus the duration at 0.050 inch. As with all intensity values, smaller numbers are faster, and larger numbers are slower.

Offset

Along with the intensity splits (open versus close), it is common for the peak lift point to not fall exactly between the lower lift opening and closing points. As with durations and intensities, the offset must be referenced to a tappet or valve lift point.

Image 1-39 is a graph of the Comp Cams 4008 tappet lift with all the measurements for intensity, offset, catalog, and sales information. Image 1-40 has the inputs from the graph highlighted in yellow with the outputs highlighted in blue. The bottom right shows the offsets at each lift. These calculations are the difference in the timing points in cam degrees. However, in crank degrees, this equals the difference in either point from the average, which is the real offset from the center at that lift. (You will learn how to use offsets for understanding valve timing points soon.)

4008 Graph Calculations

Position	Cam Angle (Deg)	Opening Half Intensities	Cam Degrees	Crank Degrees
.004" OPN	95	HYD Split	20.3	40.6
.010" OPN	100	Minor Split	15.3	30.6
.020" OPN	106	Major Split	9.3	18.6
.050" OPN	115.3	55 Deg Before Nose	.108"	INT 110 TDC Lift
.200" OPN	136.7	53 Deg Before Nose	.123"	INT 106 TDC Lift
Nose	180	53 Deg After Nose	.115"	EXH 106 TDC Lift
.200" CLS	223	55 Deg After Nose	.100"	EXH 110 TDC Lift
.050" CLS	243.2	Closing Half Intensities	Cam Degrees	Crank Degrees
.020" CLS	252	Major CLS Split	8.8	17.6
.010" CLS	257.5	Minor CLS Split	14.3	28.6
.004" CLS	262	HYD CLS Split	18.8	37.6

Tappet Lift	Duration (Crank Deg)	Total Intensity	Crank Degrees	Offset	Crank Degrees
.004"	334	Major	36.2	.050" Offset	-1.5
.010"	315	Minor	59.2	.020" Offset	-2
.020"	292	Hydraulic	78.2	.010" Offset	-2.5
.050"	255.8			.004" Offset	-3
.200"	172.6	Lobe Lift	.421"		

Image 1-40: Using the numbers for the graph in the red-shaded boxes, we can calculate many additional attributes to describe this profile compared to other designs. Both the total intensity and intensity splits shown here are at least as important as the more common duration specs. You can always go larger or smaller inside a family of lobes, but we need ways to compare different lobe families.

Specification Cards, Comp Adcole Reports, and Published Lobe Data

Refer to the published profile information and compare it to what you have learned. I have had customers pull their specification cards out of their wallets to show me the lash callout, so this is as good of a place as any to start.

Specification Cards

Image 1-41 shows the typical information that is provided with any camshaft. This grind was for a Godzilla 7.3L dyno test. Starting at the top is the part number and serial number. At Comp Cams, we keep quality inspection reports on each camshaft for several years, so that serial number is important to keep. The second line has the engine description and part number again. The part number (405-000-16) contains information about the engine family (405 = Ford Godzilla), the grind (000 is custom), and the core price information (16 is a custom roller-cam core). The description is tied to the part number.

The next section features the grind number and special instructions. Because this is a test for a future part number, the grind number is already listed. For most custom applications, the lobe identification numbers and lobe separation are on this line. Any special lifter-bore angle, journal size, or other special instructions are on the next three lines.

COMP CAMS

```
PART #: 405-000-16                        SN#:531175-21
ENGINE: CAMSHAFT, FORD 7.3 L SUPER             PART #: 405-000-16

GRIND#: GLS289HR15
SPC INSTR 1: GLS289HR15
SPC INSTR 2:
SPC INSTR 3:
                              INTAKE       EXHAUST
VALVE ADJUSTMENT             HYD          HYD
GROSS VALVE LIFT              .671         .671
DURATION @
 .006  TAPPET LIFT             289          300
VALVE TIMING      OPEN               CLOSE
@  .050     INT:     6      BTDC      46      ABDC
            EXH:    61      BBDC       1      ATDC
THESE SPECS ARE FOR CAM INSTALLED
@ 110.0  INTAKE CENTER LINE
                              INTAKE       EXHAUST
DURATION @ .050               231.00       242.00
LOBE LIFT                     .3730        .3730
LOBE SEPARATION               115.0
```

Image 1-41: I used to wonder why people might keep a camshaft specification card inside their wallet. I'm not that infatuated with them personally, but I want us all to appreciate how much information is contained on this small piece of paper.

The next lines are for the suggested starting valve adjustment or lash. Lash is typically set with feeler gauges between the rocker tip and the valve tip on overhead valve applications. For a hydraulic adjustment camshaft, the system is set with some hydraulic preload, so this is left "HYD" on both intake and exhaust.

The next lines are for the valve lift with the recommended rocker ratio. In this case, the Godzilla comes with a 1.8:1 ratio, so a 0.373-inch lobe lift rounds to 0.671-inch valve lift. The valve lift is followed by the advertised duration numbers. For this hydraulic design, the rated duration for Comp is at 0.006-inch tappet lift. This camshaft is 289 at 0.006-inch intake and 300 at 0.006-inch exhaust.

Now, we get down to the valve-timing events at 0.050 inch. Some specification cards have these listed at 0.006 inch, 0.020 inch, or whatever tappet or valve lift is used for the rated duration. I prefer the 0.050-inch numbers because they are easier to verify and correspond to when all the deflection is removed and there is airflow in the port.

Valve Timing Events

In the automotive world, we mostly speak about durations and centerlines. In the motorcycle world, they typically refer to the four-valve timing events when discussing camshaft specifications. It pains me to admit it, but they are talking about what matters most to engine performance.

However, to achieve those four points, we need to choose a profile with a given duration and clock it in the engine at a given centerline to achieve those critical opening and closing points, so there is something to be gained from each approach.

Either way that you approach camshaft specifications, understand that engines fundamentally react to when the valves open and close as well as the full motion between those events. Look back at Image 1-12 to see each event below circled and labeled.

EVO

The exhaust valve opening (EVO) is the first event after the plug fires. This event transitions the engine from the power stroke to where it uses that energy to push out the spent exhaust charge. Like duration, all valve timing points must be specified at a given lift.

You need to know three things to calculate the EVO: 1) duration at that lift, 2) the max lift centerline, and 3) the offset at that lift point. Knowing these the EVO in terms of before bottom dead center (BBDC) is:

$$\text{EVO} = \text{ECL} + (\text{Exhaust Duration} \div 2) - \text{Offset at that Duration} - 180$$

The minus 180 moves you from the before TDC (BTDC) callout of ECL to degrees BBDC, which is the standard callout for EVO. The earlier the EVO, the less exhaust pumping losses at high RPM. The later the EVO, the longer power stroke you have before using the energy to push out spent gases. Hence, tuning EVO is very important for tailoring the power and torque curves for any application.

IVO

The intake valve opening (IVO) event begins the overlap region. To calculate this valve event, we need to know the intake duration at the given lift, intake centerline, and the intake offset at that lift. The equation to calculate IVO is:

$$\text{IVO} = (\text{Intake Duration} \div 2) - \text{ICL} - \text{Offset at that Duration}$$

This equation provides the IVO in terms of degrees BTDC. This spec is very important with regard to how well the header and intake runner can communicate. It also relates closely with idle vacuum and intake piston-to-valve clearance. Emissions can be directly related to IVO.

EVC

The exhaust valve closing (EVC) event ends the overlap region. Before this valve closes, the header and intake runner can still communicate. However, the intake charge can also be robbed out of the exhaust, or the exhaust charge can be pulled back into the cylinder during the downstroke of the piston (depending on RPM if this is too late). The equation for EVC in terms of after TDC (ATDC) is:

$$\text{EVC} = (\text{Exhaust Duration} \div 2) - \text{ECL} + \text{Offset at that Duration}$$

EVC is almost as important to idle vacuum as IVO. In some marine applications, water may be ingested into the cylinder if EVC is too late. The shape of the curve down to EVC can be at least as important as the actual event to performance.

IVC

The intake valve closing (IVC) event is the most important valve event in any four-stroke engine. This correlates most closely to where a particular engine makes peak power. Three items are required to calculate the IVC: 1) duration at that lift, 2) the max lift centerline, and 3) the offset at that lift point. Knowing these, the IVC in terms of after BDC (ABDC) is:

$$\text{IVC} = \text{ICL} + (\text{Intake Duration} \div 2) + \text{Offset at that Duration} - 180$$

Closing the intake too soon stops the fresh charge when the incoming air momentum is still high enough to overcome any greater pressure in the chamber. Closing the intake too late allows the fresh charge that filled the chamber to escape back into the port. This IVC sensitivity is why advancing a camshaft tends to increase low-RPM performance, and retarding a camshaft tends to increase high-RPM performance.

Offset Effect on Valve Timing

After learning about offset and seeing it used in the valve-event calculations above, an example of how much a 1-degree offset at 0.050 inch can change the timing points is in order. In Images 1-42 and 1-43, two cams have the same 270 intake and 280 exhaust duration at 0.050 inch. A has -1.0-degree intake offset and +1.0 exhaust offset at 0.050 inch. The offsets on B are flipped. Note that the valve timing events are identical (even though A has a 115 LSA with +3 advance and B is a much tighter 113 LSA with +3 advance). Both result in the same 0.050-inch timing as a camshaft with symmetric lobe designs at 114 LSA with +3 advance.

Because every four-stroke engine is sensitive to low-lift timing points and numb to exactly where peak lift occurs, pay close attention to how lobe offset shifts timing points to properly compare various camshafts.

More on the Specifications Card

As we move past the timing events, next is the recommended intake centerline. For this camshaft, the recommended intake centerline is 110 degrees ATDC. In most cases, the camshaft is ground with the lobes indexed for this centerline. Occasionally, there is a note in the special instructions to "line up on core," which tells the grinder to be careful and remove as little material from the cam core as possible, which is more important and is specific to the timing set that the customer is using. For many OEM sets, advancing or retarding the camshaft is quite difficult. However, many aftermarket systems make this adjustment easily, and those customers may prefer the deeper effective heat-treat depth that remains if the core advance is followed.

As we move to the bottom of the specification card, we finally get back to where we started on camshaft definitions. There's often a recommended valve-spring callout under these specifications. It is a great piece of information because it identifies the valve

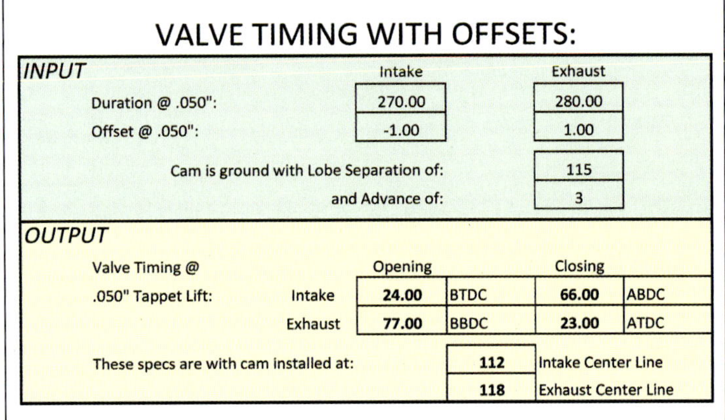

VALVE TIMING WITH OFFSETS:

INPUT		Intake		Exhaust	
Duration @ .050":		270.00		280.00	
Offset @ .050":		-1.00		1.00	
Cam is ground with Lobe Separation of:				115	
and Advance of:				3	
OUTPUT					
Valve Timing @ .050" Tappet Lift:		Opening		Closing	
	Intake	24.00	BTDC	66.00	ABDC
	Exhaust	77.00	BBDC	23.00	ATDC
These specs are with cam installed at:			112	Intake Center Line	
			118	Exhaust Center Line	

VALVE TIMING WITH OFFSETS:

INPUT		Intake		Exhaust	
Duration @ .050":		270.00		280.00	
Offset @ .050":		1.00		-1.00	
Cam is ground with Lobe Separation of:				113	
and Advance of:				3	
OUTPUT					
Valve Timing @ .050" Tappet Lift:		Opening		Closing	
	Intake	24.00	BTDC	66.00	ABDC
	Exhaust	77.00	BBDC	23.00	ATDC
These specs are with cam installed at:			110	Intake Center Line	
			116	Exhaust Center Line	

Images 1-42 and 1-43: Of all the lobe attributes, the offset is the most overlooked. Note how as little as one degree of offset can make a 115 LSA camshaft, 114 LSA camshaft, and 113 LSA camshaft act the same at 0.050 inch. As more asymmetric profiles gain popularity, we will have to understand offset. Otherwise, all of our timing points are going to be out of place.

spring with which the camshaft was initially designed and tested.

Lobe Catalogs

Moving past the specification card, look at the specifications that are contained in a typical lobe catalog. In Image 1-44, the entry for the Comp Hi-Tech Dash 5 Series is shown. The lobe that was analyzed earlier (#4008) is highlighted in this list.

Starting at the top, there's a description for Comp salesmen and engine builders. These are typically not altered over time, so the long-rod callout has been there since the 1990s. They work quite well in long-rod applications, but they were never bad in short-rod applications. We probably assumed that people using the longer rods needed the added piston-to-valve clearance and higher operating speed of this series when it was compared to the fast-opening RT series. Those were our two best-selling profiles from 1990 to 1998 for circle-track applications.

Moving past the description, notice the journal size callouts and MI that are given to the left. All roller profiles have a minimum size that can be ground without being too inverted in the flanks to grind. Having a list of available suffixes and sizes is very helpful for salesmen and engine builders when choosing a profile. This series can be made as small as "N," or a 0.900-inch base circle, so almost anyone can use these profiles.

Moving over to the right is the lobe number, rated duration (0.020 inch, seen here to the left), and the duration at 0.050 inch and 0.200 inch. Next is the lobe lift. Note this design is rated at 0.420 inch, while the design is 0.421 inch. In the 1990s, before CNC grinders were used, there was always some polishing of the master and flex in the grinder. People sent a cam back if the lift was 0.001 inch low but did not mind if it was a few tenths too large. Hence, older designs had the design lift cheated up 0.001 inch. On newer designs, rated lift is the real design lobe lift.

HI-TECH .420" ROLLERS

The Hi-Tech .420" is primarily used in oval track racing with good cylinder heads. The ramp designs are easy on valve springs, yet produce good power. They are great for long rod motors. They are also popular in bracket and marine applications where power with durability is a must. Also available in Ford Small Block and Chevy Big Block or 50mm sizes to prevent "cam growth" in the grinding process, allowing the engine builder to have more control over the tuning process.

CAMSHAFT TYPE	LOBE NUMBER	RATED DURATION	DURATION IN DEGREES		LOBE LIFT	TAPPET LIFT @ TDC		THEORETICAL VALVE LIFT @ "0" Lash ROCKER ARM RATIO		
			@ .050	@ .200		106°	110°	1.5	1.6	1.7
Hi-Tech	4001	284-5	248	165	.420	.108	.094	.630	.672	.714
Rated Duration @	4004	286-5	250	167	.420	.112	.098	.630	.672	.714
.020" Tappet Lift	4006	288-5	252	169	.420	.116	.101	.630	.672	.714
Journal = N,S,B,R...	4009	290-5	254	171	.420	.119	.105	.630	.672	.714
MI 36.2 (18.6/17.6)	**4008**	292-5	256	173	.420	.123	.108	.630	.672	.714
	4013	294-5	258	175	.420	.127	.112	.630	.672	.714
	4017	296-5	260	177	.420	.131	.116	.630	.672	.714
	4015	298-5	262	179	.420	.136	.120	.630	.672	.714
	4022	300-5	264	181	.420	.140	.124	.630	.672	.714
	4020	302-5	266	183	.420	.143	.127	.630	.672	.714
	4024	304-5	268	184	.420	.146	.130	.630	.672	.714
	4018	306-5	270	186	.420	.150	.134	.630	.672	.714
	4026	308-5	272	188	.420	.154	.138	.630	.672	.714
	4016	310-5	274	189	.420	.157	.141	.630	.672	.714
	4028	312-5	276	190	.420	.160	.144	.630	.672	.714
	4030	314-5	278	192	.420	.163	.148	.630	.672	.714
	4031	316-5	280	193	.420	.166	.151	.630	.672	.714
	4032	318-5	282	195	.420	.170	.154	.630	.672	.714

Image 1-44: A lobe list that describes a family of lobes with the same intensity and ramp designs is one of the most important reference tools for any engine builder. Everything from the description and intensity values for the whole series down to the TDC lifts for each lobe can help you choose the best lobe for your application.

TDC Lift

The next two columns are important for calculating the required piston pocket and determining how difficult it will be to fit this profile on any given centerline. By giving the tappet lift at 53 and 55 cam degrees before peak lift, the engine builder is given a measure of how much lobe lift there is at TDC overlap if this profile is installed on a 106 or 110 intake centerline. For prominent exhaust series, the TDC lift is given on the other side.

If you look at the salesman information for this profile in Image 1-45, on the right side, you can see that Comp salesmen also have access to the exhaust TDC numbers (intake side is on the left) along with the offset at 0.050 inch and at the advertised lift, which is 0.020 inch here. Note that a list of available masters and CNC programing sizes available to order a camshaft are included.

Adcole Inspection Report

Looking back at Images 1-30 and 1-31, which show an Adcole

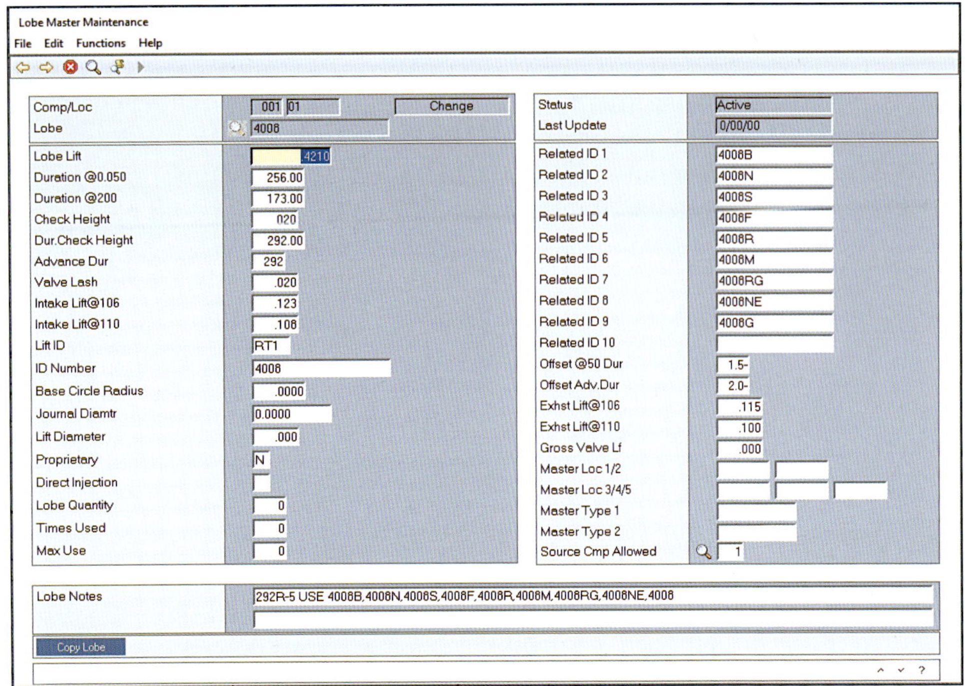

Lobe Master Maintenance

File Edit Functions Help

Comp/Loc	001 01 Change	Status	Active
Lobe	4008	Last Update	0/00/00
Lobe Lift	4210	Related ID 1	4008B
Duration @0.050	256.00	Related ID 2	4008N
Duration @200	173.00	Related ID 3	4008S
Check Height	.020	Related ID 4	4008F
Dur.Check Height	292.00	Related ID 5	4008R
Advance Dur	292	Related ID 6	4008M
Valve Lash	.020	Related ID 7	4008RG
Intake Lift@106	.123	Related ID 8	4008NE
Intake Lift@110	.106	Related ID 9	4008G
Lift ID	RT1	Related ID 10	
ID Number	4008	Offset @50 Dur	1.5-
Base Circle Radius	.0000	Offset Adv.Dur	2.0-
Journal Diamtr	0.0000	Exhst Lift@106	.115
Lift Diameter	.000	Exhst Lift@110	.100
Proprietary	N	Gross Valve Lf	.000
Direct Injection		Master Loc 1/2	
Lobe Quantity	0	Master Loc 3/4/5	
Times Used	0	Master Type 1	
Max Use	0	Master Type 2	
		Source Cmp Allowed	1

Lobe Notes: 292R-5 USE 4008B,4008N,4008S,4008F,4008R,4008M,4008RG,4008NE,4008

Copy Lobe

Image 1-45: Salespeople have additional information on each profile. Knowing the offsets and intake versus exhaust TDC lifts are important. However, knowing what program suffix sizes are currently available might be their most used bit of information.

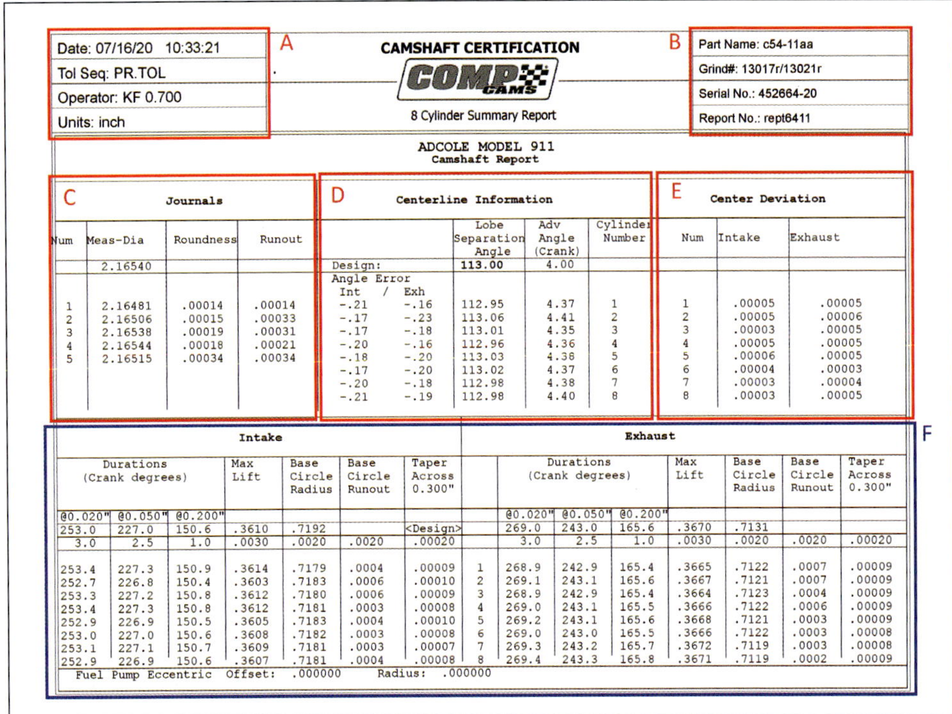

A

Date: 07/16/20 10:33:21

Tol Seq: PR.TOL

Operator: KF 0.700

Units: inch

CAMSHAFT CERTIFICATION

COMP CAMS

8 Cylinder Summary Report

B

Part Name: c54-11aa

Grind#: 13017r/13021r

Serial No.: 452664-20

Report No.: rept6411

ADCOLE MODEL 911

Camshaft Report

C

Journals

Num	Meas-Dia	Roundness	Runout
	2.16540		
1	2.16481	.00014	.00014
2	2.16506	.00015	.00033
3	2.16538	.00019	.00031
4	2.16544	.00018	.00021
5	2.16515	.00034	.00034

D

Centerline Information

		Lobe Separation Angle	Adv Angle (Crank)	Cylinder Number
Design:		113.00	4.00	
Angle Error Int	/ Exh			
-.21	-.16	112.95	4.37	1
-.17	-.23	113.06	4.41	2
-.17	-.18	113.01	4.35	3
-.20	-.16	112.96	4.36	4
-.18	-.20	113.03	4.38	5
-.17	-.20	113.02	4.37	6
-.20	-.18	112.98	4.38	7
-.21	-.19	112.98	4.40	8

E

Center Deviation

Num	Intake	Exhaust
1	.00005	.00005
2	.00005	.00006
3	.00003	.00005
4	.00005	.00005
5	.00006	.00005
6	.00004	.00003
7	.00003	.00004
8	.00003	.00005

F

Intake								Exhaust							
Durations (Crank degrees)			Max Lift	Base Circle Radius	Base Circle Runout	Taper Across 0.300"		Durations (Crank degrees)			Max Lift	Base Circle Radius	Base Circle Runout	Taper Across 0.300"
@0.020"	@0.050"	@0.200"						@0.020"	@0.050"	@0.200"				
253.0	227.0	150.6	.3610	.7192		<Design>		269.0	243.0	165.6	.3670	.7131		
3.0	2.5	1.0	.0030	.0020	.0020	.00020		3.0	2.5	1.0	.0030	.0020	.0020	.00020
253.4	227.3	150.9	.3614	.7179	.0004	.00009	1	268.9	242.9	165.4	.3665	.7122	.0007	.00009
252.7	226.8	150.4	.3603	.7183	.0006	.00010	2	269.1	243.1	165.6	.3667	.7121	.0007	.00009
253.3	227.2	150.8	.3612	.7180	.0006	.00009	3	268.9	242.9	165.4	.3664	.7123	.0004	.00009
253.4	227.3	150.8	.3612	.7181	.0003	.00008	4	269.0	243.1	165.5	.3666	.7122	.0006	.00009
252.9	226.9	150.5	.3605	.7183	.0004	.00010	5	269.2	243.1	165.6	.3668	.7121	.0003	.00009
253.0	227.0	150.6	.3608	.7182	.0003	.00008	6	269.0	243.0	165.5	.3666	.7122	.0003	.00008
253.1	227.1	150.7	.3609	.7181	.0003	.00007	7	269.3	243.2	165.7	.3672	.7119	.0003	.00008
252.9	226.9	150.6	.3607	.7181	.0004	.00008	8	269.4	243.3	165.8	.3671	.7119	.0002	.00009

Fuel Pump Eccentric Offset: .000000 Radius: .000000

Image 1-46: Knowing how to read this Adcole report ties most of what we have learned in this chapter together. With this report, the target and measured values on all the durations, lifts, centerlines, and sizes are shown. The taper and center deviation is also recorded from those three cuts we described earlier.

911 gauge in operation, we should talk about what to check on an Adcole-type camshaft gauge and what information is available on a Comp Cams report.

Adcole is a specific brand of rotary coordinate measuring machine (CMM) that is optimized to inspect camshafts with a probe head

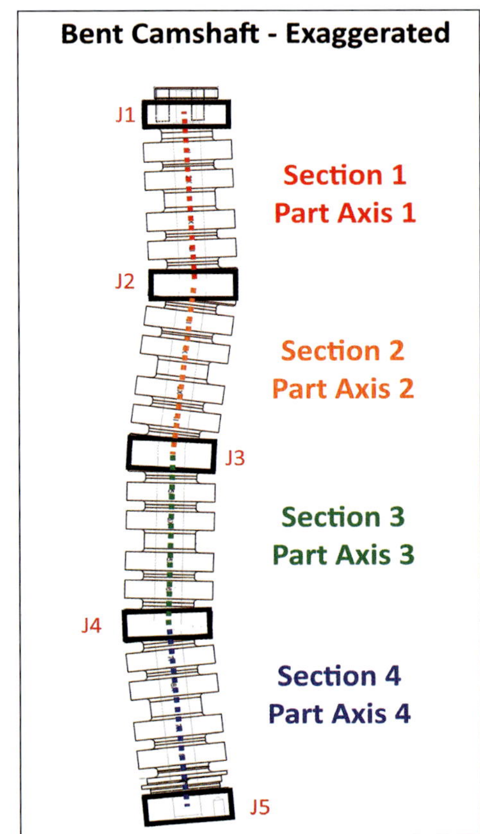

Image 1-47: Camshafts are ground off centers but run as they are held in bearings. Imagine all those 1,000-plus-pound loads going down the pushrods, through the lifters, and onto the cam face while the cam is spinning at 3,000-plus rpm and being bathed in hot oil. All of that vibration while being held in place is the world's best cam straightener. However, to check the camshaft, we first want to straighten it while still being able to separate the bent cam error from the lobe error. The Adcole gauges do that with this mathematical trick.

that matches the intended follower design. Using the correct probe prevents conversion errors as we convert from probe lift to tappet lift, and it allows us to see any surface chatter from the grinding process (like the tappet or follower riding on the camshaft will experience).

Many companies use a single generic probe and convert to the intended tappet or follower motion. Measure with the correct probe geometry whenever possible. The most important features of the Adcole gauges are the advanced mathematics for profile analysis and ultra-high precision encoders used for both the probe and rotary head. The probe can read down to around 0.0000001 inch, and the rotary head accuracy (same accuracy as above) makes my head spin.

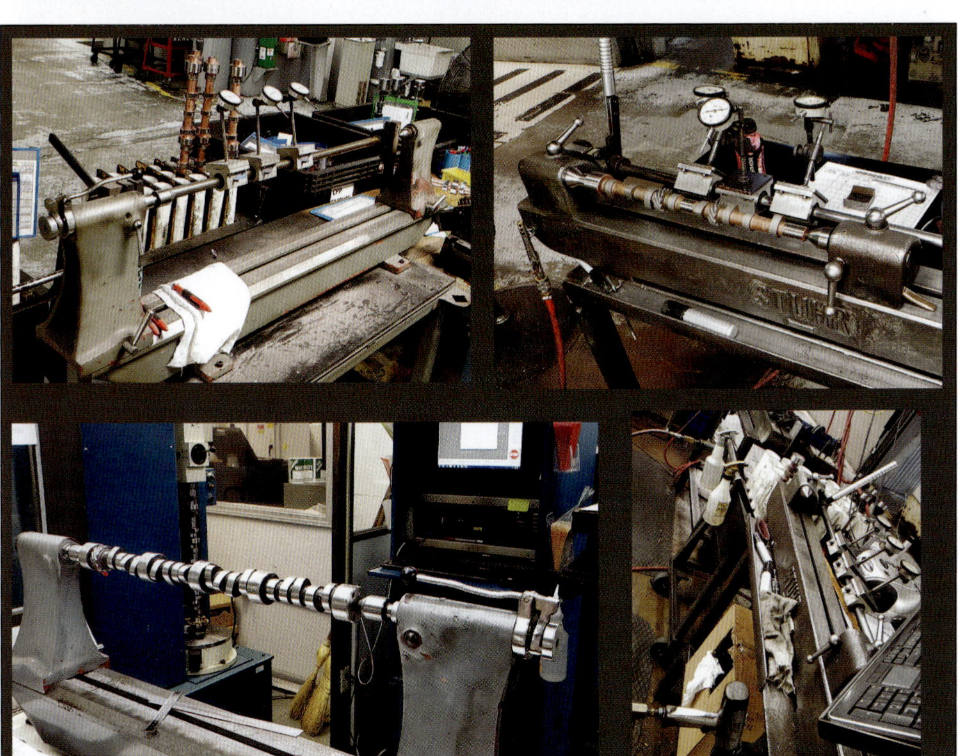

Images 1-48 and 1-49: When the lobe shapes are first milled on a cam spool or blank, stresses created and released result in some bending that must be straightened before heat treating. The heat treating process causes some internal stress, and the cams are straightened after heat treating. We have some of this after the journal grind, if the cams sit too long, and then after the lobe grind. It is pretty wild how many times a camshaft goes through straightness gauges before if goes in your engine. They pretty much stay straight after they run.

Sections A and B

Image 1-46 shows an example "8-cylinder Summary Report" for a typical V-8 overhead valve (OHV) camshaft. This is an LS test grind, but any NASCAR or Pro Stock cam uses this same "rept6411" format.

The first two sections provide the basic information about this inspection. The Section A lists the date and time, tolerances used in the first two lines, and the inspector's initials with the probe radius that was used. Here, it's 0.700 inch (a typical GM hydraulic roller lifter wheel). Lastly in Section A, it specifies that the unit of measurement used on the report is inches.

The first line of the Section B shows the camshaft core that was used for the inspection. Here, a c54-11aa was used. This file contains all the linear and angular information for the part as well as journal-diameter targets. The angular information is exactly like Image 1-26 with the calculations for LSA and advance. After loading the core information, the operator inputs the intake and exhaust designs to be measured against. In this case, they used the 13017r intake and 13021r exhaust profiles. The "r" suffix includes the design base circle size and follower wheel size. Then, the serial number and report number are listed.

Section C: Journals

Camshafts are held in the engine by the round journals of the camshaft, but we normally grind and inspect them from the center in both ends of the camshaft. This means the camshaft journals are critical to performance.

Most cam inspection systems have a very difficult time dealing with even a slightly bent camshaft. Harvey Crane used to spend half a day of his cam school showing people how to straighten a camshaft in a lathe with an axe handle so that it could be properly measured. Adcole gauges use a mathematical trick to make this straightness far less important for inspection.

Before checking the lobes, the routine starts at the bottom. Then, you check each journal on the way up the camshaft. This method creates a part axis through the center of the journals (as shown in Image 1-47) and uses simple trigonometry to convert the raw measurements of each lobe to how it would be measured between journals on its section axis. This is awesome because it checks a bent camshaft and reports how this cam acts when it is loaded in the engine. It also separates the bend from how well the lobes run true to the journals.

You would be shocked how many times a cam is checked and straightened in the manufacturing process. It may have to be straightened before and after heat treating and then again after the journals are ground. If it sits a few weeks before the lobes are ground, it needs to be straightened again before going in the grinder because the internal stresses often relieve over time. It may be straightened again after it is ground. It will be held straight in the grinder with the steady rest on the journals (as shown in Image 1-50), but as material is removed, the interval stresses can change.

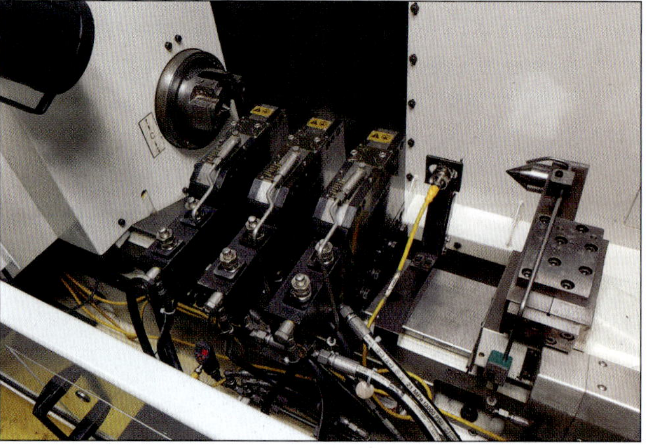

Image 1-50: Three automatic steady rests on the Landis grinder constrain the camshaft much like it is held in your engine. This is important because the cam might try to bend after a few lobes are ground, but this keeps everything centered to the journals.

Section C of the Adcole report shows the size measurement along with roundness and runout. Roundness is the error seen on a bench center if the camshaft is rotated about the journal center. The runout here is what is measured if you held the camshaft in V-blocks on the end journals and measured the runout of the center journals.

Section D: Centerlines

Along with the core, intake lobe, and exhaust lobe, the Adcole operators input the lobe separation and advance for the Adcole to create a temporary part data file to check against. Those inputs are at the top of Section D (113.00 LSA and 4.00 advance). The program compares the measured lobe angles to the target in the left column for each lobe. We calculate not only the error but also the resulting actual LSA and advance in the next two columns.

Adcole has an interesting technique for finding the lobe center. Knowing the design, these gauges fit the measured data to the design data in the highest-velocity regions. Some less-expensive gauges either look for the instant of the highest lift or curve fit around the nose. Looking at the fastest regions is far more accurate.

Note how consistently a CNC grinder hits the angles relative to each other. In this case, the cam was off by about 0.2 degrees, but every lobe was off between 0.16 degrees and 0.23 degrees. This level of angular repeatability is not possible on a manual grinder.

Section E: Center Deviation or Crown

When the Adcole inspects the lobe surface, three revolutions, or cuts, are made. The first measurement is 0.150 inch below the lobe centerline, the middle is on the centerline, and the last is 0.150 inch above the centerline. Taking lift data every tenth of a cam degree to seven decimal places (0.000000x) provides a powerful data set to analyze the surface geometry.

The center deviation calculation takes the center-cut measurement and subtracts the average of the top and bottom cut. The output is the average of these 3,600 differences. With conventional abrasives, the wheel naturally breaks down more quickly than the cam lobe during grind, so when dressing a wheel flat, the wheel wears concave. The resulting lobe face is slightly convex. With modern CBN wheels, the opposite effect is often seen. You

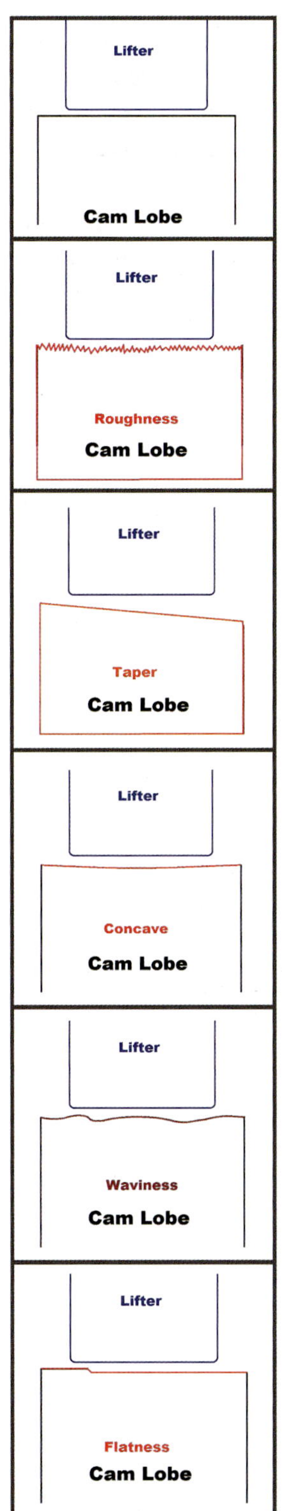

Image 1-51: When we began dialing in our mean squared error (MSE) superfinish process, we spent three years investigating cam wear and understanding how the surface texture and shape could accelerate or delay wear. We can engineer the surface for best performance by running three cuts on the Adcole on every camshaft that we grind and inspecting the dress on each machine every day.

Crown — Drop from Center

			ADCOLE Lobe	Adcole Lobe		Camshaft Lobe	Camshaft Lobe			Grinding Wheel	Grinding Wheel	
Radius (inches)	Radius (mm)		Angle to .150" Radians	Drop @ .300" W		Angle to .250" Radians	Drop @ .500" W	µm		Angle to .375" Radians	Drop @ .750" W	
50	1270		0.00300	0.00023		0.00500	0.00063	15.9		0.00750	0.00141	GM
78.74	2000		0.00191	0.00014		0.00318	0.00040	10.1		0.00476	0.00089	
100	2540		0.00150	0.00011		0.00250	0.00031	7.9		0.00375	0.00070	
118.11	3000		0.00127	0.00010		0.00212	0.00026	6.7		0.00318	0.00060	COMP
137.80	3500		0.00109	0.00008		0.00181	0.00023	5.8		0.00272	0.00051	
157.48	4000		0.00095	0.00007		0.00159	0.00020	5.0		0.00238	0.00045	
196.85	5000		0.00076	0.00006		0.00127	0.00016	4.0		0.00191	0.00036	
300	7620		0.00050	0.00004		0.00083	0.00010	2.6		0.00125	0.00023	

Image 1-52: The best surface was not shown in the previous graph but it has a slight crown. By slight, I mean a 1/10 of 0.001 inch or less drop from the center cut on the Adcole to the low and high cuts. This was not possible when I started, but with today's cubic boron nitride (CBN) wheels and CNC-controlled diamond-wheel dressers, we can create a very sophisticated lobe-face shape.

can dress the wheel flat and end up with a bathtub-shaped (concave) lobe surface.

There are numerous ways to grind a bad surface (as shown in Image 1-51). The two most common causes of failure at the edge of a roller wheel contact path is when there's a surface that is either concave or has a taper (as shown in the third and fourth sketches). To avoid being concave, the best practice is to grind the roller camshaft lobe surface a slight bit convex. This also puts the surface in compression (like an arch) instead of in tension.

Image 1-52 shows the crown target for the CNC wheel dress at Comp versus what we measured from GM. A 0.00023-inch drop between the nose and 0.150 inch on either side would be equivalent to a 50-inch radius surface. I prefer a flatter surface because too much crown results in added pressure and spalling in the lobe center over the nose. Too little will let the lifter wheel edge dig in in the flanks. By looking at the lifter track after endurance testing, you can dial in the best crown for any application. The 2,500-mm to 3,500-mm range seems to be the best in most applications.

Section E: Durations, Lift, Base Circle, and Taper

In the bottom section are the numbers that most people want first. So, starting at the bottom works well. The top line of this section provides the target values from the profile lift tables entered and described in Section B.

For example, the intake #13017R design is 253 at 0.020 inch, 227.0 at 0.050 inch, 150.6 at 0.200 inch, and 0.361-inch lobe lift on a design 0.7192-inch base circle. We can see how closely a good CNC can hit those targets. The right side is the same information for the #13021R exhaust—both as designed and as ground on cylinders 1 through 8.

Base Circle Runout

On a camshaft that moves a pump lobe (as shown in Image 1-3 and 1-4), there is a minimum lobe radius from the center, but it never needs to be constant. Looking back at Images 1-8, 1-11, and 1-12, we see four-stroke automotive cams spend

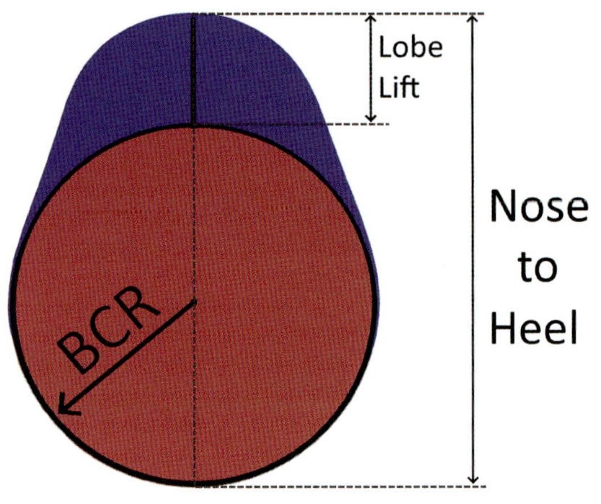

BCR = (Nose to Heel - Lobe Lift)/2

Image 1-53: When you hear the term "900 base circle," the person means a 0.900-inch base-circle diameter. There is still some lobe lift on both sides of 90 degrees from the nose, so you cannot directly check base-circle diameter with a micrometer. I am spoiled with the Adcole gauges, but you can check it the same way on a lathe or check the nose to heel and subtract lift.

a significant number of degrees camped out at their minimum radius, known as the base-circle radius.

The term "base-circle diameter" is often used to describe this minimum size. That term does not work so well, especially with race profiles, because there is always some lift above the base circle at 90 degrees from the nose. As RPM and duration increase, the lift at 90 degrees from the nose grows considerably.

As an engine builder, if you want to measure a cam's actual base-circle size, there are two options. The first is to measure the lobe or tappet lift in

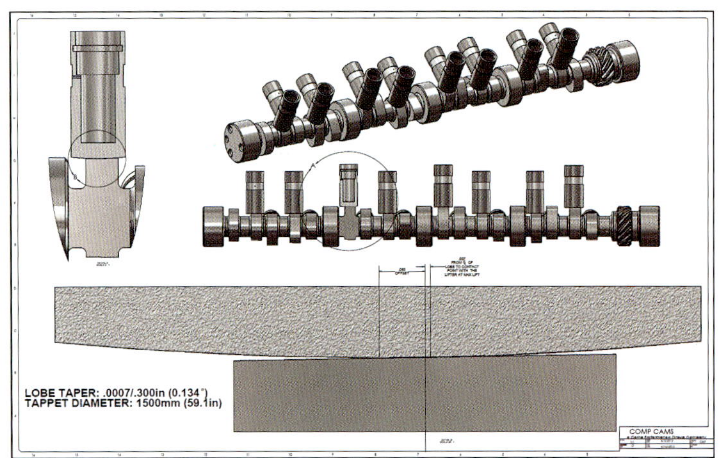

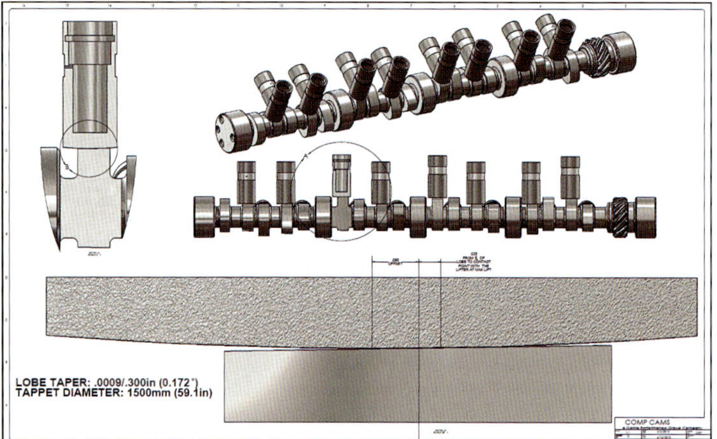

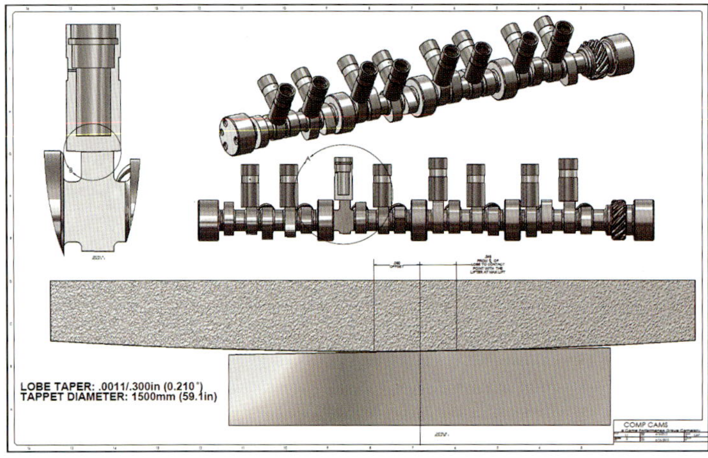

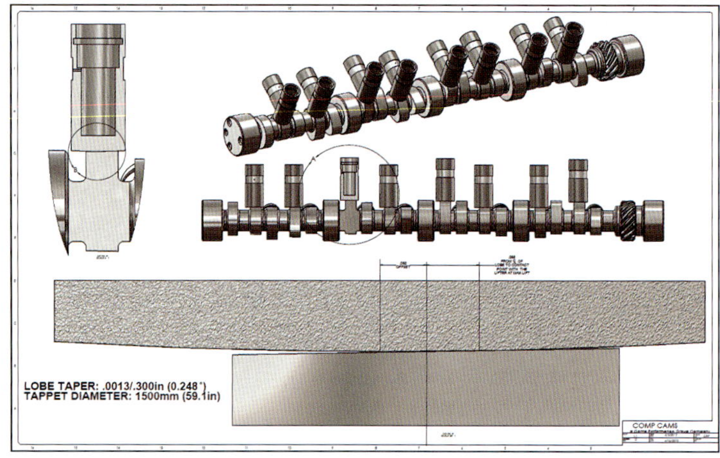

Images 1-54, 1-55, 1-56, and 1-57: Some people want to run big taper values. If an 850 carburetor is better than a 600 and a 427 small-block is better than a 305, then more taper has to be better as well. These four computer-aided design (CAD) drawings show the relationship between taper, lifter crown, and lobe offset. Running higher taper means that you need more offset, but on the engines we mainly run, too much offset runs lobes into the next lifter, and things get messy. I am all for lobe and lifter monogamy. (Images Courtesy Chris Potter)

a fixture or the engine and then use a micrometer to measure the vertical distance (Image 1-53). This distance is typically called the nose-to-heel or toe-to-heel. By subtracting the nose-to-heel from the lobe lift, you calculate the effective lobe base-circle diameter. Divide that by 2 and you have the base circle radius.

The second option is to set up the camshaft between the centers in a lathe with a dial indicator on the tool post carefully aligned through the center axis. First, use a micrometer to measure a journal diameter near the lobe that is to be measured. Then, zero your micrometer on that journal of a known radius (half the measured diameter). Move to the lobe and measure the difference in radii between the lobe base circle and the journal. This is a great chance to check the cam straightness. If you get the journals straight, measure the base-circle runout from ramp to ramp.

The Adcole is clearly my favorite way to measure the base circle because it first does that mathematical trick to make a part axis through each section. Then, you have 10 points per degree measured throughout the base circle. This results in both amazing accuracy on the size and any runout. Also, the Adcole gauge is programed with the design so that it will see any added ramp that bleeds into the base circle as base-circle error. This is impossible without knowing where the base circle is supposed to start and stop.

Taper

The Adcole gauges use an average of all 3,600 bottom-cut measurements minus all 3,600 top-cut measurements to calculate taper. On a roller cam, we want that to be nearly 0, but with a crowned surface, you will see

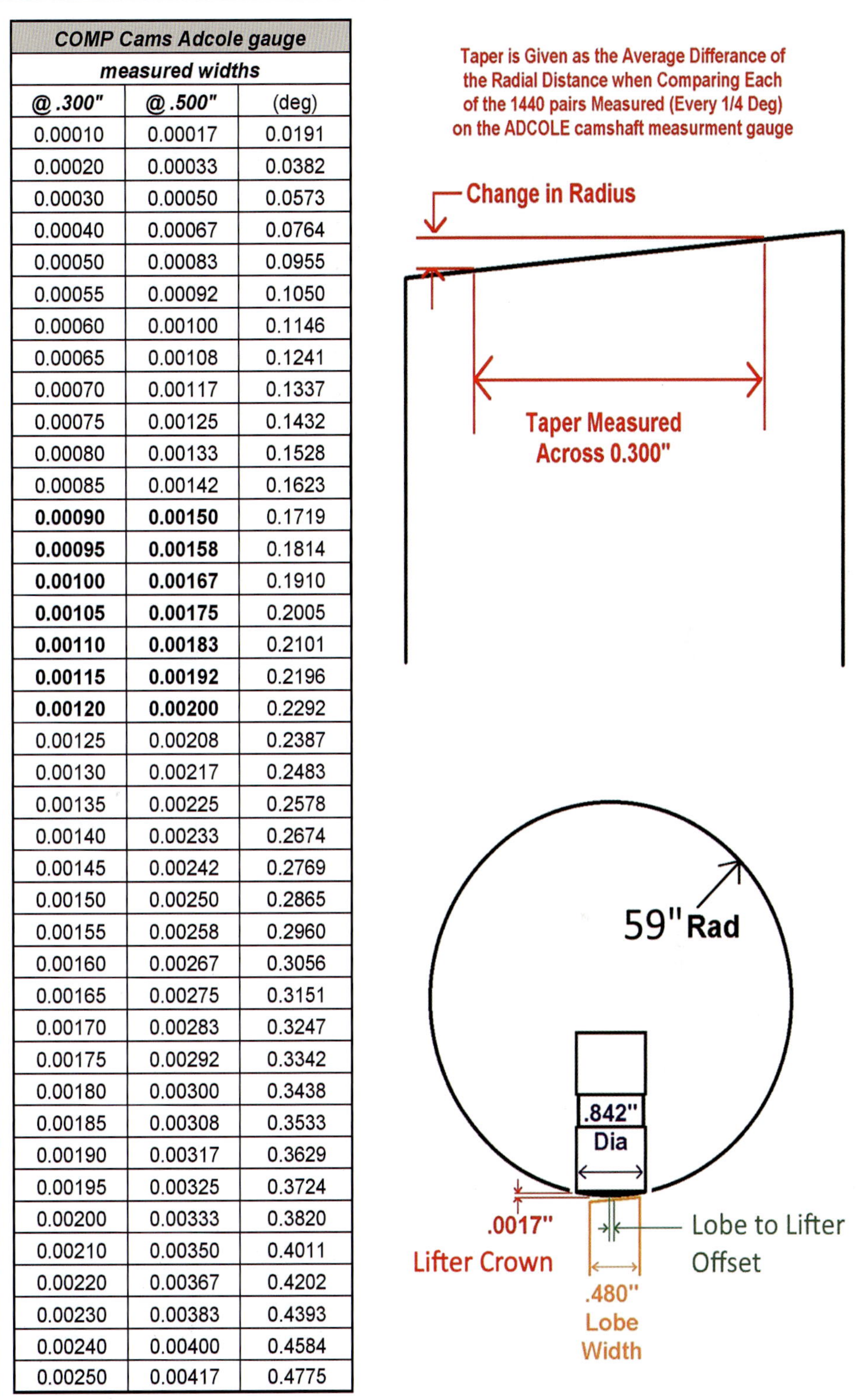

COMP Cams Adcole gauge		
measured widths		
@.300"	**@.500"**	(deg)
0.00010	0.00017	0.0191
0.00020	0.00033	0.0382
0.00030	0.00050	0.0573
0.00040	0.00067	0.0764
0.00050	0.00083	0.0955
0.00055	0.00092	0.1050
0.00060	0.00100	0.1146
0.00065	0.00108	0.1241
0.00070	0.00117	0.1337
0.00075	0.00125	0.1432
0.00080	0.00133	0.1528
0.00085	0.00142	0.1623
0.00090	**0.00150**	0.1719
0.00095	**0.00158**	0.1814
0.00100	**0.00167**	0.1910
0.00105	**0.00175**	0.2005
0.00110	**0.00183**	0.2101
0.00115	**0.00192**	0.2196
0.00120	**0.00200**	0.2292
0.00125	0.00208	0.2387
0.00130	0.00217	0.2483
0.00135	0.00225	0.2578
0.00140	0.00233	0.2674
0.00145	0.00242	0.2769
0.00150	0.00250	0.2865
0.00155	0.00258	0.2960
0.00160	0.00267	0.3056
0.00165	0.00275	0.3151
0.00170	0.00283	0.3247
0.00175	0.00292	0.3342
0.00180	0.00300	0.3438
0.00185	0.00308	0.3533
0.00190	0.00317	0.3629
0.00195	0.00325	0.3724
0.00200	0.00333	0.3820
0.00210	0.00350	0.4011
0.00220	0.00367	0.4202
0.00230	0.00383	0.4393
0.00240	0.00400	0.4584
0.00250	0.00417	0.4775

Image 1-58: This table is a great conversion for a 0.500-inch-wide check that you might make with a micrometer to the Adcole 0.300-inch-wide check. Just double the 0.500-inch number for measuring both sides at once, so 0.0040 inch with a micrometer is about 0.0012 inch on the Adcole. I prefer our low limit of 0.0009 over 0.300 inch.

an alignment error on the gauge (cuts high or low to center) as taper. Where taper really matters is on flat-tappet camshafts. The grinders need to be set up at the proper angle to verify it is hit with a flat-tappet design that uses taper and offset together to ensure rotation.

Image 1-59: I am not sure I have ever seen a flat-tappet cam fail because of heat treating or too little taper. I have seen them fail because the lifter had the wrong material, a cone face shape instead of a nice radius, or too big of a chamfer. The lifter labeled "Bad" has a face that looks just like a cone. The one labeled "Good" is spherical but not perfect. The ones with the swirl face are much better. If you look at your reflection in a lifter face, it should look like a funhouse mirror that shrinks you. If it distorts you, the face is not a sphere.

Image 1-60: If you slice and polish a flat-tappet cam core, the flame hardening drives the case all the way down into the barrel. I always wondered why I never had ground through the case of a flat-tappet regrind, but when we started sectioning flat-tappet cores, it became evident. However, when any camshaft fails, the lobe will get hot and temper that lobe. Hence, if you check the Rockwell HRC hardness after any lobe fails, it will always check at least a few points low.

Image 1-61: To wrap up taper, know that these parts come best as a matched set. The cam face and the lifter face need to be geometrically and metallurgically compatible. Lately, face is have been difficult to find.

Image 1-62: In the early 2000s, oils were the number-one contributor to cam-lobe failures. You cannot run to a parts store or big-box store and grab oil that is compatible with your flat-tappet camshaft, but this is not as big of a problem today. Keep a few cases of flat-tappet oil in your garage and a couple of quarts stashed in your car if you must run a flat-tappet camshaft.

The biggest fallacy in motorsports is the idea that more taper is better. Most GM, Ford, and Chrysler flat-tappet lifters are set up with a 50-inch bottom radius. Also, they generally have about a 0.050-inch lobe offset from the center of the lifter bore. Taper needs to be optimized for the design crown and offset (as shown in Images 1-54, 1-55, 1-56, and 1-57).

Added taper can add a little torque to the lifter that might help a bit during break-in with light springs, but it greatly reduces the surface contact and reduces life under high loads as the lower region of the lobe face becomes unused. A useful chart for comparing measured taper on a lathe or micrometer to our Adcole measurements is included in Image 1-58.

Lately, the most common problem in flat-tappet applications is the lifter face condition. Overseas suppliers often use steel faces instead of high-carbon cast iron, have excessive chamfers that let the contact point go off the edge, and often have faces that are more cone-shaped than spherical. Some of these issues are visible on the lifter faces in Image 1-59.

With any flat-tappet camshaft and lifter combination, the lobe taper needs to match the lifter crown and offset, and the material and geometry is critical. You need to run special oils in all flat-tappet applications because the United States Environmental Protection Agency (EPA) forced a reduction in wear additives that include zinc phosphates in all automotive oils that are found on store shelves today. Comp Cams has some great products, and Driven Oil is continuously testing new products to reduce flat-tappet wear during break-in and racing.

Now that you have a good understanding of camshaft terms, let's talk about what a camshaft does in the engine.

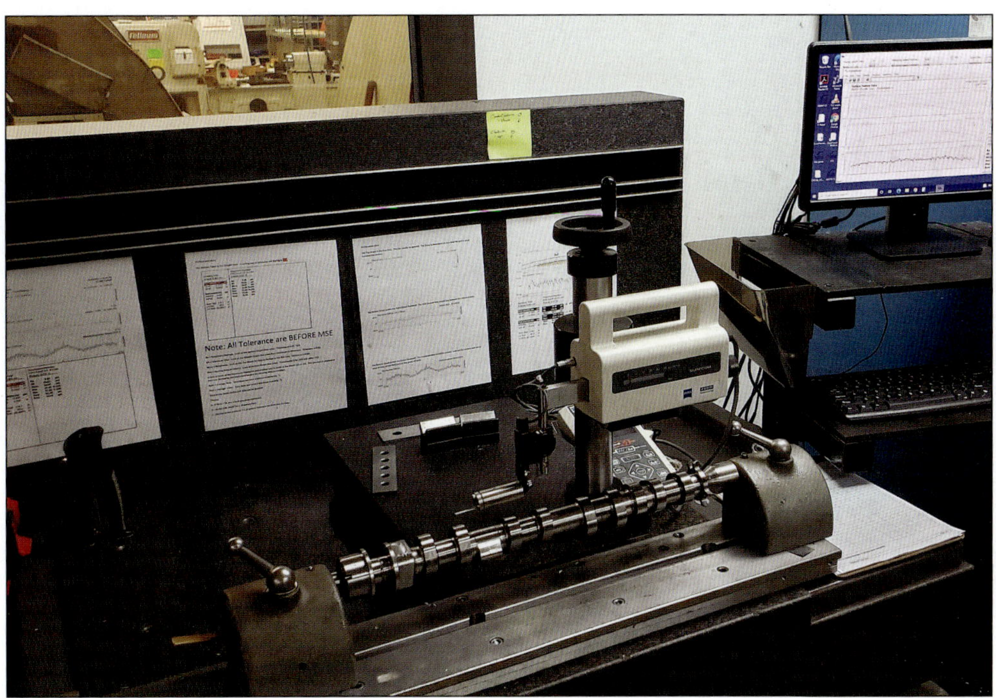

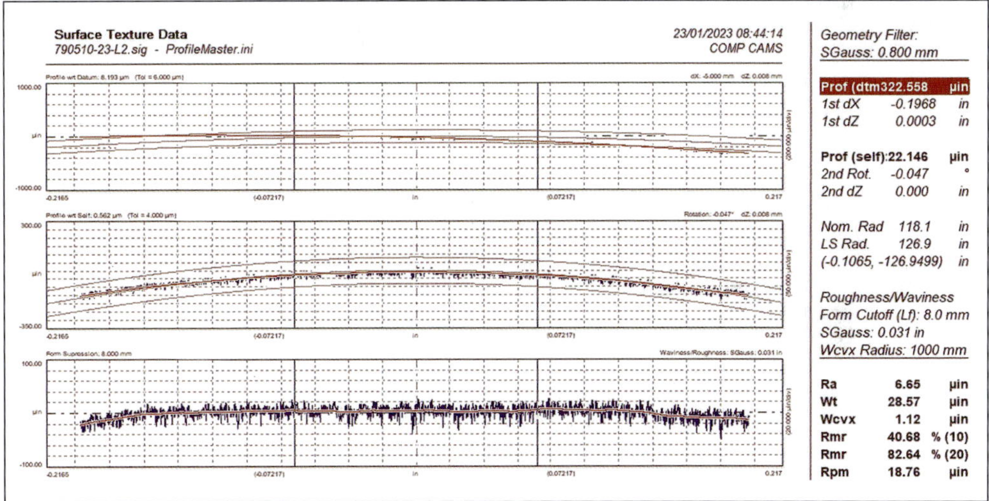

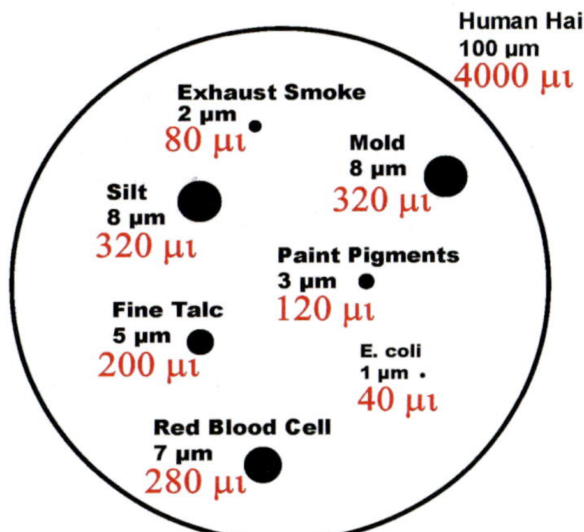

Images 1-63, 1-64, and 1-65: We measure surface contour and wear with a Zeiss Profilometer. This can measure down to 2 millionths of an inch repeatably. The bottom line on our surface reports has a minimum to maximum scale that barely fits a mold spore and equals two grains of fine talc, five particles of diesel exhaust smoke, or ten E. coli bacteria stacked on one another.

CHAPTER 2

Valvetrain Blueprinting

This chapter covers practical steps to take when setting up a valvetrain system and more advanced techniques that you may want to incorporate. I assume that you have a short-block assembled on an engine stand and the heads are almost ready to finish the long-block.

For these steps, the cylinder heads and complete valvetrain need to be on hand along with a degree wheel, dial indicator, checking springs (light flow-bench style), a selection of pushrods or adjustable versions, and a hydraulic-lifter set up as a solid with the intended preload for any hydraulic applications.

Start with a single-cylinder setup with checking springs. Everything except pushrod lengths and rocker sweep are similar on an overhead camshaft (OHC) application, but we will focus on an OHC setup.

Setting Rocker Height

The first step is looking at the rocker sweep on the valve tip to ensure the proper pivot height. The older way to do this was to use either machinist dye or a dry-erase marker on the valve tip, rotate the engine a few times, and adjust the height to minimize and center the sweep.

The problem with this approach is that you do not really watch the

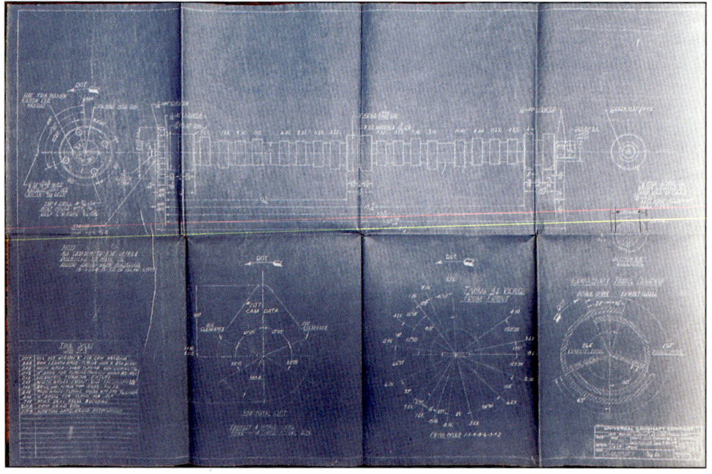

Image 2-1: When thinking of blueprinting, you may envision something like the print for a Flathead Ford 3/4 race cam by Universal Camshaft Company from 1955. However, what we are discussing is how to measure and set up your valvetrain correctly and does not require the amazing artistic talents possessed by most engineers of the mid-20th century.

Image 2-2: The blueprinting we will discuss is not engine-manufacturer specific. It deals more with dialing in the centerlines, setting up rockers, and optimizing valve springs than the different journal sizes and drive setups found on these various engine families.

action, so you cannot independently know if the height or the trunnion distance from the valve is most responsible for what causes a sweep offset. Many shaft rocker systems include a template that goes on the valve to set up the trunnion height, but I still recommend looking at the sweep so that you can alter the geometry if desired.

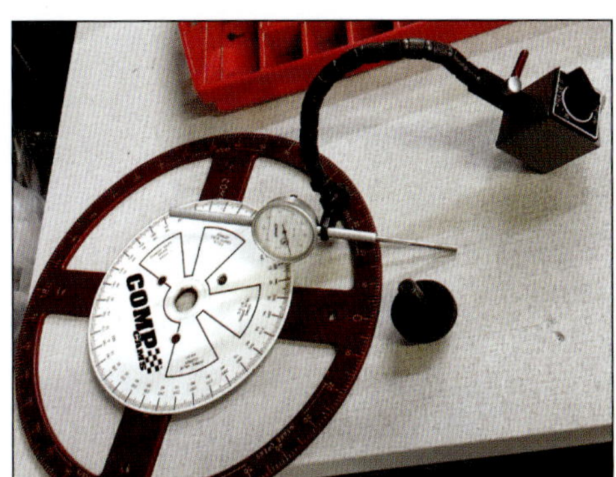

Image 2-3: A friend of mine, Jesse Smith, needed help to degree a prototype Ford Powerstroke camshaft that we had ground for him. I grabbed these two degree wheels, a dial indicator, an adjustable base, and a bolt and washer to attach the wheel as I headed out the door and to his shop. If you don't have these, I highly recommend adding them to your tool collection—but with a better stand and tips.

Image 2-5: Any sliding-tip rocker needs to sweep out from the base circle to max lift. If it changes direction for a minimum tip pattern, it will scuff and prematurely wear. This is what I mean about thinking about the action you are trying to achieve with your rocker sweep.

Image 2-6: I wish this rocker had been introduced with a roller trunnion, but it helped put Comp Cams on the map. The tip geometry was designed to mimic the OEM slider tip, so it will roll out as lift increases, just like a slider.

Images 2-7 and 2-8: The Pro Magnum steel rockers and Ultra Gold aluminum rockers share the exact same geometry as the original roller-tip rockers. If you set them up taller (more like a shaft geometry) it will increase the ratio, but it is not necessarily bad. It requires a longer pushrod and perhaps taller or shimmed studs to have enough threads engaged in the poly-lock.

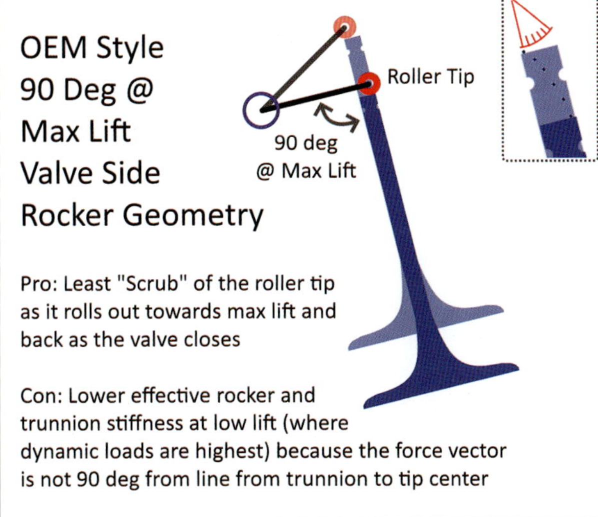

Image 2-4: When people set up pushrod lengths on stud-mounted systems or rocker heights for shaft or pedestal systems, don't just dye the tip and look at the pattern. You need to watch the sweep and think about what you are trying to achieve. Too often, someone will try to fix a small in-or-out misalignment by altering the height.

Image 2-4 shows a typical OEM or stud-mounted roller-tip geometry approach. With this layout, the roller, or slider tip, starts on the side of the valve tip closest to the trunnion and sweeps out throughout the travel. If you picture the valve tip as somewhat rough, like a set of gears, and a tip that is not easy to roll, you can see how these teeth engage outward as the lift increases. It is almost like each tooth of the rocker tip engages its own tooth on the valve tip (as sketched in the top-right box of this illustration).

Images 2-9 and 2-10: While you watch the rocker action, make sure the tips are also aligned front to back. The holes in every guide plate are oversized to allow some adjustment, but adjustable guide plates allow the engine builder to get this alignment just right.

This low-scrubbing velocity layout is required with a slider tip and was carried over in the Comp Cams roller-tip rockers that came out in the 1970s. In fact, almost all stud-mounted rockers follow the stock-type trunnion height and sweep geometry because it matches the rocker-ratio variation with the lift of stock rockers, holds up well under high endurance, and does not require a needle bearing tip.

Image 2-11: Not everyone has a sectioned small-block Chevy (SBC), but this is set up like you want for an engine to begin blueprinting. The valves are cracked with the lifters on the base circle of this single cylinder, and the valve springs have been replaced with flow-bench springs. The degree wheel is on the crank, but the pointer is not set yet.

To optimize the rocker height and watch the sweep, set up the head with checking springs on at least one cylinder with the valvetrain assembled and adjusted with both valves very slightly cracked open (0.002 to 0.005 inch) while on the base circle.

When running a hydraulic lifter, remove the check valve and spring from the bottom of the hydraulic piston inside the high-pressure chamber shown in Image 2-12. Shim the piston with washers (or whatever is handy and rigid) to the height that you intend to run with preload.

Image 2-12: I wish you didn't need to take a hydraulic lifter apart to blueprint it, but it is the best practice. After removing the retaining clip, use a pick or strong magnet to pull out the hydraulic piston. Then, remove the spring and valve that is in the high-pressure chamber. Finally, shim to the right height to crack the valves with the preload that you will run.

Once the valvetrain is assembled with the valves cracked, set up a dial indicator as close to parallel to the valve as possible with the tip near the edge of the valve-spring retainer. I recommend a 2-inch dial indicator used along with an extended-reach pointed tip. I use a fine-tip permanent marker to put a small dot on the retainer and then sweep the valve through full travel. I either turn the engine and cam or sweep the rocker to full lift by hand as I watch so that

Image 2-13: On this 7.3L Ford Godzilla engine, we did not want to take the heads on and off every time that we installed another camshaft. So, we had to let the lifters bleed down as we opened the valves to check each intake centerline. This is more time-consuming and does not allow you to check sweep and lift like you can with a modified hydraulic lifter.

Images 2-14 and 2-15: This is a much nicer indicator setup than the one I grabbed as I ran out the door. Note the pointed tip and less swear-inducing stand. If the stand moves on me, I tend to invent colorful adjectives. You also want a small-diameter extended tip so that you can mark a small dot on the retainer and see if the tip moves relative to the dot throughout the lift. When alignment is parallel to the valve, the tip contact is stationary on the retainer.

the tip does not move around on the retainer. If the contact point moves, the alignment needs adjustment until it hits the same point on the retainer at any lift.

Once the dial indicator is aligned, get a stool to sit on so that you can position your head to watch the sweep closely while rotating the engine. Having all the spark plugs removed and only running flow-bench springs (such as Comp Cams part number 4758-2) makes this much easier than fighting a high-compression race engine with triple springs.

Image 2-17 shows the stand and trunnion heights that are recommended by most shaft-mounted rocker companies. This configuration has the tip sweep out the first half of the travel and then back in the last half. In general, this geometry should have increased stiffness at lower lifts where acceleration is highest over the OEM tip geometry but benefits from lower-friction roller tips (because this configuration has the highest "wheel

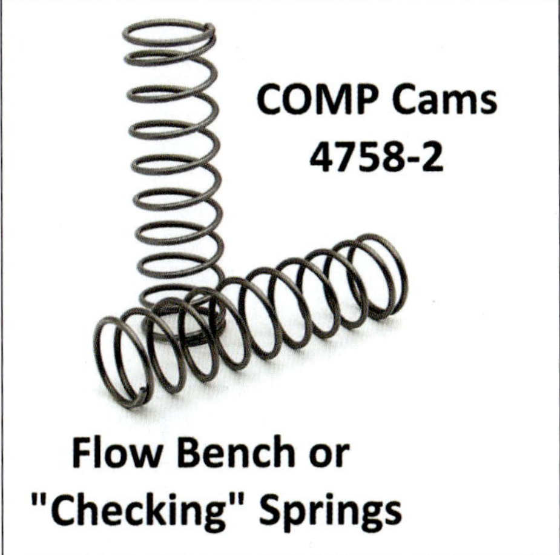

Image 2-16: Flow-bench springs, or checking springs, are required to check undeflected lift and stiffness along with making everything easier. Any light spring that fits your pocket will work. Try to find something with less than 5 pounds open load if the Comp 4578s will not fit. Lee Spring, Granger, and others have a selection.

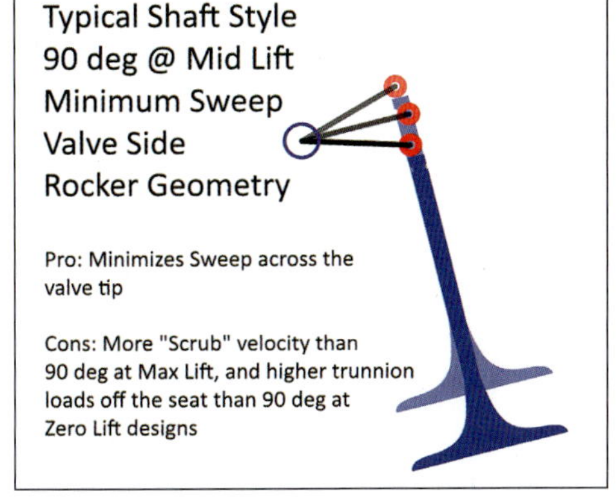

Image 2-17: Shaft rockers typically have a minimal-sweep geometry. With a low-friction tip, this design presses straight down the guide. The best Jesel and T&D rockers have a needle-bearing tip to allow this or any geometry without the tip scrubbing and wearing either the tip or the guides. With a standard tip, something between this and the OEM geometry is safer.

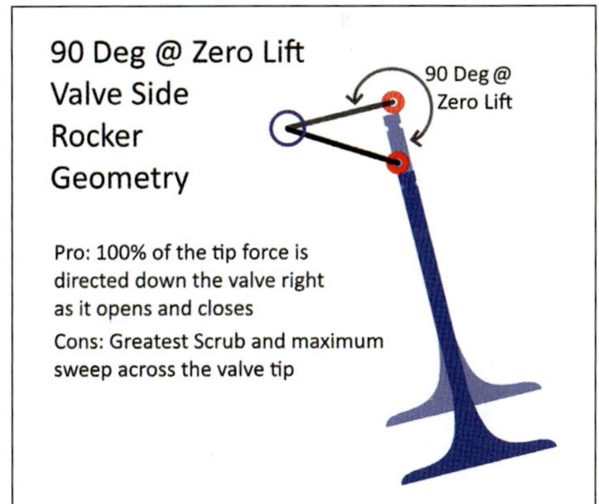

Image 2-18: With a perpendicular-at-zero-lift geometry and a needle-bearing tip, the rocker presses straight down the guide at the highest acceleration. Something between the mid lift and this geometry is best if you could ever create a truly friction-less tip.

scrub" velocity relative to the valve tip, especially at the end of sweep).

Some race teams work around a 90-degree off-the-seat approach for increased rocker stiffness at low lift, but this has the highest scrub speed. This should only be attempted with a needle-bearing-tip rocker. Pushing straight down near maximum acceleration is attractive, but the resulting friction can be problematic.

If you have slider tips, go with the OEM configuration. For most roller tips, I like to hit 90 degrees at about 2/3 lift (between OEM and 90 at max-lift geometry). This adds stiffness (low) over OEM with a smaller sweep path and a more consistent rocker ratio through the sweep. OEM geometries typically gain more than a point of ratio between low and high lift.

Setting Lash or Preload

As you set up any engine, the lash with mechanical (solid) systems or the preload with hydraulic systems must be controlled. The lash is the mechanical clearance between the valve tip and either the rocker tip or follower that activates the valve. There must be some clearance here in mechanical systems because the valve reaches operating temperature far more quickly than the head and block, which may hold the valve off the seat and destroy the interface, like a cutting torch, if a small gap remains at firing. My rule of thumb is at least 0.004-inch intake lash and 0.006-inch exhaust lash at the coldest possible temperature.

A series of unfortunate failures at the 24 Hours of Daytona following a rainstorm, red flag, and cold front taught me that tighter can be a very bad idea.

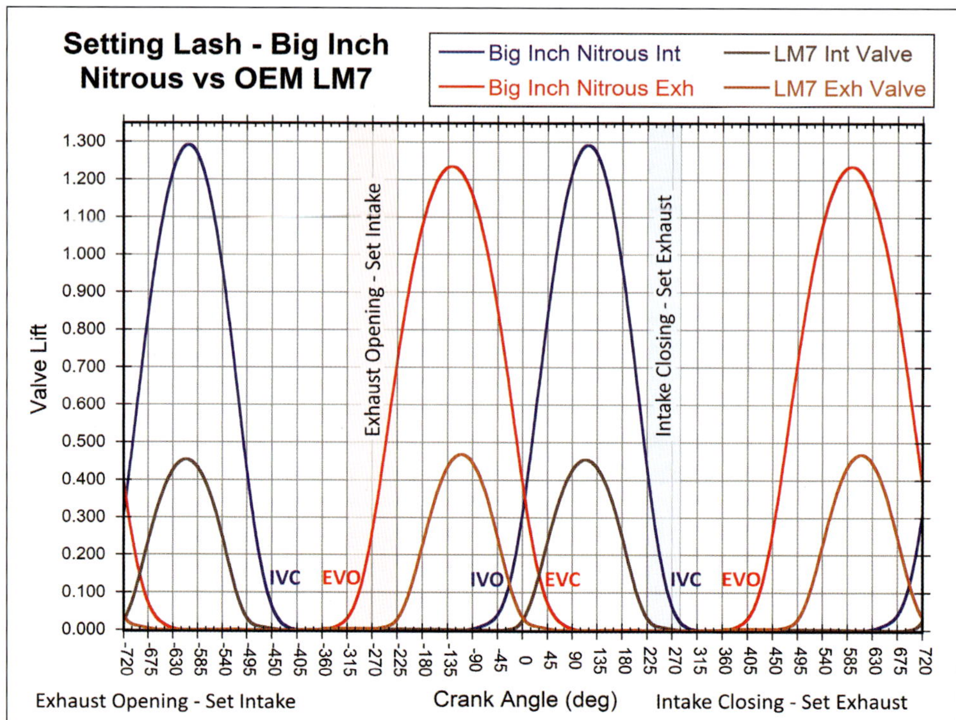

Image 2-19: This is an extreme (big-inch nitrous versus stock truck) example, but note how little time both valves are closed during racing. Also note how well the red-tinted window near EVO fits between IVC and IVO where the intake is closed. Likewise, the blue window around IVC falls between EVC and EVO while the exhaust is closed. These windows are absolutely the best place to set lash or preload.

Where to Set Lash and Preload

You will hear of quick ways to set up lash and preload where you adjust several cylinders at a time. That might be okay with some stock camshafts and applications where you don't need to be precise.

However, in any performance application, I recommend to set the intake right after EVO, and set exhaust right after IVC. For any possible four-stroke design, the intake follower will always be on the base circle at EVO.

Likewise, the exhaust follower will be on the base circle at IVC. These events are easy to watch for as you rotate the crank in the engine direction. Simply wait for the exhaust valve or pushrod to start moving on the cylinder that you are setting and

Image 2-20: Jeff Smith has probably set lash a million times. There are tools that I like from Comp Cams, LSM, and others to torque the adjuster with an Allen wrench holding the set screw to make this even easier. Note how he holds the feeler gauges. Most engine builders leave the feeler hanging while torquing the adjuster, and then they recheck the feel before removing.

adjust the intake lash or preload. Then, keep rotating after the intake is set until the intake is about to close and set the exhaust lash or preload. I recommend running one bank at a time and double-checking each cylinder on a solid.

How to Set Lash

On some overhead-finger or rocker-follower systems, it is easier to check clearance between the cam and follower pad. For most solid systems, set lash with a feeler gauge between the valve tip and rocker or follower tip. There are various ways that engine builders like the lash to feel as they insert and remove a feeler gauge. I like a sightly firm feel as the gauge is inserted, but the feeler needs to be loose enough that it can be removed from the side without excessive effort and certainly no tick from a valve closing.

Try the in-straight, wiggle, and remove-out-the-side approach. The best method is one that you can replicate and be verified within 0.002 inch. Practice until you have a matching feel for lash. If what I call a 0.018-inch lash is what you call a 0.015-inch lash, it is not the end of the world if you can reproduce your lash every time. Whenever the valvetrain shows distress or excess noise at your 0.018-inch lash, try a slightly tighter setting as that may be the cause. I try to give a +/-0.004-inch lash window on any design.

An engine was set up with the adjuster fixed using red Loctite at the Advanced Engine Technology conference in Colorado Springs. Scooter Brothers, Thomas Griffin, and I left a set of feeler gauges out. We asked everyone to feel the lash and report their measurements in a closed and locked ballot box. When the votes were counted, the total spread was almost 0.008 inch, but everyone was in the range of about 0.015 to 0.023 inch on something that was called 0.019 inch with the in-straight, wiggle, and out-the- side method that Scooter taught me.

How to Set Hydraulic Preload

Preload on a hydraulic lifter can be almost as important as lash on a solid lifter. The best method is to set up a dial indicator in line with the pushrod or adjuster (as shown in Image 2-21) to directly measure the preload. However, the common way is to tighten the adjuster or bolt down until the pushrod gets tight enough to feel drag with oily fingertips and observe the rotation to set the preload.

With a rocker that has a tail adjuster, the preload for a quarter, half, or full turn is simply one over the thread pitch divided by the number of turns (as shown in Image 2-22). If you have a trunnion bolt-down or stud adjuster, take the ratio into account (as shown in Image 2-21 and the bottom table of 2-22).

Most full-travel lifters have a 0.150-plus-inch total adjustment

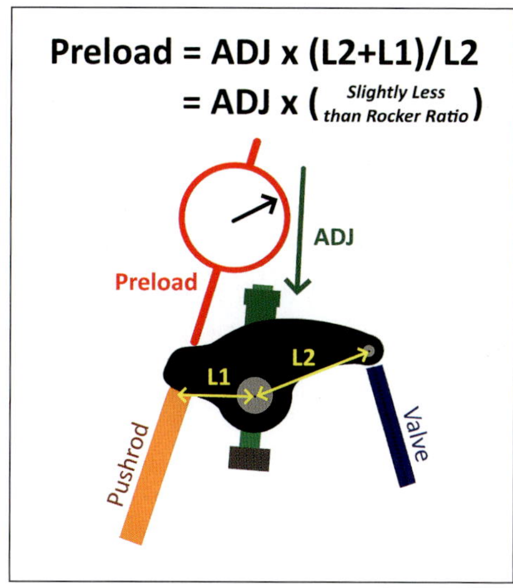

Image 2-21: This sketch shows the best way to check preload as well as the math (if you want to set it by turns at the adjuster). It does not take long to check preload the correct way, but people typically tighten the stud or bolt until they feel drag on the pushrod and then count partial turns.

Adjuster Movement in Inches vs Rotation for Common Threads and Resulting Preload

	TPI					*Metric*			
Thread Pitch	18	**20**	**24**	28	32	1.75	1.5	**1.25**	1
Quarter Turn	0.014	**0.013**	**0.010**	0.009	0.008	0.017	0.015	**0.012**	0.010
Half Turn	0.028	**0.025**	**0.021**	0.018	0.016	0.034	0.030	**0.025**	0.020
Per Turn	0.056	**0.050**	**0.042**	0.036	0.031	0.069	0.059	**0.049**	0.039
Approximate Preload at Lifter with 1.7:1 Rocker Ratio - Adjusted at Trunnion									
Quarter Turn		**0.020**	**0.017**					**0.020**	
Half Turn		**0.040**	**0.033**					**0.039**	
Per Turn		**0.080**	**0.067**					**0.079**	

Image 2-22: Note how closely the rule of thumb of 0.020-inch preload per quarter turn of trunnion adjuster turn falls in with our calculations in this table. This is just as true for a 7/16-inch x 20 TPI stud on a big-block Chevy as an 8-mm x 1.25 mm trunnion bolt on an LS—and even close on a 3/8 inch x 24 TPI.

range, whereas short-travel lifters typically have 0.050-plus-inch total adjustment range, allowing some combination of 0.050-inch pushrod-length steps to work. As preload is set deeper, the high-pressure camber volume reduces, and there is less reaming travel for the adjustment to collapse under high loads. Hence, some engine builders and I favor deep preloads.

However, going back to the 1960s Chevrolet 409, other engine builders prefer light preload to allow the engine to rev through fussy spots of 0.015- to 0.030-inch valve bounce. Hydraulic adjusters can adjust up during valve bounce and hold the valve open for an additional 30 to 50 degrees. This often resulted in a little cloud of fuel over the carburetor on dyno testing and is commonly referred to as lifter pump up, even though it is not a great description. With a well-designed profile and matched system, you should have great results with deep preload.

Calculating Optimal Spring Setup Height

Now that the dial indicator is set up to measure lift, we can properly set up the valve springs for this application. The best practice is to start with two or more sets of the valve springs that you intend to run and then check the coil bind height of each individual spring. This takes a little time, but coil bind height is probably the most difficult aspect to control when manufacturing a formed wire valve spring. Either number the springs and record the bind heights in a spreadsheet or write the bind height of each spring on the flat, ground region of the top coil. An example of where I measured and sorted two sets of 7228s with the intention to run these above their rated lift is shown in Image 2-25.

The more sets of springs you can check each time, the tighter window you can set for each group of eight that you will set aside to run together on either the intake or exhaust. For double springs, run a shim or washer the same thickness as the retainer step and check the assembly. You could also disassemble the springs and check the inner and outer separately. Typically, duals and triples are set so that the outer binds first, as this is easier to see, so disassembly is only common at the NASCAR level.

When sorting springs by bind height, I lightly oil and then cycle

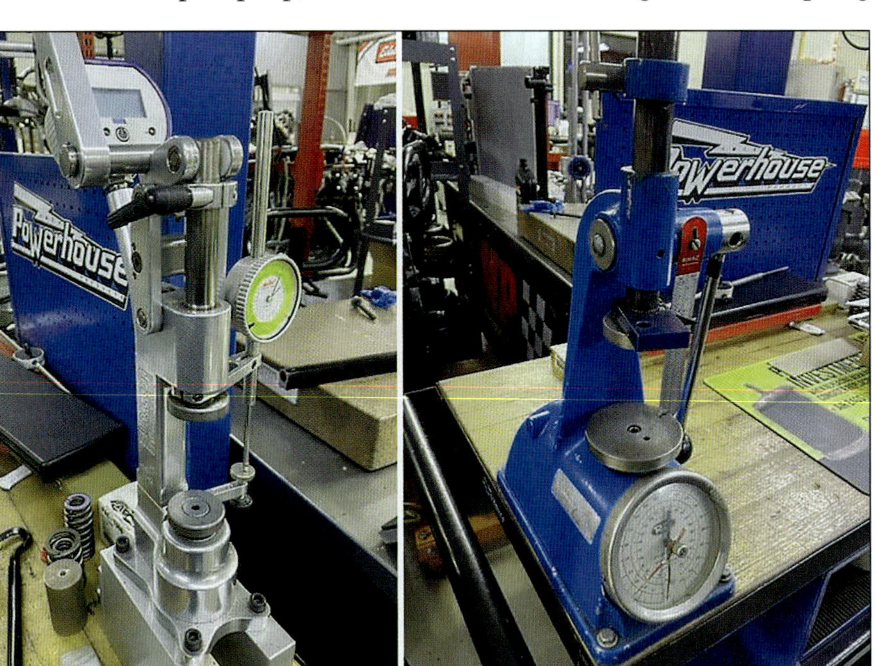

Image 2-23: We have two manual spring gauges in the research and development department so that we can set up springs quickly. Every valve spring is sorted by coil bind height, and loads are recorded before installation. If you do not have a spring gauge, you can still sort by bind height by using a simple benchtop vise. Just be very gentle as you compress, and then measure the solid height with a caliper.

Image 2-24: Performance Trends, Larson, and other companies have some awesome computer-connected valve-spring test gauges, such as this one at EFI University. If you set up heads every day in a race shop, automation makes this less tedious. Automatic or manual gauges both require you to oil the springs and cycle them before recording loads for accurate results.

7228 Valve Spring Sort Example

Open Load (lbs)	460	Gross 7228 Lift =	0.698	Net 7288 Lift =	0.684
System Stiffness	21905	Gross Check Spring Lift=	0.719	Net Check Spring Lift=	0.705

Spring #	Bind Height	Net CS Lift 0.705	Max Dist to CS Bnd 0.050	Max IH	Min Dist to CS Bnd 0.035	Min IH
13	1.035			1.790		1.775
30	1.038			1.793		1.778
21	1.040			1.795		1.780
28	1.040			1.795		1.780
24	1.045			1.800		1.785
1	1.047			1.802		1.787
19	1.047			1.802		1.787
22	1.048			1.803		1.788
29	1.048			1.803		1.788
25	1.049			1.804		1.789
20	1.050			1.805		1.790
26	1.050			1.805		1.790
31	1.050			1.805		1.790
7	1.053			1.808		1.793
17	1.054			1.809		1.794
11	1.055			1.810		1.795
12	1.055			1.810		1.795
18	1.055			1.810		1.795
23	1.055			1.810		1.795
9	1.056			1.811		1.796
4	1.060			1.815		1.800
15	1.060			1.815		1.800
10	1.062			1.817		1.802
5	1.063			1.818		1.803
32	1.063			1.818		1.803
2	1.065			1.820		1.805
14	1.065			1.820		1.805
3	1.068			1.823		1.808
6	1.069			1.824		1.809
16	1.069			1.824		1.809
8	1.070			1.825		1.810
27	1.071			1.826		1.811

Image 2-25: Dave Henninger and I both needed 7228s for heads that we were building. We combined our sets and measured each spring to establish two intake sets that could operate just above 0.680-inch lift at 1.800-inch installed height. File my above-rated lift under "don't try this at home," but the setup strategy from coil bind, which is based on gross and net lift, is extremely beneficial for any build.

Image 2-26: The proper dial indicator setup is shown. Other than going with the extended tips, I love his setup. Here, Jeff measures the system stiffness of the shaft rockers that Shane Pulido had provided for the story. So, there is a combination of real and checking springs. (Photo Courtesy Jeff Smith)

each spring to bind three times to make sure the coils move freely. I then measure the loads near the seat and open heights both as they compress and relax. Honestly, a 10-percent change in load should matter less to dynamics than a 0.030-inch difference in the distance to bind, but any good data on hand should be recorded. This provides a second sorting criteria if you run though 10 or more sets at a time at race engine shops. If the compression loads are more than a few pounds higher than the relaxing loads, re-oil the damper or springs and recheck. The fitment between inner and outer might be tight if it continues to check high on compression.

Checking Undeflected and Deflected Lift

Once the bind heights are recorded, check the max valve lift at 0 lash both with the checking spring and the real spring (as shown in Images 2-26 through 2-29). Changing the rocker design, trunnion height, and pushrod lengths changes the checking-spring lift. Rocker arms are never continuous ratios through the full sweep. Most are cheated up about a quarter to a half point so that

Image 2-27: The Comp Pro Magnum is tested both with and without stud girdles as well as the Crower shaft setup that Shane Pulido sent. The reason to start without lash and the valves cracked is that every rocker and pushrod system has a little slack in the socket and trunnion. By beginning with everything seated, you will get far more repeatable results. Also, be very careful between the two springs to set up the indicator correctly. (Photo Courtesy Jeff Smith)

Image 2-28: The dial indicator is set right on top of the retainer ridge. Unless you set up the indicator perfectly, the tip will move off this ridge and give erroneous measurements. That is why I recommend the small-diameter extended tip and put a dot on the retainer to guarantee that the tip is not moving around on top of the retainer. Once it is set up, I change the springs on the head while someone holds the indicator tip. Otherwise, I measure everything twice with two separate setups. (Photo Courtesy Jeff Smith)

Image 2-29: Running different rockers, pushrods, stands, and girdles, it is clear that the measured stiffness from these tests correlated to power, especially at high RPM. (Photo Courtesy Jeff Smith)

the deflected lift checks very close to the advertised ratio. When you change stiffness with a better rocker design, something like a stud girdle, stiffer rocker stand, or stiffer pushrod, the deflected lift is higher with less deflection.

If you want to understand the rocker ratio sweep, add a degree wheel to the crank and put the dial indicator on the lifter. Write down the angle where the lift reaches each 0.025 or 0.050 inch of tappet lift. Then, go back and check the unloaded valve lifts at each angle. Don't be surprised to see a rated 1.7:1 rocker that is under 1.6:1 off the seat and approaching 1.8:1 in the last 0.025 inch of lift motion. This is more of a pro tip for comparing the ratio sweep of a T&D versus Jesel versus Del West rocker design because every manufacturer sets up the sweep differently based on the front- and rear-side geometries.

Image 2-30: Pay close attention to how Dan Jesel incorporated the rocker stands into the strongest part of his Equal 8 cylinder heads and then had the bolts close together. This is certainly one of my favorite engines of all time, and it is my favorite valvetrain layout. If there was any possible way to improve on something this well done, it might involve incorporating some sort of steel girdle above the rockers. Good designers never leave anything alone.

Calculating System Stiffness

With the full unloaded and loaded lift both with 0 lash, you can calculate the total system stiffness that equals the pounds of load at the valve to result in a 1-inch deflection.

Jeff Smith, whom I am extremely thankful to count among my friends, has two very good articles about system stiffness. In 2018, the first article appeared in *Engine Labs*, where he used the Godbold Stiffness Rating (GSF). Another article was in *Motor Trend* from 2019.

Scan the QR code below to see Jeff Smith's 2018 article about system stiffness that appeared in *Engine Labs*.

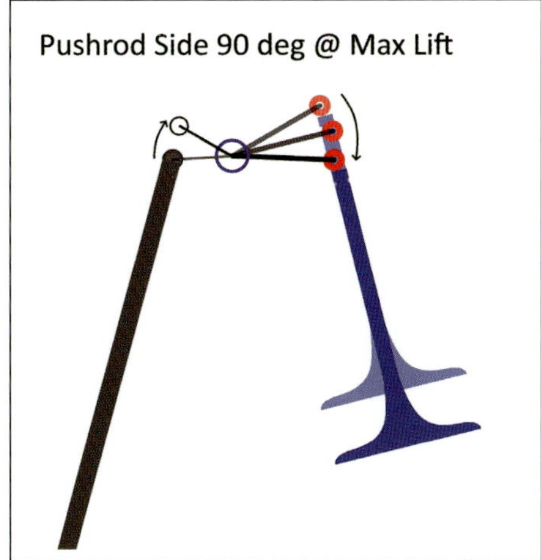

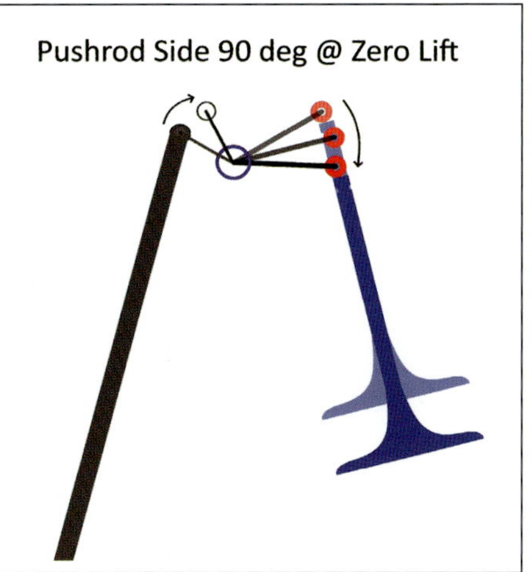

Images 2-31 and 2-32: Unless you have the opportunity to design rocker-arm bodies, the back-side geometry of any rocker is basically fixed. A screw adjuster can move it a little bit but not much. However, this side can greatly alter the ratio sweep and has been used to create designs, such as the Crane quick-lift rockers, where the low lift ratio was higher than the total ratio. Something between these two extremes might be the best approach, but then the pushrod tip changes three times each event instead of once.

Scan the QR code below to see Jeff Smith's 2019 article about system stiffness that appeared in *MotorTrend.*

To calculate the system stiffness, subtract the flow-bench spring load from the real spring load and divide that by the difference in lift. Typically, the flow-bench spring is effectively 0 pounds open, so a 600-pound open load spring that results in 0.02-inch deflection is 24,000 in-lbs stiffness as calculated from the equation below:

System Stiffness (Pounds/Inch) = (Difference in Load) ÷ (Difference in Lift)

Most stud-mounted systems fall somewhere in the 18K to 25K range, and shaft-mounted systems will typically be in the 22K to 30K range. Pedestal mounts, such as the LS3 example in Image 2-33, fall somewhere in between. Any OHV pushrod and rocker valvetrain system over 45K probably had a mismeasurement. It is extremely easy not to get the dial indicator aligned perfectly when swapping from the flow bench to the real spring, so double-checking is wise.

Knowing the loaded deflection is required to properly set up the spring. Any valve spring performs the best dynamically when it operates within a certain distance to bind. For most OHV systems, this is approximately 0.050 to 0.120 inch from bind at full lift including lash and deflection. The greater the system deflection, the

Stock LS3 Rocker Ratio Sweep & System Stiffness

LS3 Intake Ratio Sweep - Loaded

Tappet Lift	Intake Valve Stock	Stock Ratio Instant	Stock Rocker Spring Load
0.050	0.069	1.38	163.8
0.100	0.146	1.54	202.7
0.150	0.225	1.58	242.6
0.200	0.311	1.72	286.1
0.250	0.397	1.72	329.5
0.300	0.485	1.76	373.9
0.350	0.577	1.84	420.4
0.365	0.606		435.0
	Total Ratio=	1.660	

LS3 Intake Ratio Sweep - Unloaded

Tappet Lift	Intake Valve Stock	Stock Ratio Instant	Stock Deflection	Stock Rocker System Stiffness
0.050	0.068	1.36	-0.001	
0.100	0.146	1.56	0.000	
0.150	0.224	1.56	-0.001	
0.200	0.316	1.84	0.005	
0.250	0.408	1.84	0.011	
0.300	0.499	1.82	0.014	
0.350	0.595	1.92	0.018	
0.365	0.626		0.020	21751.5
	Total Ratio=	1.715		

LS3 Exhaust Ratio Sweep - Loaded

Tappet Lift	Exhaust Valve Stock	Stock Ratio Instant	Stock Rocker Spring Load
0.050	0.074	1.48	166.4
0.100	0.151	1.54	205.3
0.150	0.232	1.62	246.2
0.200	0.319	1.74	290.1
0.250	0.406	1.74	334.0
0.300	0.497	1.82	380.0
0.350	0.589	1.84	426.4
0.365	0.620		442.1
	Total Ratio=	1.699	

LS3 Exhaust Ratio Sweep - Unoaded

Tappet Lift	Exhaust Valve Stock	Stock Ratio Instant		Stock Rocker System Stiffness
0.050	0.07	1.4	-0.004	
0.100	0.147	1.54	-0.004	
0.150	0.232	1.7	0.000	
0.200	0.323	1.82	0.004	
0.250	0.415	1.84	0.009	
0.300	0.509	1.88	0.012	
0.350	0.606	1.94	0.017	
0.365	0.640		0.020	22105
	Total Ratio=	1.753		

Image 2-33: When I talk about loaded- versus checkingspring-ratio sweeps, this table shows measurements Jamison Wilcox made for an LS3. Note how the instantaneous ratios increase with lift and how the undeflected ratio is considerably higher than the 1.7:1 that everyone talks about for a stock LS3. This might take you most of a Saturday, but it is worth it as you try to understand the valvetrain system.

farther from loaded bind the system should be run. At high RPM, there will be less spring load transferred to the rocker and pushrod, as that force is used to control the motion. Hence, when dynamic lift is measured, it gets closer to the flow-bench lift minus lash as RPM increases.

Underlift

When there is 0.030-inch deflection with the real spring, Professor Gordon Blair called that "underlift." Hence, the first 0.030 inch of increased lift with RPM was not considered "loft." Instead, it's "less dynamic deflection." Until the measured dynamic lift was greater than the flow-bench spring lift minus the lash, the system is not in real loft, or separation over the nose. Because we want to dampen the valve-spring surge over the nose at high speed using the running distance to bind, the clearance should be based on the high-RPM lift and not the engine-stand lift.

Distance to Bind

Using each measured spring bind and the measured undeflected lift, most systems like to run close to 0.040 inch from undeflected lift to bind. For example, looking back at Image 2-25, you can see how I calculated system stiffness and then calculated the required installed height for each valve spring to result in a 0.035- to 0.050-inch distance to bind at the net undeflected lift. Net lift includes lash, and gross lift is without lash. For this case, I set aside the springs that bound at a shortened height for the higher-lift intake side and then used the taller coil bind springs on the lower-lift exhaust side. This allowed a spring normally rated for 0.650-inch lift to

Image 2-34: Optimizing valve-spring dynamic distance to bind is probably one of the best tools I know for professional-level race teams, but it has been difficult for most Sportsman racers to explore. Ben Strader at EFI University now offers Spintron testing at a price around twice what you might spend for a day of high-level dyno tuning. Running 0.040 inch from undeflected net lift is a great start, but he can help you dial that in for any spring and system.

be run slightly above 0.680 inch in my 1.800-inch-max-installed-height heads.

Conical valve springs, such as the Comp Cams 7228 and 7230, are extremely sensitive to distance to bind because the coils nest inside one another and do a great job dampening over the nose when they come together under control. Lightweight dual springs are almost as sensitive to distance to bind. Heavier springs might run better with slightly more room. However, only very old spring designs should be run at high speed with more than 0.100-inch clearance to bind at max undeflected lift. Running the springs tighter gives the system a great opportunity to reset.

My wife used to teach first through third grades at a Montessori school. I have seen her gently place her hand on a wiggly boy's shoulder and he instantly calmed down. That's exactly our goal with distance to bind. Too far to bind, and the spring continues to surge unabatedly. Too tight, and we might be slapping it and create greater agitation. Either ask your spring manufacturer or get someone like Benjamin Strader at EFI University to test your system at various heights on a Spintron if you ever want to dial this in the way that it is done in most professional race series. High-speed video of valve springs running at various distances to bind is very informative.

Measuring and Setting Installed Height

Now that we know coil bind heights, have measured the intake and exhaust side lift with the real and checking springs, and have calculated a target installed height based on distance to bind, it is time to set up the heads. For this, use a spring height gauge, such as those shown

Images 2-35, 2-36, and 2-37: Knowing where you want to set up your springs based on net undeflected lift and coil bind is awesome, but you still need to hit that target height. I have tried most height gauges and snap gauges. So far, these height gauges from PAC are my favorite. Remember, trying to produce something better than you can measure it is known as guessing.

from PAC in Images 2-35, 2-36, and 2-37. Use the intended spring seats, valve locks, and valve-spring retainers and choose the correct shims under the seats to set each installed height. Write the installed height on the rail next to each spring as it is set up (as shown in Image 2-38).

Image 2-38: Once you set up each valve-spring installation height, the best practice is to write the height on the valve-cover rail as demonstrated by Eric and Anthony at Horsepower Research (HPR). I know this seems simple, but then you can get a phone call and remember exactly where you were in the process and help place assorted valve springs.

Degreeing a Camshaft

While we have the dial indicators in place from finding peak lift, it is the perfect time to both verify the centerlines (commonly called degreeing the camshaft) and check piston-to-valve clearance. The first question is "Should I degree my camshaft?"

The two potential negatives of not taking the time to degree a camshaft are loss of performance and possible piston-to-valve interference.

If you are off by 4 crank degrees, the loss of performance is going to be in the neighborhood of 10 ft-lbs on a 400 ft-lb/400-hp application—but only on the extreme ends of the torque curve. That is a big deal in racing, but it's probably not dramatically bad on the street.

However, those 4 degrees will reduce piston-to-valve clearance by about 0.030 inch on either the exhaust or intake. If you were already tight, checking the camshaft intake centerline can save your engine. If you assemble enough engines,

Image 2-39: This is Jesse's Ford Powerstroke. It took a little work to attach the small wheel and set up the pointer, but we were degreeing the cam within 30 minutes. There was no easy way to fit the preferred large wheel on the partially dressed engine.

Image 2-41: I am turning the 7.3L slowly in the direction of normal rotation until the piston gently hits the spark-plug stop about 34.3 degrees before TDC. No pistons or piston stops were harmed during the taking of these pictures.

Image 2-40: I prefer the blue head-off piston stop, but the gold spark-plug style works great if you can take your time. If you know someone or are someone who is always going too fast and breaking things, it is probably best to keep the spark-plug style out of reach.

eventually you will install a camshaft timing set with the alignment a tooth off. If you degree every camshaft, you will always catch this mistake.

Comp Cams and Edelbrock degrees every camshaft for testing because the changes we look for are typically within the range of 10 ft-lbs. However, with all the components that can contribute to the centerline moving a degree or two, it is a great habit for anyone to add to their engine-building process.

The first step is to put a degree wheel on the crank with a pointer and then add a piston stop to the number-one cylinder. The head-off style that bolts to the deck and uses another bolt in the middle to stop the piston is better than a spark-plug

Image 2-42: Going back around counterclockwise to the piston stop on the other side of TDC, the piston made firm contact with the stop at 34.0 degrees ATDC. From here, I move the pointer between the two measurements (about 34.15 degrees) and re-verify the clockwise stop until I am satisfied that both measurements are equal on the opposite sides of zero.

style, but you can use either style as long as you are careful as the piston approaches TDC.

I just eyeball to set the degree wheel pointer close to 0 at TDC without the piston stop. Then, I turn the engine in the direction of normal rotation to drop the piston about 1 inch and add the piston stop. Then, slowly turning the engine the opposite direction, I gently hit the piston stop and check the degree wheel reading (as shown in Image 2-41).

Once I record the number, I rotate it about three-quarters of a turn in the running direction and then slow down to gently hit the stop on the BTDC side. If you have the TDC pointer correct, the BTDC side shown in Image 2-42 will match the distance from TDC seen on the ATDC check in Image 2-41. If it is off, move the pointer or wheel half the difference and verify by retouching the stops

Image 2-43: I removed the piston stop and have moved to checking the max-lift intake centerline. This takes a little patience, as I must wait for the lifter to bleed down as it comes up the ramp. I am doing this while tuning clockwise, as I don't have much faith in the stock chain tensioner if I try to turn it counterclockwise.

Image 2-44: By now, my patience is spent, and I have given the cam-degree job to Jamison Wilcox. Note how he is carefully watching the indicator as he rotates the engine. When he bumps the crank to hit the exact lift target before or after peak lift, he will look at the degree wheel and record the angle with respect to TDC.

Image 2-45: The indicator was zeroed at peak lift with the hydraulic lifter bottomed out. We are tuning it until 0.050 inch before peak lift as we find TDC. The alignment looks a little off, which is okay for finding the centerlines but will cause a mess for undeflected versus deflected lift measurements. However, this apparent misalignment is probably the angle of the camera.

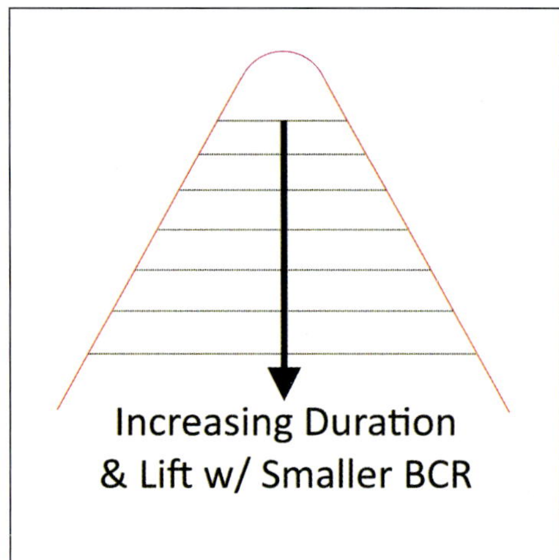

Image 2-46: In the days of flat-tappet camshafts, most cams had the same centerlines (110 LSA +4 advance was very common for street and 106 LSA +0 advance for race), and the lift and duration moved with one another as I am trying to show with these rounded triangles. As lift increased, I went smaller on the base circle and farther down so durations increased.

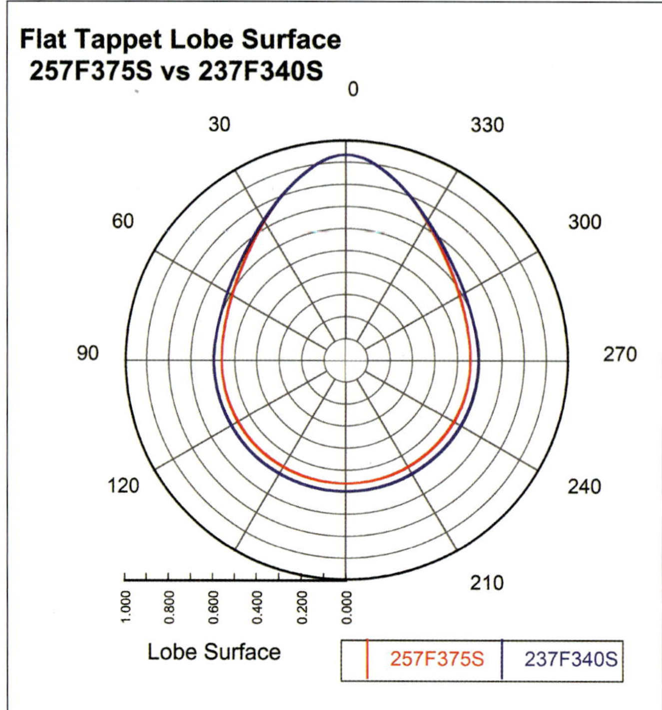

Image 2-47: This is easier to see looking at real lobe surfaces. The blue design is a 237 at 0.050-inch lobe with 0.340-inch lift. The red design is a 257 at 0.050-inch lobe with 0.375-inch lift. Both are made to fit inside a Chevy 1.868-inch journal. Note how both noses are the same. The larger-duration design has a smaller base circle, like a pyramid with a larger base. The red design has a great deal more lift around TDC because of the larger duration and not because of the lift.

from both directions to ensure that you have TDC set.

Max-Lift Centerlines

For degreeing any camshaft, I prefer measuring the intake max-lift centerline and then confirm the exhaust (rather than checking the four low-lift events). The high-lift region will be moving faster and is more accurately confirmed.

Rotate the engine in the normal direction until the dial indicator on the retainer shows max intake lift. If you are forced to check using an active hydraulic lifter, wait until the lifter stops bleeding down and the valve stops. Then, measure the crank angle (after TDC) at 0.050 inch and 0.100 inch below max lift as you rotate in the normal direction. Continue turning in the normal direction to keep the timing set in tension all the way around about 1.5 rotations until the valve is opening again. If it is a hydraulic, let the lifter bleed down again to about half lift. Then check the angle at 0.100 inch and 0.050 inch from max lift on the way up in terms of degrees after TDC. You can then verify the closing numbers.

The intake centerline is the average of the "before" and "after" numbers. If you measure 0.050 inch down on the opening side at 80 degrees ATDC and the closing side at 140 ATDC, the intake centerline is (80 + 140) ÷ 2, or 110 ATDC. The 0.100-inch down measurement is more repeatable than the 0.050 inch, but the 0.050 inch is less likely to have any offset relative to the peak. Averaging both numbers is a great technique to get a number that you can trust. If they are more than a degree different, double-check your work.

On the exhaust side, repeat what you did on the intake side, but now you will work in terms of before TDC. Watch your degree-wheel numbers, as some have two sets and all flip at 180. Count by 10s from the 0 mark to make sure that you keep all of the centerline measurements in terms of TDC and not BDC.

Once you have the centerlines measured, advance or retard the camshaft numerous ways (depending on the application). We discuss the how and why in Chapter 3, but for blueprinting, we simply need to know where it is installed.

Piston-to-Valve Clearance

Attempted violations of the space-time continuum are severely punished. This is especially true when we allow the piston and any valve to occupy the same real estate at the same time inside the combustion chamber.

To be safe, we need enough room to account for piston rock, crank whip, and any timing system fluctuations. The standard answer to, "How

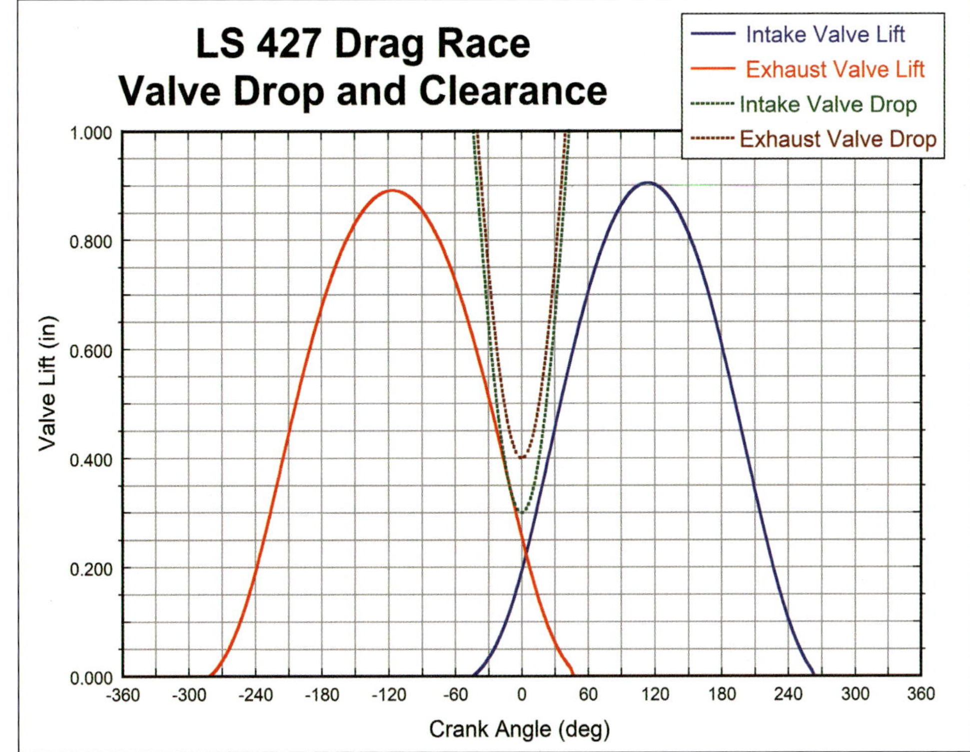

Image 2-48: Looking at valve motion for a 427 LS race camshaft (solid lines) versus the piston clearance (dashed lines), see how the piston-to-valve clearance will always be closest in that 5 to 15 degrees from TDC range? The exhaust is closer BTDC and the intake ATDC. Because of the added exhaust duration, this piston has deeper reliefs on the exhaust and/or the valve is deeper in the chamber from the deck.

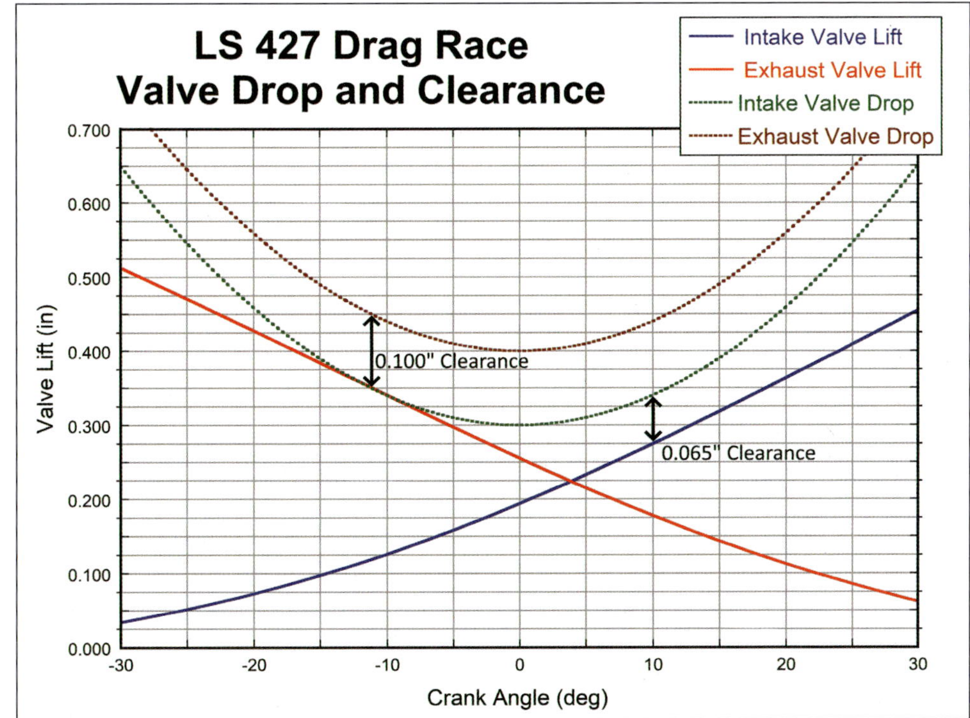

much room do I need?" is 0.080-inch intake and at least 0.100-inch exhaust (at Comp Cams). On the intake side, the valve chases the piston, and you may be safe being closer. I have seen the laser markings of a Pro Stock valve leave a shadow on a piston top. The engine builder might have said it had 0.040-inch piston-to-valve clearance, but that includes 0.020 inch of deflection. If that system was checked with a light flow-bench spring, I bet it would be very close to 0 clearance at 0 lash and 0 deflection.

There is something almost magical as the intake valve and piston are very close together during the early part of the intake stroke. With a great deal of intake piston-to-valve clearance, the volume between the valve and piston acts like a dampener of the pressure drop from the piston rushing down. However, with tight intake piston-to-valve clearance, it is almost like the intake port sees the whole piston dropping with the valve as one large surface, thus creating a stronger signal to the intake port.

There is a huge misconception on piston-to-valve clearance, as many engine builders associate piston-to-valve clearance with peak valve lift. This made some sense in earlier days with flat-tappet camshafts. To keep the lobe nose radius the same, most lobe designs grew lobe lift by roughly 0.006 inch every 4

Image 2-49: Zoomed in on overlap, you can see the 0.065-inch intake and 0.100-inch exhaust clearance. Looking at the intake clearance on the exhaust valve, there will always be about 5 degrees to either side of TDC where the piston and valve move together before the piston runs off and leaves the valve.

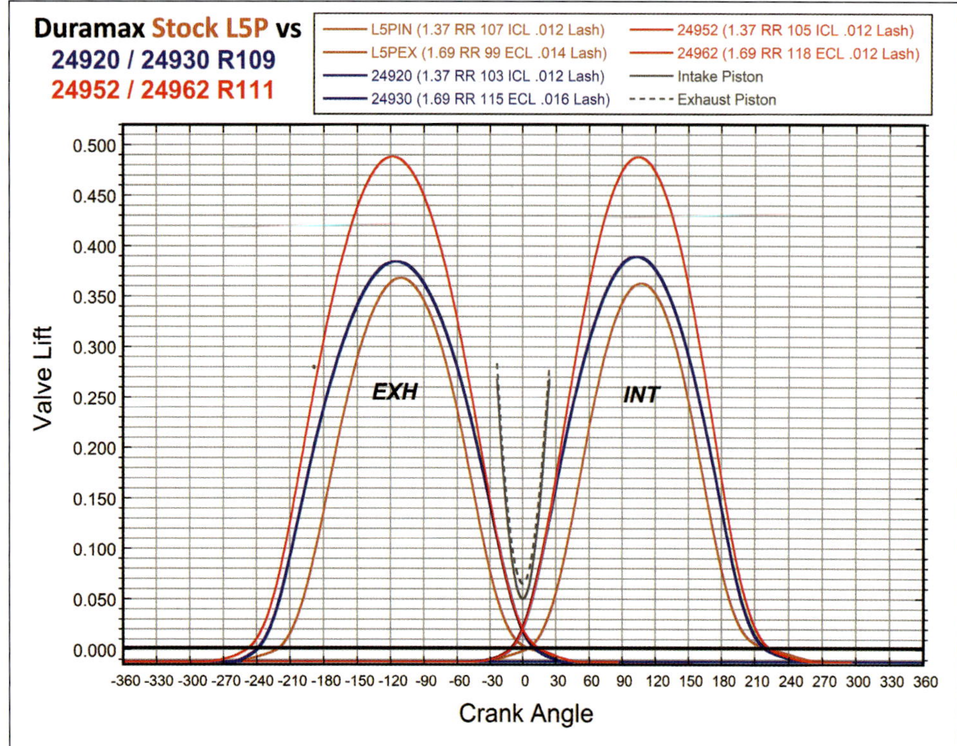

Image 2-50: Note that the red camshaft grind for a stock L5P Duramax piston has 0.100 inch more peak lift than the blue grind, but both of these camshafts have nearly the same piston-to-valve clearance. Because of the tighter clearance at TDC, this diesel application will be closest before it reaches 10 degrees on either side of TDC.

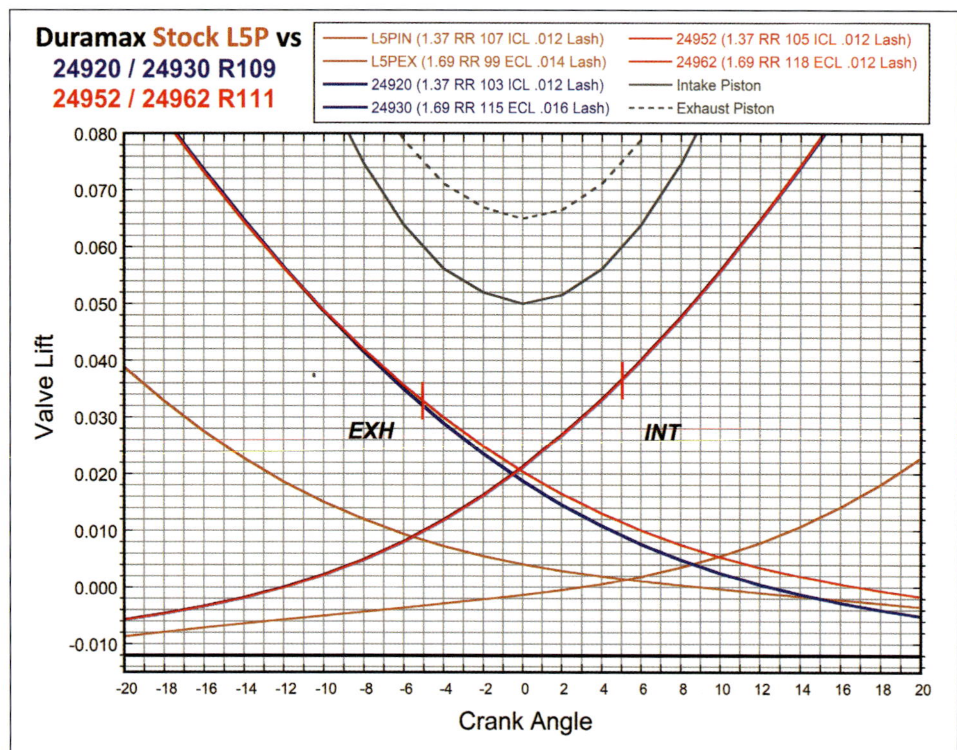

Image 2-51: Zooming in on the overlap region of these Duramax camshaft grinds, we are closest in the 4- to 8-degree window. The relatively long stroke and tight piston-to-valve clearance make everything closer sooner on these applications. Also, note how similar the clearance is between camshafts with 25-percent different max lift.

degrees of duration. Also at that time, lobe separation was seen as something rather magic and rarely varied for a given application. In those cases, most 0.550-inch camshafts had very similar piston-to-valve clearance.

The problem with this approach today is it ignores where piston-to-valve clearance is closest. Depending on the rod-to-stroke ratio and lobe quickness, minimum piston-to-valve clearance generally occurs near 10 degrees BTDC on the exhaust and 10 degrees ATDC in the intake. In this region, the valve and piston velocity are equal so they move together and change very little distance over several degrees. Diesel applications with little valve drop tend to be closest around 5 degrees on either side of TDC. Pro Stock applications with very fast high-lift camshafts and short strokes can have a minimum clearance as far as 15 degrees from TDC.

Duration, lobe quickness, offset, and centerline determines piston-to-valve clearance (not peak lift) as the piston likely approaches 2 inches down the bore before peak valve lift is reached.

Mapping Valve Drop

While blueprinting the valvetrain, it is a great time to know just how much room is available by checking the valve drop every five degrees

Image 2-52: This shows how to properly clay a piston. The clay on top leaves excellent imprints of how close the valve came to these piston reliefs, both axially and radially. (Photo Courtesy Mike Magda)

Image 2-53: With part of the clay cut with a razor blade and removed, it is easy to use a caliper to measure thicknesses. If the valve relief had been deep into the piston crown, the radial clearance might be more important. This becomes very important if you run something with a different valve layout, such as an LS7 head with an LS3 relief piston. (Photo Courtesy Mike Magda)

between 15 BTDC and 15 ATDC. First, find TDC as described earlier. With a dial indicator on the retainer and the pushrods or camshaft removed, push down each valve by hand from the valve seat until it touches the piston at 15 BTDC, 10 BTDC, 5 BTDC, TDC, 5 ATDC, 10 ATDC, and 15 ATDC. If you have TDC correct and the piston does not rock excessively, your BTDC and ATDC numbers should be equal.

Once you have your valve-drop numbers, subtract the required clearance from those to determine the max valve lift you can have in each region. At Comp and many cam companies, we can give you the tappet lift for any camshaft at +/-10 degrees from TDC. It takes a little work (and maybe an email from sales to our engineering department), but we want to help. We publish the TDC lift at 106 and 110 centerlines. Subtract those to know about how fast the tappet lift changes every 4 degrees in that region and then use the slope to find the tappet lift a few

Image 2-54: If you are not worried about radial clearance and know about how much your system defects at low lift, simply use the checking spring, set the lash, and push the valve down every 5 degrees around TDC to see how it moves from undeflected lift until the valve connects the piston. This can also be done with the real spring, but you need to use something like a head-on spring checker to overcome the higher loads. With the flow-bench springs, this is very easy.

degrees earlier or later. If calling or emailing seems easier, please go that route.

While controlling the tappet lift on either side of TDC is easy by optimizing the centerlines and profiles, we don't know exactly what ratio your rockers will check at low lift (we discussed how they vary through a sweep) or how much your system deflects. Hence, we need some help from the engine builder on those aspects to optimize a race engine. It is generally easier to start with a known piston-to-valve clearance for a given camshaft and use that to determine the clearance with any other camshaft. This is something we can do for our sales team through engineering at Comp Cams.

How to Check Piston-to-Valve Clearance

There are two ways I recommend for checking piston-to-valve clearance. With a hydraulic, you have to either make a solid version of your hydraulic body (as we discussed in "Degreeing a Camshaft") or give your cam company the valve drop numbers that we covered and discuss the clearance targets with the theoretical rocker and no deflection.

The traditional method is to clay the piston. This uses modeling clay applied to the piston top about a quarter-inch thick on top of the valve-relief regions. With this applied, bolt on the heads with a used gasket, assemble the valvetrain, and turn the engine a few times. Remove the heads and use a razor blade to slice the clay at the deepest valve indentation location as demonstrated by Mike Magda in Image 2-52. At this point, a set of digital or dial calipers can be used to verify clearance. The benefit of this method is that you can see both radial and axial clearance.

The easier way is to use the light flow-bench valve springs we used for centerlines, undeflected lift, and stiffness. With used head gaskets and the assembled valvetrain, you find TDC and then set up the dial indicator like we did for max lift. The only difference is that now we are going to measure the clearance from valve lift produced by the cam every 5 degrees on the close side of TDC (after for intake and before for exhaust) at 15, 10, and 5 degrees. At each of these angles, push the rocker down until it touches the piston (as shown in Image 2-54).

I personally like to measure all the 5-degree drops, add the pushrods to measure lift, and then map piston-to-valve clearance all at one time while I have the degree wheel set up, dial indicator in place, and flow-bench springs attached. Going back and forth with these different blueprint steps over three different days can be frustrating. If I know the pocket is optimized for my valve and chamber, I only use the drop method. If you need to check radial clearance on the pocket, you need to clay the piston.

Advanced Blueprinting

Just in case everything so far was too easy, here are some professional-level ways to quantify the relationship between system stiffness and system mass.

Valve-Side System Mass

On the valve side of the rocker, the system mass includes the sum of the valve, locks, and retainer, along with approximately one-third the total mass of the valve spring.

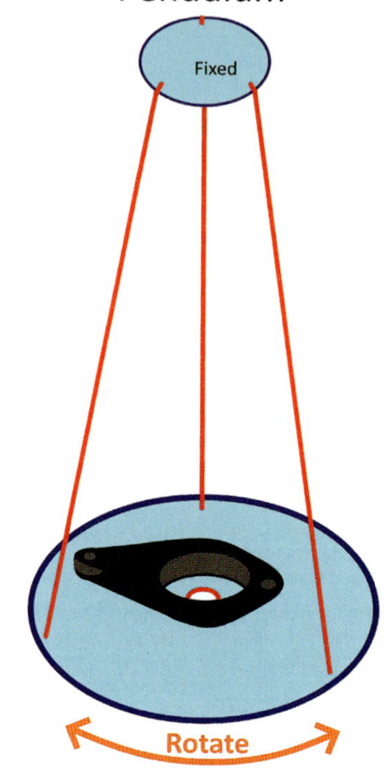

Image 2-55: This three-wire pendulum is an expensive and accurate way for anyone to check the moment of inertia (MOI). I have a few old CDs that need to become MOI gauges. Instead of calculating the MOI from frequency (as you might find in a physics experiment Google search), I prefer calibrating the gauge with known MOI.

This reasoning is too long to fully explain, but the top coil moves with the retainer, so it's 100 percent of its mass. The bottom coil hopefully does not move at all, so 0 percent of its mass is active.

Numerous experiments and papers on the dynamic mass of a cylindrical spring point us to using one-third of total mass as a great approximation. For a conical or beehive spring, the top coils (most active) are lighter than the bottom coils, so one-quarter the total mass is more appropriate. Other than the spring approximation, these numbers only require measurements on a gram scale.

Pushrod Side

The pushrod-side contribution can be calculated by measuring the mass of the pushrod and lifter and dividing that sum by the rocker ratio. It should be apparent this reduced scaling of mass is because the pushrod-side components are moving slower by the rocker-ratio factor.

Hence, the spring force required to control this mass will be reduced by the ratio. Some people believe pushrod-side mass does not matter. If you are over-sprung (far more open load than required), there can be some truth to this thought. Pushrod and lifter mass does not lead to increased deflection and pole vaulting of the rocker and pushrod. However, there will be increased camshaft deflection, and the spring still is required to control this mass in the negative-acceleration regions. Simply put, it matters.

The Effective Rocker Mass

The system mass due to the rocker itself is a bit more difficult to calculate unless you have a solid model drawn with computer-aided design (CAD). Here, you want to find the moment of inertia (MOI), which can be divided by the square of the distance from the rocker pivot to the valve-tip center to provide the rocker contribution to effective system mass.

I'm sure someone is asking, "What is MOI?" Basically, mass is a body's resistance to translational acceleration, as defined by $\boldsymbol{F} = m\boldsymbol{a}$. Why that relates 1:1 with what we measure as gravitational mass on a gram scale or bathroom scale is a great talk with a group of physics geeks. I won't bore you, but research that on your own if you ever have insomnia.

If mass is a body's resistance to translational motion, then MOI is a body's resistance to rotational acceleration. When the valve is moved, the pushrod and valve translate, but the rocker rotates. To treat rotational mass like translational mass, we need to find the MOI.

Measuring Rocker MOI

The best approach to experimentally measure MOI for a rocker arm starts with something like a three-wire pendulum. One can be made with three pieces of fishing line and two disks, both with three holes evenly spaced on their perimeters. The top disk should be a smaller diameter (anything in the 2-inch rage will be fine) and needs to be fixed under something like a shelf or rigid bracket. The bottom disk needs to be as light as possible and have a large enough diameter to easily fit the rocker body with the trunnion centered. Many craft stores have thin, 4-inch wooden disks that will work, or you can use balsa wood if you want to go the extra mile. Another option is to use an old compact disc (CD) if you can figure out

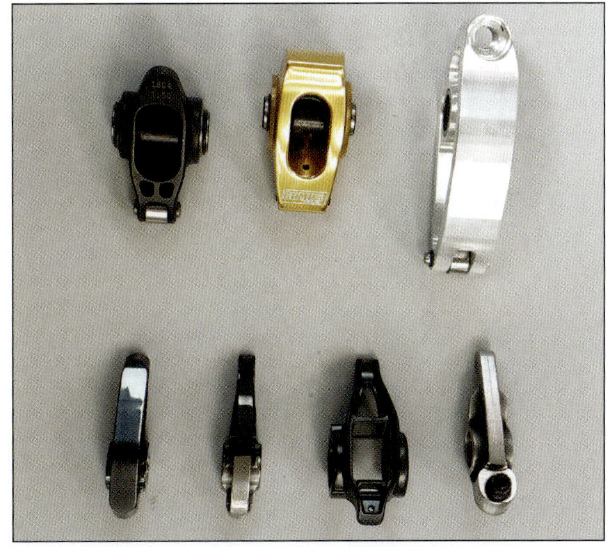

Images 2-56 and 2-57: There are so many ways to design a rocker. The MOI definitely matters. The black rockers on the bottom right of the photo on the right were designed by Dr. Charles Jenckes, made by Del West, and run by DEI when turning a cup engine at 11,000 rpm. Each design here has a unique stiffness and unique MOI. The higher the stiffness divided by MOI, the better a rocker design. Adjusters on the back are always an MOI penalty and include a possible critical failure point.

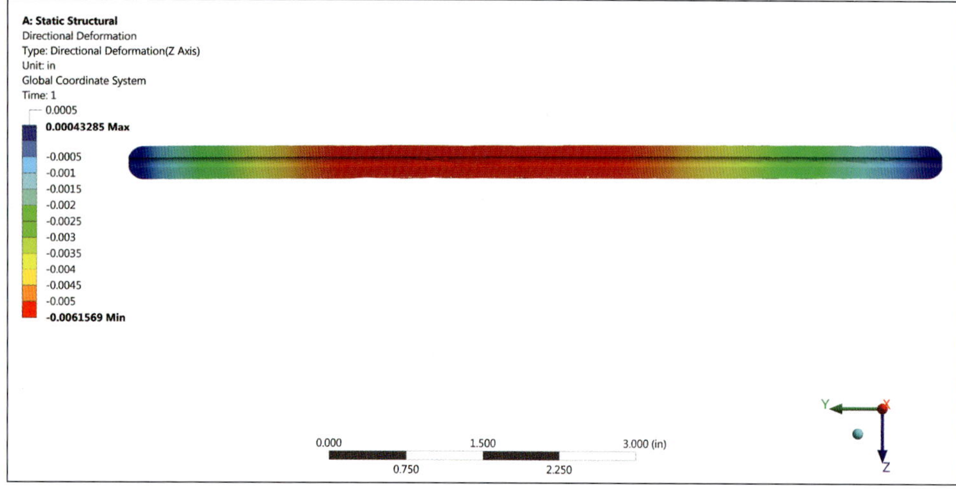

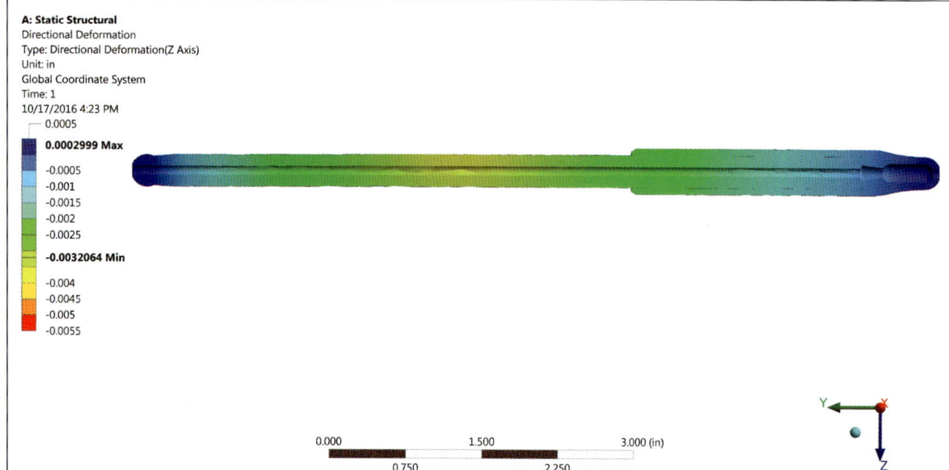

Images 2-58 and 2-59: When we model pushrod stiffness, we always add a light torque about one end and load the system over 1,000 pounds. These graphs show how much stiffer the two-piece XD-A adjustable pushrod is above a standard 5/16-inch pushrod.

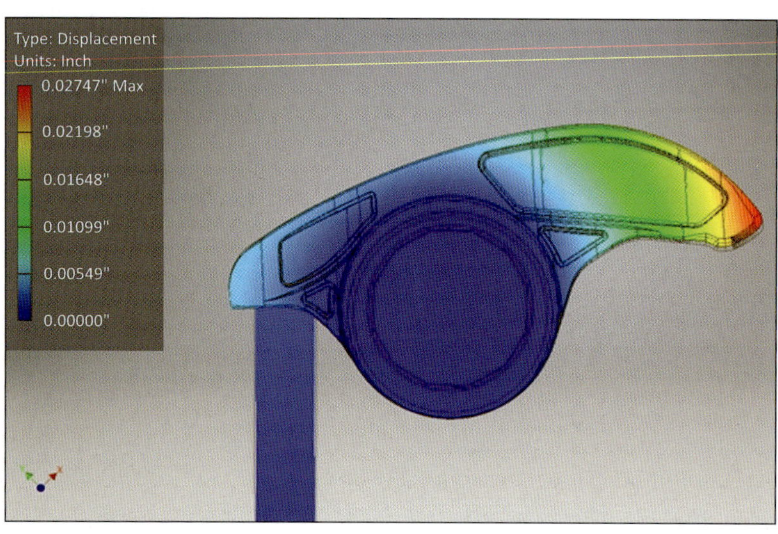

Image 2-60: After the pushrod, the next-most-flexible piece of most overhead camshaft (OHC) valvetrain systems is the rocker arm. This tip was flexing about 0.025 inch under typical loads, even assuming no trunnion deflection.

how to drill the holes.

Tie the bottom disk to the top with three pieces of fishing line through the perimeter holes (as shown in Image 2-55). Distribute the load as evenly as possible while keeping both disks flat to the horizon. Any length can work, but 18 to 24 inches should make the required measurements easiest. Mark the center of the bottom disk to properly center the rocker and standard about the axis of rotation. For an MOI standard, I like to use washers. These are inexpensive and their MOI (I_w) is:

$$I_w = \frac{1}{2} m (r_1 2 + r_2 2)$$

The symbol "m" is the mass of the washer, "r_1" is the outside radius (diameter divided by two), and "r_2" is the inside radius. Use the radii and not the diameter measurements in your calculations. Otherwise, the numbers with be off dramatically. I have found this out the hard way.

To find the MOI, place the rocker without the trunnion on the center of the bottom disk with the trunnion hole centered on the disk along the vertical axis. You probably need some two-sided tape to hold it in place, but you want to use as little as practical and leave it there when using washers. Twist the disk with the rocker about 20 degrees and release. Use a stopwatch to time 10 or more oscillations. Once you have that time per cycle (period or frequency) of the pendulum rotation with the rocker, either match that time or bracket it with a combination of washers.

With an assortment of washers, you should be able to find a combination of washers with very close to the same period as the rocker. The washers must be stacked on the disk center with the hole axis in the vertical

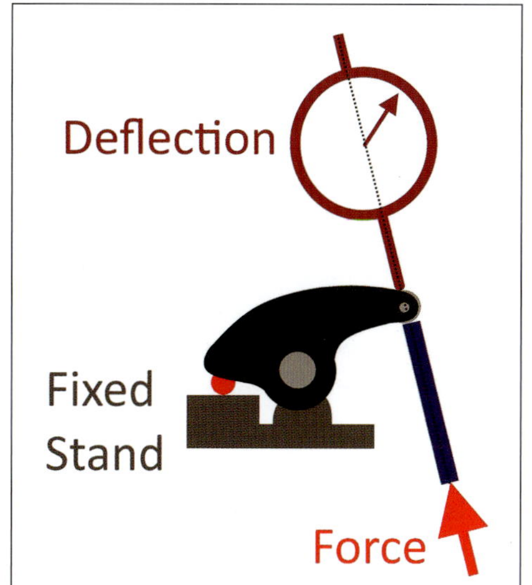

Image 2-61: This stand allows you to measure the rocker flex independently of the other valvetrain pieces. When the pushrods are flexing, it may be difficult to compare rockers on the engine. However, if the pushrods are flexing that much, you might want to look at them before the rockers.

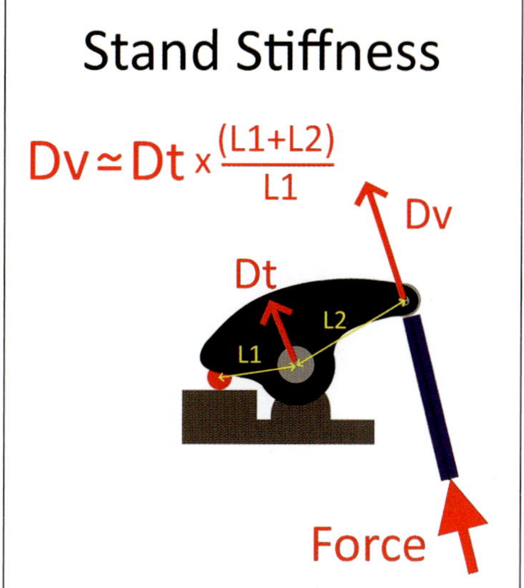

Image 2-62: The most overlooked flex point in good valvetrain systems is often the rocker trunnion. These are under tremendous load, and the shaft, bearings, and stands can all play a role. The focus here is generally independent of MOI and valvetrain mass too.

Image 2-63: For stud-mounted systems, stud girdles are a great way to decrease the trunnion flex. This constrains the rockers more back and forth than up and down, but you never want the rockers dancing above the heads.

direction. If the rocker rotates too quickly to accurately time 10 torsional oscillations, use longer lines. Both longer lines and higher masses reduce the oscillation frequency. Once you have a close match, use the calculation above for the MOI of each washer then add up the combination that matched the MOI of the rocker.

Weigh and measure the washers you use, as there can be considerable variance. For comparison, a Grade 2 USS 1/2-inch washer MOI should be close to 3 kg x mm^2, and a USS 3/4-inch washer will run close to 19 kg x mm^2.

As for the MOI, when testing various rocker bodies, a factory LS rocker body should be roughly 32 kg x mm^2 MOI. Most stud- or shaft-mounted roller-tip rocker arms are significantly higher MOI, often in the 50 to 120 kg x mm^2 range, or higher for very large engines, especially those with heavy adjusters. For an idea of the range of variance, see Images 2-55, 2-56, and 2-57.

Converting MOI to Effective Valve-Side Mass

Once you have the MOI of the rocker arm and you want to know the effective valve-side mass, divide the MOI by the square of the distance from the trunnion center to the tip center. Most OHV rockers have a trunnion to tip distance of 1.5 to 1.9 inches (38 to 48 mm). If we take the MOI of the LS rocker above and divide it by the approximate 1.55-inch or 39-mm tip distance squared, the effective mass of the rocker at the valve tip will be approximately 21 grams.

Note that, here, the rocker mass is roughly one-fifth the mass of the valve itself, which is certainly too much to ignore. It is not surprising that a roller tip will add to that effective mass, as will any adjuster on the back side. Typically, the pushrod and rocker are the two most-flexible components in an OHV valvetrain.

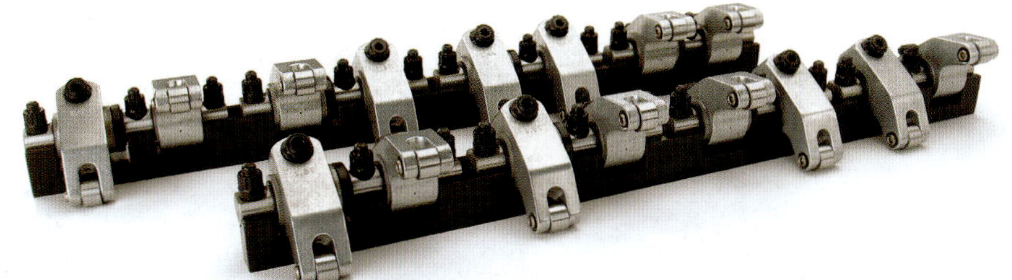

Image 2-64: A good shaft system often has a solid-steel stand to support the head and hold the rockers firmly in place. If you wanted to improve something like this stand, you probably want to go to narrower rocker bodies so that the bolts holding the rocker shafts could be closer together. Still, this is a huge step up from a stud-mounted system.

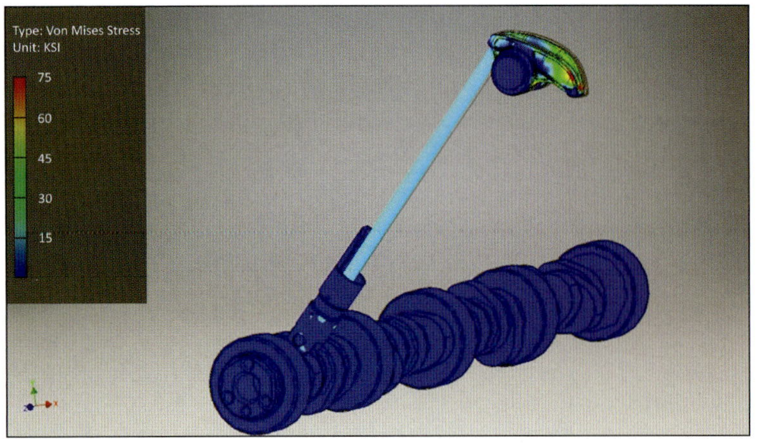

Image 2-65: Measuring system stiffness is better than looking at each component because we get to see how everything works together. This includes the camshaft flex, lifters, pushrods, rocker support, and rocker arm. When we model the entire system in finite element analysis (FEA), we want to see the same deflection we measured. Otherwise, we probably missed at least one constraint, such as the rocker support or head flex.

Hence, we always want to increase their stiffness, but when doing so, be careful the percentage change in system stiffness increases by more than you are increasing the effective mass at the valve.

Please remember that the rocker mass is not important unless someone is throwing the rocker at you or you need to take a few grams off the engine, but the rocker MOI is paramount. Mass toward the center of the trunnion moves slowly, but mass toward the ends moves quickly as the rocker oscillates and the valve opens and closes.

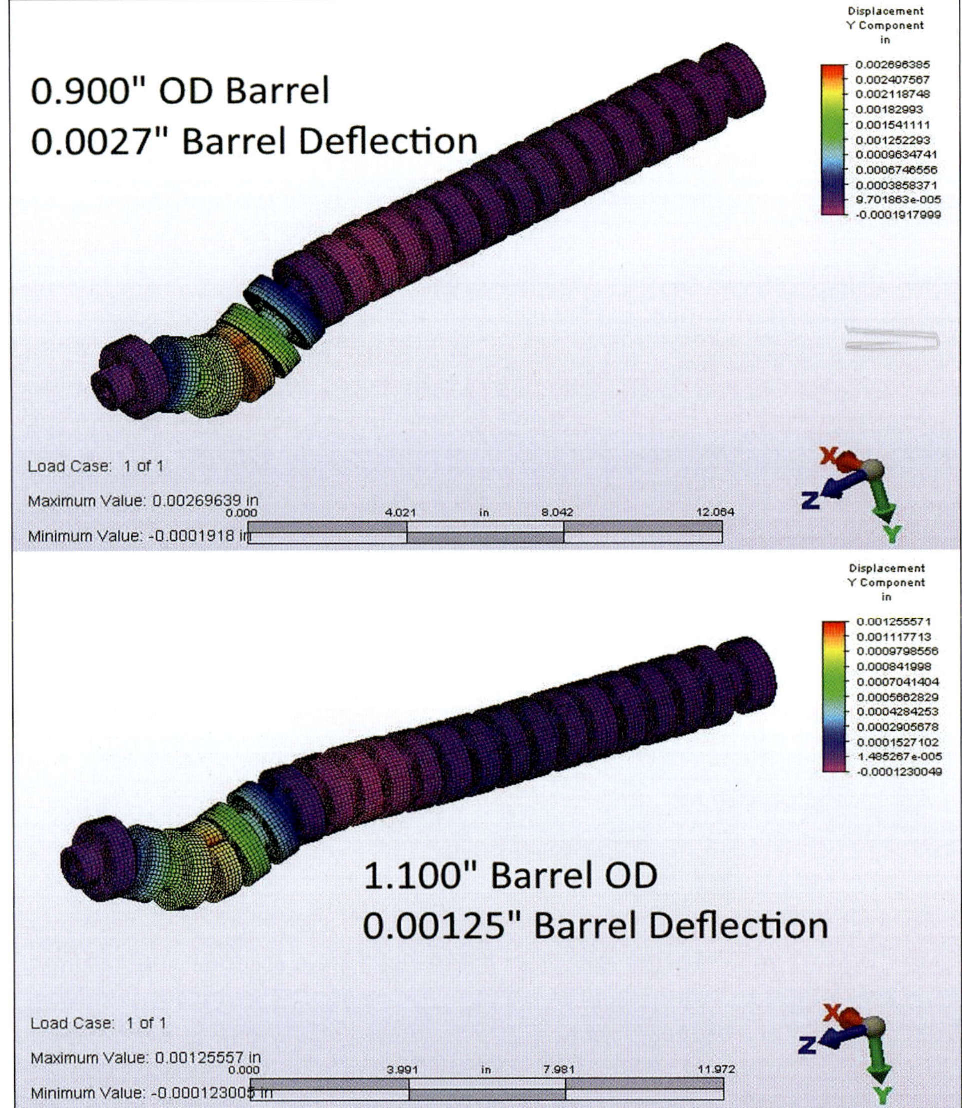

Specific Stiffness

I alluded to our goal in the sections above, but we should make our evaluation target clear. If you want to compare different combinations, the best quantitative measure I know was created by my good friend, Dr. Charles Jenckes, when he was at DEI and Del West. Jenckes first measured the rocker-arm stiffness with a constrained ball in the pushrod seat, a fixed trunnion, and the valve stem loaded (as shown in Image 2-61).

With an apparatus like this, you can change the ball height and measure the stiffness in any part of the rocker sweep. Once the stiffness was measured and the MOI was

Image 2-66: When we first started running FEA, we modeled camshafts with measured loads and different barrel diameters for a Ford cup team. Around this same time, Grumpy Jenkins had talked the NHRA into allowing the Ford-sized 2.125-inch journals to be used in big-block Chevy applications. Note the 0.0015-inch difference in cam distortion between 0.900- and 1.100-inch barrels.

determined, Jenckes divided the stiffness by the MOI to determine the specific stiffness of various rocker designs. He first worked to maximize the specific stiffness of a base design and make both stiffer, and therefore heavier, versions like the base design in certain percentage increments and test those on a Spintron and Dyno. His goal was to optimize the rocker design around the valve mass, RPM, and valve spring of any given valvetrain package. Note that the stand stiffness in both this test and a running engine is going to be significant.

Now that we know how to measure the entire system stiffness and system's effective mass, we can take Dr. Jenckes's rocker arm approach and apply it to the entire valvetrain system instead of a singular component. If you take a selection of rocker arms and measure the system deflection and calculate stiffness with each and then measure the MOI of each and calculate the MOI of each, you now have the total system stiffness and total system effective mass. Then, divide those numbers for each combination.

Because I typically measure system stiffness in lbs/inch and valvetrain mass in grams, one of those needs to be converted. I tend to swap the grams over to pounds because 454 is one of those numbers that is easy for me to remember, having grown up in the heyday of the big-block Chevy. Divide the mass in grams by 453.5924 to get the system mass in pounds. Then, divide the system stiffness by the system effective mass. Your answer for system specific stiffness should come out in the units of 1/inch or $inch^{-1}$. Note that mass cancels when you divide system stiffness by system effective mass.

Dimensional Analysis of Specific Stiffness

If you are surprised about losing the mass units, think about how powerful this measurement and calculation can be when comparing different systems. For example, a weed trimmer engine with a very light valvetrain and therefore less required stiffness can be compared in a meaningful way with a large diesel engine on a ship.

For a more pertinent comparison for this book, you can not only compare two different LS engines but can also look at those compared to a big-block Chevy, a Chrysler Hemi, or even various NASCAR engines. As valves, springs, and other components become lighter, it makes intuitive sense that the rocker arm needs to be lighter. By taking this approach, you have a better way to compare systems over the typical "Well, that looks about right" method that many people have used in the past.

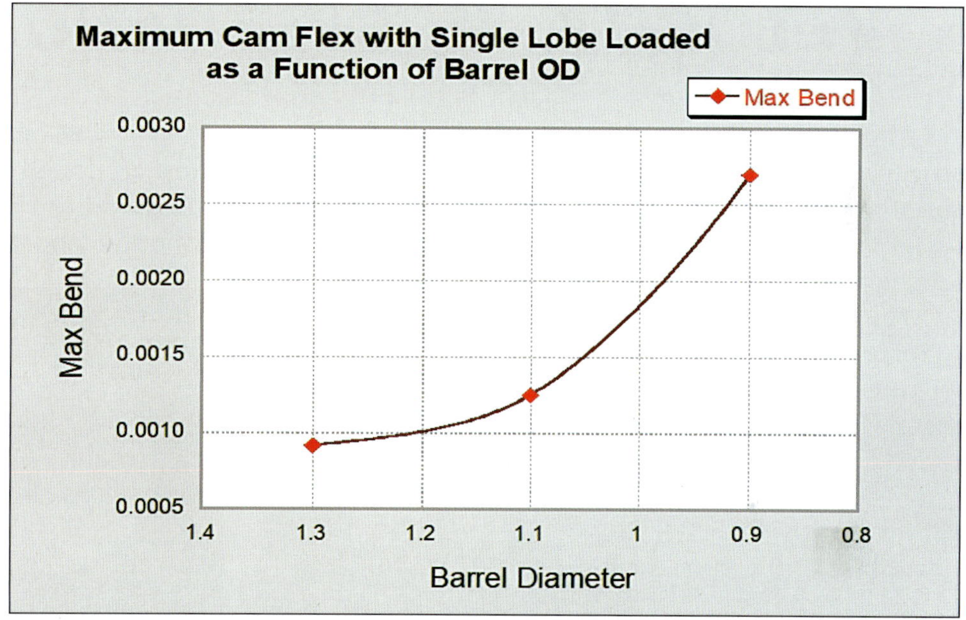

Image 2-67: This graph shows why most professional series run 1.250-plus-inch barrel sizes. It will make you sick to your stomach to think about the cam deflection with a long-stroke small-block Chevy and 0.900-inch barrel camshaft. Having 1.100 inches is better, but once you get around 1.250 inches, the cam typically doesn't flex nearly as much as the pushrod and rocker arm.

324-30 Pro Stock				
Lift	Dur	1.8:1	1.8:1	1.8:1
	Lobe	0" Lash	0.028"	0.032"
0.006"	360.4	370.7	326.1	322.2
0.020"	324.1	344.5	313.8	310.9
0.050"	**289.1**	312.3	**295.1**	**293.1**
0.200"	207.1	248.9	240.8	239.7
0.400"	117.9	197.7	191.2	190.2

Image 2-68: That 0.0015-inch reduced bend on the cam core acted just like 0.004-inch tighter lash in the Grumpy Jenkins case. He called and told me we had ground the camshaft 4 degrees too big. He checked it with a dial indicator and found that it was correct. That led to a new lobe optimized for the newly increased valvetrain system stiffness.

CHAPTER 3

A Dynamic Understanding of Profiles: Velocity, Acceleration, and Jerk

After explanations of the camshaft terms found on specification cards, in lobe catalogs, and on inspection sheets, and looking over valvetrain setup or blueprinting, we need to investigate some of the important design details you have likely heard repeatedly but are rarely shown.

There are two dynamic behaviors with camshafts that are extremely important but poorly understood. We will dive rather deep into the dynamics of airflow in subsequent chapters, but here I want to lay a foundation for the dynamics of valve motion.

Image 3-1: The appearance of a camshaft changes very little, even with dramatic differences in resulting motion. A keen eye might see that the second camshaft from the right on the front row is probably spicier than the rest of these coming out of superfinish. This chapter covers ways to quantify and understand profile aggressiveness.

Valves in any engine are a lot like teenage kids. The camshaft design is like the parent that can tell the valve what to do, but there is always deflection and resistance to motion, and sometimes the valve can go flying off in

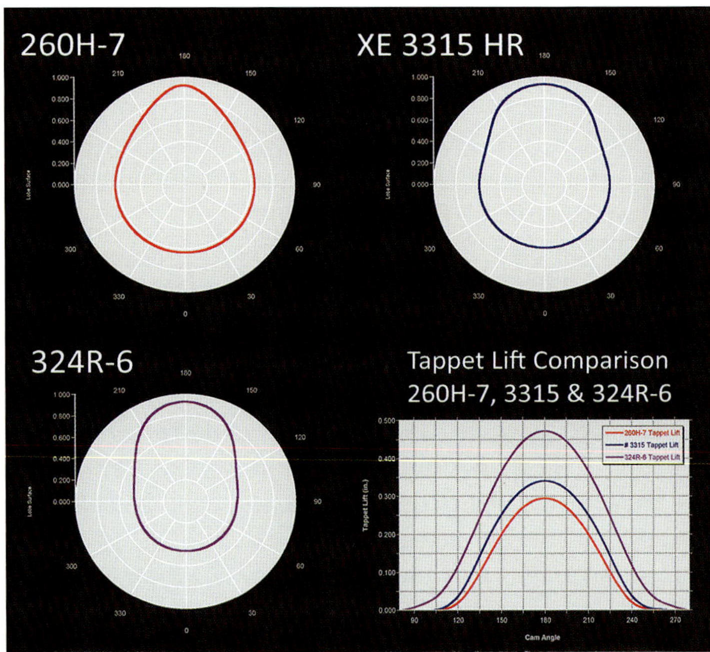

Image 3-2: I made this display for our NHRA trailer that shows how looking at the lobe surface is different from looking at the tappet motion. The red is a common 260 high-energy flat-tappet profile, the blue is an Xtreme Energy hydraulic roller, and the purple is a common Competition Eliminator profile from the 1990s. These all had to fit inside the same 1.868-inch Chevy journal envelope, so to go higher, the base circle has to get smaller.

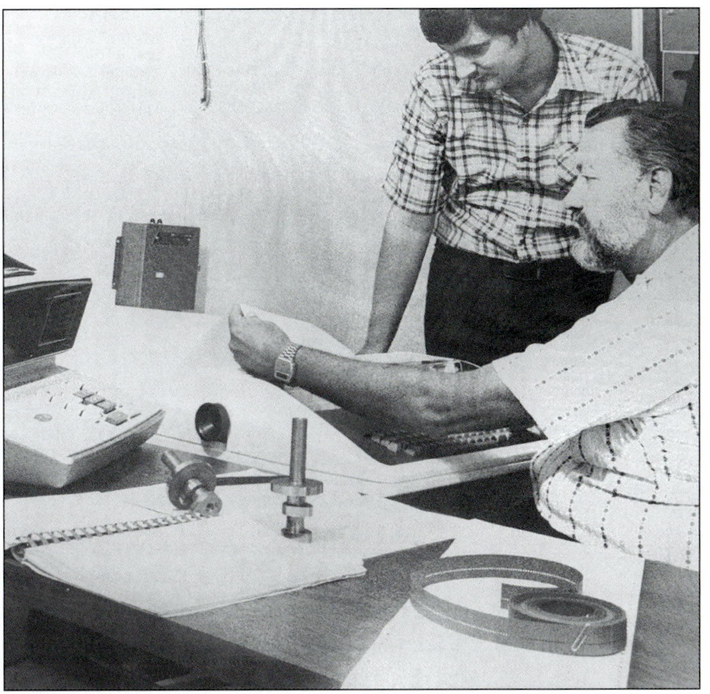

Image 3-3: Harvey Crane is one of my most important mentors and a dearly missed friend. I used to call him the CIA (camshaft information agency). Harvey measured camshafts more closely than anyone and looked at every tiny detail of what made each unique.

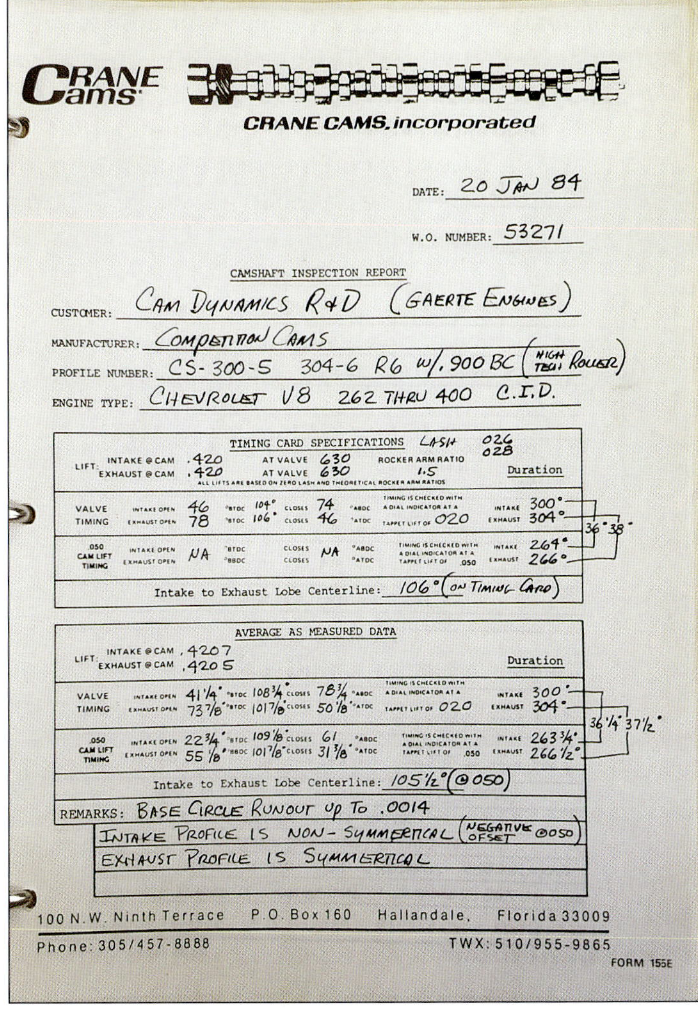

CRANE Cams

CRANE CAMS, incorporated

DATE: 20 JAN 84

W.O. NUMBER: 53271

CAMSHAFT INSPECTION REPORT

CUSTOMER: CAM DYNAMICS R&D (GAERTE ENGINES)

MANUFACTURER: COMPETITION CAMS

PROFILE NUMBER: CS-300-5 304-6 R6 w/.900 BC (HIGH TECH ROLLER)

ENGINE TYPE: CHEVROLET V8 262 THRU 400 C.I.D.

TIMING CARD SPECIFICATIONS LASH 026 028

LIFT: INTAKE @ CAM .420 AT VALVE 630 ROCKER ARM RATIO 1.5
EXHAUST @ CAM .420 AT VALVE 630

ALL LIFTS ARE BASED ON ZERO LASH AND THEORETICAL ROCKER ARM RATIOS

		Open		Closes		Timing	Duration
VALVE TIMING	INTAKE OPEN	46 °BTDC	104°	CLOSES 74 °ABDC		TIMING IS CHECKED WITH A DIAL INDICATOR AT A TAPPET LIFT OF 020	INTAKE 300°
	EXHAUST OPEN	78 °BTDC	106°	CLOSES 46 °ATDC			EXHAUST 304°
.050 CAM LIFT TIMING	INTAKE OPEN	NA °BTDC		CLOSES NA °ABDC		TIMING IS CHECKED WITH A DIAL INDICATOR AT A TAPPET LIFT OF .050	INTAKE 264°
	EXHAUST OPEN	°BBDC		CLOSES °ATDC			EXHAUST 266°

36° 38°

Intake to Exhaust Lobe Centerline: 106° (ON TIMING CARD)

AVERAGE AS MEASURED DATA

LIFT: INTAKE @ CAM .4207
EXHAUST @ CAM .4205

		Open		Closes	Timing	Duration
VALVE TIMING	INTAKE OPEN	41 1/4° °BTDC	108 3/4°	CLOSES 78 3/4 °ABDC	TIMING IS CHECKED WITH A DIAL INDICATOR AT A TAPPET LIFT OF 020	INTAKE 300°
	EXHAUST OPEN	73 7/8° °BTDC	101 7/8°	CLOSES 50 1/8° °ATDC		EXHAUST 304°
.050 CAM LIFT TIMING	INTAKE OPEN	22 3/4° °BTDC	109 1/8°	CLOSES 61 °ABDC	TIMING IS CHECKED WITH A DIAL INDICATOR AT A TAPPET LIFT OF .050	INTAKE 263 3/4°
	EXHAUST OPEN	55 1/8° °BBDC	101 7/8°	CLOSES 31 3/8° °ATDC		EXHAUST 266 1/2°

36 1/4° 37 1/2°

Intake to Exhaust Lobe Centerline: 105 1/2° (@ 050)

REMARKS: BASE CIRCLE RUNOUT UP TO .0014
INTAKE PROFILE IS NON-SYMMERTICAL (NEGATIVE OFSET @050)
EXHAUST PROFILE IS SYMMERTICAL

100 N.W. Ninth Terrace P.O. Box 160 Hallandale, Florida 33009
Phone: 305/457-8888 TWX: 510/955-9865
FORM 155E

Image 3-4: One of the profiles we will examine (#4008) was dissected by Harvey in 1984. This inspection report has more cam designers involved than any I have seen when digging through Harvey's records. The camshaft was ground at Comp Cams (John McWhirter) for Gaerte Engines (Earl Gaerte) and then somehow acquired by Cam Dynamics (Mark Heffington), who sent it to Crane Cams (Harvey) to be analyzed. My mentor did a great job digging through all the details.

uncontrolled ways. Every part of the valvetrain system acts like an individual spring by bending, flexing, storing energy, and then releasing it—often when you least wish. People talk about aggressiveness when speaking about how quickly a camshaft tries to move a valve, but is there a better description?

To quantify both energy and applied forces, let's climb up on the well-trod shoulders of Gottfried Leibniz, Johann Bernoulli, and Sir Isaac Newton to let them explain how velocity and acceleration are important to cam design.

Velocity

To take the first step, we are using both measured data from a GM 5.3L camshaft and design data from the 4008 Hi-Tech -5 design that we have been discussing. While the Hi-Tech is still successfully used today, it has been widely measured, analyzed, and copied since about 1984.

Looking at Image 3-5, the 5.3L measured intake tappet lift is in the standard format of tappet lift versus cam angle. I drew a green line tangent to the surface at 165 degrees. On the right, I calculated the slope of that line as close as I could eyeball it at that angle. Using the rise/run formula, we approximate the slope and velocity of the lifter as 0.0033-inch lift per camshaft degree. With that in mind, we define tappet velocity as follows:

$$\text{Tappet Velocity} = \text{Change in Lift} \div \text{Change in Angle}$$

Velocity is the rate of change of position. You have probably seen the standard Newtonian definition of velocity as change in position

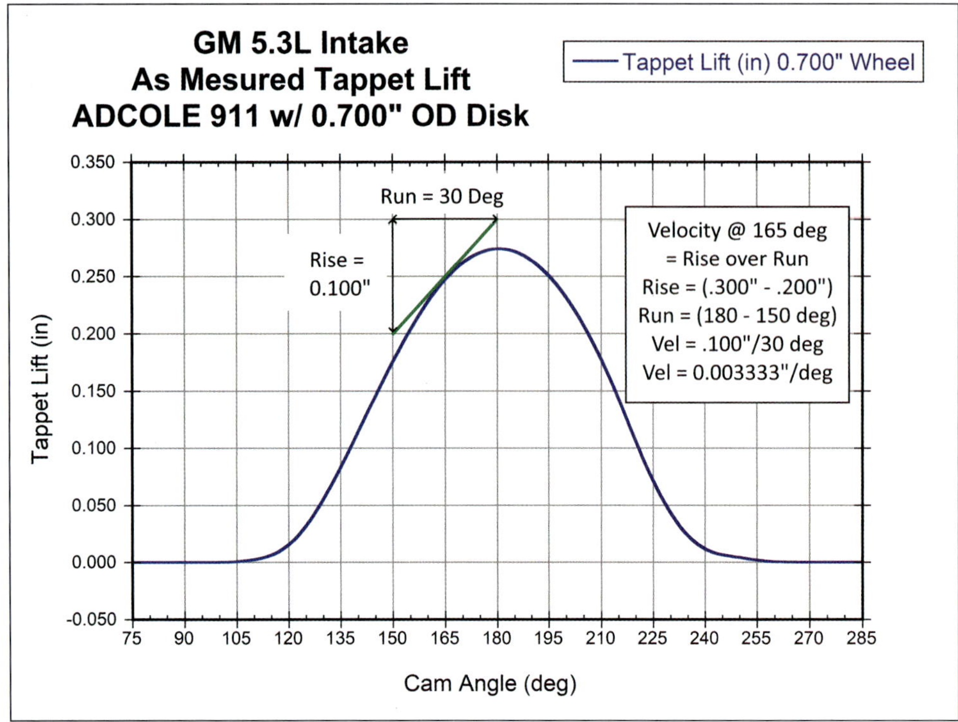

Image 3-5: A cam design is not really the lobe but the lift it produces. The first factor to describe profile aggressiveness is measuring the slope of the lift curve at every degree. Draw a tangent line at any point on the curve, and the velocity is the rise over run of that line (as shown on the right side).

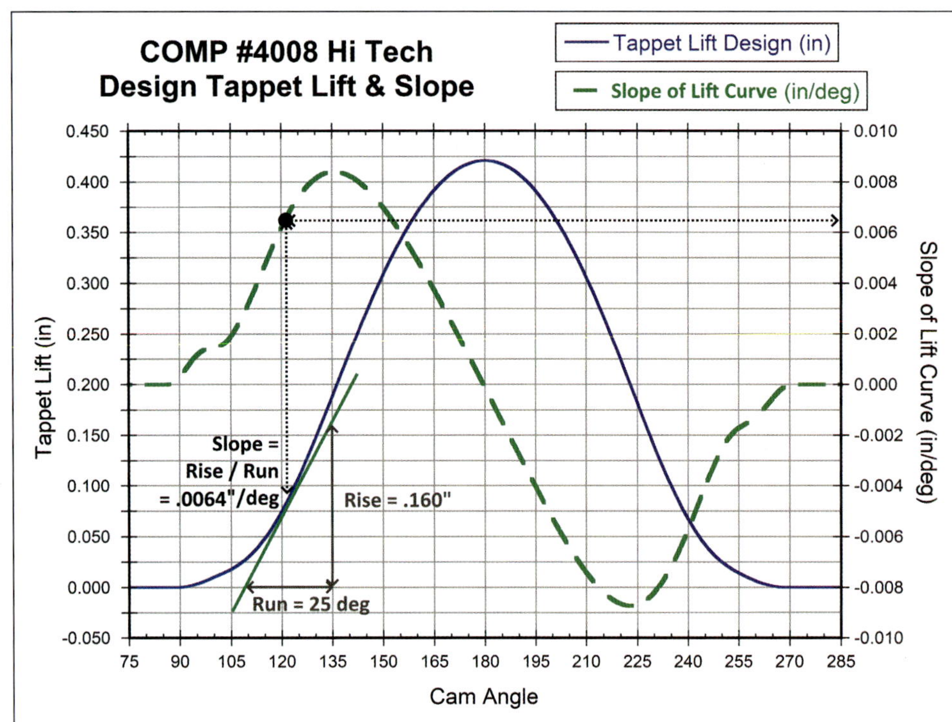

Image 3-6: Moving from the OEM design to a race design, I made the same tangent line earlier on the opening side at 122 degrees. The slope measured at different angles is shown as a dashed green line.

over a change in time or Dx ÷ Dt. Because camshafts are ground with an angular reference frame, we tend to use angular velocity instead of time-based measurements.

However, we can calculate the degrees turned per second by taking RPM ÷ 60 to know revolutions per second. Then, multiply that by 180 to calculate the degrees per second because the cam only goes halfway around each engine revolution. Multiplying the velocity in inches per degree by the angular velocity in degrees per second provides the valve velocity in inches per second.

In Image 3-6, I plotted this same rise/run for the Comp Cams 4008 profile, this time with a dotted line added to show the slope of the lift curve at every degree as a green dotted line. If we make this slope measurement accurately at every angle, we can plot this as the tappet velocity in inches per degree (as shown for the 5.3L camshaft in Image 3-7 and the 4008 in 3-8).

Kinetic Energy

The velocity curve is far more important dynamically than anything we learn looking at the common camshaft specs. Kinetic energy was defined by Leibniz and Bernoulli as the energy a body possesses due to its motion and is expressed mathematically as: $KE = \frac{1}{2} m V^2$.

This equation says that a change in valve velocity is more important than a change in the valve mass when determining valve-spring selection. To explain a little more about why, let's look at the four shaded regions in Image 3-9. In Region A, the camshaft provides the energy flow into the tappet, valve, and system from the time the lifter begins to move until the tappet and valve reach maximum

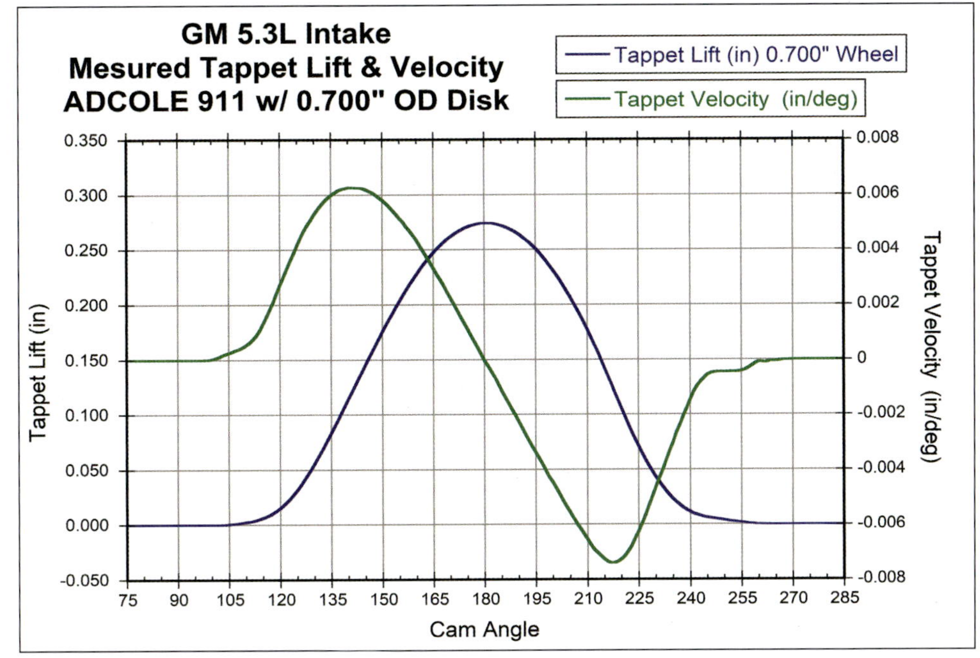

Image 3-7: The easier way to describe that slope of the lift curve is the derivative or rate of change. Mathematical tools to engineers and physicists are like Snap-on tools for auto mechanics. I'm going to pull out my derivative tool and hit the blue curve to calculate the slope and velocity at every degree and plot that in green for the OEM GM 5.3L intake profile.

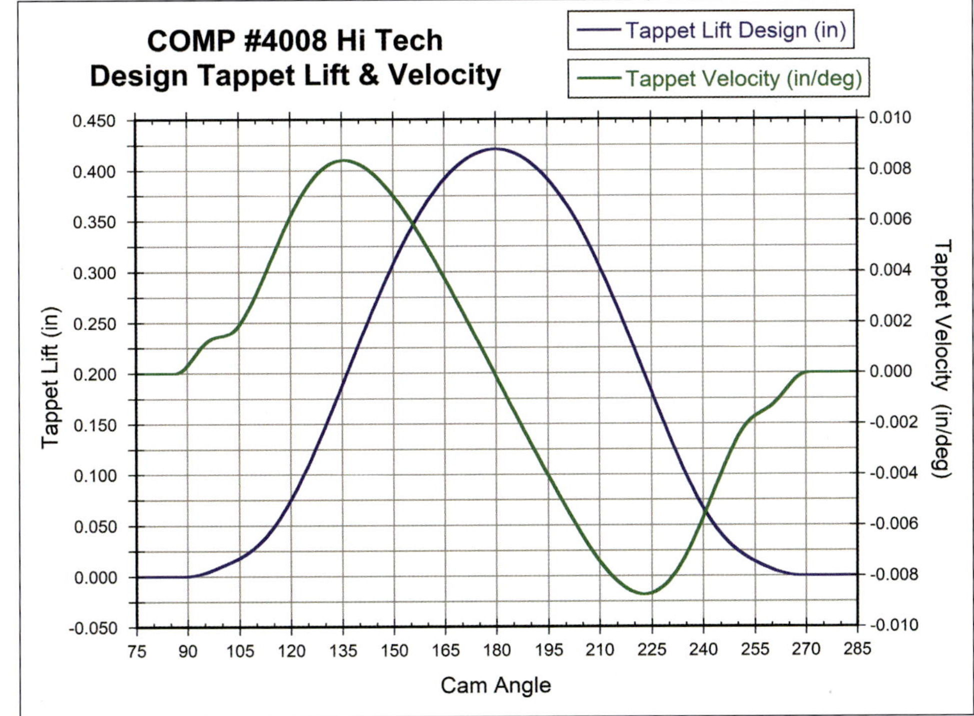

Image 3-8: While the derivative tool is handy, look at the #4008 profile as well. The maximum velocity is significantly higher in this case than the OEM design. Like The Bandit, *this tappet and valve have a long way to go and a short time to get there, so we should expect higher tappet speeds.*

opening velocity and maximum opening kinetic energy.

If you think of the Carroll Shelby–style 0 to 100 to 0 test, this yellow section is the 0 to 100 mph segment, and the camshaft driven by the timing set is the powertrain. As the tappet passes maximum velocity (V_{max}) around 140 degrees, what happens to the valvetrain system is analogous to swapping your feet from the accelerator to the brake pedal. Generally, if the spring does not absorb this kinetic energy, while the bind and retainer guide might help a bit, the piston top is eventually going to be asked to do the job of stopping the valve.

As we cross over from Region B to Region C, the spring goes from storing the kinetic energy as potential energy to releasing that stored potential energy back as kinetic energy in the opposite direction. This is a mirror image of our 0-100-0 example, as the valve-spring brakes store energy like a rubber band on the opening side instead of converting it to heat or thermal energy like the brakes on a Cobra. After max lift, this energy release sends the vehicle, tappet, and valve backward toward the starting position.

As we cross from Regions C to D, we swap our foot back from the valve-spring pedal to the camshaft pedal, except now the camshaft must slow the tappet and valve. This slowing is another way of converting the kinetic energy of the tappet and valve, but here it is transferred to kinetic energy in the camshaft that will be transmitted through the timing set back to the crankshaft.

Amazingly, the cumulative effect from the crankshaft's point of view from this total energy transfer is quite small. While the crankshaft

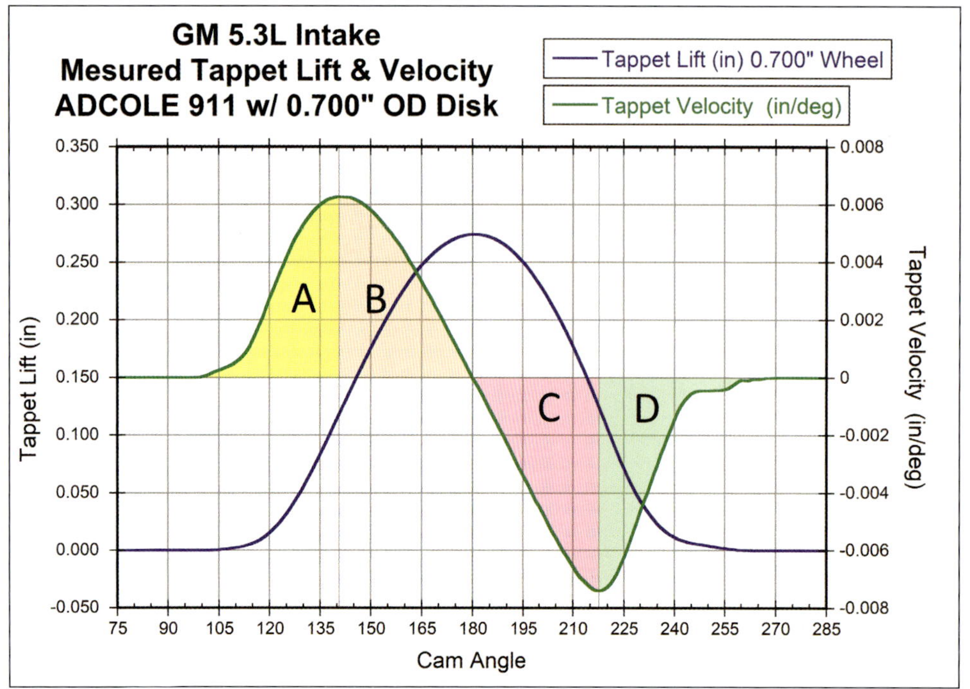

Image 3-9: The best way to begin our look into valve dynamics is to look at the energy flow from the profile to the valve spring and then back in each of these four regions. We noted the higher velocities for a race profile. Now, think about the valve-spring size and loads on a stock GM 5.3L engine versus what is required in most roller-cam circle-track applications.

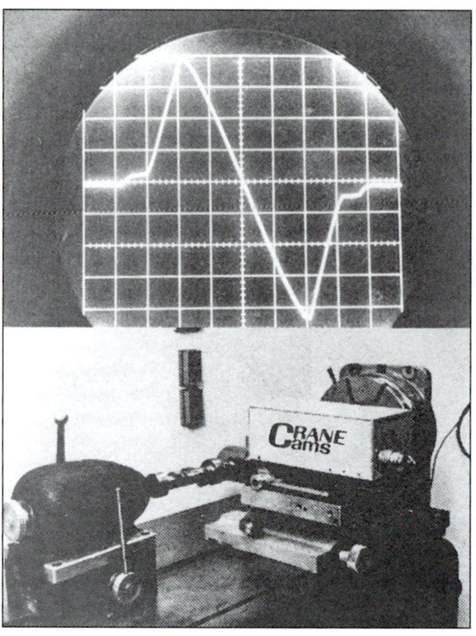

Image 3-10: Understanding the importance of velocity in camshaft design is not new. Harvey Crane used a World War II bombsight stand coupled with the most accurate encoder that he could find and an oscilloscope in the 1960s to make this highly accurate measurement gauge. The accuracy was not needed for duration, but it is critical to accurately measure velocity.

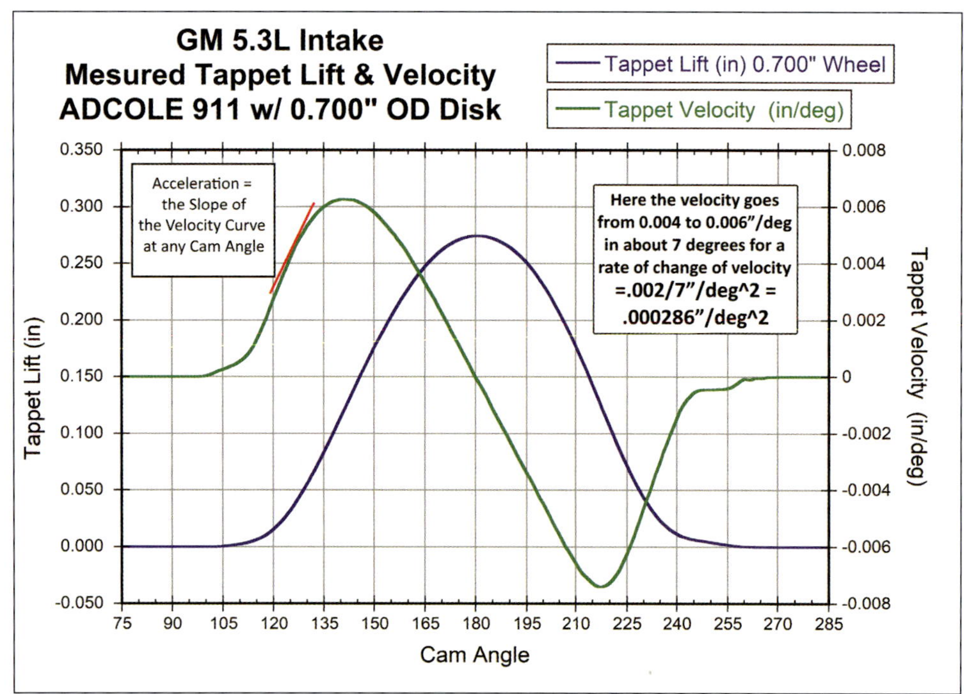

Image 3-11: We measure velocity to learn about energy transfer, but the forces on the system are proportional to the rate of change (slope or derivative) of the velocity curve. We apply the same tangent line technique to our velocity curve to calculate the rate of change at that angle.

had to do work to open the valve, except from a small tax of friction in the valvetrain and heat created internally in the valve spring, most of the work to open the valve will be given back to the crank on the closing side.

Acceleration

Knowing that velocity is the slope of the position curve, you may already have known or guessed that acceleration is the slope of the velocity curve. A line tangent to velocity is shown in Image 3-11. Examining the tangent line I drew around 127 degrees, the velocity increases from 0.004 to 0.006 inch/degrees in about 7 degrees for an eyeball rate of

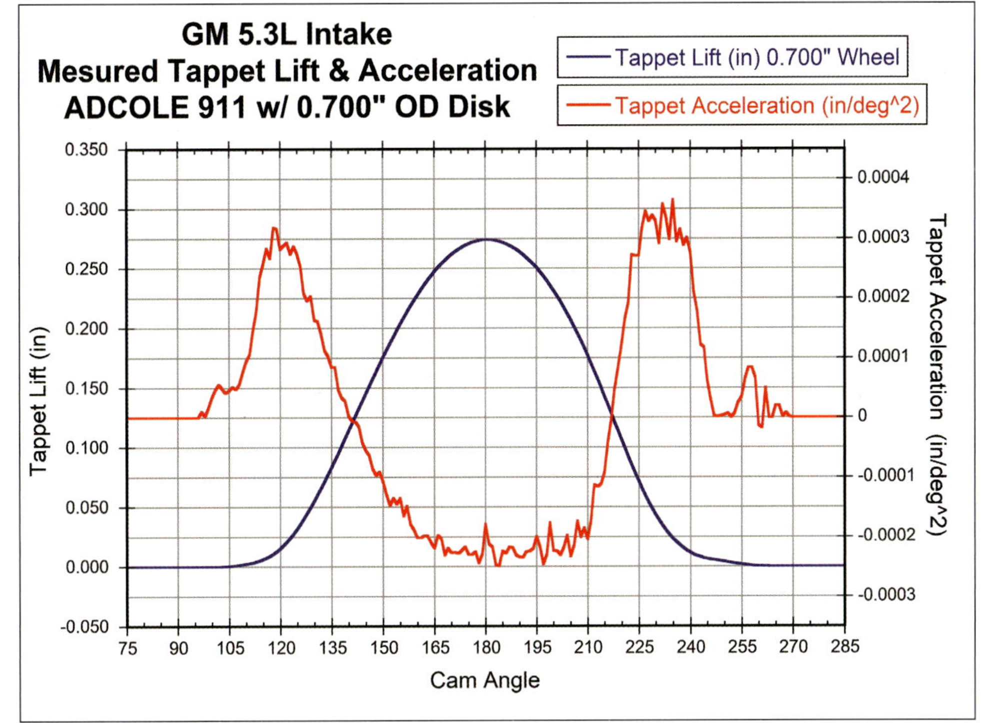

Image 3-12: With machine vibrations, camshaft vibrations, and accuracy limits, you will always be able to see error in any measured acceleration curve. This Adcole data is precise enough to show what is there without filtering. Unfortunately, there is not a good commercial option available to most engine builders to measure to the level required. This is the measured acceleration in red for the GM 5.3L intake profile.

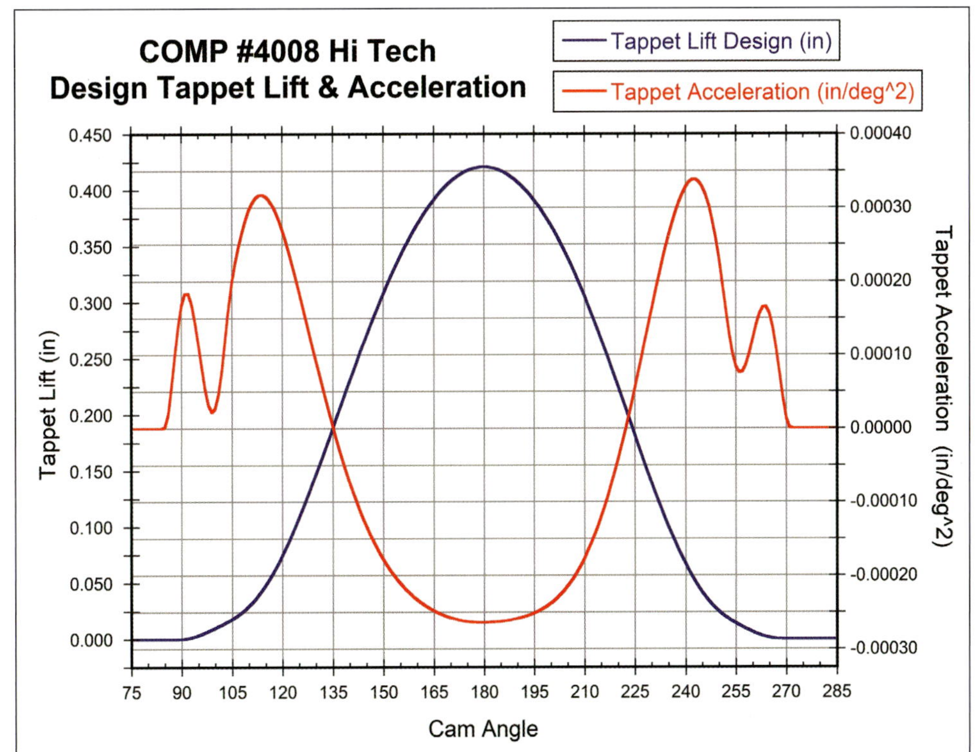

Image 3-13: Going from measured to design acceleration is almost like cheating. This is the curve for the #4008. While we were significantly higher on velocity with the race profile, the lower RPM OEM design is a little quicker at peak closing acceleration. Thinking about how acceleration is given in inches per degree squared, which grows as the square of RPM, we should not be very surprised. High-RPM profiles must have controlled acceleration rates.

change of velocity of 0.002/7 inch/deg^2 = 0.000286 inch/deg^2. Our angular based tappet acceleration is defined as follows:

Tappet Acceleration = Change in Velocity ÷ Change in Angle

Acceleration is the rate of change of velocity. When we carefully plot the measured acceleration at each degree, we get Image 3-12, which is in excellent agreement to that eyeballed tangent line and approximated slope at 127 degrees.

Every time we go one step deeper down into these slopes or derivatives for you calculus geeks, any error in position measurements or manufacturing quickly snowballs. If we had a 20-percent error on velocity from point to point with that +/-0.001-inch position uncertainty, the resulting possible acceleration error is roughly +/-0.002 inch/deg^2, or more than 5 times off our acceleration plot scale of +0.00045 to -0.00035 inch/deg^2.

That is why we are forced to measure and manufacture to such a high precision. We need to be able to both look carefully and control our acceleration. Some readers are probably yelling Sir Isaac Newton's second law of motion at the book at this point, so let's go ahead and state why

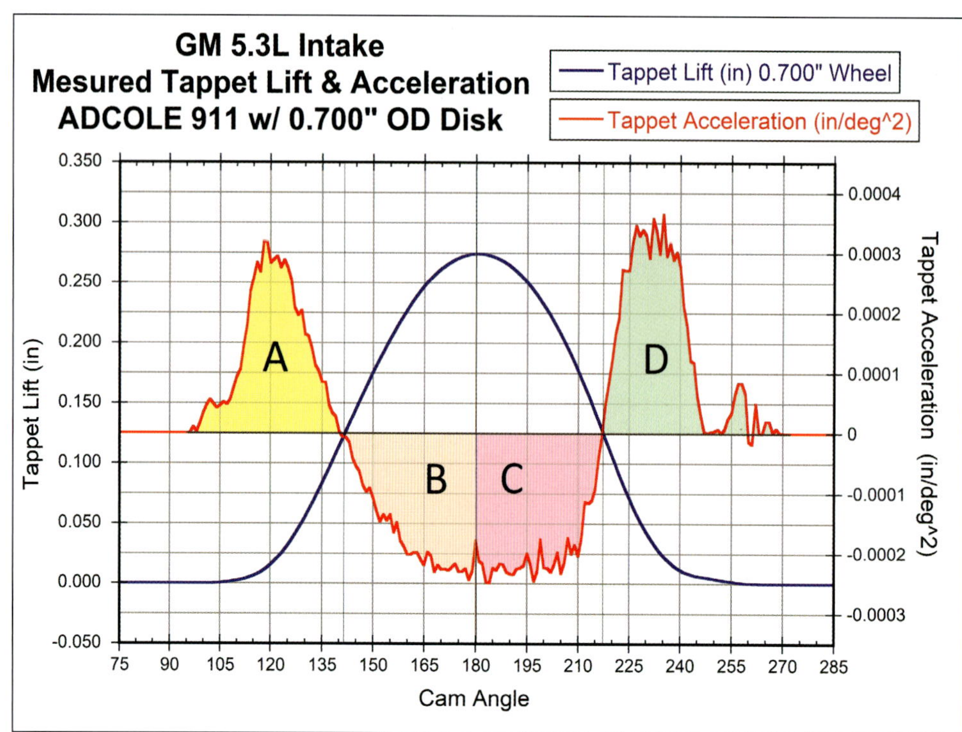

Image 3-14: Going back to our same 0-100-0 velocity regions, note how total force flows from the pushrod to the system in the positive-acceleration regions and from the spring to the system in the negative-acceleration regions becomes clearer. Thomas Griffin used to tell me that I was able to design the positive parts with my profile, but he had to control the negative with his spring designs. It is a little more complicated than that, as the camshaft can excite the spring in Regions A and D and be limited by the spring's available dynamic forces in B and C.

acceleration matters so much to cam design: $\boldsymbol{F} = m\boldsymbol{a}$.

You may note that "F" and "a" are in bold italics above. It is the standard way for physicists to notate we are dealing with vectors. Both the acceleration ($\boldsymbol{a}$) and force ($\boldsymbol{F}$) have a definite direction, unlike the energy equations we dealt with for velocity, which is also a vector, but its square is scaler.

The first reason that I care so much about acceleration is because the forces on the system are directly proportional to acceleration. Not only that, but at high speed, those forces will grow wildly with engine speed because we are designing and measuring our tappet accelerations in inches per degree^2. To convert from angular (inches/degree/degree) to time-based acceleration (inches/second/second), we need to multiply by how many degrees pass each second twice.

Because valvetrain loads are time based, the forces on the components grow as the square of RPM. If I want to take an engine that had the components designed for the forces experienced around 4,000

Theoretical Pushrod Force Assuming with Zero Clearance and Zero Deflection

Valve Mass	120	grams				
Retainer Mass	15	grams				
Lock Mass	5	grams				
Spring Mass	150	grams				
Effective Spring Mass	50	grams				
Effective Rocker Mass	30	grams				
Total Effective Mass	220	grams				
Tappet Acceleration	0.00035	"/deg^2				
Rocker Ratio	1.7					
Valve Acceleration	0.0006	"/deg^2				
Valve Acceleration	0.015	mm/deg^2				
Engine RPM	4500		6000		7500	
Engine RPS	75.00		100.00		125.00	
Camshaft Deg per Sec	13500		18000		22500	
Valve Acceleration	2754344.3	mm/s^2	4896612	mm/s^2	7650956	mm/s^2
Valve Acceleration	2754	M/s^2	4897	M/s^2	7651	M/s^2
Valve Tip Force Req	606	Newtons	1077	Newtons	1683	Newtons
Valve Tip Force Req	136	Lbf	242	Lbf	378	Lbf
Inertial Pushrod Force	232	Lbf	412	Lbf	643	Lbf
Valve Spring Seat Load	150	Lbf	150	Lbf	150	Lbf
Rocker Side Spring Force	255	Lbf	255	Lbf	255	Lbf
Total Pushrod Force	487	Lbf	667	Lbf	898	Lbf

Image 3-15: Professor Jack Taylor spent four years training me to always make a good approximation based on my knowledge before taking any measurement. I use Excel to estimate the minimum pushrod forces at each RPM based on the valve side and rocker mass, tappet acceleration, and rocker ratios. I do most calculations in metric units and then convert back to imperial.

rpm engine speeds and have the same forces at 8,000 rpm, I have to reduce the peak inch/deg^2 accelerations by a factor of 4.

Looking at the acceleration curve for the slower opening/faster closing Comp Cams Hi-Tech 4008 Race profile in Image 3-13, the peak angular acceleration is lower than the production GM 5.3L design. Knowing the GM truck engine was developed to operate below its factory 6,000-rpm rev limiter but the Hi-Tech roller profile was developed to live between 7,000 and 9,000 rpm, this lower peak angular acceleration makes sense. The time-based acceleration rates and forces are far higher on the race application. The slower opening of this design was developed to excite valve springs less at very high RPM, which is a common design characteristic of newer profiles.

Positive Opening Acceleration

Acceleration has to do with loads, so let's talk about what we use to apply those loads by returning to the gas-pedal and brake-pedal analogies that were used for velocity while looking at the same four regions from the velocity curve but with those shown in Image 3-14 of the acceleration curve.

The opening-side positive-acceleration Region A is certainly the gas or accelerator pedal and corresponds to the loads that the cam lobe and tappet applies to the pushrod, rocker, valve, lock retainer, and active part of the spring as the valve starts to open in a conventional OHV arrangement.

Before, I wrote about which pedal we pushed but not *how much* we were pushing it. The acceleration curve tells us how aggressively the gas or brake pedal is applied. You might

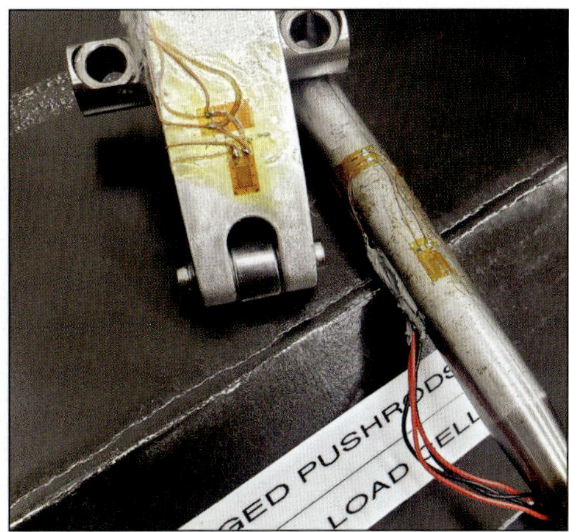

Image 3-16: Measuring those dynamic loads is far easier than you might imagine. The only difficult aspect is finding a data acquisition system that can record something every degree inside your operating range. Once you have that bit, gluing a strain gauge to basically any component can tell you the load experienced. We calibrate the rockers and pushrods outside the engine in a press before the dynamics test.

Image 3-17: Here is a zoomed-in view of the strain gauge glued on an LS rocker. As the rocker deforms, the wires compress in this gauge to reduce the path length and resistance. Once calibrated, we must route those wires to a data question system, such as the National Instruments unit, to record load.

Image 3-18: Not only can rockers and pushrods be measured, but here you can see tiny strain gauges glued onto an outer-valve spring and a load cell that can be placed under a valve spring. The strain gauge is inexpensive to buy but difficult to adhere, and it tends to come off. Also, the wires can get pulled into the head when the spring rotates. The load cell is easier but costs significantly more and tends to die if you drive the system out of control.

be shocked to learn that the maximum measured pushrod loading due to acceleration is greater than 1,000 pounds of force, even in street/strip applications.

These huge loads make sense, as a quick calculation shows a 0.00035 inch/deg^2 acceleration and common component masses resulting in over 667 pounds of force at 6,000 rpm and 898 pounds of force at 7,500 rpm as seen in Image 3-15. You might expect this loading to be higher than actual and difficult to directly measure, but both assumptions are incorrect. Because we assumed the rocker, pushrod, and valvetrain system were infinitely stiff and have 0 clearances

Image 3-19: Our earliest motoring test, where you drive the valvetrain with an external drive, was one small-block Chevy going through two manual transmissions to another one without pistons to test the valvetrain. That system puts pushrods in low earth orbit if you selected the wrong gears. This is a later unit that Thomas Griffin used for his master's thesis. The electric drive ran directly to the camshaft and only drove one cylinder. Because of torsional vibrations from only one pair of lifters, he had to add a harmonic dampener to the camshaft to act like it would when activating all eight cylinders. Tracking was done with an Optron system that required a slot in the cylinder and head to record an interface on the valve edge.

Image 3-21: Every year, we gain capabilities on the Spintron test cells. One cell is used primarily for durability testing, but the other cell almost always has some dynamic test running. You can see the control desk with the National Instruments data acquisition system underneath. Their lab view software makes routines easy that were difficult in the past writhing routines rather easy. AVL, A&D, and EFI University all have commercial systems available today.

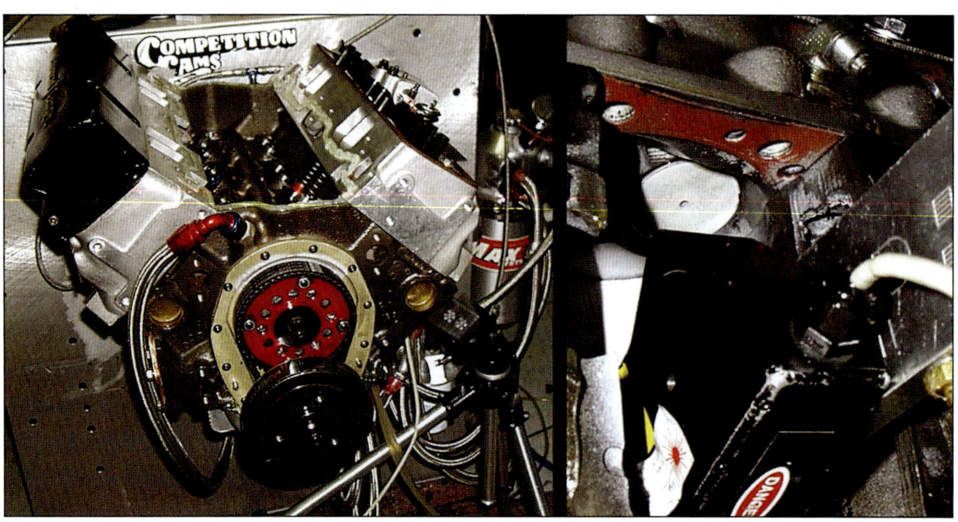

Image 3-20: When Bob Fox developed the first Spintron test system with a 50-hp electric motor, we were one of the first three customers. The internal dry sump, laser-tracking software that used a standard head, and ability to drive all eight cylinders were huge steps forward. Learning to design camshafts when we could track valve motion and measure loads directly was a huge benefit.

in those quasi-static calculations, the real numbers are significantly higher.

To measure these loads, we typically glue a wire-strain gauge to the pushrod and rocker (as shown in Images 3-16, 3-17, and 3-18). Strain gauge or load cell signals are amplified and run into a high-speed data-acquisition system. Early on, we used an oscilloscope to capture this signal, then a Nicolet Odyssey, and now a Nation Instruments system. There are also data systems you can buy from both AVL and A&D Technology for the 1-degree resolution at high-RPM signal processing required.

With component gauging and signal processing, we measure component loading in both of the motoring cells (Spintron cells), where the valvetrain is driven by an electric motor and in actual running engines on the dyno to see how these loads change with cylinder pressure. The motoring case is nice in that

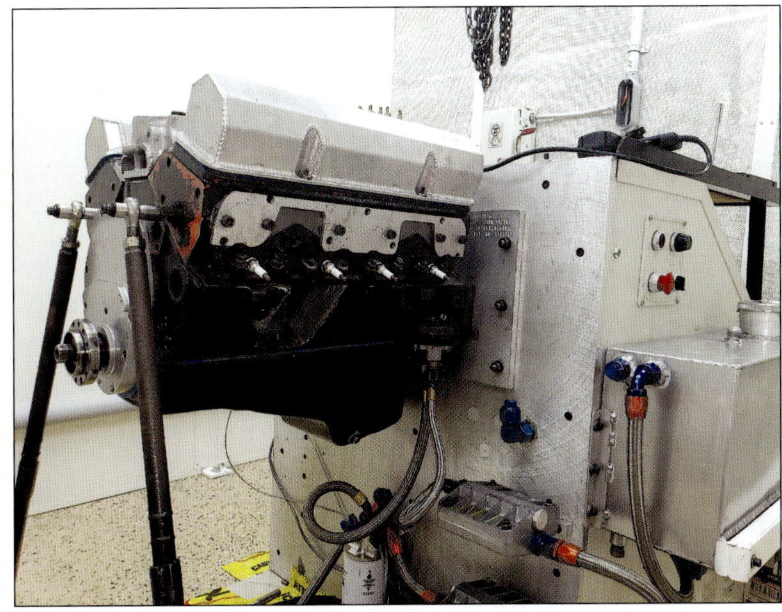

***Image 3-22:** Inside one of our new insulated Spintron test rooms, this small-block Chevy has a window cut to allow a tracking laser to be placed in the number-3 cylinder bore. This allows us to track the valves. In place of a normal crankshaft, a dummy mandrel is driven by the newer 75-hp AC drive. This goes through the normal timing set, turns the camshafts, and simulates the valvetrain on a running engine.*

component failures are far less expensive, and we can put a laser in the cylinder bore and track the valve motion without a piston in the way (as shown in Image 3-22).

Image 3-23 provides the measured data from a circle-track application that is running a lobe much like the Hi-Tech example at 8,000 and 8,500 rpm. Even if we cheat up our acceleration numbers by over 20 percent in the quasi-static excel calculation to simulate lash and increase the masses to accurately

Theoretical Race Pushrod Force Assuming with Zero Clearance and Zero Deflection

Valve Mass	100	grams				
Retainer Mass	20	grams				
Lock Mass	5	grams				
Spring Mass	200	grams				
Effective Spring Mass	50	grams				
Effective Rocker Mass	50	grams				
Total Effective Mass	225	grams				
Tappet Acceleration	0.0004	"/deg^2	*Increased above desgn to compensate for lash*			
Rocker Ratio	1.8					
Valve Acceleration	0.0007	"/deg^2				
Valve Acceleration	0.018	mm/deg^2				
Engine RPM	8000		8500		9000	
Engine RPS	133.33		141.67		150.00	
Camshaft Deg per Sec	24000		25500		27000	
Valve Acceleration	10533888	mm/s^2	11891772	mm/s^2	13331952	mm/s^2
Valve Acceleration	10534	M/s^2	11892	M/s^2	13332	M/s^2
Valve Tip Force Req	2370	Newtons	2676	Newtons	3000	Newtons
Valve Tip Force Req	533	Lbf	602	Lbf	674	Lbf
Inertial Pushrod Force	959	Lbf	1083	Lbf	1214	Lbf
Valve Spring Seat Load	250	Lbf	250	Lbf	250	Lbf
Rocker Side Spring Force	450	Lbf	450	Lbf	450	Lbf
Total Pushrod Force	1409	Lbf	1533	Lbf	1664	Lbf

***Image 3-24:** To help confirm our measurements, do the same math that we ran for the street load excel sheet with the race parameters. Theoretically, it is 1,409 pounds, where we saw a bit over 2,000 pounds with the load cell. We know the lash and deflection is going to make our calculation more of a lower limit than a real expectation. As we hit 8,500 rpm in the test, note that the pushrod saw zero load a few times over the nose. Yes, that means we had real separation! Like any fall, separation is not a problem, but the sudden stop as you come back together can hurt. That is why we predicted 1,533 pounds minimum load at 8,500 rpm without separation or lash but measured 3,500-plus pounds.*

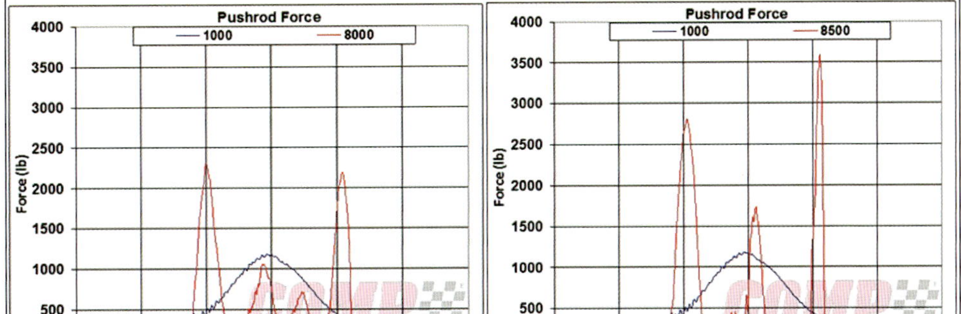

***Image 3-23:** I'm not sure about you, but when I hold a 3/8-inch OD pushrod in my hand, it does not seem possible that it would live under 2,000-plus-pound force spikes for perhaps a million cycles—never mind the 3,500-plus-pound force that it sees here at 8,500 rpm. That is probably why we have checked so many pushrods and rockers. If it helps, that blue line at 1,000 rpm is almost exactly the spring load times the rocker ratio, or exactly what you expect at low RPM.*

reflect a race application to get the chart in Image 3-24, the quasi-static calculation is off by approximately 50 percent. The reason the real loads are higher goes back to my initial lazy teenager example.

When we applied the 1,400 ft-lbs on the pushrod, the valve did not immediately do what we asked. Energy was stored in the pushrod as with a pole vaulter in track and field, but this runner speeds up as he plants this pole. Together, this leads to the much higher loads measured than calculated without deflection.

By 8,500 rpm, when this system starts to get unhappy, the calculated load of 1,533 ft-lbs is off by almost a factor of two on the opening and more than that on the closing. At this point, the spring coil surge is working against the pushrod, and there is separation and some crashing over the nose and on the closing side. The point of this is to see that the static acceleration sets more of the minimal dynamic loads than the maximum values.

Limiting the acceleration and velocity in the lash or hydraulic take-up region is how a cam profile designer can develop a profile that will maintain stability at higher engine speeds. Stiffer pushrods and rocker arms can also improve this situation. Here is one last note before we move to Region B. This deflection robs us of duration at higher RPM. Not many people think they are running variable-duration camshafts, but reality always creates changing duration. As engine speeds increase, loads go up faster than the predicted square of engine speed. These loads lead to higher deflection. This higher deflection reduces the duration at the valve. Hence, just when you want your camshaft to act larger, it shrinks.

Going from Positive to Negative Acceleration (Swapping Feet)

If the tappet and pushrod were the accelerator pedal in Region A, I bet you guessed the valve spring again is the brakes and applies force in the opposite direction in Region B, and the magnitude of acceleration is like brake line pressure. In fact, we can think of the acceleration curve as a three-segment relay race with two people running. The tappet, pushrod, and rocker run the first segment (Region A) and then the valve spring runs two segments back-to-back through Regions B and C. As we pass into the final segment, Region D, the valve spring hands the baton of control back over to the pushrod and camshaft. The only problem with this analogy is that those first runners can set the valve spring in resonance if we try to move too fast in Region A.

If we have already slapped the spring so hard in Region A that it is surging violently, there will not be enough load to match the force required for our design's negative acceleration (deceleration). If there is not enough load available from the spring to keep the tappet on the camshaft, there is separation. If you look back at the 8,000-rpm pushrod load

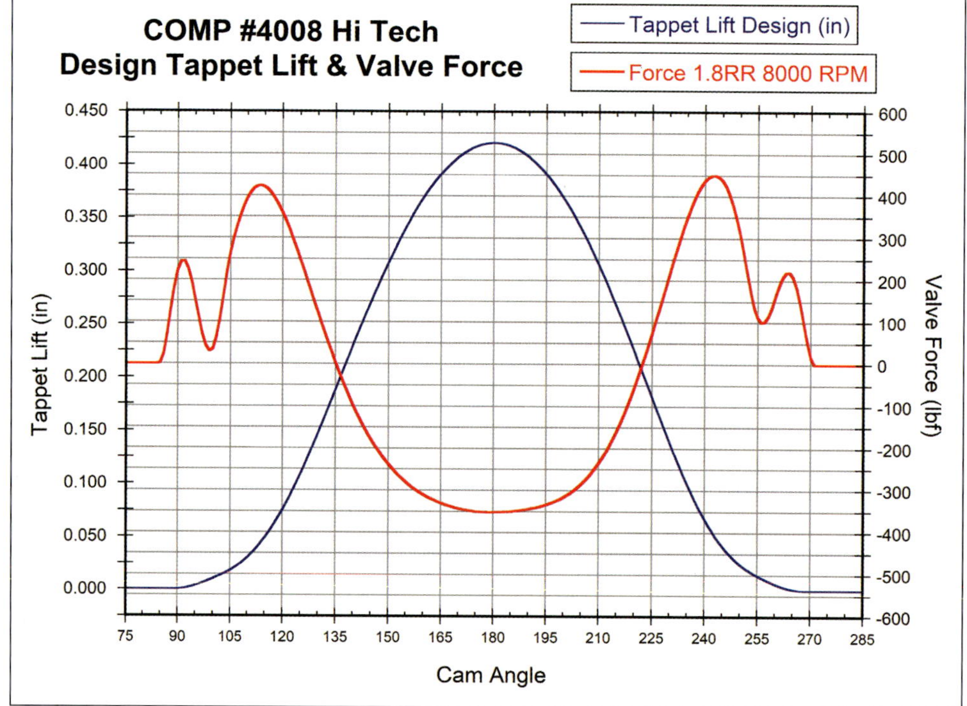

Image 3-25: Valve force is less than pushrod force because of the ratio. In this graph, we calculate the force required at the valve to create this exact design valve lift, assuming no lash and no deflection. Instead of a normal valvetrain system, if we had some sort of electric coil or other device to move the valve, these are the instantaneous forces required. People think I am against electronic valve-control systems. Nothing could be further from the truth. It is fun to sit at my computer and design how I want the valve to move at each RPM and throttle position. Unfortunately, the current camless valve-control systems really don't have the energy or efficiency to drive the valve directly in a way that is sufficient for automotive racing.

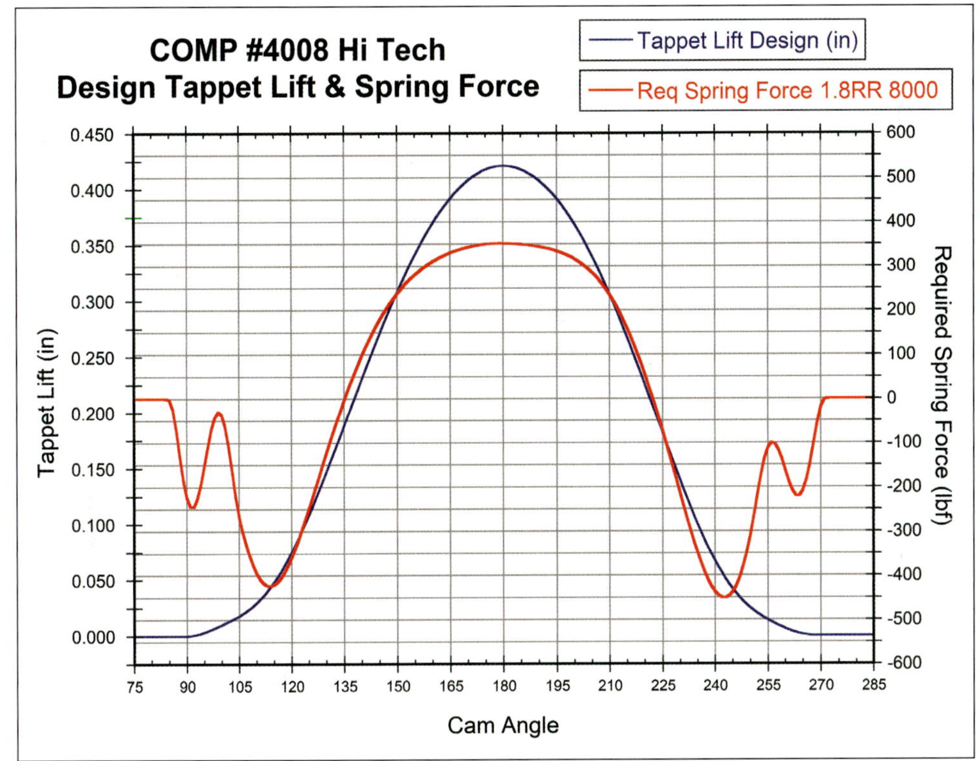

Image 3-26: Looking at these valve forces from the valve spring's point of view is like I thought it would be to live in Australia when I was a little kid. All the loads are upside down compared to how I think of it from the camshaft design side. Knowing Newton's third law (for every action there is an equal and opposite reaction), we should not be surprised that this graph is the last red curve flipped upside down. However, it helps knowing that you need at least 350 pounds of real open load to control this valve at 8,000 rpm. If we see less than this with that load cell under the spring, regardless of what the catalog says, the system goes ballistic.

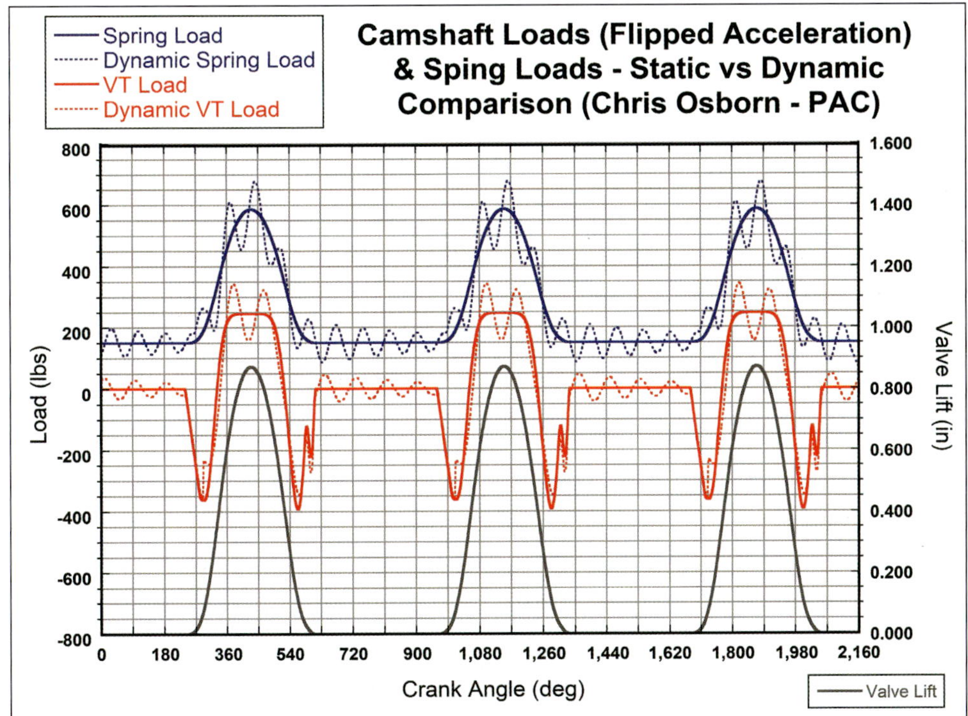

Image 3-27: I know that Chris Osborn is not from Down Under—even if he looks at acceleration upside down from my cam design point of view. This is a quicker profile than the 4008 with a nose shape that is not as nice. The solid blue line is what the spring provides without any surge or vibration at 8,000 rpm. The solid red line is what the cam profile requests if there was not lash, deflection, or vibration.

plot from Image 3-23, the pushrod force goes to 0 twice on the opening side, spikes near max lift, and then goes back to 0 a few times on the closing side too.

Here, we can see exactly what happens when a spring cannot supply enough force to keep everything together so that it will follow the profile. We could even use that 225-gram effective mass and convert the acceleration from angular based to time based and convert our acceleration to force through Newton's second law ($\boldsymbol{F} = m\boldsymbol{a}$) and create Image 3-25. This looks exactly like the acceleration plot, just scaled as the corresponding force to create that acceleration at 8,000 rpm.

Nose Acceleration and Spring Load

With these pushrod load plots and the thought of spring loads and surge fresh in our minds, let's go back to Regions B and C of the acceleration plot. We can say that if the available spring load or static spring load minus what we lose due to spring surge is greater than the magnitude

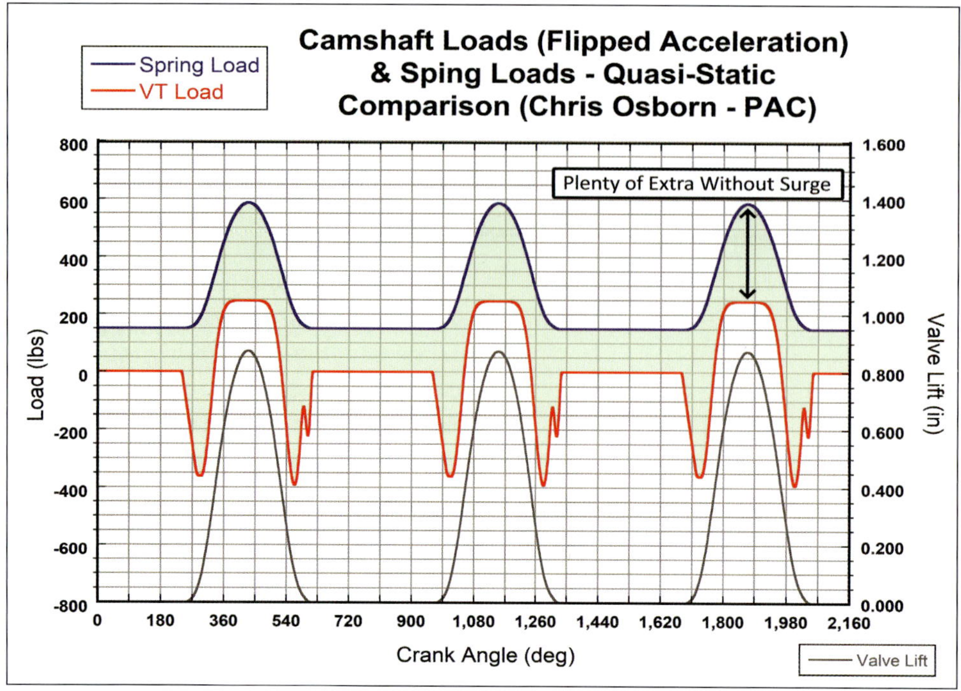

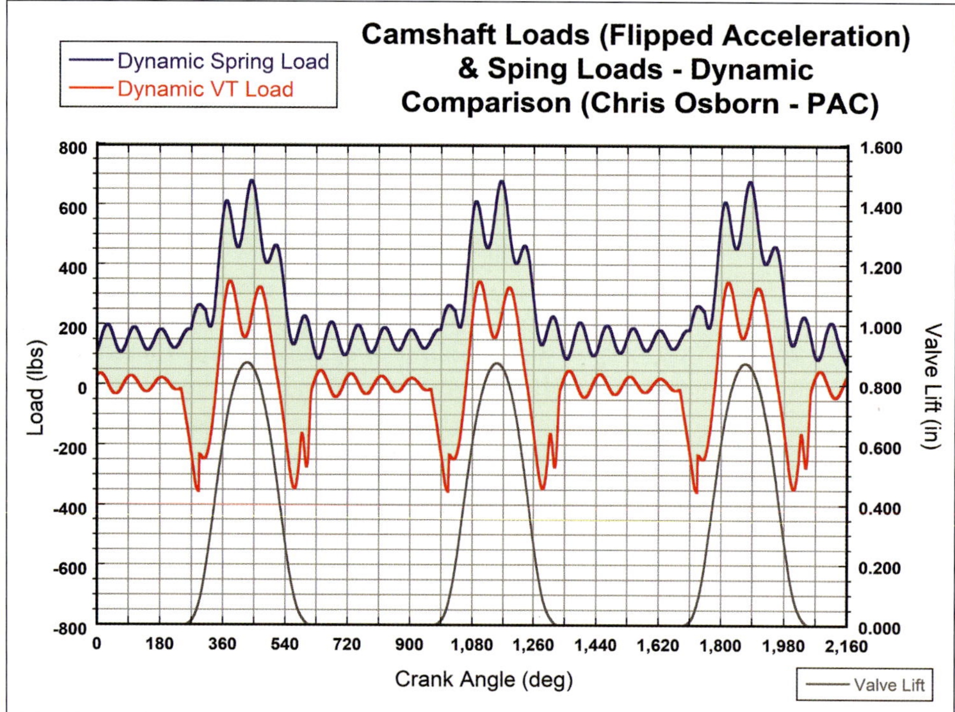

Image 3-29: Once we focus on the vibration, deflection, surge, and real-life messiness of the dashed lines of Image 3-26, it becomes clear that the extra 330 pounds that dropped to 200 pounds is more like 75 pounds past peak lift on the closing side. If I knew all the masses and life was not messy, I could tell anyone the open loads needed for any cam profile given the system mass and RPM. Unfortunately, the differences between the quasi-static solid lines of Image 3-26 and dashed lines with all the messiness are very difficult to model and change with every spring design and valvetrain system.

Image 3-28: Note that there's an extra 330-pound load over the nose. Because the profile nose acceleration does not match the spring force (too flat), the real extra load is more like 200 pounds at around 0.600-inch valve lift. A little design work on that nose acceleration shape makes this a much easier system to control.

of the negative acceleration multiplied by the effective mass, then the system will be in control.

Newton's third law of motion might not be as well-known as his second, but it is just as important. The third law states that for every action (force) there is an equal and opposite reaction (opposing force). For valvetrain systems, the valve spring provides the equal and opposite force (as shown in Image 3-26, which shows these required forces at 8,000 rpm from the valve spring's point of view).

In physics language, we are in control at a given RPM and cam angle if the available spring force (***F***) holding the system together is greater than the "m***a***" that our profile requires. My friend Chris Osborn at PAC created a model of static and dynamic spring loads to compare to the inverted camshaft acceleration curve shown in Image 3-27. Here, the solid lines are the spring loads and cam acceleration assuming no spring surge of vibrations in the valvetrain and the dashed lines include the dynamic behavior of each subsystem.

When someone asks about the required spring load for any camshaft and valvetrain system, most engineers think about something more like Image 3-28, where the surge and natural frequencies are ignored. This tends to be rather simple to calculate, but people often look at the maximum profile nose acceleration shown with the arrow in Image 3-28. Note that 60 to 80 degrees before and after max lift there is a significantly smaller margin of safety (green shaded distance between the blue and red curves). However, for this

Image 3-30: To measure what is occurring with each coil, note how we attached strain gauges to individual coils. This lets us see the real loads, balance the stress evenly from coil to coil, and ensure we had the load required for control at high speed. I can't overstate how much this helped when developing the conical valve springs.

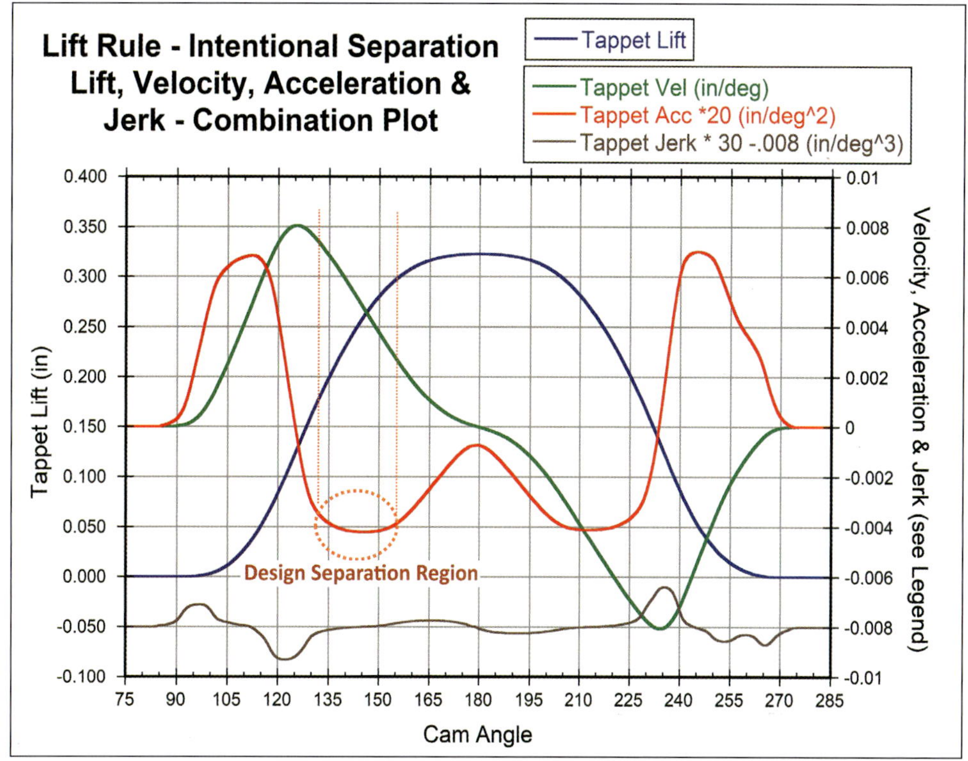

Image 3-31: Sometimes we want to drive the system out of control. Some sanctioning bodies believe they can save racers money with a lift rule. Nothing could be further from the truth. If someone sets a lift rule, we can go from that flat-nose acceleration shape of VA-26 to a double negative hump (as shown in this graph), which results in a design separation region on the opening and a "hope" region on the closing. I say "hope" because at too low or too high of an RPM, it stops working and the system crashes. If this system is not coming back together by 225 degrees, there are going to be extreme pushrod loads when it crashes around 240 to 255 degrees, like we saw earlier but far worse.

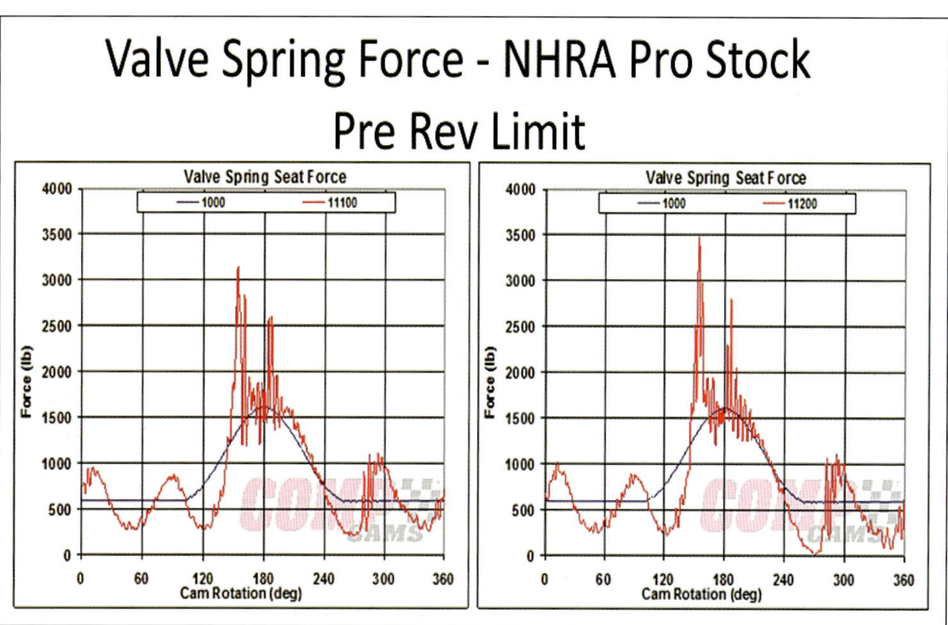

Image 3-32: What a difference 100 rpm can make, even at 11,000 rpm. The spikes in the measured spring seat load data result from coil impacts. The coils literally collide at high speed. At 11,200 rpm, the spring surge was so great that we lost all the 600-pound spring load that we started with at 1,000 rpm. It was not that we killed the spring, but it could not keep up with the valve. If you watched this on a high-speed video, you might see the bottom coil pick itself up as the valve closes. For high engine speeds, high-frequency springs are needed to keep up with the valve motion.

Going Deeper: Jerk and Software

We have not talked about jerk so far, but it is the cornerstone for the next step of improvements.

Tappet Jerk = Change in Acceleration ÷ Change in Angle

Jerk is the rate of change of acceleration. Going back to the 0 to 100 to 0 analogy, jerk is how quickly each pedal is moved. If you have ever driven a road-race car, you know if you go full throttle right up to the breaking point and then hit the brakes, it upsets the chassis, and the car does not want to turn.

If you start lifting the accelerator pedal smoothly even a second earlier and then push firmly but controlled on the brakes, the car performs much better and reacts far more predictably as you turn the steering wheel. NASCAR teams monitor the throttle position along with brake-line pressure and steering angles to help coach drivers on how to make these transitions smoothly yet rapidly without upsetting their suspension.

For the valvetrain, jerk is both how rapidly acceleration transitions and how much impact the components experience. Jerk also has tremendous influence on the harmonic content that the profile transfers to the valve spring.

The jerk curve for the Comp 4008 is shown in Image 3-34, followed by the common plotting convention that Harvey Crane introduced with the lift, velocity, acceleration, and jerk on one graph in Image 3-35. Note that jerk is shifted down to keep it from being jumbled with velocity and acceleration. This combination plot is the graphical format we will use going forward to look at any cam motion design.

Modern camshaft design software and the analysis tools used focus on designing the acceleration curve primarily with a close eye to both velocity and jerk while targeting certain lift and duration goals. There are several useful programs available. Gama Technologies now includes GT V-Train inside its GT-suite. However, I typically use 4stHEAD, which was developed by Professor Gordon Blair and Dr. Charles McCartan from the school of mechanical and aerospace engineering at Queen's University in Belfast.

I want to express my appreciation for their assistance and how the tools they developed have contributed significantly toward improvements in combustion engine performance and efficiency over more than a decade. ■

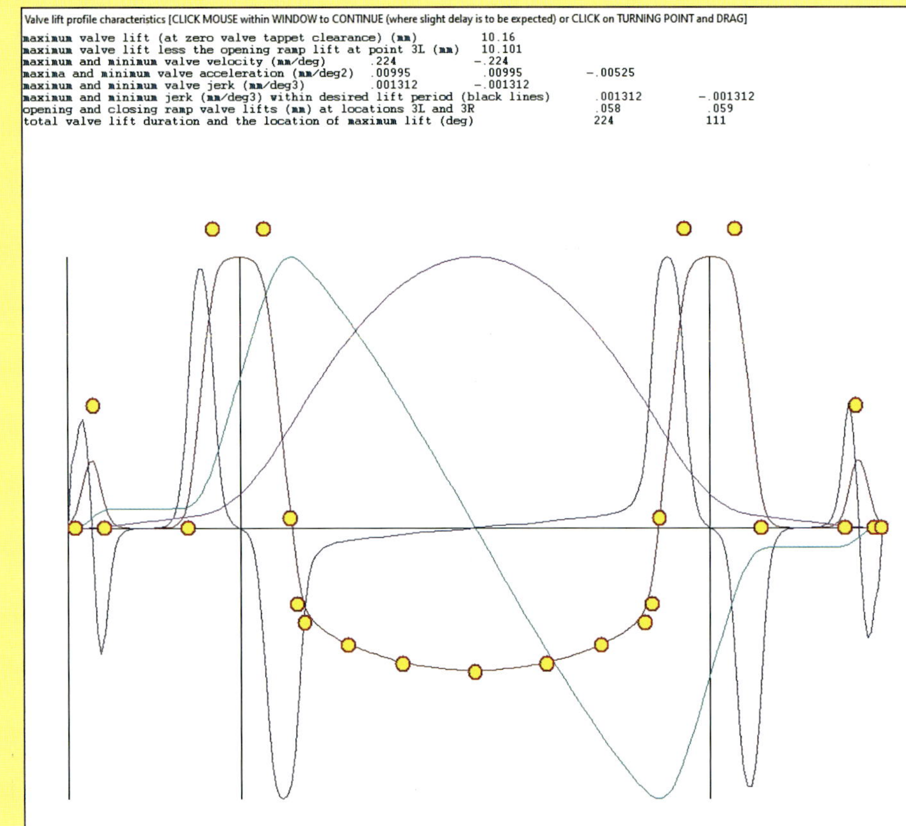

Image 3-41: By moving the 12 acceleration nodes in our current 4stHEAD software, I can mimic almost any camshaft design style from the past and create all new ideas—some good and some not so good. This graph shows the nodes positioned to create a modified trapezoidal design. The graphical presentation is close to the format that both Harvey and I use (but without the jerk curve offset). There is some very useful maximum and minimum information on the top as you tweak the nodes in this software.

Image 3-33: I often joke there should be a ratio to score cylinder heads based off the percentage of the valve diameter you can see when looking down the intake port. Great heads seem to always be north of 75 percent. This Pro Stock Dodge Hemi is close to 90 percent. The chamber might not be as efficient as the GM splayed valve design, but at high RPM, this port makes up the difference and then some.

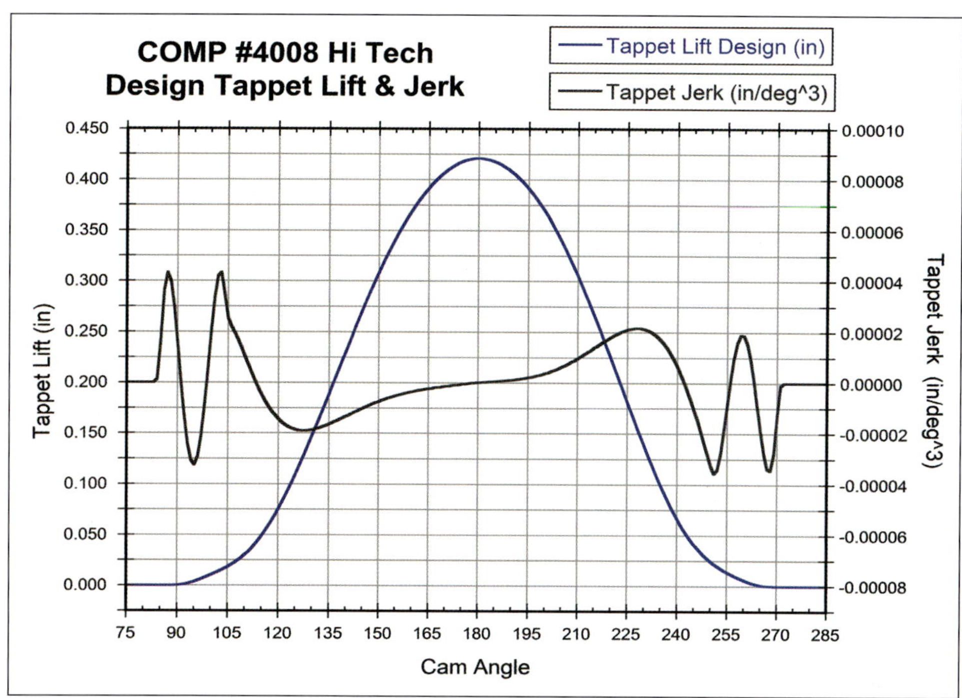

Image 3-34: Going deeper into profile design and derivatives, it is necessary to look at "jerk." Here, we see how quickly acceleration is changing and forces are being applied or removed with the #4008 design. Most of the jumpy ends are the transitions into the lash original ramps. For the main section, the jerk is below 0.00002 inch/degree³. These low jerk rates set this series above the common designs of that era.

RPM, valvetrain mass, and design acceleration, we are quite safe when we ignore the dynamic coil behavior.

However, in the real world, the valve spring wiggles like a bowl of jelly when the valve is quickly opened, which results in surging coils and a strong wave running through the resulting available load to control the valve (as shown with the blue line in Image 3-29). Not only does the spring vibrate but the entire

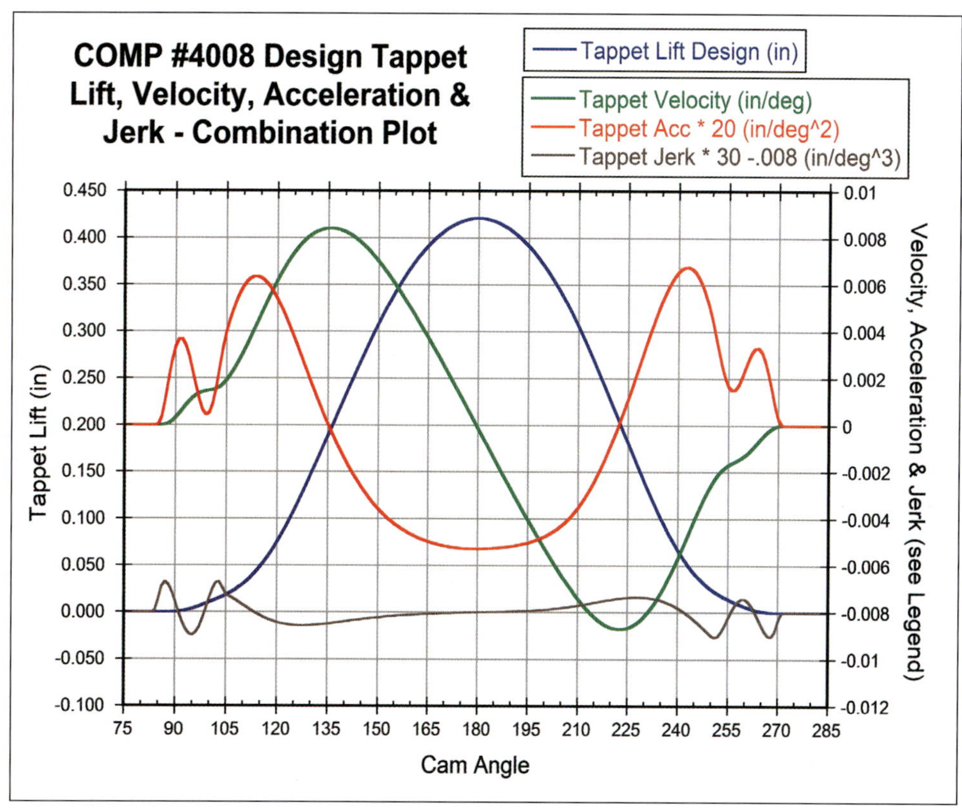

Image 3-35: This is the common format I learned from Harvey Crane that I use for plotting and evaluating lobe designs. When all the curves on this plot look smooth, there will be relatively low harmonic content in the profile. Earlier designs have far more abrupt transitions.

valvetrain system also has its own natural frequency and stiffness contributions to required control force (as shown with the red line in Image 3-29). See how much smaller the gaps are in the green safety region.

The excess spring force (think of it as the available balance in a checking account at your bank) can be quickly measured on a Spintron or Dyno with a calibrated strain-gauged pushrod like was shown in Image 3-25. Just like when reading your monthly statement, we always want some cushion here all the way from peak opening velocity to peak closing velocity (Regions B and C).

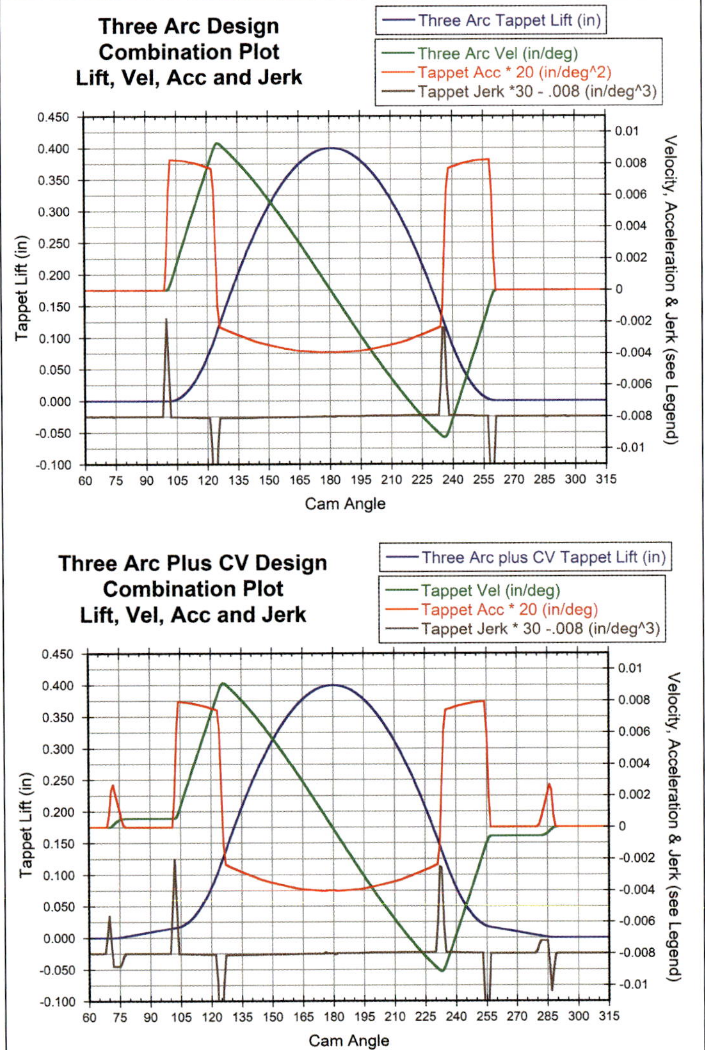

Image 3-36: This shows the harsh transitions of a geometrically developed three-arc profile and a later three-arc-plus-CV ramp profile. The jerk of these designs is only constrained by my graphic smoothing and design software. It would be infinite if it could have been manufactured. The saving grace of these designs was the smoothing of the older cam-grinding machines. Note that the peak positive acceleration and nose accelerations were both limited by the geometry of the arcs.

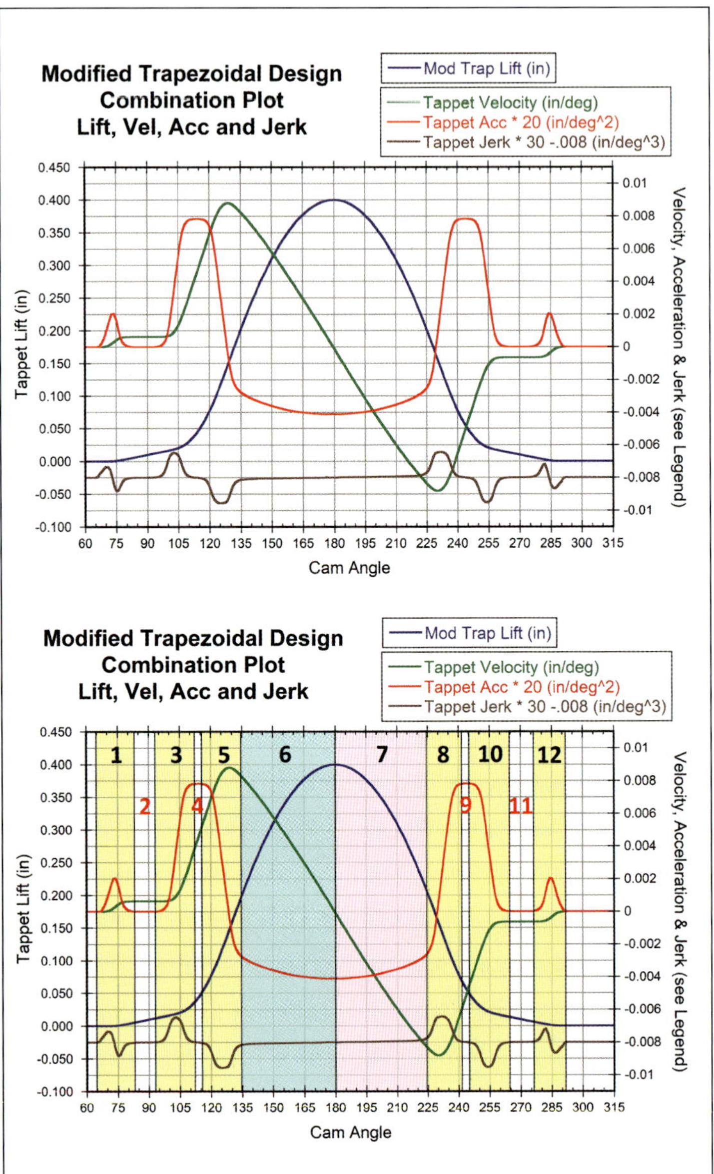

Image 3-37: This shows what is known as a modified trapezoidal design. These designs are created with several factors in mind: 1) smooth transitions between constant velocity ramps, 2) limited jerk to constant positive acceleration, 3) limited jerk to max velocity, and 4) a constant radius of curvature or spring matching shaped nose. The opening side and closing can have the same or different segments. Note the 12 design regions. Most of the original Ed Winfield and early Isky profiles were developed with this technique. Many European designs still use this approach.

The only applications where we knowingly try to force pushrod loads to 0 are lift-rule classes, such as NHRA Stock Eliminator and a few circle-track classes. To get around the measured static lift limit, we knowingly run two strong negative acceleration peaks (one on either side of max lift) that are both greater magnitude (more negative) than the valve spring is able to control at speed (as shown in Image 3-31). This design of acceleration curve shape guarantees separation in the orange-circled region and valve loft to result in a higher lift than when measured statically.

The real issue with this lofting approach is not tossing the valve. Throwing it higher is never that difficult, but like any fall, it is the sudden stop that hurts. At the right speed, everything comes together nicely on the closing side and no damage occurs. At a slower speed, it can crash near the nose and damage the camshaft and lifter. At too high of a speed, the valve will clear the entire closing side, and we are back to using the piston for valve control.

For 99-plus-percent of applications, we want the negative acceleration rounded at the nose and closely matched around the available open spring loads throughout Regions B and C. This keeps the pushrod lightly loaded and everything following nicely along, keeping all the valvetrain parts together. Note that from the acceleration point of view, Regions B and C really are not different.

Closing-Side Positive Acceleration

Now, we finally made it to Region D of the acceleration plot. The runner who started this race by carrying the team through Region A has hopefully been riding along nicely while getting a breather through Regions B and C and should now be ready to take back the baton. As soon as we cross peak closing velocity, the camshaft system needs to slow the valve to a low velocity before it contacts the seat. There will be significant deflection in this region resulting from the high forces and limited system stiffness.

The closing side sees higher loads than the opening, even with a symmetric profile. The highest loads I have seen in a controlled system were just over 10,000 pounds of force for an NHRA Pro Stock application. Before this spike, there was some slight separation in Region C, but not so much that we let the piston stop our valve.

Closing Loads Past the Buckling Point

Think about those types of load. We were seeing pushrod loading basically four times higher than the weight of that Pro Stock car. For street applications with 5/16-inch pushrods, it is not uncommon to see the pushrod loads on the closing side exceed the buckling load of the pushrod.

About now, I'm sure eyes are rolling. How could that possibly be true? We have seen that it is possible to exceed the pushrod buckling loads on both sides millions of times without a catastrophic failure. The trick to this is understanding how a pushrod can buckle. All pushrods are far, far stronger and stiffer in pure compression than in bending.

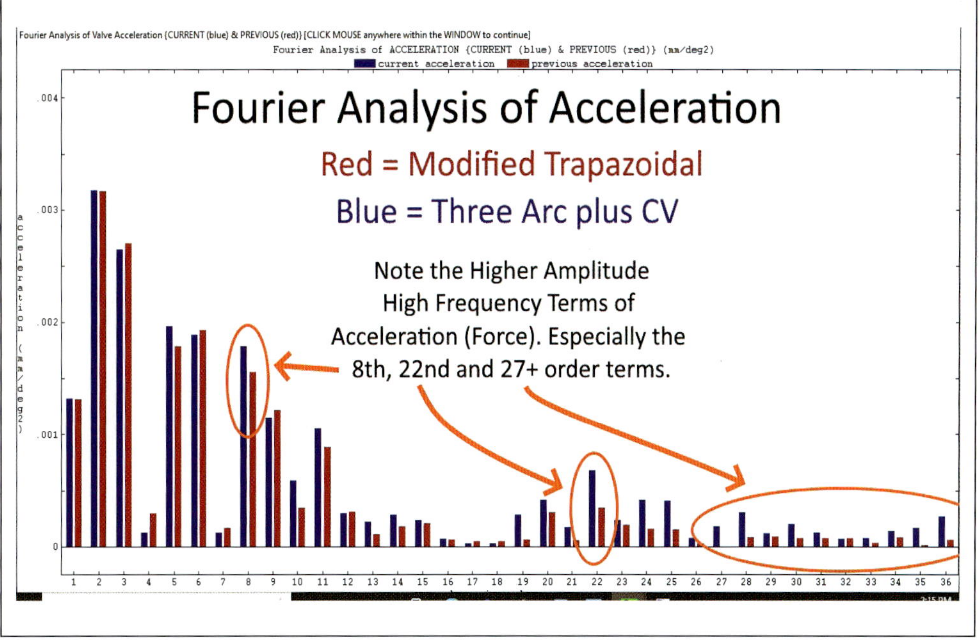

***Image 3-38:** In addition to the huge jerk differences between the new modified trapezoidal and old three-arc designs, note how this shows itself in drive frequency. Jon Batiste Fourier developed a theory of how any function or curve can be constructed of a series of sine waves. We can use this to see what spring frequencies a cam design will excite. When you get out to the 22nd order and higher, the older designs still have spikes that excite the spring at a quarter of the engine speed of a newer design. High jerk results in high order terms.*

Unfortunately, we always apply a bending moment on the rocker end as the ball or cup tip tries to rotate the pushrod end through the rocker sweep. To reduce this torque, there are a number of drag-race pushrods with a bronze cup and a small radius ball adjuster on the rocker. Regardless of how much you try to reduce the torque, there is always enough there to start bending the pushrod. As soon as you get any bending started, the applied compression loads take over trying to further bend the pushrods.

Hence, when we measure pushrod loads higher than what can cause failure if it was loaded that much on a press, what keeps it from failing? The answer is: it did not have time. There was certainly enough force, but as seen in the graphs, the pushrod loads are only near those peaks for maybe 10 to 15 cam degrees. The camshaft turns 24,000 degrees per second at 8,000 rpm. Hence, 20 degrees go by in 1/1,200th of a second or a little more than eight-tenths of millisecond.

When excessive force was applied, the middle of the pushrod tried to move out to the point that the steel tube went into plastic deformation and totally gave way. However, before it bent very far, those loads were gone and everything was alright again. Pushrods in highly loaded operation can be the boy who cried wolf of the automotive world.

Keeping It on the Seat

Focusing on that final pulse in the far right of Region D, this is required for the constant-velocity closing ramp that we noticed in the velocity plots. As a cam designer, I will tailor this last part of the curve (245 to 265 degrees) around stiffness, RPM, noise constraints, endurance requirements, valve-seat erosion concerns, seat angle, materials, lash or hydraulic-lifter performance, spring seat loads, and several other factors. You may think I forgot about our spring after the handoff between Regions C and D, but we need it again in this final part of Region D.

The valve is always going to close with some velocity, which is typically rather high. The valve-seat angle helps catch the valve, but the head flexes almost like a drumhead. Again, we are dealing with stored energy and have to keep the valve head from jumping back off the seat as the valve-head shape springs back with the valve-spring seat load. The valve spring is going through quite a lot on this return trip, even as it closes. When the camshaft took over to rapidly slow the system, the valve-spring coils had to slow down with everything else, and they probably ran into one another at high speed.

There is considerable coil collision and vibration in this region, like we discussed over the nose, but perhaps even higher amplitude, as there is more overall average room between coils at low lift. There are some great high-speed videos online for spring surge, but perhaps more useful is a plot from a load cell under the intake valve spring of an NHRA Pro Stock Spintron engine around 11,000 rpm before the dark days of the 10,500-rpm rev limiter. This test used a piezo electric load cell under the spring seat (shown in Image 3-18). In Image 3-32, the spring load

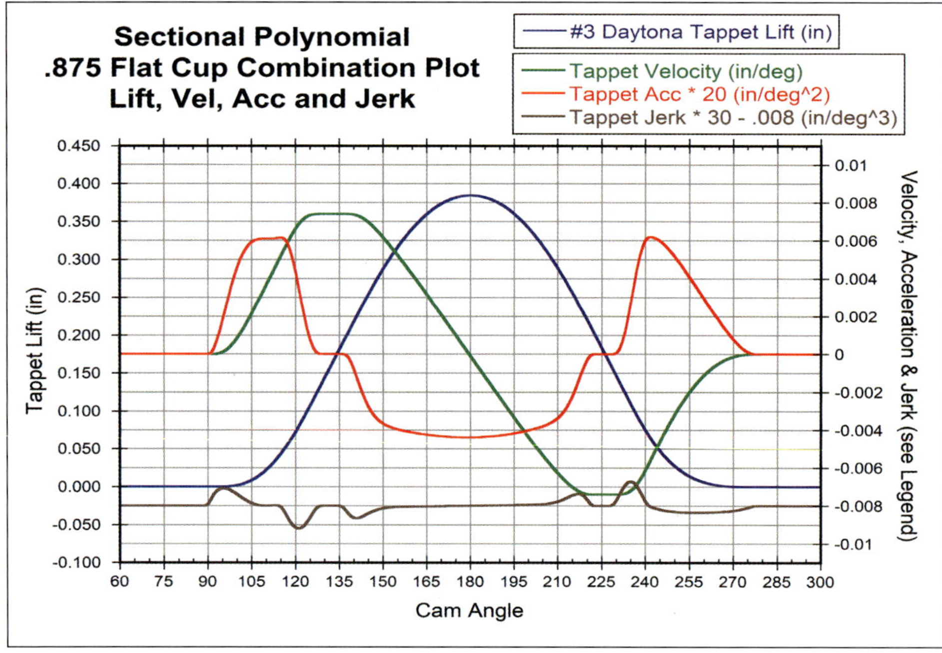

Image 3-39: When I started cam design, the profiles were made from several eight-term polynomial sections that were linked together. This design won the Daytona 500 and was made from 12 sections linked together so smoothly that I sometimes forget where I put the blends. Note the ramp-less opening design, which favors the older modified trapezoidal designs, along with constant maximum-velocity sections to stay right on the edge of the 0.875-inch flat-tappet limit. The closing is nearly constant jerk, which was a Comp Cams fingerprint for several of the most successful flat-tappet cup designs.

is at 1,000 rpm in blue, along with it at 11,100 rpm in red on the left plot, and 11,200 rpm in red on the right.

This was from Roy Johnson's championship-winning Pro Stock Dodge Hemi. This engine had an intake port that was large enough to support 12,000 rpm, so maximizing area under the lift curve while maintaining valvetrain stability into the tachometer's stratosphere was pretty much the limiting factor to performance. Note in the graph that even with nearly 600 pounds of seat load shown at 1,000 rpm in blue, the dynamic load with spring surge was only about 200 at 11,100 and basically 0 at 11,200 rpm. If you are thinking that 0 is not enough, you are 100-percent correct.

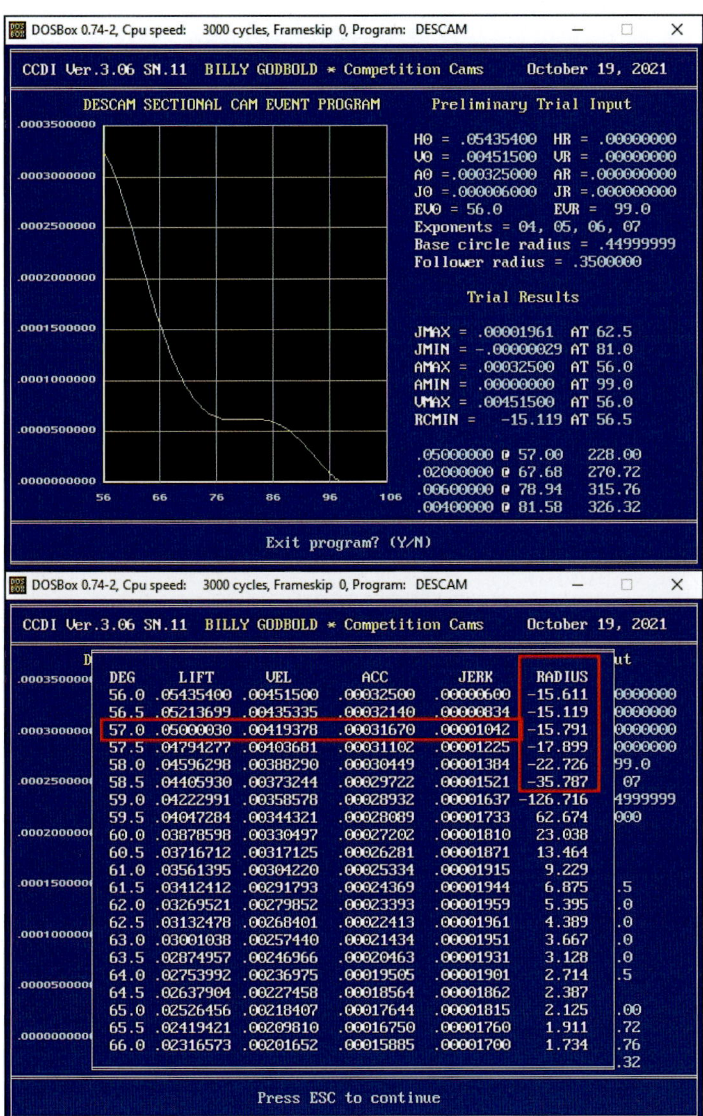

Image 3-40: These are the input and output pages from Harvey Crane's design software. This is the input for a roller-cam ramp that goes from 0 to just past 0.050-inch tappet lift and could be opening or closing. Note that it outputs the radius of curvature, which was an important limit for small-journal roller designs, just as max velocity was a huge constraint in flat-tappet designs.

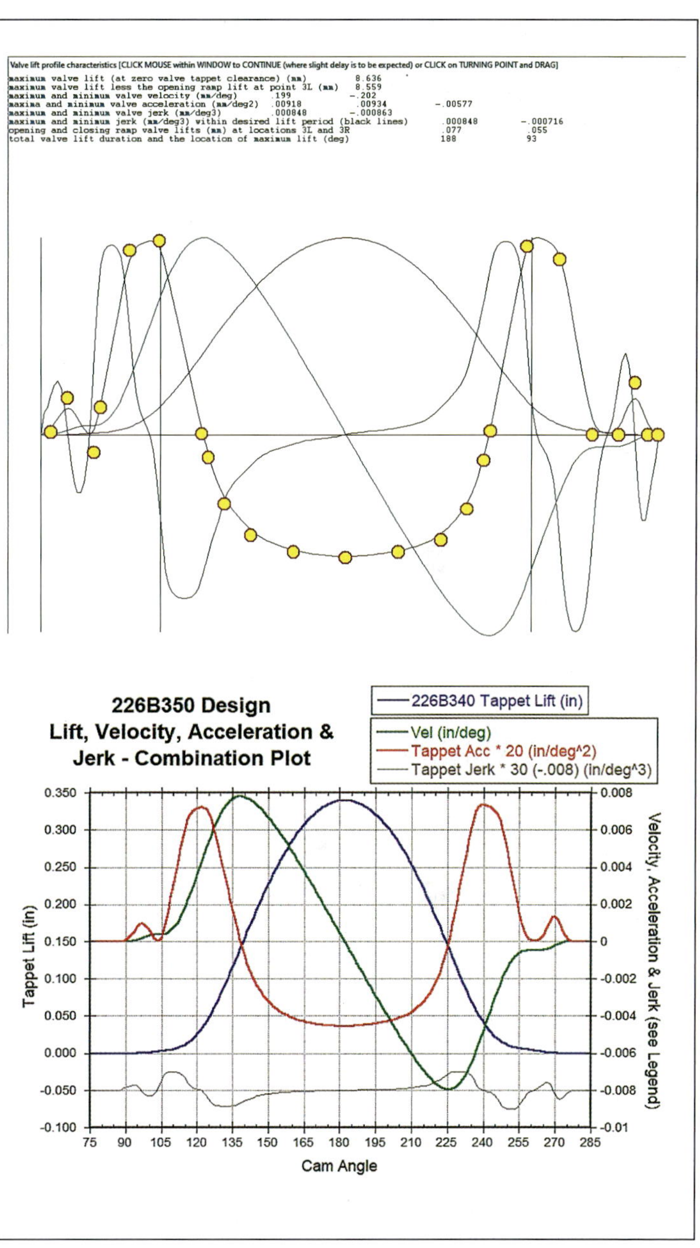

Image 3-42: This illustration shows how 4stHEAD can be used to make a design closer to the GM 5.3L example, except with more lift and duration. The ramps are tweaked a bit too. This software gives the designer the ability to mimic almost anything and then tweak it to be different wherever someone thinks a change might be better. By coupling this type of software with a CNC grinder, Spintron, and Dyno, you can have some fun throwing designs around to determine the best option.

Energy and Four-Stroke Engine Fundamentals

The camshaft is often called the heart or mind of a performance engine. It is like a great football coach who gets the most out of every player or a music conductor who ties the symphony together. As we continue to study camshafts, common understanding is needed regarding how engines function and what the camshaft needs to optimize.

Some people argue about the definition of an engine versus a motor. A quick look at the *Merriam-Webster Dictionary* puts most of that to rest, but I also favor the definition of an "engine" for our purposes, as it gets down to our main goal. We need a machine for converting any of the various forms of energy into mechanical work.

Several years ago, Dr. Derek Splitter, who works with the combustion and fuel science group at the National Transportation Research Center, gave us a great tour of Oak Ridge National Lab. His building is a few miles from the main campus, so Dr. Splitter joked that they were off campus because that they "just burn stuff" in comparison to other Oak Ridge research teams that create new isotopes and probe materials with a neutron beam. However, they have had access to run that neutron beam through a running engine to allow them to take a good look inside.

I'm a little embarrassed to admit that it took me years to appreciate the fundamental truth of Dr. Splitter's statement. Internal-combustion engines fundamentally deal with how well we can combine fuel with air, burn this combination, and then convert the released thermal energy into work. If we want camshafts that make more power, we need to do a better job burning stuff.

Follow the Energy

Gasoline, as well as diesel, is a remarkably stable fuel with an amazing energy density. There is about 116,000 British Thermal Units (BTUs) of heat that can be released from each gallon of gasoline, or roughly 12,000 watt hours per kilogram in metric units. In typical hot-rod units, this means that each pound of fuel has the potential to create about 7.4 hp continuously for 1 hour or 444 hp for 1 minute. In comparison, today's best automotive batteries can store about 250 watt hours of energy per kilogram (or 9 hp for 1 minute).

However, there are two important things we must account for with the energy density of gasoline and similar fuels. The first is air. For

Image 4-1: Combustion can be beautiful. This inefficient combustion in my fire ring creates more interesting colors than extremely efficient combustion. However, we care more about the work done at the flywheel than the colors in the chamber when we use spark to initiate a reaction between the compressed gasoline vapor and oxygen inside our internal-combustion engines.

Image 4-2: This 5-gallon jug of gasoline can contain enough chemical energy to produce 233 hp for 1 hour or 2,330 hp for 6 minutes. We never extract all the chemical energy as work at the flywheel, but 777 hp for 6 minutes is a reasonable target.

gasoline, 14.7 pounds of air needs to mix with each pound of fuel to extract that stored chemical energy. The second is efficiency. While electric motors might be 90-percent efficient when converting stored electric potential energy into work, combustion engines are typically limited to about 33-percent efficiency when converting stored chemical energy into work.

Regarding this air mass contribution, we are surrounded by a vast sea of air on the earth's surface, so we typically don't need to carry oxygen with us in most applications. However, coaxing this surrounding air into the combustion chamber and then getting maximum efficiency out of the burn is where camshafts come into play.

Image 4-3: Gasoline is not the only item that we need to convert the potential energy into thermal energy. It also requires 14-plus times the mass of air to react. Normally there is plenty of air around us, but there is less at 12,000 feet. We were on our way from Durango toward Pikes Peak, where the average pressure and density is only 60 percent of what is typically seen near sea level. Gasoline engines are not as attractive if you need to carry your own air.

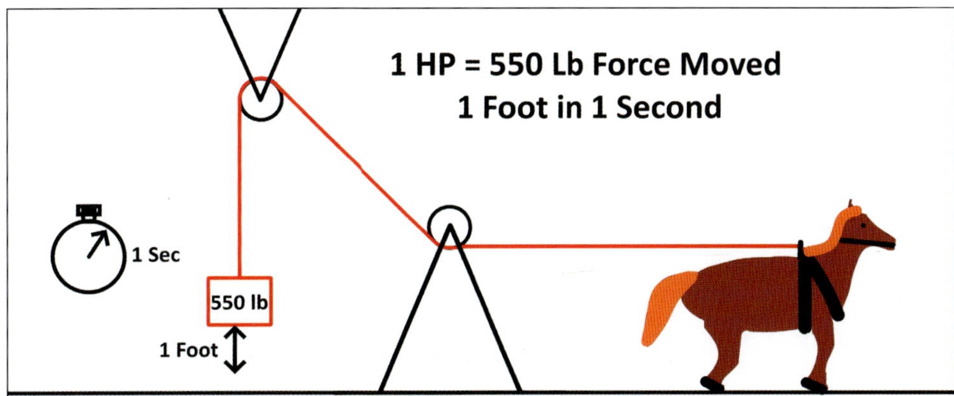

Image 4-4: A horse may produce almost 15 hp for a few seconds, and many people can produce more than 1 hp for a short time. However, the term "horsepower" matched what a single horse could sustain over several hours.

What is Horsepower?

Because we are going to talk about horsepower throughout this book, we should define this term.

In the 1700s, James Watt measured how quickly a horse could continuously turn a 12-foot mill wheel. After some collaboration and looking at the forces and speeds, 1 hp was set at 33,000 ft-lbs per minute. This is the same work as a horse lifting a 550-pound weight one foot every second. This unit became very useful for comparing average work done by a team of horses to any engine.

For reciprocating engines, torque is measured instead of force because we are dealing with rotation, not translation. To bring horsepower into terms of rotational torque, divide that linear 33,000 ft-lbs/min by the circumference of a circle (2ϖr). Then, multiply by the RPM. Using this with a slight bit of rounding to calculate horsepower, measure the torque and RPM. Then, calculate the power as:

HP = Torque (ft-lbs) x RPM ÷ 5,252

I have read a thousand weird reasons why people said their horsepower and torque curves crossed at 5,252 rpm when plotted on the same scale. I hope you see that is simply the definition of horsepower. If you look at most engine dynos, there is a load cell setup to measure force a certain distance out from water brake center that is otherwise free to rotate. This load cell is typically calibrated by hanging weights at some distance and then used by the dyno software to measure toque at each engine speed. By using the formula above, power is calculated from torque and RPM.

Why is power generally more important than torque? That is rather simple. I weigh about 200 pounds. If you give me a strong enough 12-foot pole and a fulcrum 1 foot from the end, I can lean my body mass over the long end and slowly pick up a 22,000-pound mass. This means that with this lever, I can produce more than twice the peak torque about that pivot than a Top Fuel engine creates at its flywheel. However, that same Top Fuel engine produces well over 6,000 ft-lbs torque at 8,000 rpm, whereas I could not make a full revolution of that 12-foot pole in 1 minute.

Simply put, we can gear flywheel torque to make basically any wheel torque we desire but at slower and slower wheel RPM. However, regardless of how you gear a system, the power never increases. You always lose a little to friction in any transmission and drivetrain.

My Oldsmobile friends like to ask me if I care more about torque or power. My response is that I want all the torque, but I also want it to keep producing at very high RPM. In truth, just give me power, and I will figure out the right gearing to move any vehicle.

BSFC and Efficiency

Going back to the 7.4 hp hours of stored chemical energy available to create heat in each pound of gasoline, how much work can we extract at the flywheel? While people in combustion research or F1 may talk about combustion efficiency, almost every engine dyno measures this efficiency a different way. Going back to the dyno cell, in addition to our load cell and tachometer, most good test cells will have a high-precision fuel-flow gauge somewhere past the regulator to measure the fuel consumed by the engine. This data is captured along with torque, RPM, and the other engine parameters during the dyno test. The system will the divide the horsepower at that RPM by the fuel flow in lbs/hr to calculate what is formally called brake-specific fuel consumption (BSFC).

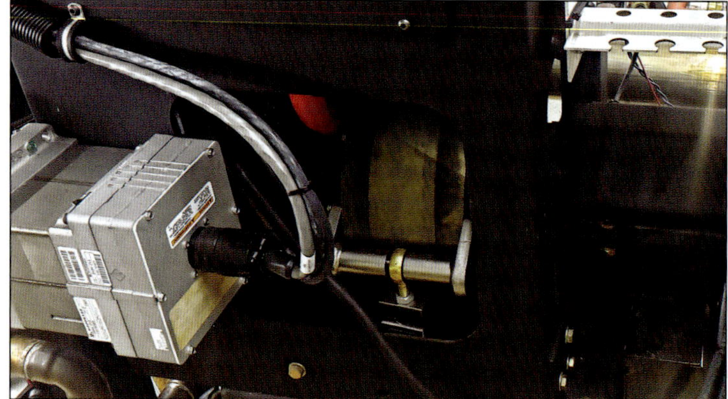

Images 4-5 and 4-6: Sometimes people do not understand that water-brake dyno typically does not measure power from water flow but allows the adsorber to rotate and then uses a loadcell to measure the force required to hold the brake in place. This 18-degree-headed small-block Chevy is a nice talking point when we discuss cylinder heads too.

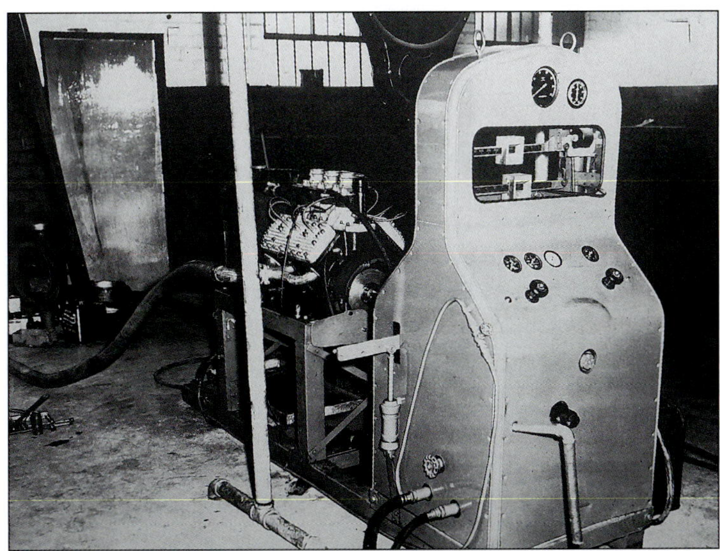

Image 4-7: The lever arm and manual balance scale on the first Edelbrock engine dynamometer makes the torque arm and load measurement easy to see. The operator needs to load the engine and adjust the beam until the RPM is steady.

Image 4-8: This is another early dyno at Edelbrock, but it is later than the first. I would have loved to see Vic test engines with this monster. There must be something to measure load and calculate torque on that large water brake.

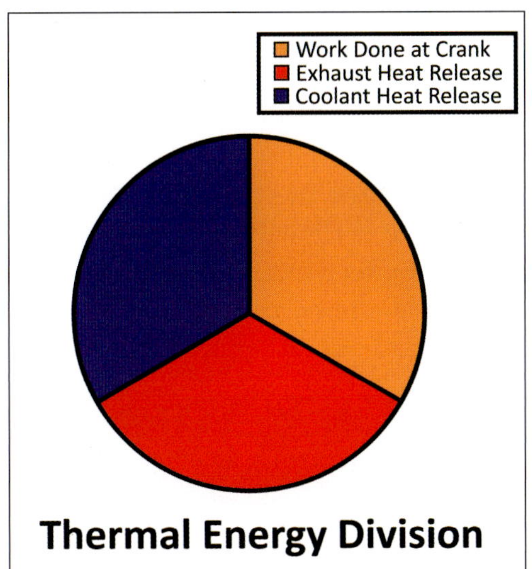

Image 4-9: My favorite analogy that describes where combustion thermal energy flows is a pizza shared among three people. The people are Carl (the crank), Xavier (the exhaust), and Bob (the block, piston, and head, typically flowing to the coolant system). We will learn how to feed Carl more than the typical 33 percent of this pizza so that he can move us faster. We will then find the best way to share the rest between Xavier and Bob.

Gasoline BSFC to Efficiency

BSCF	HP/(Lb/h)	Efficiency
0.275	3.636	49.1%
0.300	3.333	45.0%
0.325	3.077	41.6%
0.350	2.857	38.6%
0.375	2.667	36.0%
0.400	2.500	33.8%
0.450	2.222	30.0%
0.500	2.000	27.0%
0.550	1.818	24.6%
0.600	1.667	22.5%
0.650	1.538	20.8%
0.700	1.429	19.3%

Image 4-10: In racing engines, if fuel flow is not limited, we often use some of the fuel for cooling and other benefits, knowing that it will never release thermal energy. Hence, a 0.500 brake-specific fuel consumption (BSFC) that only has 27-percent total efficiency might be well over 33-percent thermally efficient. Basically, you don't need to beat yourself up over high BFSC until someone limits the size of your tank.

Most modern gasoline engines are about 33-percent thermally efficient, which means for every pound of fuel that burns, a third of the energy goes to the crank and 67 percent is lost. Generally, about half of the lost energy escapes out the exhaust and the other half goes into the water or is radiated from the engine. The BSFC of these 1/3, 1/3, 1/3 engines will be somewhere in the 0.420 to 0.460 BSFC (hp per lbs/hr) depending on the air-fuel ratio. In Formula 1, where fuel flow is regulated, these engines hit right at 50-percent thermal efficiency. Half the thermal energy is converted to work and the other half is left as heat. For gasoline, if every drop burned, it would probably be in an astonishing low 0.3 BSFC range. For most performance and race engines, anything under 0.41 BSFC is outstanding. I have heard of a few in the 0.38 range but have never seen any under 0.39 BSFC. With oxygenated fuels and/or intentionally running a little rich, it is not uncommon to be above 0.5 BSFC in great running engines. Image 4-10 features a table of how efficiency and the BSFC number relate for gasoline engines.

If the BSFC numbers are good, we know we are doing a good job extracting energy from the fuel, especially if air-fuel ratios are maintained and changes in BSFC are carefully observed when the camshaft or other components are changed.

Air-Fuel Ratios

There is a major reason why you should look at O_2 readings whenever possible along with BSFC. One of my favorite mental pictures is to think of the combustion chamber pre-spark like an eighth-grade dance. The compression is the music, the spark plug is the lighting, and the chamber geometry is the dance floor. However, we are going to focus on the kids dancing. Let's call our air "girls" and our fuel in the chamber "boys."

It is useful to introduce a very important term from chemistry: stoichiometry. Any stoichiometric mixture has a perfect balance of reactants. This means that for every molecule of fuel in the chamber, there is the perfect amount of oxygen from the air ingested or any other source so that every molecule of fuel finds its dancing partner(s). Given perfect mixing and enough time, when a stoichiometric mixture combusts (burns), the resulting product (gas) does not have a single oxygen or fuel molecule remaining.

For gasoline, we already mentioned the stoichiometric air to fuel mass ratio is 14.7:1. For methanol, that ratio is about 6.4:1, ethanol is about 9:1, and E85 is closer to 9.8:1 but varies with the imperfect blends found at most E85 pumps. To make our life a little easier and take away some of the variation with fuels, instead of talking about air-fuel ratios, most tuners and engine builders find it easier to talk about lambda exhaust gas measurements. The lambda or Greek "λ" is simply the actual air-fuel ratio divided by the stoichiometric air-fuel ratio of whatever given fuel you are using:

$$\lambda = \text{AFR (actual)} \div \text{AFR (stoichiometric)}$$

With a basic understanding of lambda and stoichiometric ratios, let's go back to the eighth-grade dance. In the analogy, if there are 20-percent more girls than boys, then lambda is 1.2 and the dance floor is very lean. If there are 20-percent fewer girls than boys, lambda is 0.8, and we are rich. In our analogy, energy is only released from the reaction when a boy dances with a girl. To be like most engines outside of fuel flow limited F1, we see that the boys (fuel) are relatively easy to let in the dance, but we struggle to coax a limited number of girls (air) to attend.

This analogy helps visualize why most engines perform best with lambda values in the 0.85 to 0.95 range instead of a true lambda 1.00 balance. Think back to what I mentioned about perfect mixing and unlimited time. Neither the dance or the engine cycle will have unlimited time or perfect mixing. In the combustion chamber, the girls are going to be spread out rather uniformly, but

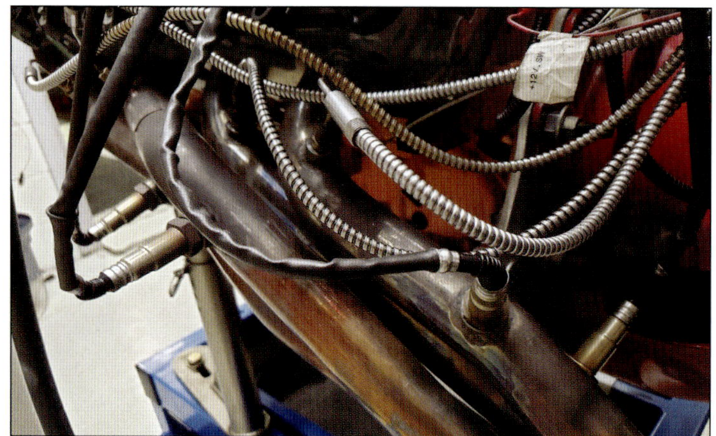

Images 4-11 and 4-12: All of our dyno headers are fitted with both exhaust gas temperature (EGT) and wideband O_2 sensors on each primary tube. Using the wideband O_2 measurements to let us know the air-to-fuel ratios in each cylinder can help find airflow or fueling discrepancies. If we know the fuel flow into that cylinder from something like injector pulse width (IPW), we can back out airflow. There are typically one or two additional O_2 sensors in the collector to provide average data to the electronic control unit (ECU). Collecting data is easier than ever, so why not know what is going on with each cylinder?

the boys are prone to clump together and can get in each other's way. If we keep adding boys, every girl will be more likely to find a dancing partner, but the extra boys will soak up much of the additional energy released. A dance is by no means a perfect analogy, but I find it useful. However, if you don't, please feel free to just think of air and fuel.

There are far more things going on with the reactions from spark to kernel to flame front than we can fully cover. It is simplified in Image 4-13, where we see all the molecules involved in a complete reaction between a pair of well-known and rather simple octane molecules as they react with 25 oxygen molecules. Octane is a simple form of gasoline with eight carbons linked together with 18 hydrogen atoms. Not shown are the intermediate reactions involving the surrounding nitrogen and other molecules, or how product gases from those initial chemical reactions interact. Other factors, including dissociation, such as reverse combustion, also points you a bit rich for peak power, even if you can achieve a perfectly homogeneous mixture.

In any case, know that the real combustion process is rather complex, and some extra fuel above the stoichiometric balance always helps. However, we only release the stored energy from the fuel when it reacts (burns) with oxygen.

To a degree, we have gone all over the world to come to a simple conclusion that I am sure you have heard before. In many ways, four-stroke engines are limited by how good of a job they do pumping air (filling up the dance floor with O_2). In truth, the two real limits are how well they pump air and how efficient they are at converting the chemical energy of the air-and-fuel mixture into potential energy used to do work.

The Otto Cycle

Now we get to talk about the interesting part where camshafts come into play. What can we do to get more air into the combustion chamber?

In 1876, German engineer Nikolaus August Otto built the first four-stroke internal-combustion engine. Every spark ignition four-stroke piston engine from the smallest handheld grass trimmer to today's Mountain Motor Pro Stock

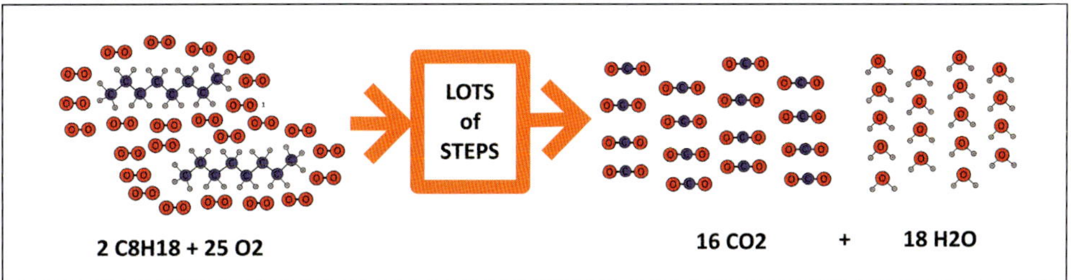

Image 4-13: An elementary-school dance can be compared to a gasoline reaction at the molecular level. The ends of this octane hydrocarbon chain can begin reacting without every other O_2 molecule in place. The analogy of adding a few extra boys to the chamber helps me understand. Just realize that more is going on at the molecular level.

Image 4-14: This piston from Ben Strader's Spinal Tap *LS engine was developed to go more than 11,000 rpm on the dyno with more than 1 inch of valve lift. The idea began with a discussion about the NHRA's 10,500-rpm limit in Pro Stock and how we could show everyone how easily an 11,000-rpm engine can be built. Spoiler alert: it's difficult.*

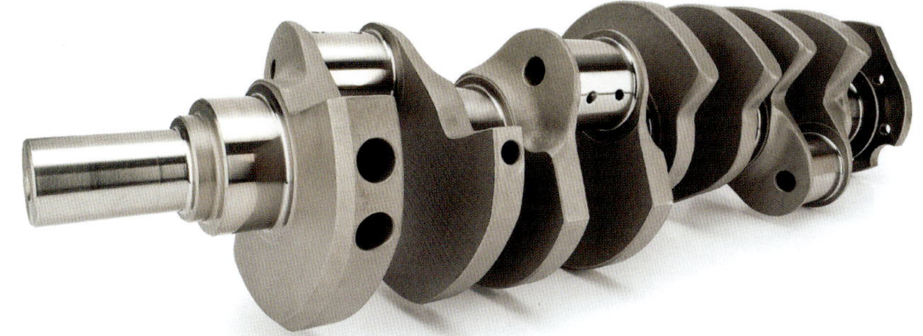

Image 4-15: The energy in gasoline is used to create thermal energy, and it performs work on the piston that is transferred to the crankshaft. We are learning about the Otto cycle because it provides an overview of how the engine needs to ingest air, add fuel, release energy, and then transfer it to something like this Lunati signature crankshaft.

Image 4-16: Before looking at simplified sketches of a crank, rod, piston, and ring assembly to describe the Otto cycle, a mental picture of the real bits (such as these in a Lunati LS rotating assembly) is helpful. These connecting rods transfer the work done on the piston to the crankshaft.

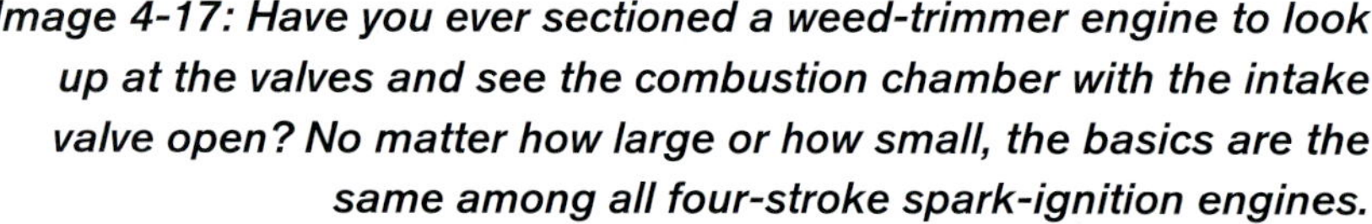

Image 4-17: Have you ever sectioned a weed-trimmer engine to look up at the valves and see the combustion chamber with the intake valve open? No matter how large or how small, the basics are the same among all four-stroke spark-ignition engines.

Image 4-18: On this Briggs & Stratton 5-hp flathead engine, see how the valves and ports are inside the block instead of the cylinder head? Most of the combustion chamber is moved over to the side instead of directly over the piston. This configuration is far less efficient than a modern overhead valve (OHV) or overhead camshaft (OHC) chamber, but these are fun in a cart or junior dragster.

Image 4-19: The scale is different, but the basics of Sonny's 940-ci 1,700-plus-hp street engine is the same as the weed-trimmer engine. Everything is larger, but the physics are the same.

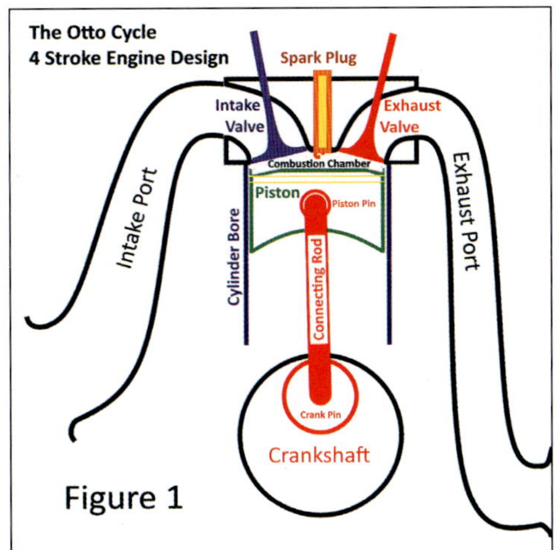

Image 4-20: This simple sketch shows a typical four-stroke, spark-ignition, internal-combustion engine and its subsystems.

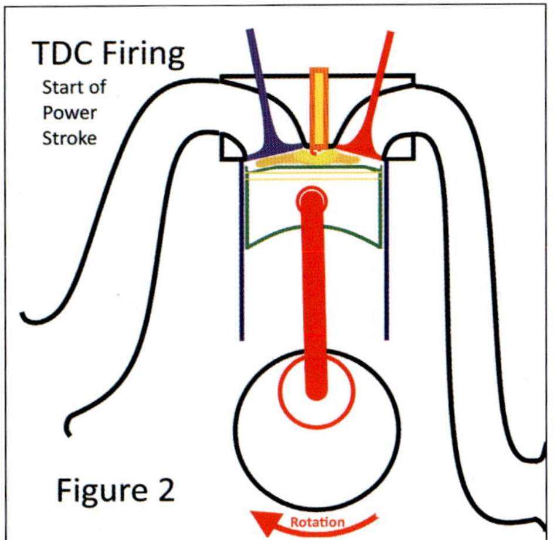

Image 4-21: TDC firing is the starting point for most graphs, plots, and sketches moving forward in this book. Here, the piston has just reached TDC (or the top of its travel in the cylinder bore) right after (maybe 20 to 40 degrees) the plug fires. The piston now changes direction to go back down for the power stroke.

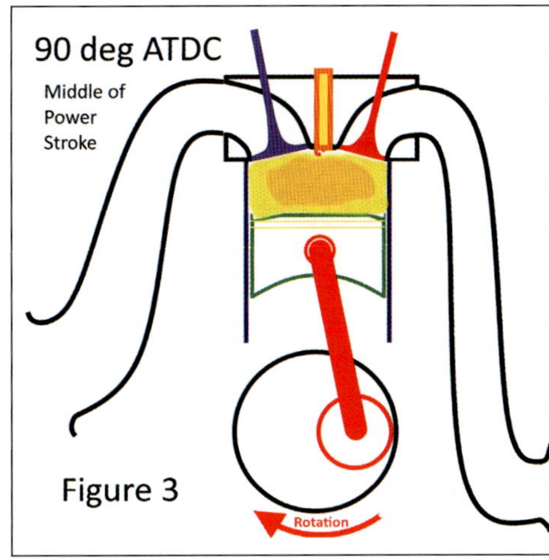

Image 4-22: The piston is approximately halfway down the bore. Most of the work on the piston has already been done at this point. Even though we have the most leverage in this region, like when pulling perpendicular to the end of a wrench, the combustion pressure has dropped significantly as the volume is now roughly six times larger than it was at TDC. In many racing engines, the exhaust valve would have already cracked at this point.

and beyond are built around this same general layout. A piston is connected to a crankshaft by a connecting rod reciprocating down and up in a bore, which employs the same thermodynamic principles.

Four Strokes of the Ideal Otto Cycle

The idealized Otto cycle is generally taught with a few assumptions that make the math much easier. First, it is assumed that the chemical energy is all converted instantaneously to thermal (heat) energy at the plug firing (TDC). Second, it assumes no heat is transferred between the combustion chamber and walls (piston, head, or bore). Third, it assumes all sealing is perfect. Fourth, it assumes everything in the chamber follows something called the ideal gas law (pressure times volume equals temperature times a constant). Fifth, it assumes there are no flow restrictions whenever either of the valves is open on the inlet and exhaust strokes, and there is no mixing in-between. Lastly, the ideal engine is assumed to be frictionless. We will introduce these four strokes in the ideal case and later we will see how this compares to the real case.

Power Stroke

In the ideal case, spark occurs at TDC and a complete burn happens instantaneously. For the next 180 degrees, both valves stay closed. Pressure drops are only due to the increasing volume as the piston moves farther away from TDC, not to any heat transfer. The fancy engineering term for this is adiabatic expansion. It is also assumes that no gases get out past the rings, valves, or otherwise.

Exhaust Stroke

At BDC, the exhaust valve opens immediately and completely, and the pressure in the chamber drops to the outside ambient pressure typically assumed to be 1 atmospheric

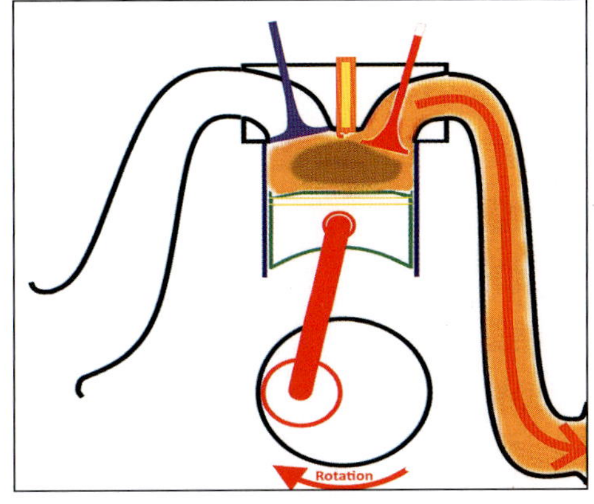

Image 4-23: With the crankshaft 90 degrees past the bottom of travel (BDC), we are now using work from the crankshaft to push out the remaining exhaust gases. In a race engine, we try to get rid of most of the exhaust mass while the piston is much closer to the bottom of the stroke. In another 20 degrees, the piston will achieve maximum velocity on the upstroke.

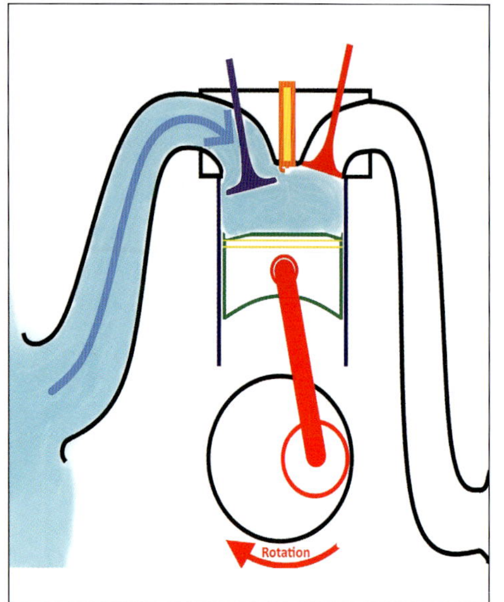

Image 4-24: At 90 degrees past TDC and near both maximum lift and the middle of the intake stroke, we can visualize the cylinder being filled by a fresh charge of air and fuel. In our ideal model, we assume there's no pressure across the valve during the intake stroke. However, in real life, we know we only induce air velocity through a change in pressure. Unfortunately, in real life, we are heating the incoming air with the hot head, piston, and bore walls.

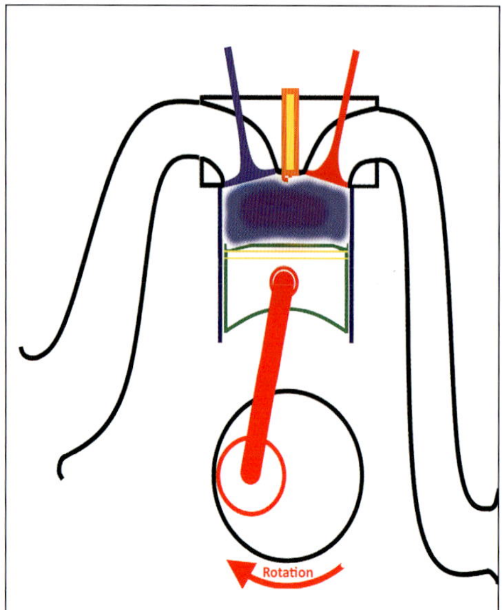

Image 4-25: We are 90 degrees up on the compression stroke, or a full revolution from what we talked about on the exhaust stroke. At this point, we have done all we can do from a camshaft point of view until after we light the mixture and go through the next power stroke, at least until the point we actually open the exhaust. The compression stroke of the ideal Otto cycle is probably the closest of the four ideal strokes to what is seen in the real world.

pressure (ATM). The piston then returns to TDC without having to push any remaining gases out of the way with no exhaust pumping work or losses as we assume no flow restrictions. Hence, the combustion chamber stays at a constant pressure (isobaric) of one ATM during the complete exhaust stroke.

Intake Stroke

At TDC, the exhaust valve shuts, and the intake valve completely opens instantaneously. The chamber again stays at the same 1 ATM of the exhaust stroke for the full TDC-to-BDC intake stroke (isobaric) but now fills from the intake port without requiring any pumping work. With these assumptions, the cylinder and combustion chamber will be 100-percent full, with a fresh air and fuel charge of one ATM at BDC.

Compression Stroke

At BDC, the intake valve instantaneously closes. As the crank continues to rotate, the captured air and fuel is squeezed as the piston rises in the bore. On this stroke, we again assume there's no heat transfer (adiabatic compression) or lost mass. The pressure in the chamber rises

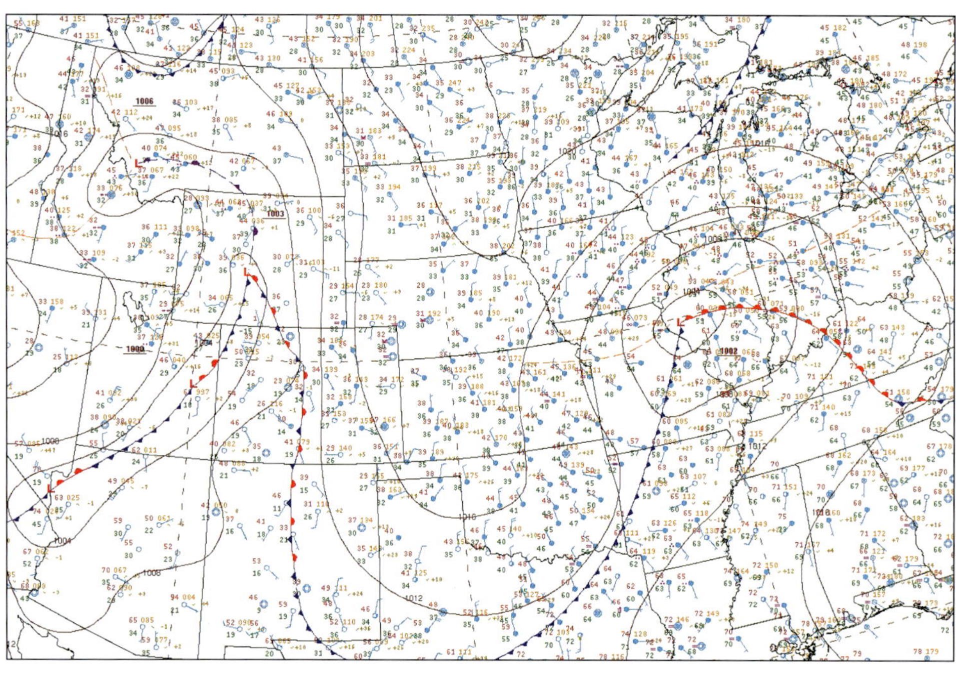

Image 4-26: Weather forecasting and modeling relies heavily on understanding atmospheric pressure. Looking at the spacing between isobars (lines) of constant atmospheric pressure, meteorologists can accurately predict the resulting windspeed and direction. Simply put, all gases will naturally flow from high pressure toward low pressure. If we want airflow in the engine, we need pressure differences, which is the topic of the next chapter.

exponentially with the reduction of volume and follows the ideal gas law. In this ideal model, the pressure jumps immediately at the end of the compression stroke as the piston reaches TDC, and all the chemical energy stored in the air-fuel mixture is converted instantaneously into thermal energy with a corresponding increase of cylinder pressure.

Ideal versus Real

While the ideal model above is great for both understanding the four strokes independently (and it makes the math easy), several assumptions are clearly not true. The first incorrect assumption is when either valve is open, the pressure in the chamber will be the same as outside the engine. This is not correct, as we know pressure differences are required to create airflow. Weather maps show high pressure (H) and low pressure (L) along with the isobar lines of constant pressure around each. The wind moves perpendicular to the isobars and travels from high to low pressure. The more closely spaced the lines are and the more pressure change, the higher the wind speed. Regardless if we consider wind or port flow, the high-to-low pressure flow of air always holds true.

Less-restrictive ports help us approach the ideal case, especially at low RPM. This is one of the many places where an OEM engineer trying to minimize pumping losses for fuel economy has common port flow goals with a race engine builder trying to maximize power.

Another major factor that the ideal model oversimplifies deals with the speed of heat release. In the ideal case, all of the energy stored in the fuel is released instantaneously at TDC. If you have ever set timing on an engine, you know there is some lag, as you likely set the spark to occur at about 15- to 35-plus degrees before the piston reaches TDC for best full-throttle power. This limited speed of combustion forces the engine tuner to find the best timing setting, which has the least pressure fighting the piston as it rises toward TDC but also results in the best total heat release and power during the following power stroke.

Note the oversimplification of no heat transfer, but heat always flows from higher temperatures to lower temperatures. This often means heat flows through the head, piston, and cylinder walls in exactly the wrong direction for the best performance. During the inlet stroke, heat is added and reduces the air density inside the chamber, which makes it more difficult to fill. During the power stroke, heat that we want doing work on the piston is lost, as it is transferred through the head and cylinder walls to the coolant.

Similarly, for instant energy release, the idle model assumes instantaneous valve openings and closings at the start and end of the exhaust and inlet strokes. Not only does this not work with the whole idea of $\boldsymbol{F} = m\boldsymbol{a}$ without infinite forces but overlap allows interaction or communication between the inlet and exhaust systems.

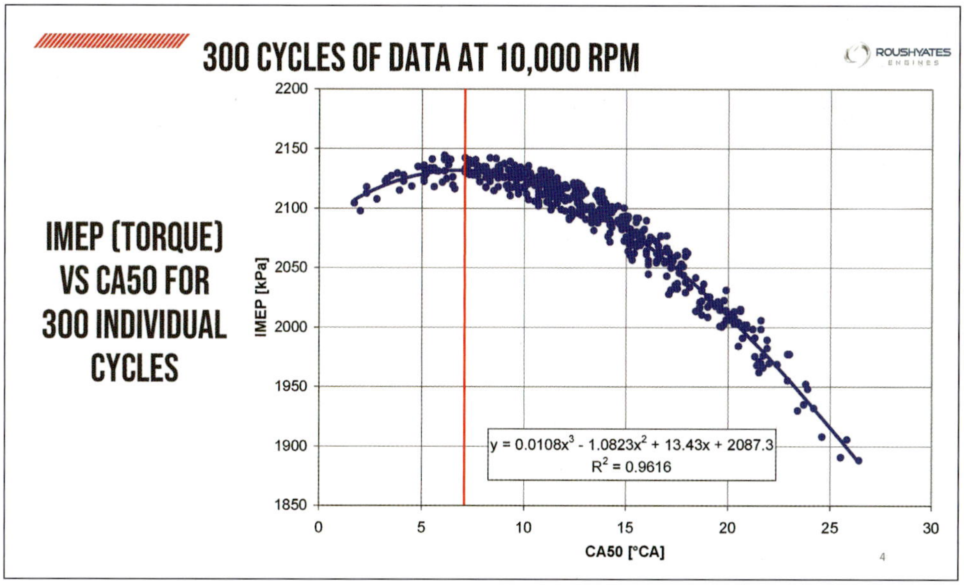

Image 4-27: The fancy term for the crank angle when 50 percent of the thermal energy is released is "CA50." We discuss using cylinder-pressure data to find this point in Chapter 5. Gary Patterson from Roush Yates supplied this data that shows 300 firing events at 10,000 rpm. Indicated mean effective pressure (IMEP) is the torque that this cylinder produces, and you can see performance drop as the CA50 point moves past 8 degrees ATDC. Slower and faster burn rates between firing events is quite common in all spark-ignition engines.

Volumetric Efficiency

If you were to go back to the early years of four-stroke design and ask people studying these engines, "How well can someone possibly fill the cylinder," the answer is likely to be something like 50 or 75 percent due to flow restrictions.

Knowing that we need air to

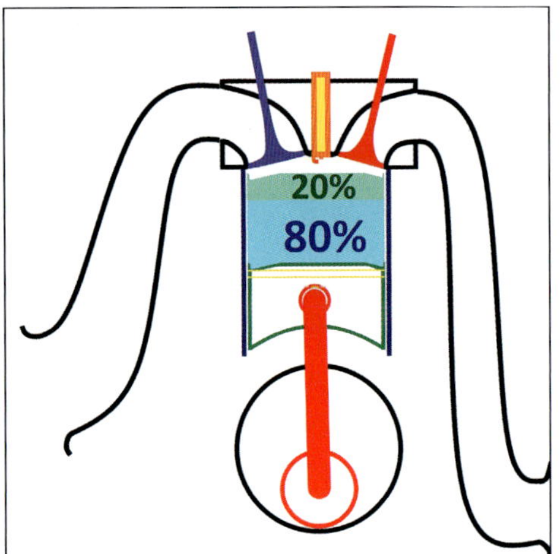

Image 4-28: Eighty-percent VE is the volume displaced by the piston from TDC to BDC with 80 percent filled and 20 percent empty. In a real engine, the cylinder is still filling well into the piston upstroke, so when discussing VE, we are actually talking about the equivalent mass ingested relative to total displacement and not the actual volume filled.

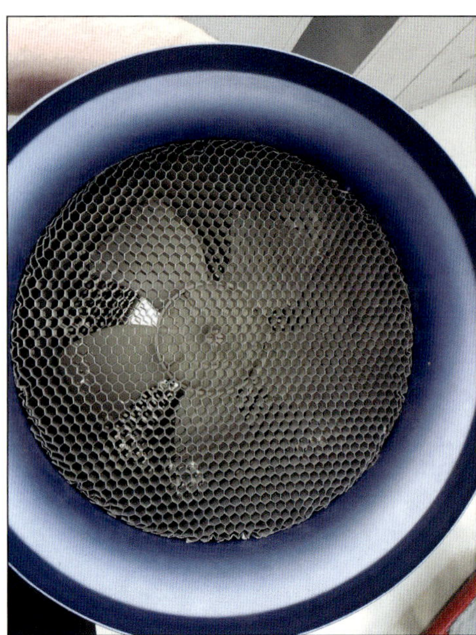

Images 4-29 and 4-30: To measure airflow directly, SuperFlow and other manufacturers make various air hats with flow straighteners and a low-friction fan blade to measure the speed and mass of the air flowing through the engine. These work best on a step test where you hold the engine steady for a few seconds at each RPM before recording a torque measurement because the fan blades have inertia and measured airflow will lag. Often, we use the quicker fuel flow and O_2 measurements to approximate airflow during a faster sweep test, which is easier on the engine and dyno. Having both available to compare is the best practice when you want to know the real VE.

make power, let's introduce the common term for this filling percentage. For four-stroke combustion engines, volumetric efficiency (VE) is defined as the volume of air at outside pressure and temperature that moves through the engine in four complete strokes (two crank revolutions) compared to the measured displacement of that engine (area of piston x stroke x number of cylinders) and given as a percentage. Volumetric efficiency is often seen in fuel-injection tables for each RPM as VE and corresponds directly to the amount of fuel needed that cycle to achieve a given air to fuel mass ratio target (AFR). As we optimize our camshaft to bring more air into the combustion chamber, we work to increase volumetric efficiency.

Since VE is the percent of total displacement filled by air each two revolutions, we can use displacement

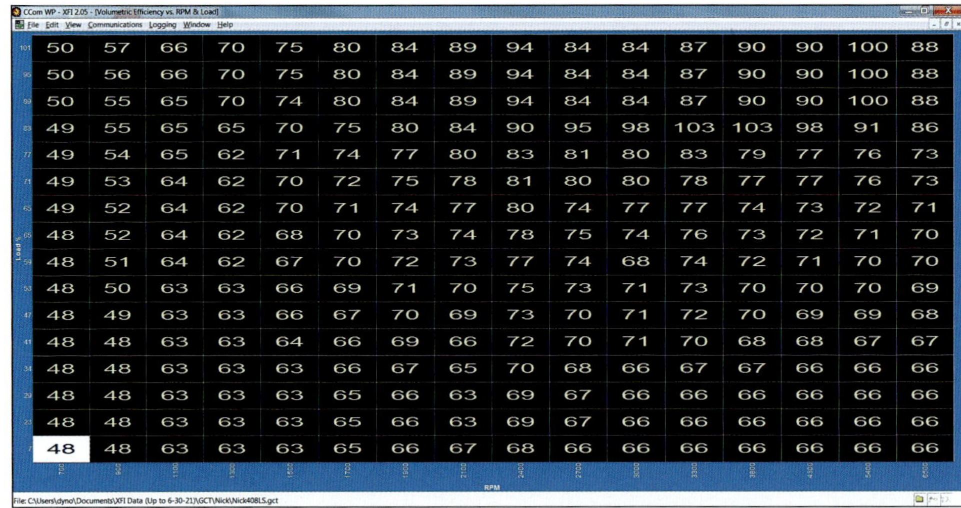

50	57	66	70	75	80	84	89	94	84	84	87	90	90	100	88
50	56	66	70	75	80	84	89	94	84	84	87	90	90	100	88
50	55	65	70	74	80	84	89	94	84	84	87	90	90	100	88
49	55	65	65	70	75	80	84	90	95	98	103	103	98	91	86
49	54	65	62	71	74	77	80	83	81	80	83	79	77	76	73
49	53	64	62	70	72	75	78	81	80	80	78	77	77	76	73
49	52	64	62	70	71	74	77	80	74	77	77	74	73	72	71
48	52	64	62	68	70	73	74	78	75	74	76	73	72	71	70
48	51	64	62	67	70	72	73	77	74	68	74	72	71	70	70
48	50	63	63	66	69	71	70	75	73	71	73	70	70	70	69
48	49	63	63	66	67	70	69	73	70	71	72	70	69	69	68
48	48	63	63	64	66	69	66	72	70	71	70	68	68	67	67
48	48	63	63	63	66	67	65	70	68	66	67	67	66	66	66
48	48	63	63	63	65	66	63	69	67	66	66	66	66	66	66
48	48	63	63	63	65	66	63	69	67	66	66	66	66	66	66
48	48	63	63	63	65	66	67	68	66	66	66	66	66	66	66

Image 4-31: VE charts tell the EFI system how well it fills the cylinder. Each cell represents the VE percent for that given RPM and manifold pressure. With this table, the FAST XFI system knows how to target the fuel. Typically, we use O_2 sensors and a target AFR value for this table. Having a very good table certainly helps the EFI system and the engine. Some cells are above 100 percent, and peak VE occurs near peak torque (not peak power). The added attention at 83 percent indicates that this engine was restricted by the throttle opening.

multiplied by the RPM multiplied by VE to determine the total airflow into any engine. Honestly, this is how most aftermarket electronic fuel-injection (EFI) systems work today. It's used along with an air-fuel target to calculate the fuel flow and injector pulse width (IPW).

Knowing this, it's understandable why sanctioning bodies often limit displacement, RPM, or airflow with something like a restrictor plate. Those factors directly limit the airflow into any engine and limit the energy available.

Image 4-32: I don't like sonic chokes because they set a hard limit on drawn air mass flow. Understanding that air mass is required to make power explains why NASCAR restrictor plates were so effective for lowering speeds on superspeedways. Spenny Clendenen sent this 7/8-inch test plate from Richard Childress Racing (RCR) to Chris Brown.

Scan the QR code below to learn more about Spenny Clendenen of Richard Childress Racing.

Displacement, RPM, and VE are the first three knobs to increase airflow. Then, divide that airflow by the best power AFR target to know the fuel flow for that RPM. Multiplying the matching fuel flow by the BSFC provides the predicted power of any engine. Therefore, BSFC is our fourth knob to make more power. Images 4-32 and 4-33 show how we can put these together and calculate the power for almost any application.

Going forward, we want to optimize a camshaft for the displacement and RPM of any engine based on the components used, thereby improving both the volumetric efficiency and brake specific fuel consumption.

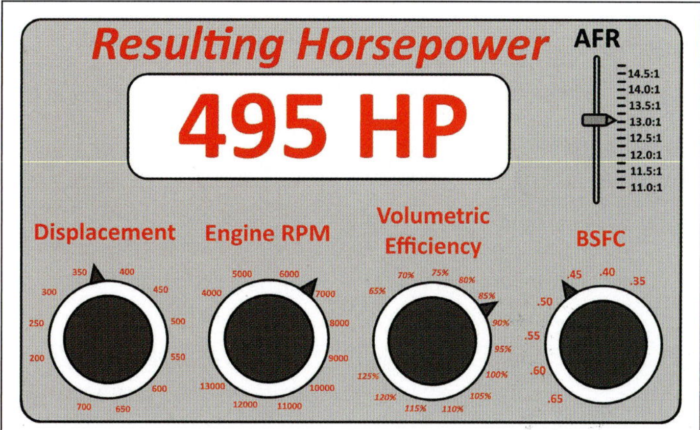

Image 4-33: This fake control panel shows the only tools that are available for increased performance. If the high-lift (0.200-inch) duration and peak lift are increased while maintaining stability with a new profile that has the same seat timing, it should increase VE. The greater filling may also improve the BSFC. The same is true for a better cylinder head port. Likewise, we can reduce friction or increase combustion efficiency and improve BSFC at a given AFR. Those two knobs on the left are easy to change, but they are also the items that sanctioning bodies target first.

Billy's How Much Power Sanity Check!

Engine Disp (L)	Engine Disp (ci)	RPM	ci per Min /2	VE	Total Engine CFM at VE Demand	Lbs. Air per Min	Lbs. Air Per Hour	AFR (x:1)	Lbs. Fuel Per Hour	BSFC	HP
6.2	378.3	5000	945868.0	90	493	39.8	2385.4	13.0	183.5	0.45	407.8
6.2	378.3	6000	1135041.6	90	591	47.7	2862.4	13.0	220.2	0.45	489.3
6.2	378.3	7000	1324215.2	90	690	55.7	3339.5	13.0	256.9	0.45	570.9
6.2	378.3	8000	1513388.8	90	788	63.6	3816.6	13.0	293.6	0.45	652.4
6.2	378.3	9000	1702562.3	90	887	71.6	4293.6	13.0	330.3	0.45	734.0
6.2	378.3	10000	1891735.9	90	985	79.5	4770.7	13.0	367.0	0.45	815.5

Image 4-34: When the Corvette C8 was introduced, a popular magazine released an article with a too-good-to-be-true chassis dyno result on the LT1 engine. Instead of letting it go, I created and posted this Excel calculation on Facebook. Note how RPM x Displacement ÷ 2 = ci/min, which can be multiplied by the VE and converted to air CFM. Knowing the pounds of air in a cubic foot, convert it, and then divide air mass flow by the AFR for pounds of fuel. Now, divide that by a reasonably great BSFC and we have horsepower. I was not alone in my skepticism of the dyno result, and the publication soon explained its dyno calibration issue.

Under Pressure

Image 5-1: A chapter on pressure in a book about camshafts may seem odd, but to get the camshaft timing points optimized, consider how each valve event changes the pressure in the chamber and runners.

The song "Under Pressure" by Queen and David Bowie can be loosely tied to performance engines. Every four-stroke engine is powered by a piston that is under pressure.

For mechanical systems in physics, there are many details that are difficult to fully investigate with the energy-style approach that was covered in Chapter 4. Hence, the next classical approach is to look at the driving forces that move any dynamic system. For internal-combustion engines, there is one critical attribute that forces the piston down during the power stroke and provides the signal for all airflow. That attribute is pressure.

Pressure is the most direct way of looking at what is going on inside the cylinder. Work is defined as force multiplied by distance. Hence, the work done on the piston is the total force on the top (pressure times piston top surface area) multiplied by the distance traveled.

Image 5-2: The pressure on top of the piston drives the piston and crank. The larger the bore and surface area, the greater the force is for a given pressure. The longer the stroke, the greater distance that force is applied and the greater amount of work done.

Image 5-3: This Top Fuel piston sees extreme pressures. The average pressure during the power stroke, known as brake mean effective pressure (BMEP), to make 14,000 hp at 8,000 rpm is more than 2,700 psi (190 bar). In comparison, the peak pressure of a naturally aspirated top-level drag-race engine is just over 100 bar for several degrees. When looking at the peak pressure curves of most engines, think about the average pressure being almost twice as high in a Top Fuel engine, and you will quickly understand why the parts are so beefy.

In times past, I went through all the trigonometry and looked at the rod angle and crank angle to calculate instantaneous force vectors and torque from cylinder pressure. This is fun for math geeks, but it is easier and more useful to use force multiplied by distance.

Because piston force is not constant, we need to plot the pressure curve versus piston motion and measure the area under this curve. Math geeks call it "taking the integral of force over a distance," but we don't have to use calculus terms.

Pressure is what creates work and power. Engineers have been looking at cylinder pressure versus crank angle for a very long time. In the World War II era, this was often done with a recording drum on the crank and a needle attached to copper line with a port in the chamber. Very much like drum record making, they

Images 5-4 and 5-5: Sometimes, all that awesomeness escapes.

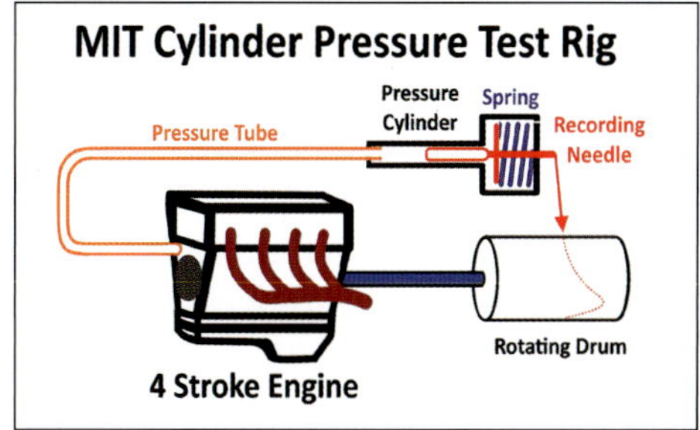

Images 5-7 and 5-8: Knowing that the Otto cycle goes back to 1876 and deals with pressure driving the piston, we should not be surprised that researchers took pressure measurements before World War II. There is an even better description of this device in Volume 1, Chapter 5 of Charles Fayette Taylor's The Internal Combustion Engine in Theory and Practice. *If you can't get enough of engine theory and thermodynamics, read both volumes.*

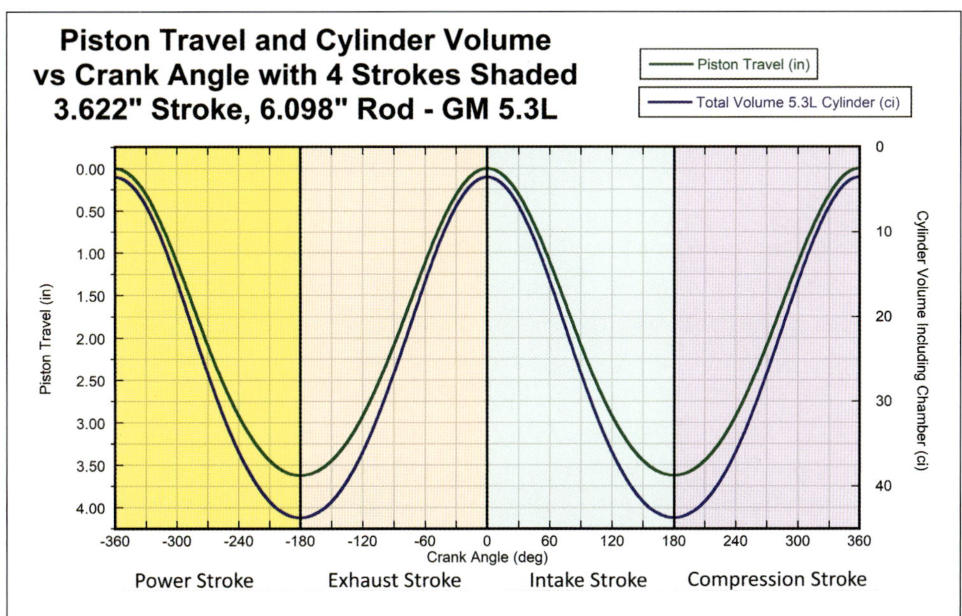

Image 5-6: Instead of looking at the force multiplied by the distance to calculate the work being done, the pressure multiplied by the volume provides the same result. Because we are going to be measuring pressure in terms of crank angle, we need the calculation for volume at each crank angle used in this graph to plot pressure versus volume. The shape of this curve is not a sine wave. It would be with an infinitely long rod, but piston motion changes with rod-to-stroke ratio.

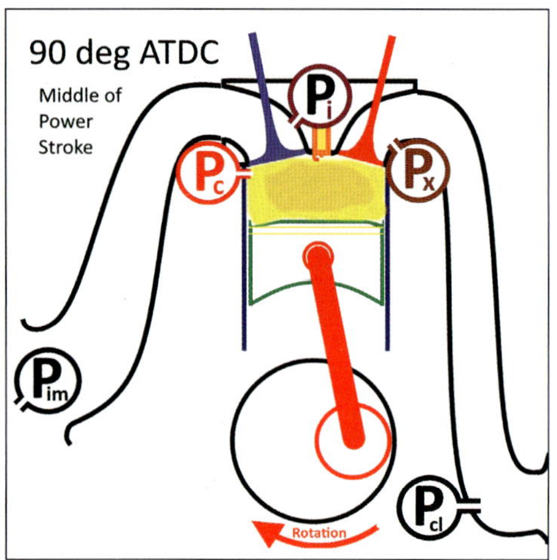

Image 5-9: Each "P" in this illustration represents a place where we want to know and try to control the pressure inside the engine. We need to think about pressure inside the engine like race teams do in Formula 1 cars. The team can build the best car in the world, but the driver controls the vehicle. Pressure in the chamber (P_c) drives the piston. The difference in pressure between P_i and P_c and then between P_c and P_x drives the airflow into then out of any engine. Pressure also drives the air in each runner. I am showing only five gauges in this sketch, but sometimes we run several pressure probes in one runner to measure the speed and direction of the pressure waves.

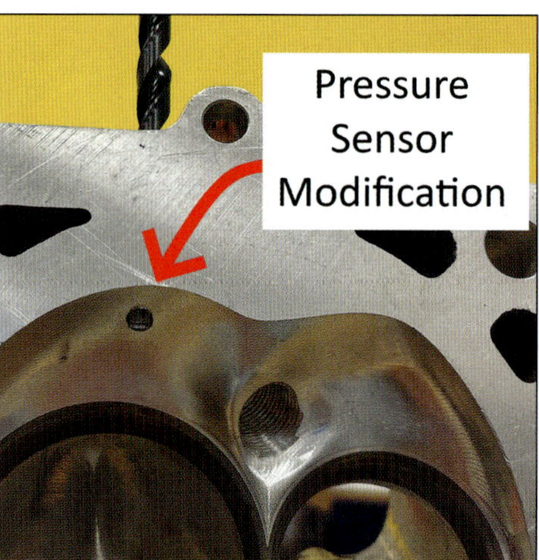

Image 5-10: To get clean pressure data, a probe in the chamber is required. Fortunately, tools are available to drill the access through the deck region in one shot. EFI University has selected a region reasonably far off the wall while still maintaining some distance from both the intake valve seat and spark plug. After drilling this stepped hole, all that is needed is to tap the bottom and install the pressure probe.

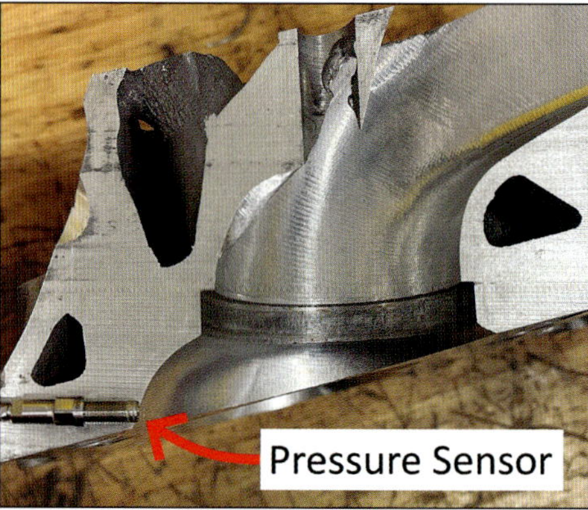

Image 5-11: EFI University sliced up a head and took a picture showing this cross section so that we can see the pressure sensor as it was installed, along with the aluminum support and coolant passage. Unfortunately, sacrificing a few heads is the best practice to find the regions where you achieve a good position in the chamber without running through a water jacket. These small pressure sensors are available through AVL, A&D, and Kistler.

loaded an engine at a given RPM and then opened the passageway that engaged the recording needle on the drum that spun with the crank. While rather complex, this mechanical system worked quite well and left a curve that represented pressure to be measured at each drum and crank angle.

Today, we typically use electronic gauges set up for the temperature and pressure ranges of the region being investigated. The five primary regions are the intake manifold (P_{im}), intake-valve bowl (P_i), combustion chamber (P_c), exhaust-valve bowl (P_x), and header collector (P_{cl}) (as shown in Image 5-9). We will start by diving into cylinder pressure measurements in the combustion chamber (P_c), which are typically made using small sensors made by AVL, Kistler, and others that enter through the deck (as shown in Image 5-10 and 5-11 from EFI University). There are some spark plugs with integral pressure sensors, but the spark creates a thermal shock and resonance in that cavity that can hide what is really going on globally.

Measured and Theoretical Otto Pressure versus Crank Angle

In Chapter 4, I wrote about how oversimplified the Otto model is. However, is it still useful? To answer that question, let's look at both the theoretical cylinder pressure and measured cylinder pressure data supplied by Dr. Robert Prucka at Clemson University's International Center for Automotive Research (CU-ICAR).

The pressure data from CU-ICAR that we are using is from a GM 5.3L near peak torque, which is always near the best filling and peak efficiency. As you can see in Image 5-12, graphing ideal versus real pressure over the factory 5.3L camshaft's valve lift at each degree, and then again with these pressures overlayed with volume in Image 5-13, the simple model is very close to the measured values except in a few key regions.

The first item that jumps out is that the much higher theoretical pressure is over the first 15 degrees. Here, the slower actual heat release dramatically reduces the peak pressure com-

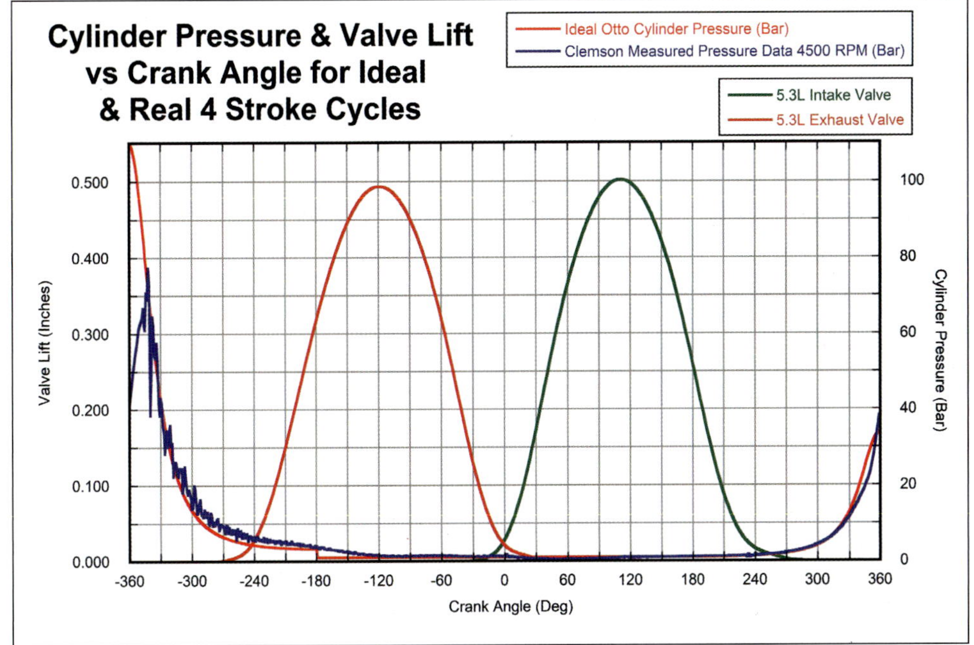

Image 5-12: It's time to throw something rather interesting on top of our 720-degree cylinder volume chart. The red curve is the theoretical ideal Otto cylinder pressure compared to the measured cylinder pressure provided by Clemson University in blue. The first and last 30 degrees are certainly off a good bit, but the rest is certainly close enough to make the ideal model useful. We see another rather large jump right at -180 degrees, but I'm not sure how big the exhaust valve needs to be in real life to drop pressure that rapidly.

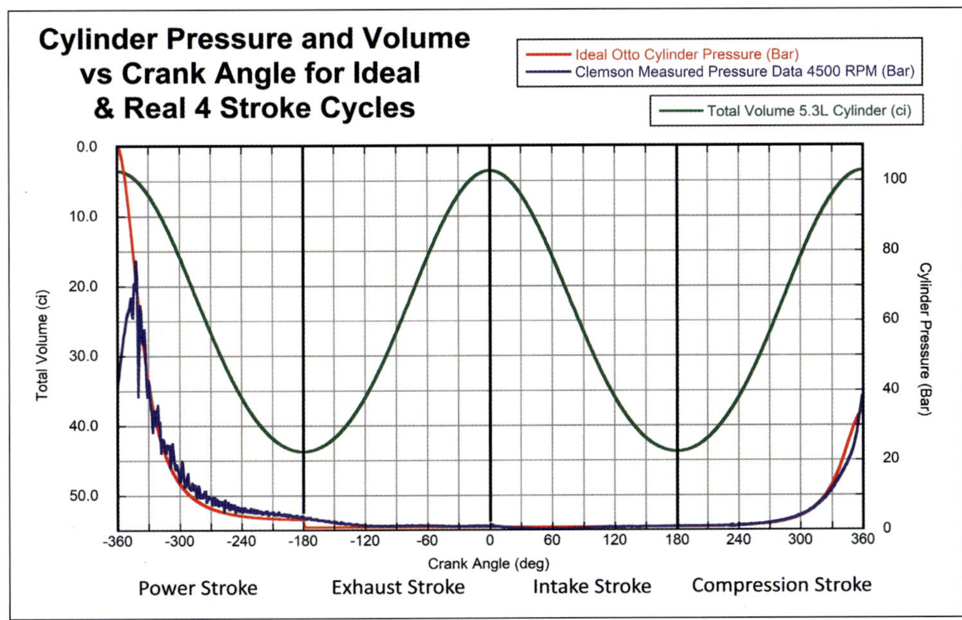

Image 5-13: Moving to the overlay of these pressure curves on top of the volume curve opens our next step. Pressure versus crank angle is very interesting. However, calculating the work being done, seeing where to move events, or even calculating the mass fraction burned is not easy with this format. But, when we plot pressure versus volume, we have an even more useful tool.

pared to the instantaneous model, which means the real engine is less prone to lifting the heads, destroying the bearings, knocking out ring lands, or any of the numerous common failures when the applied forces from excessive cylinder pressure exceeds the material strength of what holds the engine together.

Continuing left to right, the next item that stands out is that the ideal model drops to lower pressure for the last half of the classical power stroke. This is because of both the continued heat release from the fuel and the heat transfer back from the hot walls of the cylinder and chamber. Then, we see one of the impossibilities of the ideal system at BDC when the pressure drops instantaneously to 1 bar at -180 degrees.

In comparison, a change in slope of the measured data is seen much earlier in the real data. As the exhaust valve begins to open, the exhaust port (in this application, about 60 degrees before BDC depending on when what lift you call "open"), the pressure drops slowly in comparison to the model. It always stays slightly above 1 bar throughout the exhaust stroke.

Next, past TDC 0, look closely to see that while the ideal model stays at one bar, the measured pressure data drops well below 1 ATM. This drop in pressure corresponds to "intake pumping losses" as the piston goes down and lowers the cylinder pressure to create the pressure difference that draws in a fresh charge. OEM engineers' efforts to minimize these pumping losses have been wonderful for hot rodding, as this has led to vastly increased cylinder-head intake flow on all the newest American V-8 engines, including the GM LS Gen III and LT Gen V, Chrysler

Hemi, and Ford Coyote and Godzilla engines. All have intake port flow some 50-plus-percent greater than similar displacement engines from 20 years earlier, in large part to try and reduce this pressure drop and pumping losses.

Finally, the compression stroke is very close to the ideal until the last 30 degrees. From 330 to around 345 degrees, the ideal model pressure rises higher, as it does not account for heat loss to the chamber or gases escaping around the rings. In the last 15 degrees, the actual pressure slope rapidly increases and catches back up as the plug sparks and combustion begins.

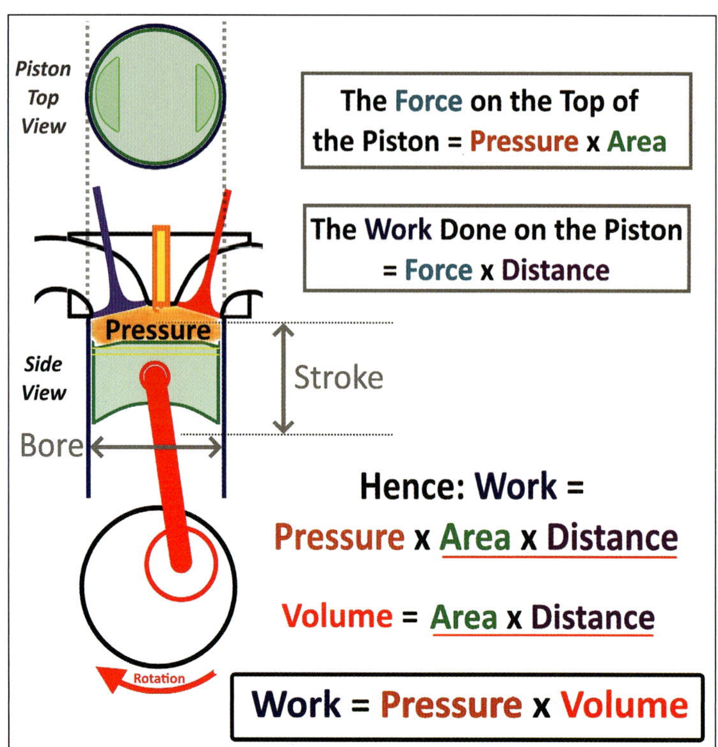

Image 5-14: Breaking down the math a little deeper, you can see how the average pressure over the distance traveled equals the work done on the piston. Because we know that Power = Work ÷ Time, we can see how mean pressure is going to be proportional to torque, agreeing with Gary Patterson's CA50 Chapter 4 slide. (See Image 4-27.)

PV Diagrams

If we want to calculate work done on the piston where "W" is work, "F" is force, "A" is piston-top area, "V" is chamber volume, "P" is pressure, and "d" is the piston movement, we know the following about work, force, and volume:

Work: $W = F \times d$

Force: $F = A \times P$

Volume: $V = A \times d$; Therefore: $A = V \div d$

When we put $A = V \div d$ into the second equation, we get $F = V \div d \times P$. When we put that equation for F into the top equation, we get $W = V \div d \times P \times d$, which simplifies to: $W = V \times P$.

We just learned that the work on the piston is simply cylinder volume multiplied by cylinder pressure. We can do the same thing for our graph as with the equations above and take that volume versus crank angle data and pressure versus crank angle data and now plot pressure with respect to volume instead of crank angle to get the cool plot of "P" versus "V" in

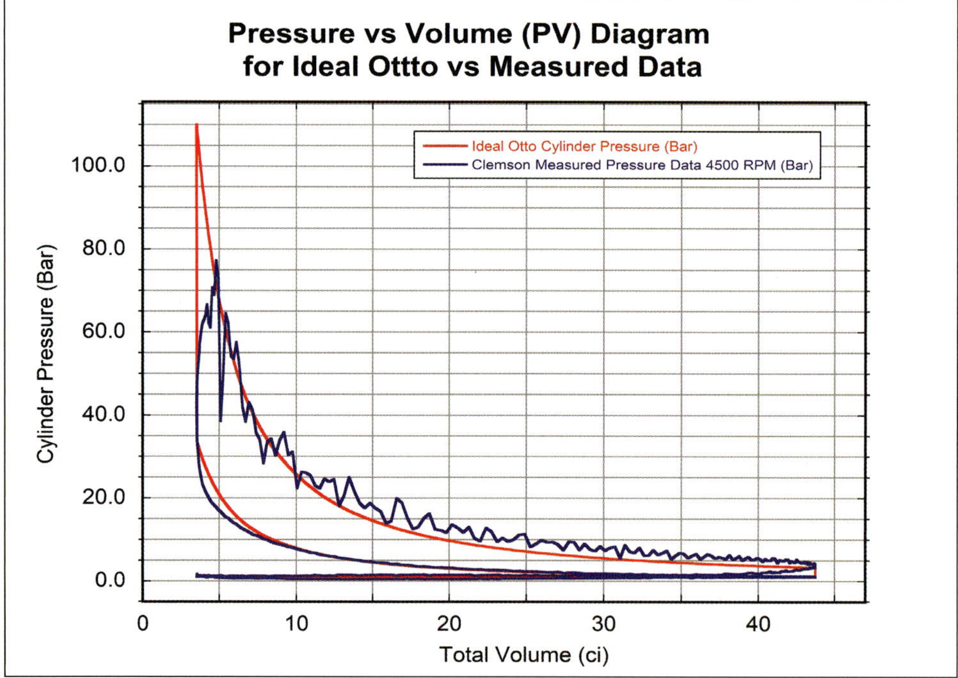

Image 5-15: This style of pressure-versus-volume plot may be one of the most useful tools that original equipment manufacturers have to analyze engines. If you were to go back to the turn of the 20th century, engineers made something like a drum-style recorder on the crank with a mechanical gauge that moved the recording stylus so they could record this data. Over the last several decades, this style of plot has become more commonplace in all of racing. It has trickled down from Formula 1 to NASCAR and Pro Stock drag racing.

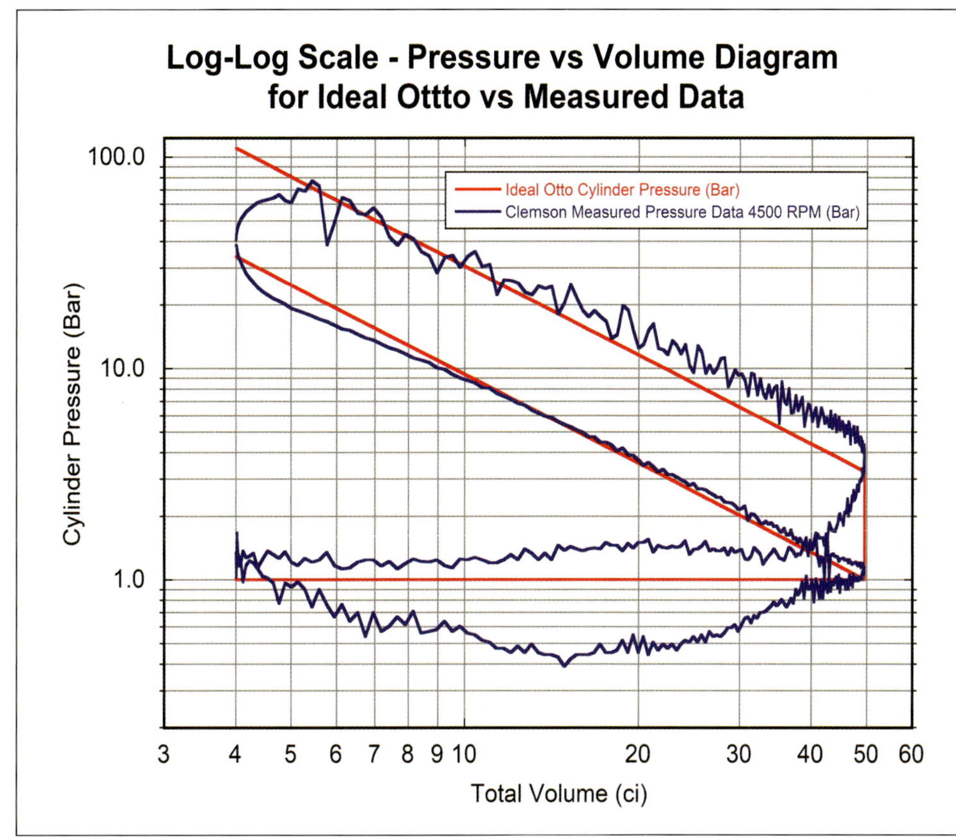

Image 5-16: Changing the pressure scale from linear to logarithmic makes it more difficult to do area estimations in your head. However, the benefit is that we can examine both the high-peak cylinder pressure and peak work region at the top along with the lower-pressure regions where the valve events occur at the bottom on a single graph. This makes the pumping loop much easier to examine. The reason my ideal slopes are not right is that I used the specific heat for plain air in my calculation. If you ran it with the correct values for the air-fuel mixture and the exhaust gases, the Otto model slopes would match almost perfectly.

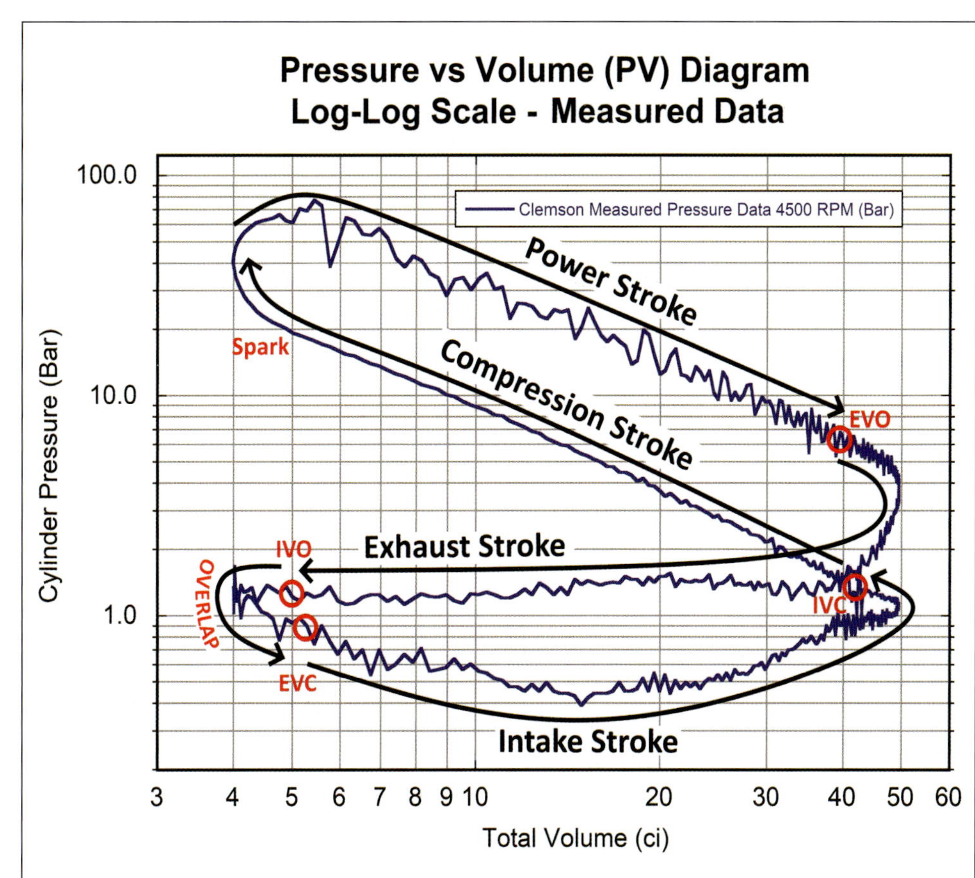

Image 5-17: When I began working with PV diagrams, I knew they were extremely valuable for understanding work, but figuring out where everything was on this graph made my head spin. Adding these arrows helped me find the valve events. To make life easier, the intake closing tends to show itself (as shown from the spike in pressure at IVC). Sound waves are simply pressure waves. If you have ever been near a Spintron operating at speed, you know that valve closing makes a very audible and measurable sound wave that we can pick up inside the chamber with a cylinder-pressure sensor.

Image 5-15. Because power is defined as work per unit time, these areas will be directly proportional to the torque at that engine speed. Otherwise, we can multiply the area times RPM (just like torque) to calculate the power from the area.

The linear scale plot is correct and proportional, but for camshaft development, the bottom region is most interesting. We still want to look at the high pressure too. To make it easier to see both in one plot, the most common technique is to use a log scale on the Y-axis (pressure) and X-Axis (volume). This log-scale version is shown in Image 5-16. Note how this scaling helps us examine the bottom loop. The exhaust and intake strokes are quite different than the flat red line going back and forth at 1 bar for the ideal model. To begin, know that the far left (minimum volume) is TDC and the far right is BDC.

Reading The PV Diagram

To make the pressure volume (PV) diagram easier to understand, I will take out the ideal lines and draw arrows to show both valve events and the direction we are traveling around this oddly shaped, twisted figure-eight course in Image 5-17. Start at the top left-hand corner, TDC, just after the spark plug fires. On any PV diagram, the far left (minimum volume) is TDC and the far right (maximum volume) is BDC.

From TDC firing, follow the black line down the pressure curve that represents the power stroke. This line ends around 30 ci of volume as the exhaust opens to allow the pressure to drop more rapidly.

After EVO, a new block line is added from EVO that twists around to IVO to represent the exhaust stroke. Right before we make it to the far-left side, the intake valve opens. Note that before this happens, pressure drops in the chamber. Some of the drop is from the slowing piston and some is due to exhaust wave tuning with a negative wave making its way back right before intake opening. As the intake opens, the overlap region begins and the piston changes direction. The overlap region ends with a small red-circled pressure blip when the exhaust closes.

Continuing the path, follow the line left to right on the intake stroke. Here, there is much lower pressures as the piston rushes down and drops pressure to create the differential needed for the high port velocity required to fill the cylinder. Note the lowest chamber pressure is in that same 70 degree or 15-ci region where the piston moves the fastest. As the path reaches the far right at BDC of the intake stroke, the blue line changes direction again. Then, there is a much larger blip (circled in red) when the intake valve closes.

The intake valve doesn't have a higher closing velocity, but just as shown in the EFI university picture, the probe is much closer to the valve and the head is larger. Note that the chamber pressure at IVC is greater than the 1 bar assumed in the ideal model. It is even slightly over 1 bar at BDC. If you have seen a modern 5.3L truck intake manifold, you might guess why. This intake has very long runners that are tuned to be extremely good right around this 4,500-rpm peak torque region.

Moving along from when the intake valve closes at IVC back to the left toward TDC, the pressure rises in a way that closely matches the ideal model. There is still some heat and energy transfer between the trapped charge and the walls, and some gases will sneak past the rings. I did not include the fuel heat capacity in my ideal calculations.

However, from the camshaft and valvetrain point of view, once the inlet valve closes, we are along for the ride. Then, right before TDC, the slope changes. First, it is gradual as the spark creates a small kernel. This quickly grows into a rapidly expanding combustion flame front. Congratulations! You have made one full loop around a PV diagram.

Using the PV Diagram

Now that you can follow the twisted figure-eight of a PV diagram, how can this understanding be used to make more power? The best thing about PV diagrams is they basically show the torque at that RPM before paying any taxes, including friction internally or externally. The area of the top loop is the work done on the piston by the pressure from heat release (as shown in Image 5-18).

Likewise, the bottom loop represents the losses due to pumping. From the loop crossover back left, the piston does work to push out exhaust gases. Then, as the piston changes direction at TDC, the crank has to work to bring the pressure down below 1 ATM to create the low-pressure signal that results in flow into the chamber. One important note is that the area of the top loop with the log pressure scale looks similar but is roughly 100 times larger than the bottom loop. The skew of the log scale makes this graph easy to examine but can trick you into putting more interest into the bottom than the top loop, where you are doing the most work.

For a camshaft designer, the emphasis on the bottom of the loop

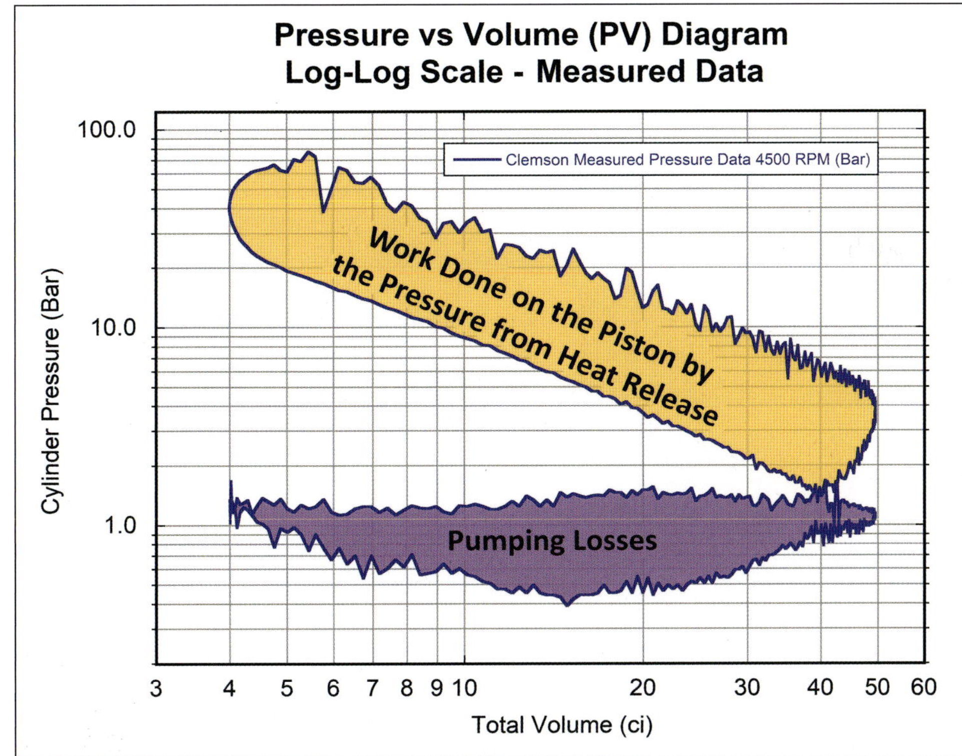

Image 5-18: This PV plot with the shaded areas is the most useful mental tool that I know for improving our understanding of how valve events change torque and power. I can't overstate how helpful thinking about the goal of increasing the top area and reducing the bottom area are to each change that we make to the engine and especially the changes that we make to the camshaft.

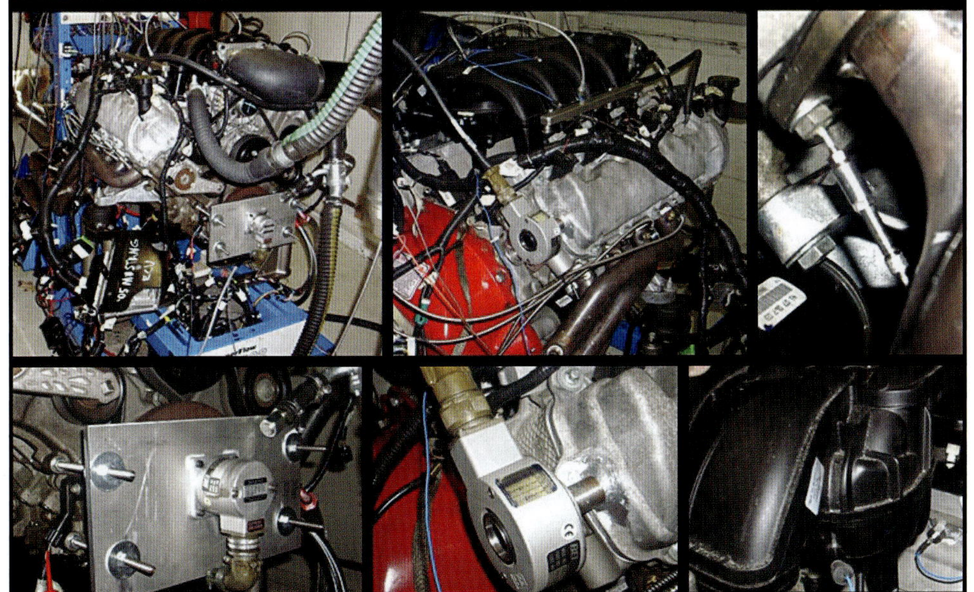

Image 5-19: We can certainly try to measure so much that we don't need a model. With plenum, port, and chamber pressure, you can see the waves moving through and try to estimate the port velocities, but there is a far better approach. I describe the best engineering practice as a three-legged stool: 1) your tribal knowledge, 2) experimental results, and 3) computer models. If you tie these three legs together by improving the models with testing and improving your tribal knowledge from both, you complete the circle and will move ahead much faster than someone with all their weight on one or two legs.

is not much of a problem. Almost everything that we can directly change is in the bottom region. The first job at any RPM is to trap as much air mass as possible at IVC. Once that mass is trapped, the piston and rotating assembly will do their job by squeezing those gases during the compression stroke.

The pressure before spark is correspondingly higher if more mass is trapped at IVC, but for a large part, the valvetrain system is along for the ride from IVC until EVO. Numerous factors come into play once the plug sparks. How well the combustion chamber is designed, if the AFR is optimized, how rapidly the fuel reacts, and how well the tuner set the timing all factor into combustion. However, from the cam-design side, the primary goal is to trap the most mass at IVC.

Moving around the PV diagram, we next come to the valve event that is farthest up the pressure curve by a very significant margin in many cases. Welcome to EVO. While the importance of IVC might be important and simple to understand, this graphical representation helps most of all when trying to understand how to balance EVO.

Better Understanding of EVO: 427 LS Simulation

Using an engine simulation and the PV plots, we are going to explore how large changes in EVO change the PV loops and performance. I put together a fairly high-end 427-ci LS7-based drag-race engine with good CNC heads (65 percent exhaust to intake ratio [E/I]), new MMO and MMX low-shock solid-roller profiles, 1.9:1 ratios, about 0.900-inch lift,

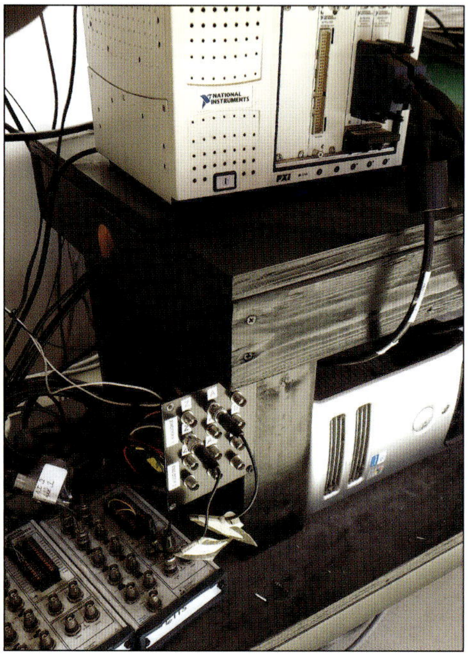

Image 5-20: In addition to good sensors, you must take data at crank degree resolution to make good decisions from cylinder or port pressure data. AVL, A&D, National Instruments, and EFI University have systems that are up to this job, but know that none of these systems are inexpensive.

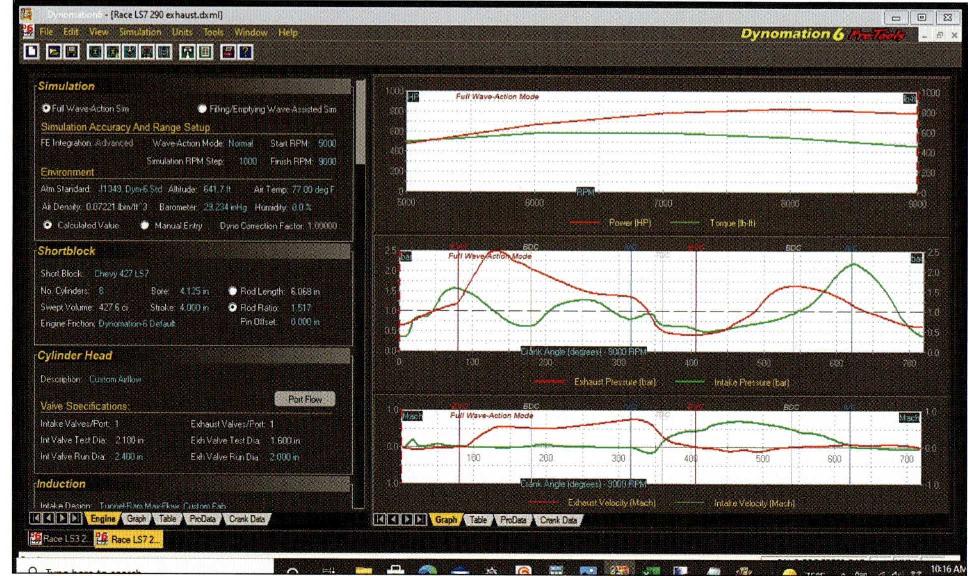

Image 5-21: This screen capture of the main screen on Dynomation 6 shows where we set up our LS7 drag-race engine with the port flow, runner lengths, displacement, and dozens of questions about the configuration. While this can take some time, it is at least a hundred times faster than setting up a model and a thousand times cheaper than building and testing engines for each change. I never use these models to find out how much power something will produce or to iterate exactly what cam will be best. However, I use it to see how items, such as cylinder pressure and port velocities, change with various component configurations. That peek behind the curtain is invaluable and helps with understanding, especially where measurements are difficult to obtain.

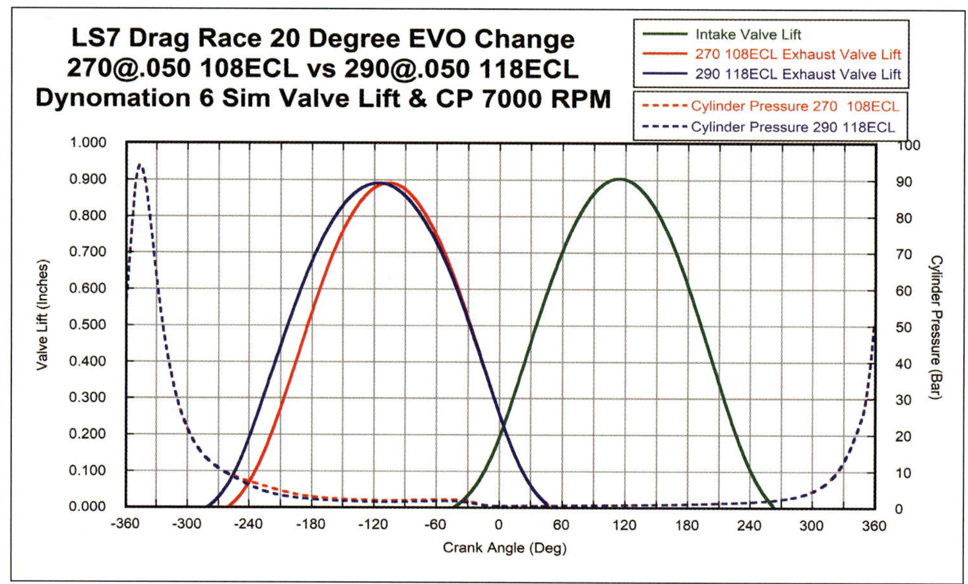

Image 5-22: Here, we have a valve motion plot with much larger race motion. Note the lift scale and much larger overlap triangle. I believe the best camshaft changes we can make are when we change one valve event while holding the other three constant as shown with the bigger (blue) and smaller (red) exhaust designs. Here, we move the exhaust centerline by 10 degrees to maintain the same exhaust closing with the 20-degree-different-duration designs and allow us to explore what changing the exhaust opening will do to cylinder pressure.

12.5:1 compression, and a custom tunnel-ram intake.

To not break the bank, we are not going to build and test this engine. Not only would it be expensive, but I want to do some things I know are wrong to demonstrate how EVO really works. The simulation tool I am using is the Dynomation 6.

With Dynomation, we can find the velocity in each port along with mass flow, intake-port pressure, exhaust-port pressure, cylinder pressure, and numerous other details, along with the simulated dyno curves, which I personally find the least interesting and informative. What simulations do so well is help us understand some of the why's and what's that are normally hidden behind the curtain without testing an engine.

Let's take a close look at the Dynomation 6 (Image 5-21) program after running a simulation. On the left, the top graph is power and torque with a cursor for what RPM we are examining on the next two plots. The middle plot has the exhaust and intake port pressure right behind each valve. The last plot includes the intake and exhaust port velocities. However, instead of using the Dynomation plots, we are going to have the program output the data and plot the results ourselves.

The question I want to answer is, "How does a 20-degree-later EVO change our PV diagrams and performance?" I chose a huge step to clearly change our PV diagrams and engine performance. I always wonder about people moving EVO by 1 or 2 degrees. There is always a win and a loss when moving EVO. Moving it later helps increase the power stroke, but later allows less free time to get the exhaust to leave the dance

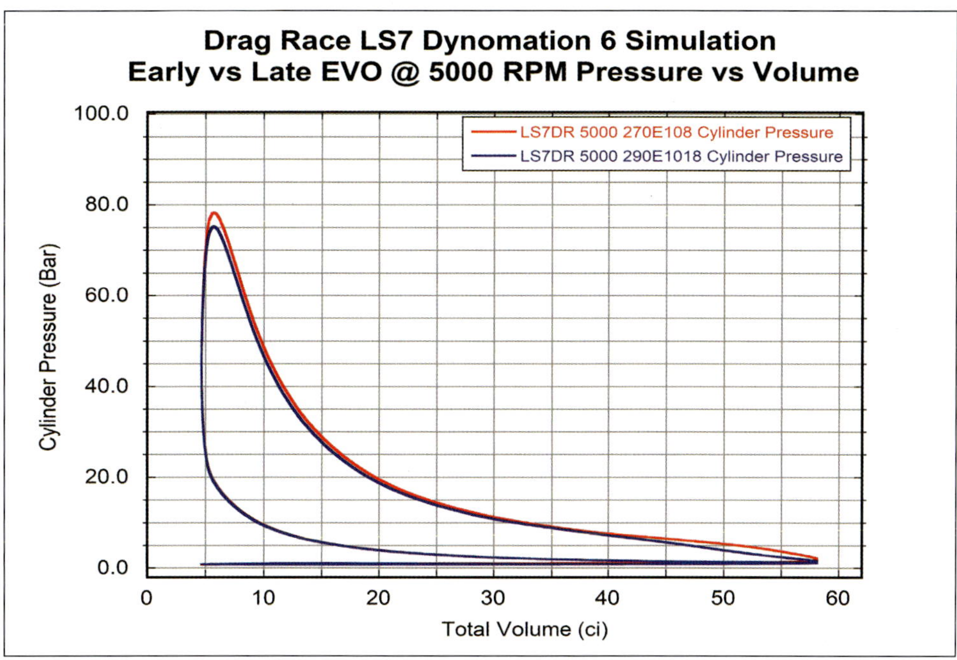

Image 5-23: Dynomation outputs the pressure and volume in a text format that is easy to input into any graphics program to plot. Note how closely the peak pressure is to the factory engine, but now we make these same pressures at a higher RPM and in a larger engine. With simulated data, we don't see the noise from experimental systems.

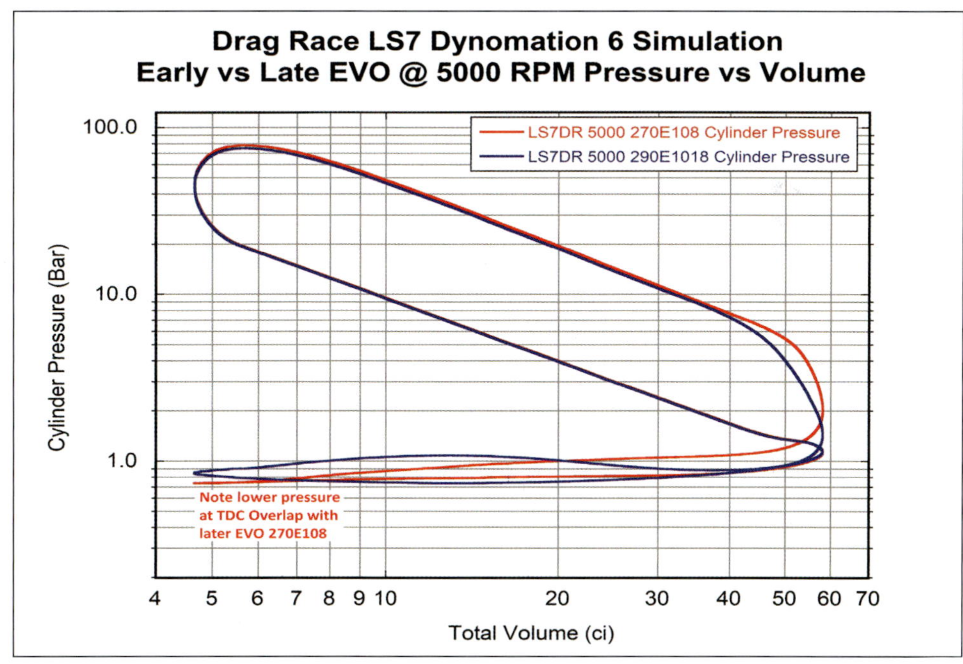

Image 5-24: In log-log format, we see the lower exhaust pressure near TDC overlap. This is due to the header tuning well with the EVO and helps build momentum to better fill the cylinder and create higher peak pressure on the top red curve. Pay careful attention to how the earlier simulated exhaust opening changes the shape of the tail of the power stroke and completely shifts the pumping loop.

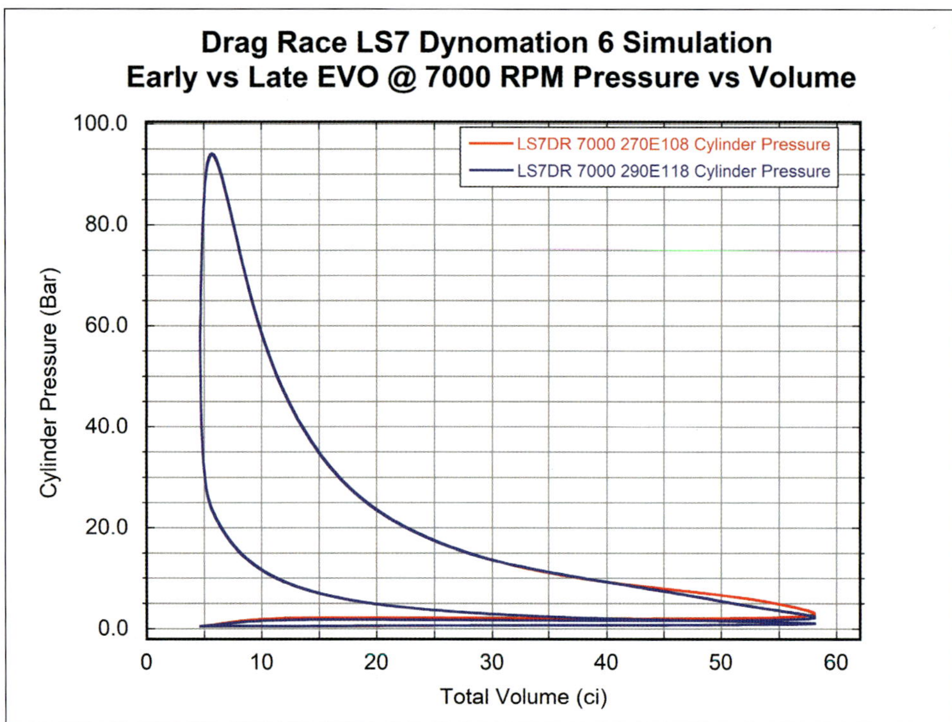

Image 5-25: At 7,000 rpm, there is a great example of the give and take of the exhaust opening. When we open the exhaust valve earlier, we take from the power stroke and top work loop.

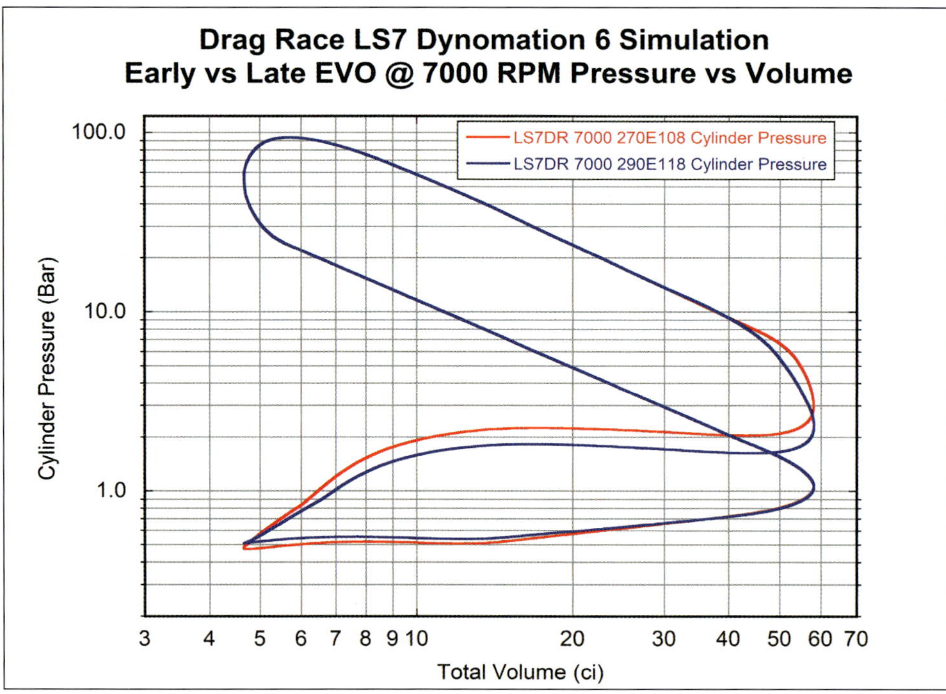

Image 5-26: We reduce the losses in the pumping loop to give us almost the same area back in the form of less work from the crank to push out the exhaust. Lower exhaust pressure during overlap allows more filling in this region and allows higher pressure and less work during the intake stroke (raising the floor of the pumping loop).

floor before the piston pushes out what remains.

Setting up the Test and Chewing on the Results

For our virtual test, one might guess that something around a 269 intake and 280 exhaust duration at 0.050-inch lift is close to the right cam. However, we want to run two wrong cams to see how pressure changes. Both will use a 269 MMO intake on a 110 intake centerline. The late exhaust opening will have a 270 MMX exhaust on 108 ECL, and the early exhaust opening will have a 290 MMX exhaust on a 118 ECL.

This 20-degree exhaust duration change with a 10-degree centerline change results in exactly the same exhaust closing and intake motion, which isolates the difference to only the exhaust opening side. Image 5-22 is back to our normal valve motion (as modeled) cam plot from -360 to +360 crank degrees with the smaller exhaust/later EVO in red and the larger exhaust profile/earlier EVO in blue. The difference in exhaust profiles (red versus blue solid lines) is evident. Notice the change in cylinder pressures (dotted lines) during the last part of the power stroke and throughout the exhaust stroke, shown at 7,000 rpm.

Instead of looking at this in crank degrees, let's use our new tool of looking at both linear and log PV diagrams at 5,000, 7,000, and 9,000 rpm. I am choosing these steps for the wrong cam EVO because a drag-race application such as this might spend significant time at 5,000 rpm on the converter and finish through the lights at 9,000 rpm. Starting with the 5,000-rpm PV diagrams, with the 270 exhaust in red and the 290 exhaust in blue, see how quickly cylinder pres-

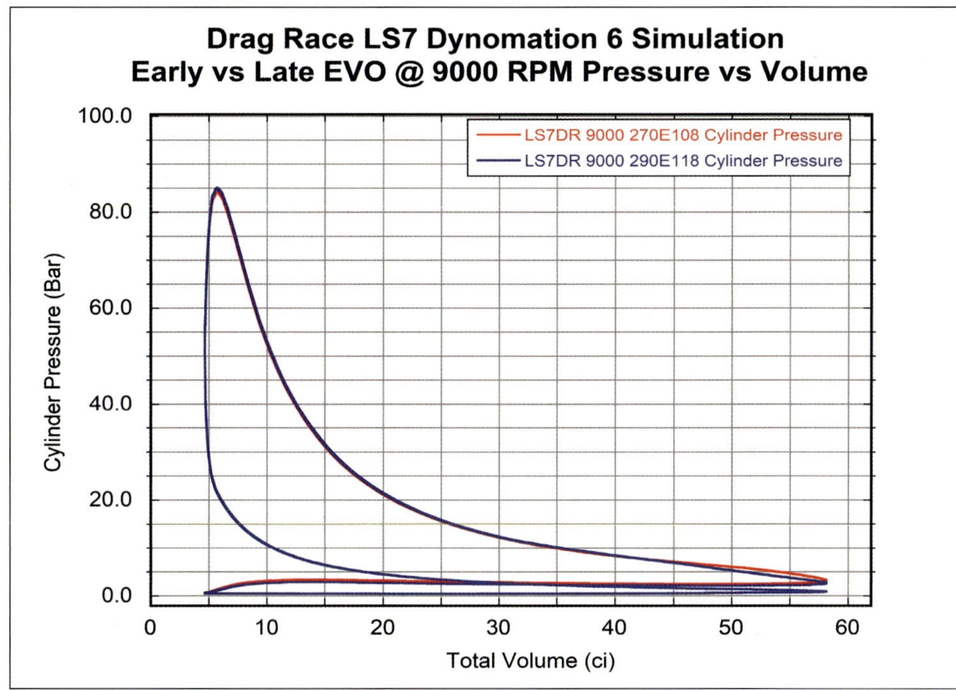

Image 5-27: At 9,000 rpm, we moved from just about a tie between two camshafts to a big win from big blue. Here, the difference in pumping losses finally jumps out on the linear scale.

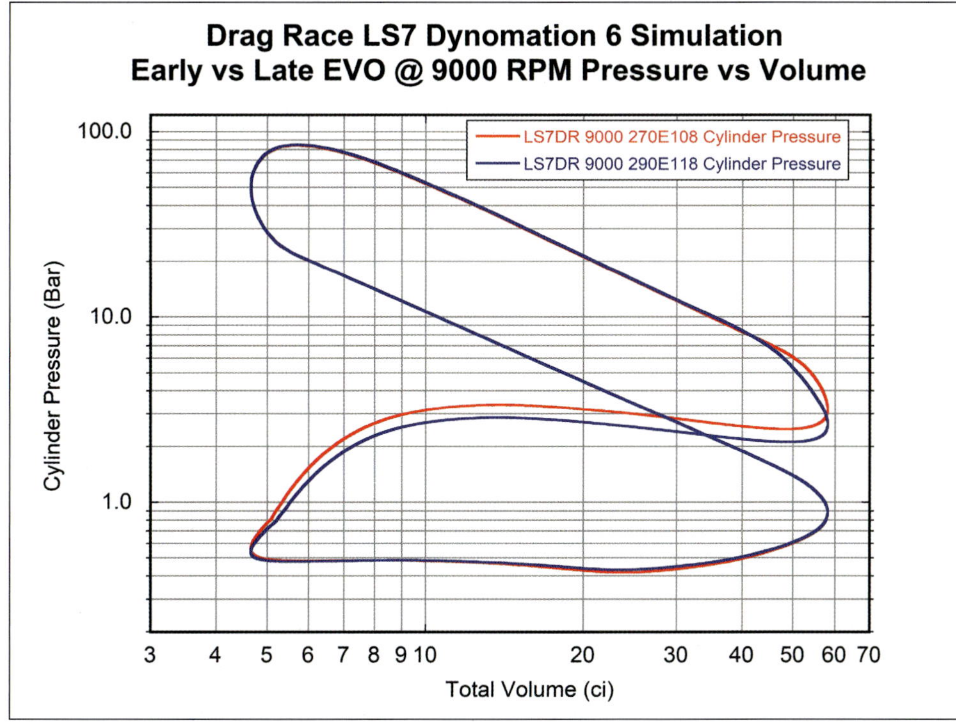

Image 5-28: Going to the log scale, the pumping loop for the smaller, late EVO design is larger than with the dropped exhaust-stroke pressure that resulted from the earlier exhaust opening. Both exhaust designs are the wrong size, so this experiment might be a waste of valuable time in a dyno cell, but it is rather quick, easy, and useful in a simulation.

sure drops at the tail end of the power stroke (around 40 ci) in Image 5-23.

The zoomed-in log plot in Image 5-24 shows the reduced top work loop. Note the bottom pumping loops are small in both cases. There is something weird that has to do with wave tuning at the left side of the pumping loop. The earlier EVO led to the reflective wave coming back at the wrong time for this RPM, which results in higher pressure at overlap for this application. With proper wave tuning, the negative exhaust pulse should arrive near overlap to coax the intake in, whereas this had a high pressure come in and pushed the intake the wrong way.

If you study the graph, our model predicts that this will result in more exhaust gases being ingested during overlap. Even though the red curve and blue curve show similar filling at IVC, the 290 exhaust fills more with exhaust gases than the 270, not due to more overlap, as that is the same, but due to poor wave tuning. Together, at 5,000 rpm, the later EVO 270 exhaust was much better in terms of work done on the piston. This is very important in many 2- and 3-speed drag cars, as the launch is critical for best performance, and they spend significant time at the converter stall RPM.

Images 5-25 and 5-26 are at 7,000 rpm with this same labeling convention. First, the top part of the pressure curves are basically identical in both the linear and log views. The second thing to notice is how drastically the big change of EVO jumps out on the log plot. You can see exactly where the 290 exhaust opens and pressure starts dropping like a rock.

While the top "work done" loop is reduced, both pumping loops grew compared to those at 5,000 rpm.

The earlier-opening 290/118 exhaust has a dramatically smaller pumping loop. Looking at the top loop, it is evident the 270/108 did a better job working on the piston, but the 290/118 required much less work to remove the remaining combusted gases (exhaust). Looking at these PV diagrams, you can correctly guess that the overall results are extremely close.

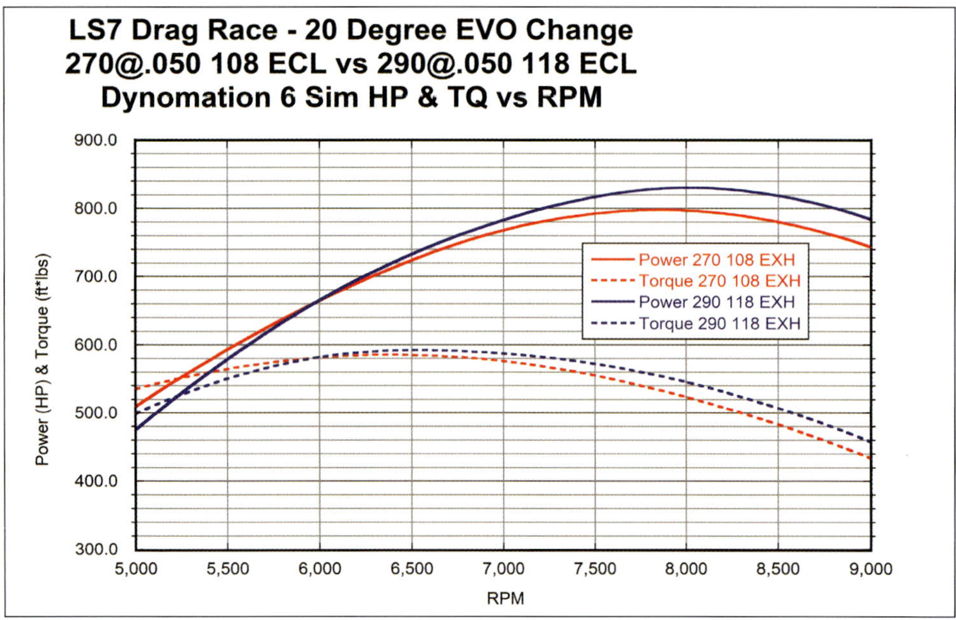

Image 5-29: I do not use this simulation tool for absolute power estimates, but I also assume that showing output this time is useful. I only simulated 1,000-rpm steps, so these very smooth curves are the best fit for those widely spaced data points. However, the match at 6,000 rpm was real, and we were very close at 7,000 rpm, which was exactly as we guessed from the PV diagrams.

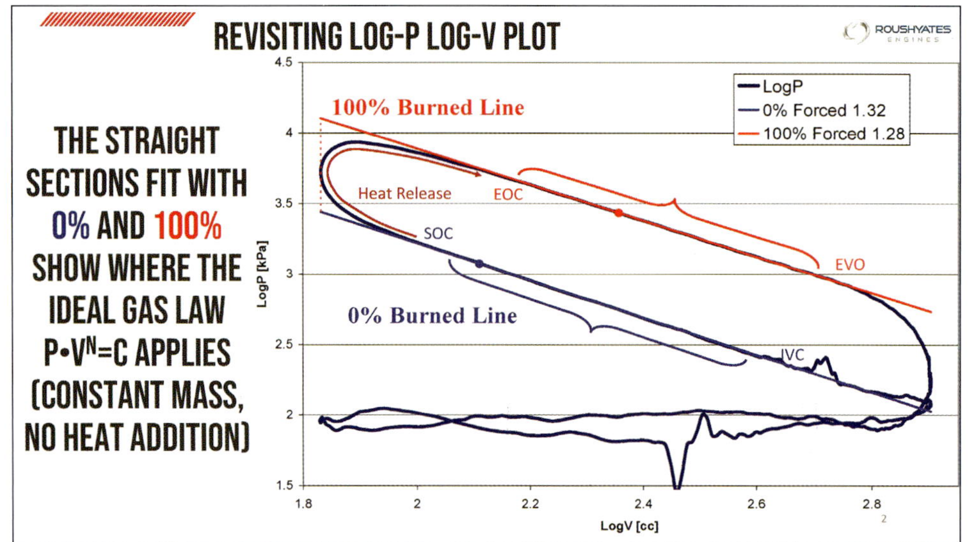

Image 5-30: At very high speed, there is less heat transfer to the walls, piston, and chamber, so this 10,000-rpm race engine more closely mimics our ideal Otto from IVC to SOC, and then from EOC to EVO than the 4,500-rpm 5.3L. Adding the blue line up (blue ride) and red line down (red ride) is a great tool for camshaft development because it helps us see where we lock ourselves in at IVC and jump off at EVO. (Graphic Courtesy Doug Yates and Gary Patterson)

Lastly, Images 5-27 and 5-28 are for 9,000 rpm. Here, something cool has happened that we can see with the top loop on the log curve. While pressure is still dropping at the early EVO, the pressure drops so considerably further for the entire exhaust stroke. Effectively, the floor dropped on our top "work done" loop enough so that the early-opening 290/118 is now winning on the top loop. On the bottom loop, there is a significantly larger pumping loop on the red curves because the dropped floor of the exhaust stroke on the work done loop is also the ceiling of the pumping loop. Clearly, the 290/118 is the overall winner by a landslide at 9,000 rpm.

The takeaway is seeing how small changes in either direction from optimal EVO will rob from one loop and pay the other. Hence, I typically make at least 4-degree changes in EVO when testing camshafts. However, if you are dramatically off on EVO, both loops can be hurt (see the 290/118 at 5,000 and the 270/108 at 9,000). Again, I chose these durations and EVOs to show you wrong—but in a way not nearly so unbelievable that this information is not useful.

The simulated power of each camshaft is shown in Image 5-28. These two camshafts made the same power at 6,000 rpm, but the late-EVO 270/108 is 40 ft-lbs higher at 5,000 rpm. Likewise, the early-EVO 290/118 camshaft is 40 hp higher at 9,000 rpm.

If we were to put these camshafts in drag cars that operate from 5,000 to

9,000 rpm, the specific vehicle configuration would determine which was better. A very heavy car with a Powerglide that camped on the converter would be quicker with the 270/108 exhaust, but a lighter car (especially with a 4-speed or a transmission with more gears), might be dramatically better with the 290/118. However, almost any imaginable combination is better with an EVO somewhere in-between these extremes.

Hopping on the Rides

Gary Patterson provided measured data (Image 5-30) from a single cycle of a race engine at 10,000 rpm. Note the red and blue lines that Gary added to these curves. From a camshaft perspective, it's like jumping on a ride at an amusement park. Note that at IVC (see the spike from the valve closing), air stops moving in or out of the chamber. Lock in for a ride on the blue line up from that point, all the way until the spark plug fires at the start of combustion (SOC). Then, we change roller coasters and jump from the blue uphill track to the red downhill ride. Combustion finishes at end of combustion (EOC). We are locked in the red path all the way down until EVO.

What we do with camshaft optimization is pick when to open the exhaust, try to keep it out of the way, let the mixing of overlap connect the intake and exhaust, keep the intake valve out of the way during intake stroke filling, and try to close the intake at the right time to shift the blue ride as high as possible. Making that top loop big and the bottom loop small is the goal, and selecting those events, optimizing the lift curves, and keeping everything stable is how we achieve improvement.

For camshaft development, look mostly at the bottom of straight segments where the intake closes and exhaust opens. The ignition and chamber people spend their time looking at how they swap rides up top.

Today, this technology is moving from the major universities and top professional race teams to an even wider audience. EFI University is starting to take measurements on customer engines with its Plex System shown in Image 5-32. Note the same compression and expansion lines. Use these to evaluate the valve timing points for this application and RPM.

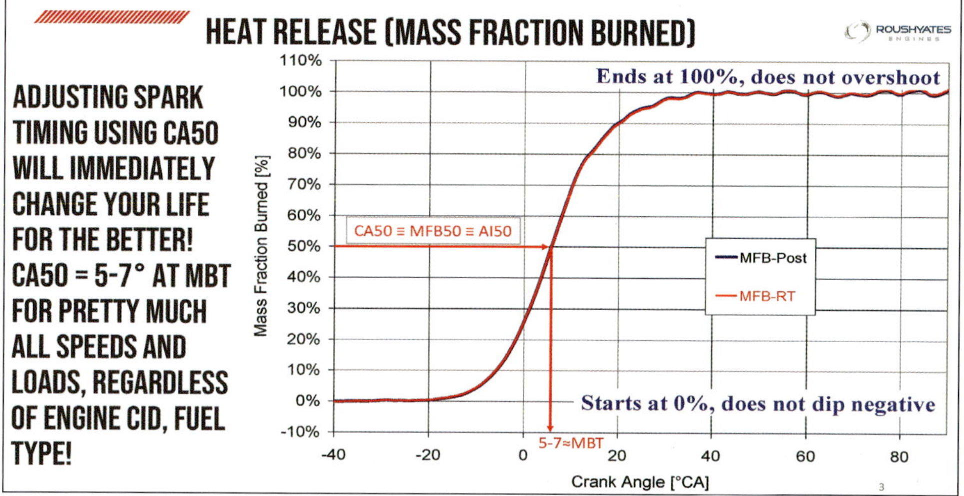

Image 5-31: This is the jump from the blue line (0-percent burn) to the red line (100-percent burn) from the last graph but in crank degrees. Most engines make their best power at any RPM when 50-percent burn occurs at 8 degrees after TDC. We reach 50-percent burn when the pressure is halfway between the blue and red sloped lines. (Graphic Courtesy Doug Yates and Gary Patterson)

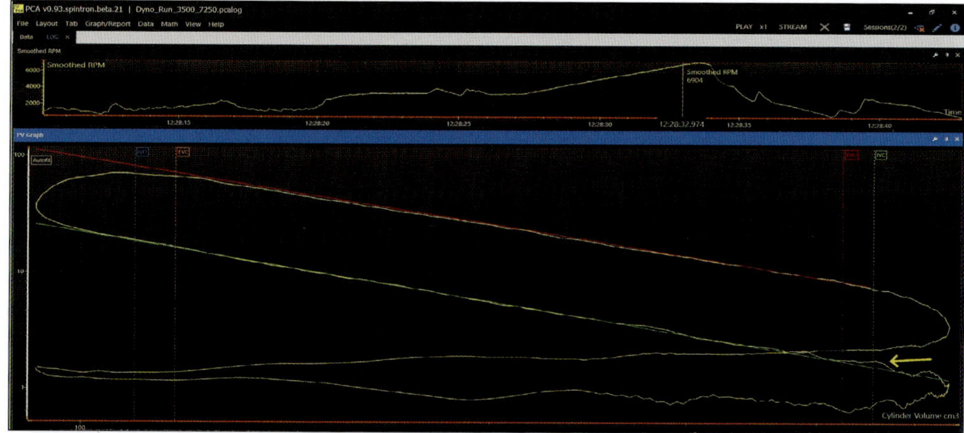

Image 5-32: Ben Strader sent this plot from the EFI University plex cylinder pressure system to show how to use cylinder pressure measurements to determine valve event changes. The cylinder pressure jumped above the bottom green line and then fell back down. With a properly timed intake closing, this engine would have made more peak power. However, it was supposed to close at the right time (see IVC line). My guess is the intake valve is bouncing to allow cylinder pressure to escape.

Understanding Valve Events

After looking over pressure volume (PV) diagrams, we are at a great point to have a general overview of how each valve event changes performance of the engine. The best approach is to break it into three parts: EVO, overlap, and IVC.

We'll start with the EVO. This time, we will use a plot of an NHRA Pro Stock camshaft that ran before the rev limiters were introduced in 2016. For reference, I am adding the Otto cycle lines and labels to the camshaft plot in Image 6-2.

***Image 6-1:** You never know who you might meet at the Performance Racing Industry (PRI) trade show in Indianapolis. While eating breakfast, someone who I deeply respect, Ed "Isky" Iskenderian, sat down at the table beside me and started talking about a presentation he was about to give a few hours later. It could not have been more enjoyable, as he went through each of his points on four-stroke valve events. The pioneering work that Ed has done for camshaft events and engine airflow is outstanding. He is truly a treasure to our industry.*

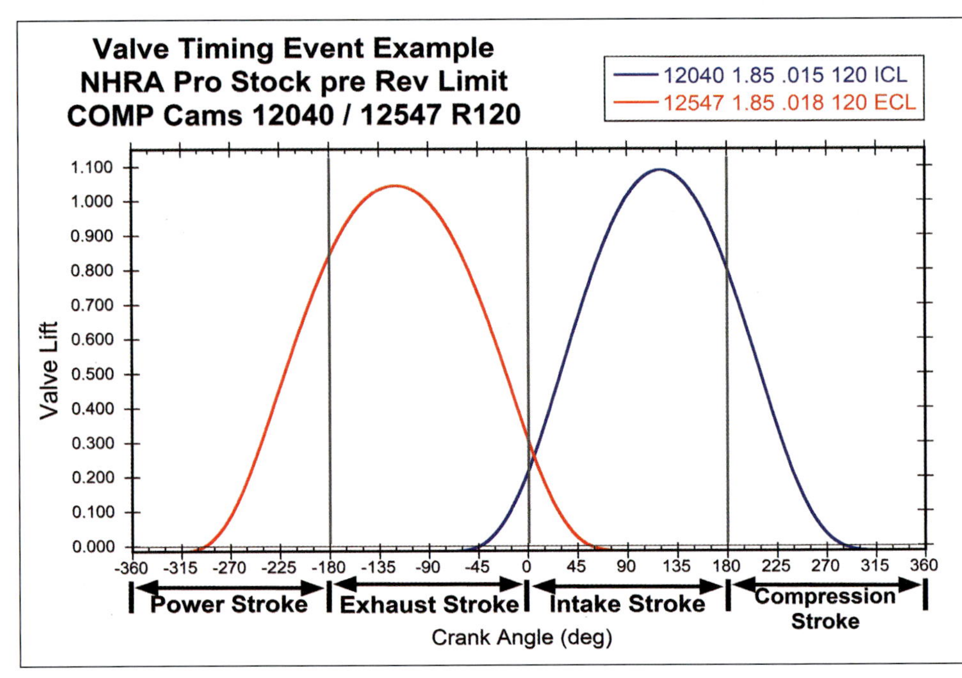

***Image 6-2:** If you want to see a valve motion plot of something that is big, real, and has made awesome power in competition engines, you will love this plot. This is a few years (and rule changes) old, but it is either very close or on top of what was run in championship-winning Pro Stock engines. You may think this overlap is huge. In a way it is, but with two massive Dominators feeding 500 ci at 11,000 rpm, the engine would have liked more overlap if greater valve reliefs would not have made a mess of combustion efficiency. When running less dome and shallower reliefs, BSFC increased at high RPM more than VE suffered from less overlap moving less air.*

EVO

The EVO occurs well before the middle of the exhaust stroke. Recall how much of the area of the top work loop occurred in the first half of the volume sweep and see how cylinder pressure does not drop immediately at EVO. Don't be surprised that a 500-ci engine operating just past 11,000 rpm has a very early EVO. These camshafts don't have the earliest EVOs in motorsports, as these are surpassed by the large-displacement Pro Mod nitrous engines.

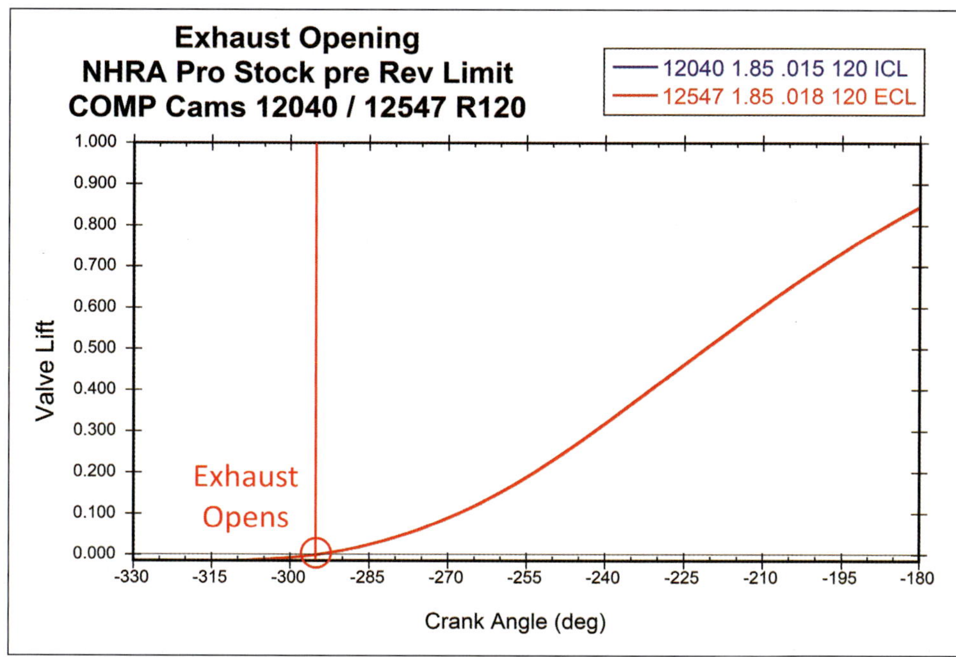

Image 6-3: Zooming in from -330 to -180 degrees, focus on the EVO to BDC region. The red vertical line at EVO represents the end of the pure power stroke. To the left, all the pressure was being used to force down the piston and drive the crank. As soon as that line is crossed, cylinder pressure is used for forcing out the spent exhaust gases while the remaining pressure will continue to do work on the piston. As we reach the right side of this graph, the piston begins its upstroke, and the remaining mass and pressure requires work from the crankshaft.

When the exhaust valve is opened, the exhaust gases begin to exit rapidly and cause a high-pressure wave to travel down the exhaust port at the speed of sound. Inside the chamber, the pressure begins to drop rapidly. Instead of using cylinder

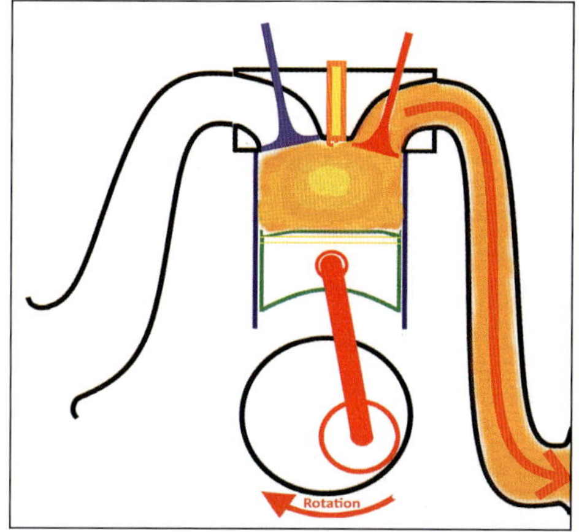

Image 6-4: The exhaust opens early in the power stroke of real engines. This early exhaust opening greatly reduces the power required to push the remaining spent mass out later. It only reduces the work done during the power stroke a small amount when timed correctly for the given RPM and cylinder head exhaust flow.

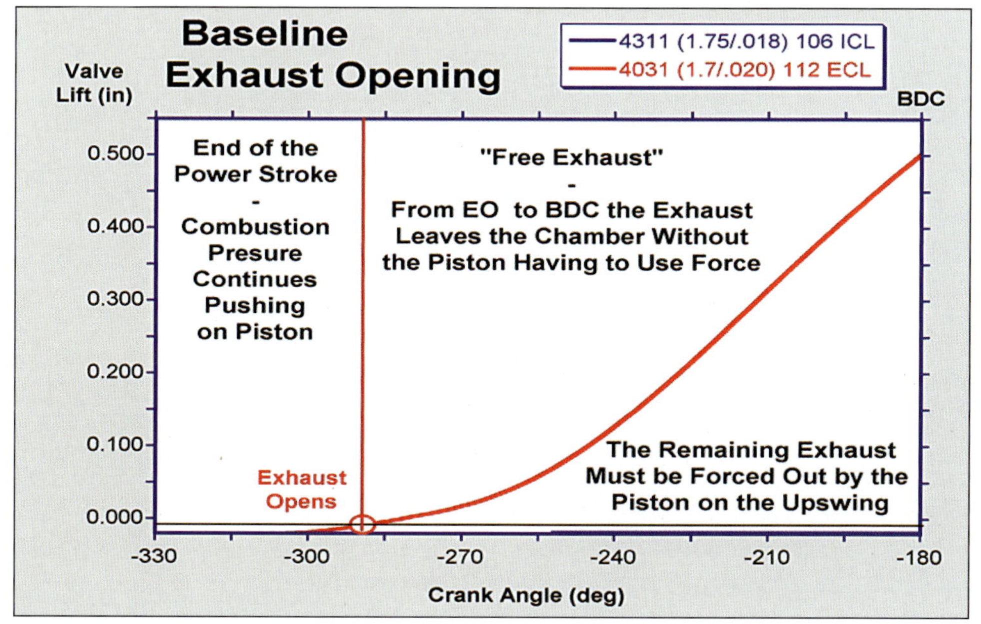

Image 6-5: Even on something like an 8,500-rpm circle-track engine, we try to open the exhaust more than 100 degrees BBDC. This makes sense thinking back to cylinder pressure, as we have dropped from around the 90-bar peak to around 9 bar by EVO. Using some of the combustion energy keeps us from having to rob as much work from the crank to push this exhaust mass out later.

pressure to push down the piston, we now use that pressure to push out the exhaust gases. This dramatically reduces the trapped mass that has to be pushed out with work from the crankshaft when the piston returns to TDC during the exhaust stroke.

When I first started working with camshafts, a late EVO was often described as under-scavenged. The mental picture created was that there was too much remaining exhaust gases during the intake stroke. While there can be a tiny bit more of these remaining exhaust gas residuals, depending on EVO, this has more to do with wave tuning in Chapter 7. The real losses from too late of an EVO are from the work done to push out remaining gases while the piston is rapidly moving back to TDC during the exhaust stroke. You do not have to worry about a late EVO creating a dirty chamber, as the piston pushes out almost all the exhaust gases. However, how much work required to push out the remaining exhaust gases is linked to EVO.

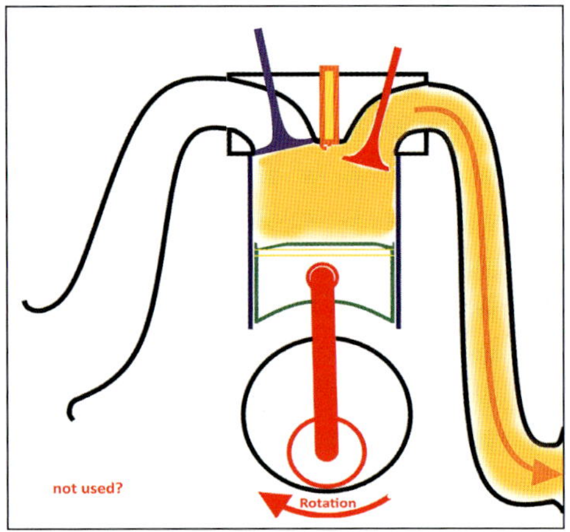

Image 6-6: The more mass that is moved from EVO until the piston quits hanging out around BDC (where it is slowest due to rod-to-stroke relationships), the less work the crank does to push the rest out and make room for a fresh intake charge. In this BDC region, the exhaust valve needs to be as far out of the way as possible without upsetting the valve spring or opening the exhaust so soon that we lose too much of the top PV loop.

Finally, we need to know that the timing and speed of the EVO point is key to both the volume and tone of the exhaust note and can affect the shape of the pressure wave. It is not just the point of EVO that matters. The shape of that curve from EVO to BDC makes a huge difference in how much mass we can get out of the chamber and how the engine responds to different collectors or headers.

Overlap

I like considering IVO and EVC together as they form an overlap triangle, which is almost like a stroke itself in our performance and racing engines. At IVO, both valves are open and allow the intake and exhaust systems to link with one another to improve efficiency. The earlier we open the intake, the easier it is to have the door open wider later when the piston reaches peak velocity about 70 degrees after TDC. For this to work properly, the EVO and header lengths need to be optimized to return a negative wave to the chamber at IVO. This is commonly achieved with most racing headers in the operating range.

I'm sure you have heard that tighter lobe separation cams are peakier. The truth of that statement has to do with how all the events are moved. The increased overlap is key in that where the exhaust and intake are tuned (typically around peak torque), they have more time to work together. A better test is to try different overlap triangles without changing EVO and IVC, or change EVO and IVC without changing overlap.

If the engine's airflow is restricted somewhere other than the cylinder head, you may have to be concerned about excessive overlap allowing too much of the inlet charge out of the exhaust. For most open engines, the overlap is geometrically limited by piston-to-valve clearance, not lost intake mass out the exhaust. If the piston is well designed to maximize BSFC, it's almost certain to be limited by valve clearance.

The reliefs decrease compression and add complexity to the piston top geometry, both of which slow combustion. If you add much dome to the piston top, it adds even more complexity to the chamber. The reason why the original big-block Chevy chambers typically ran best with 40-plus of timing has everything to do with the flame having to go over the hills and through the woods to complete combustion. A modern chamber requires far less ignition lead to do the job.

Exhaust Valve Opening Overview

- EVO occurs near the middle of the power stroke
- Exhaust begins exiting the chamber
- Cylinder pressure drops rapidly
- Combustion pressure is used to force out exhaust, not force down piston (blow down)
- Later exhaust openings increase low-RPM torque by lengthening power stroke
- Earlier exhaust openings give more time to remove exhaust for free near BDC

Understand that too much overlap reduces the vacuum signal and causes excessive misfire at idle, but some give a nice-sounding lope. This is especially important when driving a race car around the pits or developing a camshaft that passes emissions. When overlap is tuned for maximum performance inside a high-RPM operating range, the engine is not going to perform well at much lower RPM.

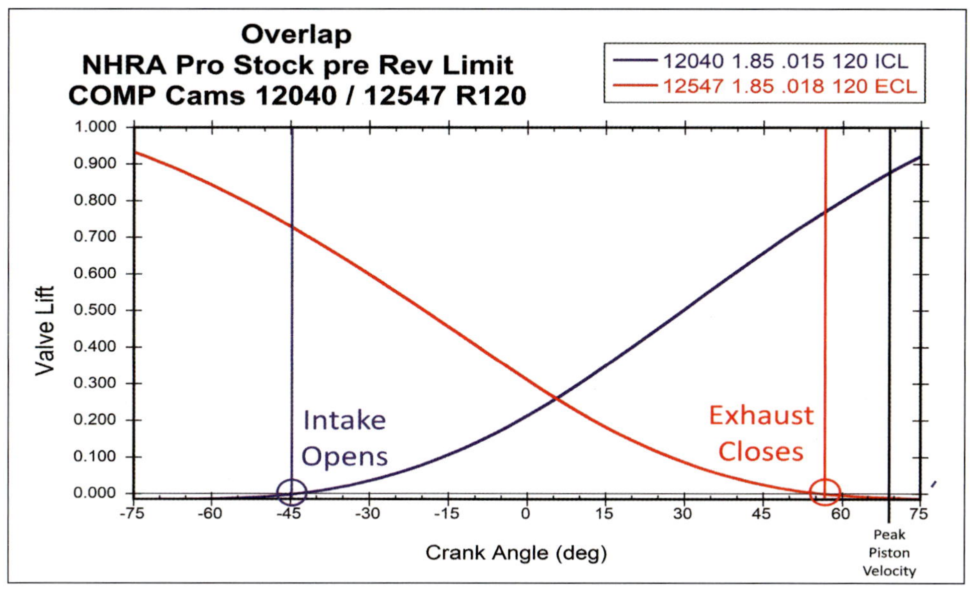

Image 6-7: By focusing on the overlap region of the Pro Stock cam (from -75 to +75 crank degrees), we can see how much exhaust lift we have when the intake cracks open and how much intake lift there is when the exhaust finally closes. This 0.700-inch-lift range at the end of the overlap is greater than most street performance and some race camshafts. During overlap, the intake and exhaust system can communicate and result in a complex coupled system, where small changes on one side will alter the wave tuning and can greatly affect the other side. Finally, note where in relation to intake opening that peak piston velocity occurs (near +68 degrees). The piston velocity is the driver for most of our pressure drop.

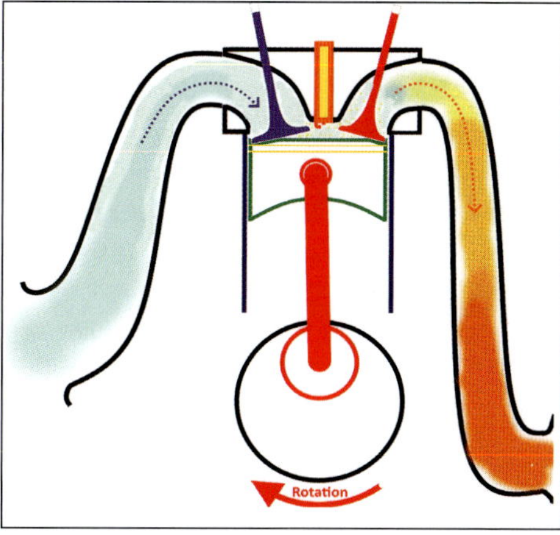

Image 6-8: Returning to our original engine sketch can help you understand how greatly the overlap connects the two sides. Note how this Hemi cylinder head configuration creates a line-of-sight path from the intake out the exhaust without requiring much movement through the cylinder. This path makes the overlap more sensitive on both Hemi and Pent Roof 4V heads. Finally, note the valve pockets required even in the simple sketch. In most open race engines, the practical depth of these pockets (without upsetting the ring package, compression, and/or piston top geometry) typically becomes the limiting factor as to how much overlap will be used.

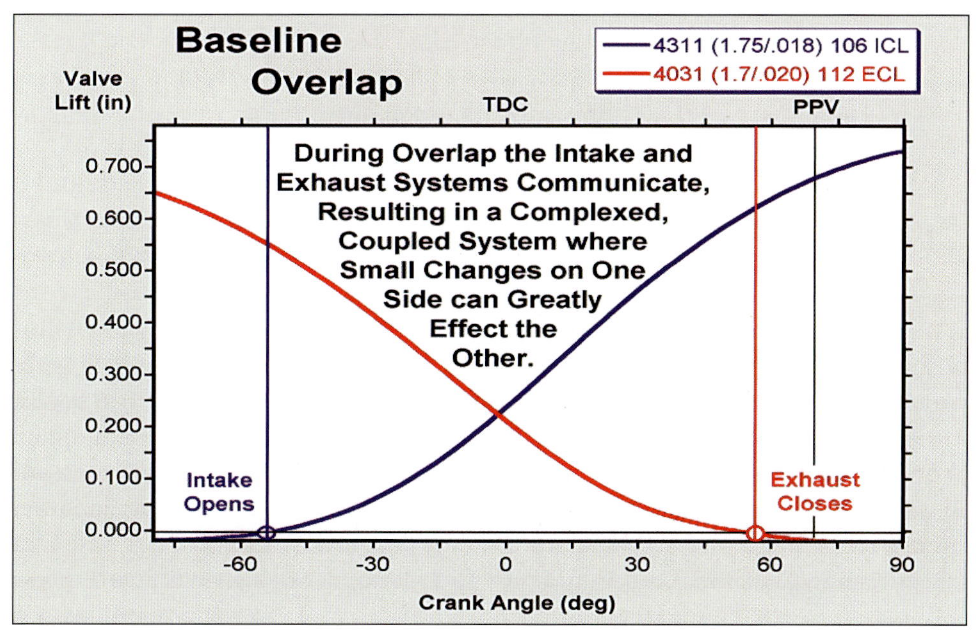

Image 6-9: Looking at the circle-track camshaft, the overlap is moved forward a little compared to the Pro Stock because this application was limited by a compression limit that allowed more intake room. However, the bottom triangle is similar (0.230-inch high versus 0.270-inch high at crossover). Note how much more lift the exhaust has on the Pro Stock when the intake cracks open, and how much more lift the intake has when the exhaust closes.

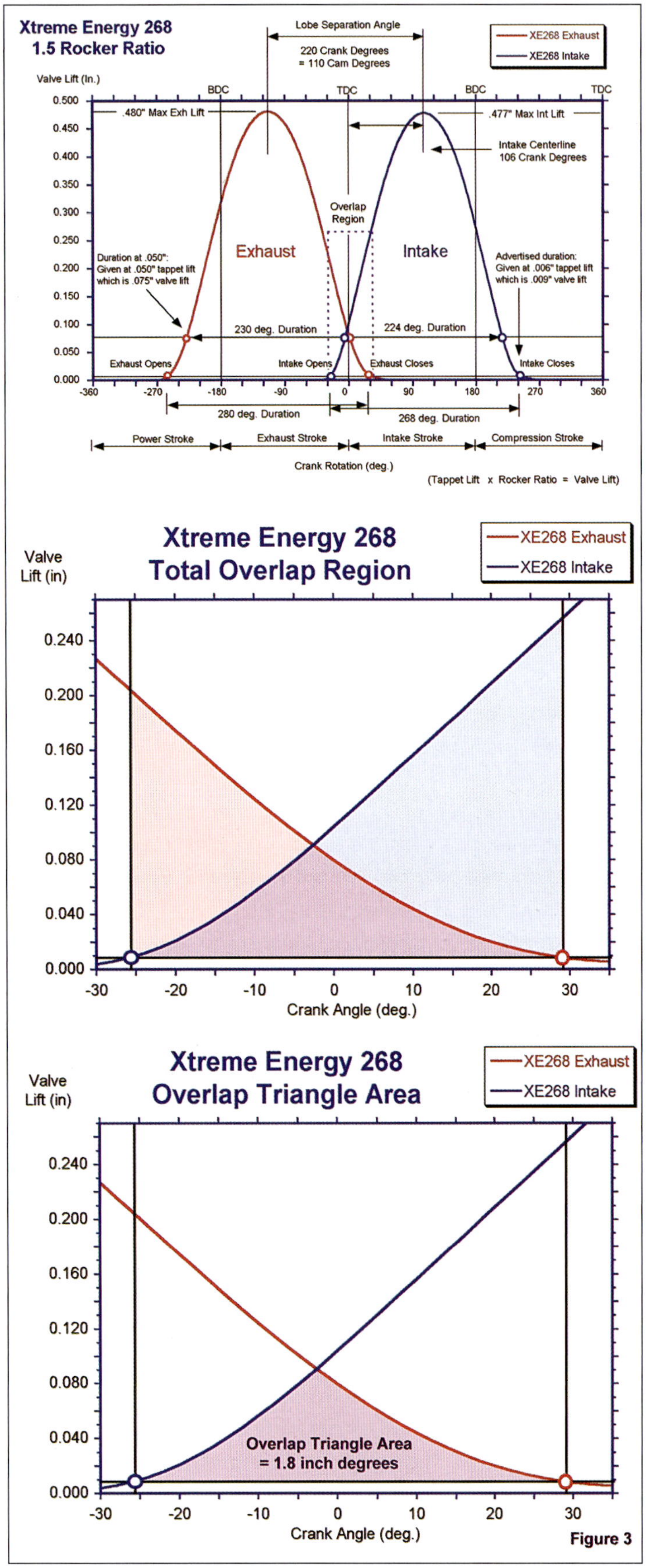

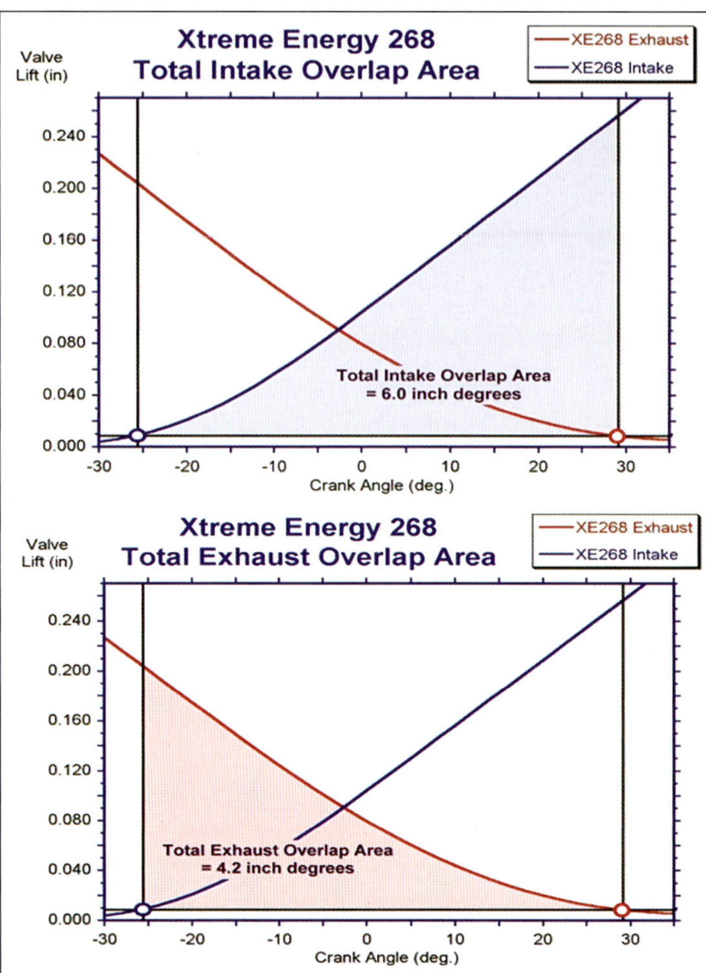

Image 6-10: When idle vacuum becomes the limiting factor for overlap, pay close attention to the area of the small triangle as well as the exhaust-closing and intake-opening shapes. People ask if it is overlap duration, the lift at split overlap, the middle triangle area, or how the middle triangle is advanced relative to TDC. Unfortunately, it all plays a part, as well as the lift of the other valve.

As with EVO, the shape of the overlap triangle can be more important if we look at the duration or area. By tailoring the exhaust-closing ramp and the intake-opening ramp, the shape can be optimized.

A slow ramp or closing rate at EVC can be beneficial for a few reasons. First, as the valve approaches the seat, the curtain area around the head reduces, and this small cross-sectional area can speed flow, like putting your thumb on the end of a garden hose. Bernoulli's equation explains how in airstreams, high velocity results in low pressure. Slowing down to stay in this high-velocity lift region a few degrees longer can result in more pressure drop to motivate the intake charge at the cost of

Overlap Overview

- IVO begins overlap
- During overlap, both valves are open
- Remaining pressure in chamber at IVO can cause reversion of exhaust and misfire
- Overlap and early IVO can result in internal EGR
- Exhaust leaving can result in lower cylinder pressure and signal to intake
- The earlier the intake opens, the easier it is to maximize lift at peak piston velocity, but you must be careful to avoid intake piston-to-valve interference later
- The shape of the overlap may be more important than the duration or area
- The overlap requirements of an engine are dependent on the chamber design and desired idle characteristics
- As the exhaust valve closes, the exhaust valve curtain area is greatly reduced
- Exhaust velocity increases through the smaller area, resulting in low pressure (Bernoulli)
- Although the exhaust gas velocity at the seat is high, the mass flow may be low
- Hence, slower closing exhaust lobes may be preferred for various applications
- Slower closing also reduces exhaust seat erosion and noise

some increase in the amount of intake charge mass that escapes out the exhaust. If the opening is small enough, perhaps there's a longer signal with less mass loss.

Finally, because the exhaust valve is quite hot and steeper seat angles are often helpful, a slower-closing exhaust helps reduce seat wear and erosion. Exhaust seat wear is typically more of an issue than intake seat wear, where cooler air and fuel help reduce erosion. Finally, a slower closing can reduce EVC noise. This is mostly important on street applications, but this drawback of requiring slower closing sometimes becomes a performance benefit.

IVC

IVC is the most important valve timing event. When the intake valve closes, air stops flowing into the chamber and pressure increases as the piston rises. This point generally determines the power range more than any other camshaft attribute. Early intake closing tunes in the power earlier because it traps more air at low speed before it can turn around and exit back into the manifold. Later intake closings allow more air to enter at high RPM when the momentum of the intake charge allows air to fill even as the piston rises.

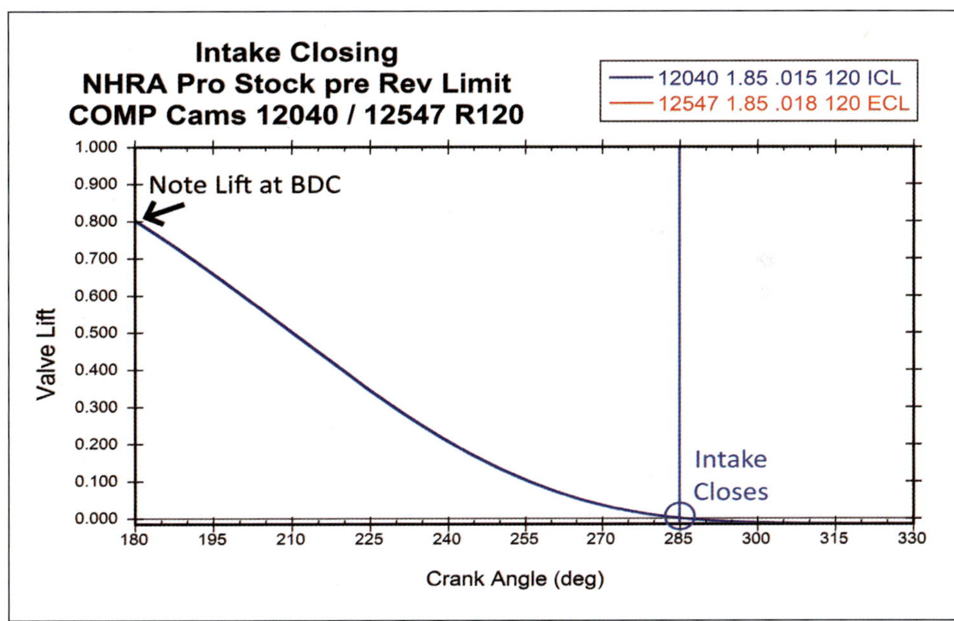

***Image 6-11:** Note how late the intake closing occurs in an 11,000-rpm application. Not only is the cylinder still filling as the piston starts rising, but peak port velocity happens well after peak piston velocity in high-RPM engines. As RPM increases, the intake port velocity peak continues to fall farther behind peak signal at 68 degrees—first to peak lift and then closer to BDC. Here, the door is still open almost 0.800 inch at the bottom of the stroke. The momentum of the incoming air and fuel charge can overcome slightly higher cylinder pressure than port pressure for a short time. We are tuning the intake-runner length to have a pressure wave return to the inlet valve near IVC to allow us to force a bit more inside.*

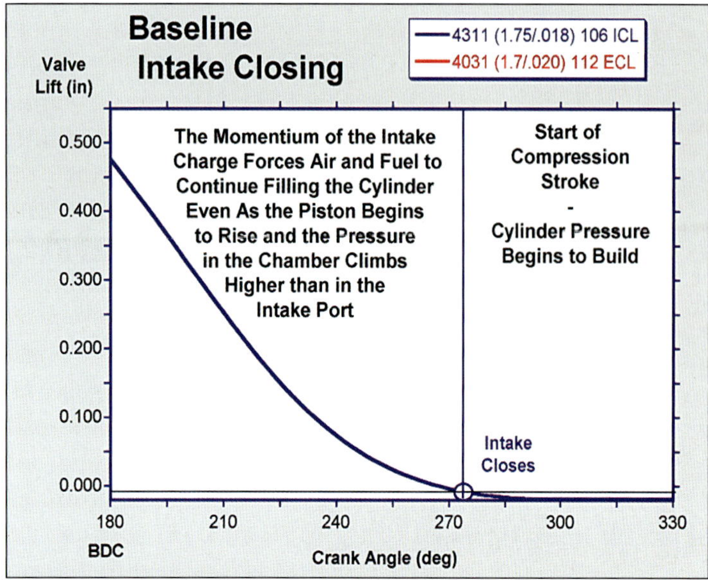

Image 6-12: At IVC, there is a significant difference in valve timing between an 11,000-rpm Pro Stock and this 8,500-rpm circle track engine. Here, the closing is about 12 to 13 degrees earlier. We talked about how the piston almost camps out at BDC after EVO. The same thing is happening here before IVC. The time that a piston with a smaller rod-to-stroke ratio seems to sit at the bottom is an excellent opportunity to keep filling the cylinder. Once the piston starts rushing upward, pressure builds and filling stops.

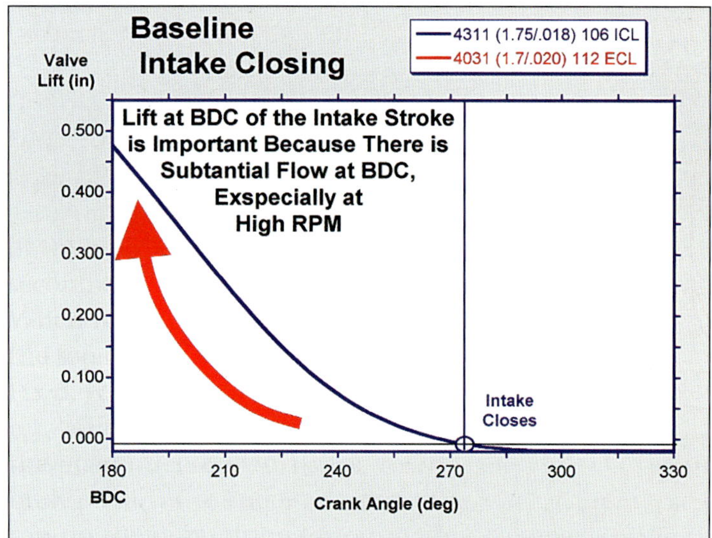

Image 6-13: Not only has the closing point moved, but note how the BDC lift dropped from 0.800 inch on the Pro Stock down to under 0.500 inch for this circle-track camshaft. Of all the camshaft specs that you should investigate, intake lift at BDC is probably the most overlooked by all but the very best engine builders.

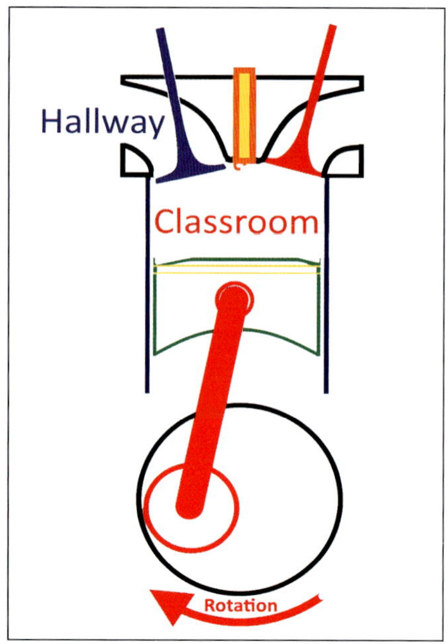

Image 6-14: The region near IVC is shown but with the intake tract off, the word "Hallway" added, and the combustion chamber labeled as "Classroom." A large section of Chapter 7 is about how we build pressure in the hallway to overcome pressure in the chamber as long as possible to fill the chamber.

Kindergarten

My favorite analogy for how IVC and all the events work together goes back to my kindergarten classroom. Mrs. Edwards' classroom had two doors: one to the playground and one to the hallway. Whenever I was in that classroom, all I wanted to do was get out to the playground. The more she talked, the more I wanted out. For this analogy, the classroom is the combustion chamber, the playground is the exhaust port and outside world, and the hallway is the intake port and intake manifold. In our model, the hallway is always filled with kindergarteners who want to go to the playground. The door to the hallway is the intake valve, and the door to the playground is the exhaust valve.

As the class eager for exercise, Mrs. Edwards (camshaft) finally shows some mercy and opens the playground door, and the class starts flowing out as quickly as possible. As the class thins out, the teacher opens the door to the hallway (intake). Seeing the playground fun, the kindergarteners from the hallway start rushing through. A few lucky ones get all the way through, but now the teacher is shutting the playground door—but not so fast that a few don't have hope of making it across. Even after the playground door is closed, there is more room in the classroom than the hallway, and students are following one another inside.

Unfortunately for these students, the teacher starts writing on the board. The pressure builds inside, and seeing what's happening, many of the kids start sprinting back toward the hallway (intake) door. A few will make it

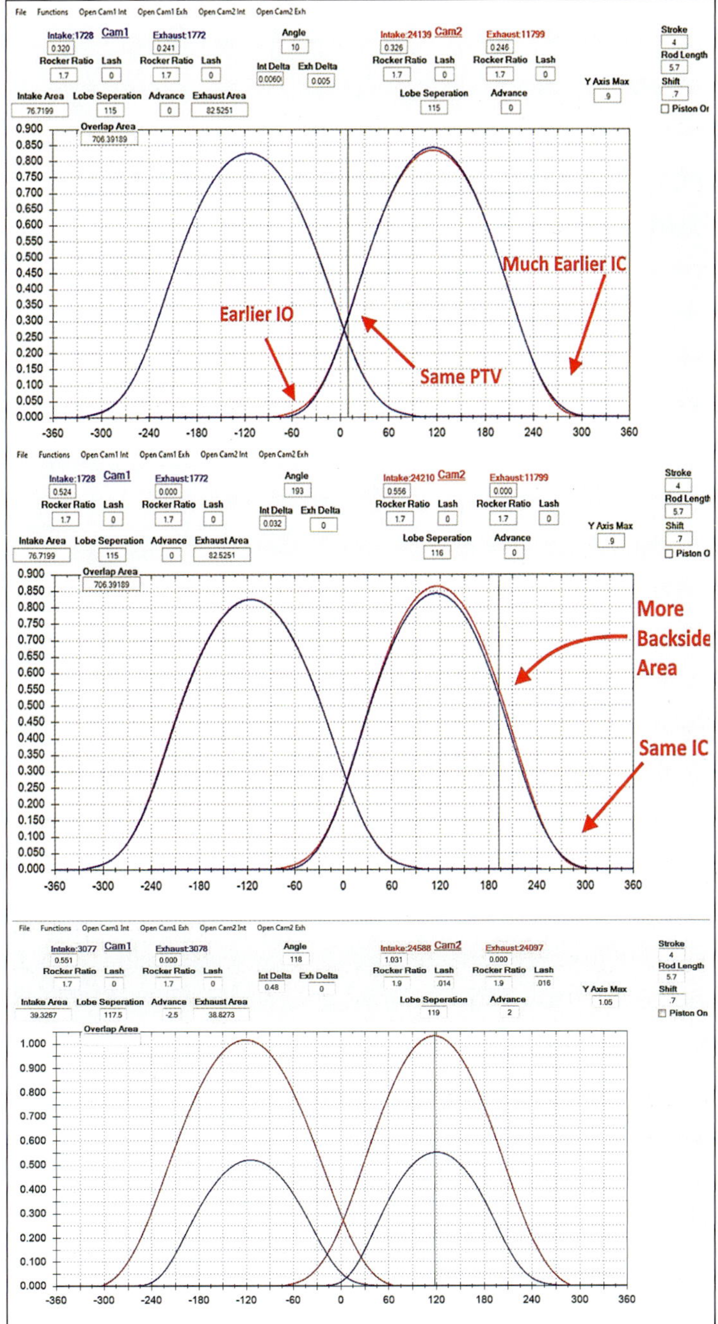

Image 6-15: Much like Bob Glidden's Fairmont camshaft, the new low-shock lobe profiles add a take-up ramp to the front side to upset the spring less and allow the door to be closed faster on the closing side. The top graph shows that if you match normal duration and centerline specs, the low shock should close earlier and only add low-speed torque. However, if you get the events correct, like the second graph, you can add more lift on the backside. Lastly, note how much all of the valve events move between a stock LS3 camshaft and Ben Strader's low-shock camshaft for Spinal Tap, the 11,000-rpm LS.

Intake Valve Closing Overview

- This is the most important valve event
- Once the intake valve closes, air stops moving into the chamber and cylinder pressure builds
- Earlier intake closings make better low-RPM torque by trapping air in the chamber
- Later intake closings give the air more time to enter the chamber at high RPM
- At low RPM, the air column momentum is less, and flow changes direction soon after BDC
- Maximizing intake lift and backside area near BDC is extremely important for best fill

out, and that is great for them and okay with the teacher, as there are limits to how quickly she can shut the door. If she got a few more in earlier by having the door more open during high flow than she lost with her limited closing rate, that is a good trade. What she wants is to teach the largest number of students.

Here is a little more information to describe why keeping the door open wide longer is important. In 1978, Bob Glidden raced a Ford Fairmont in Pro Stock for part of the season and never lost in the car. From what I understand, there is a cam aspect to that story. At the time, fast-opening and slow-closing lobes were very popular. He was running one, but an intake master was installed backward when grinding one camshaft, and that was part of what made the Fairmont engine so good.

After Bob sent the cam back at the end of the season, we made many faster-closing designs. Why was faster closing better? First, shutting the door quickly trapped more of the inlet charge. That is simple, but the second part might be more important. When you have a faster-closing ramp, there can be more lift at BDC for the same IVC. This was the magic. Even 20-plus years later, I know engine builders who look at the intake lift at BDC as a way of comparing intake lobe designs. Just like with Mrs. Edwards, closing the door faster can have multiple benefits, but we need to keep the valvetrain stable.

When you start applying what you have learned in these first chapters, keep in mind the critical importance of IVC. With just a few dyno tests while trying different intake centerlines or lash points, you should be able to quickly find the optimal IVC. Going forward, if you don't change the cylinder head ports, intake manifold, exhaust header, or operating range, the best IVC in this engine will be the same for all camshafts.

CHAPTER 7

Wave Tuning

Most performance and racing engine enthusiasts have heard about wave tuning, but there are few good explanations about how it works and even fewer resources that cover how valve events and wave tuning work together. The biggest synergy from the combination of Edelbrock and Comp engineering teams has been working together on combined intake manifold and camshaft designs.

The most commonly known attributes of wave tuning are: 1) longer header or intake runner lengths improve low-end torque and 2) shorter runners improve high-end horsepower. However, there are hardly any mentions that EVO is almost as important as RPM to optimizing header length (as shown in Image 5-24 of Chapter 5) or how all four valve events play an important role.

***Image 7-1:** Valve events, header lengths, engine speed, and intake lengths all work together to move VE far above the early targets of 75 percent. Today, most of the best production engines are near 100 percent in the region around peak torque, even with overlap severely restricted by the startup test (before the catalytic converters light) and other emissions restrictions. A big shout-out to Holley for this awesome April Fools' Day joke, which was made real with the Sky-Ram. The* **Engine Masters** *crew put this on the dyno at Westech Performance with awesome gains at low RPM, but power fell hard past 5,000 rpm.*

Starting at EVO

The key to understanding wave tuning is to focus on pressure spikes or strong dips in the bowl region behind each valve at each event. Because gases always flow from high pressure to low pressure, the resulting pressure waves are used to enhance engine airflow.

Looking back at the PV diagrams from Chapter 5, for both the OEM truck and the Race LS application, EVO occurs while the cylinder pressure is still in the 6- to 10-bar range (over 88 psi). Applications that add power can be significantly higher, and Top Fuel applications are far higher yet. While this pressure can make exhaust valve dynamic control more difficult, using this energy and the resulting pressure wave is our key to pushing VE well beyond 100 percent.

As the exhaust valve opens, a very strong high-pressure wave moves down the exhaust pipe at the speed of sound.

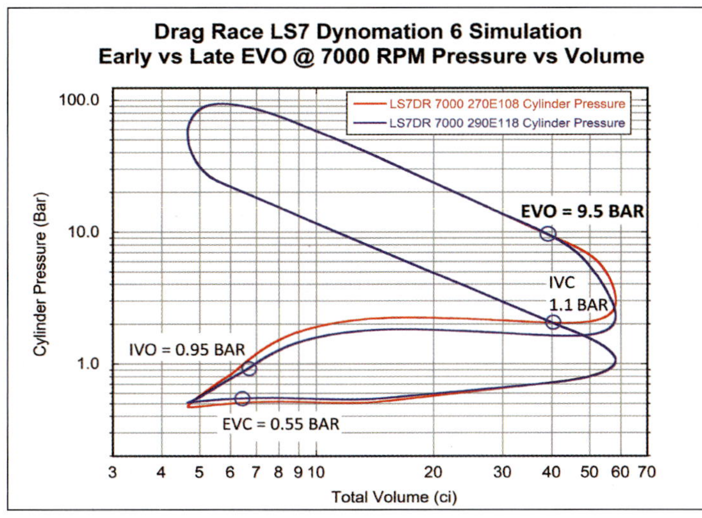

Image 7-2: Of the 4 valve events, 1 occurs at a chamber pressure approaching 10 times the other 4. With the valve event pressures for the Chapter 5 simulation labeled for the earlier EVO 290 exhaust camshaft, note the 9.5-bar pressure at EVO. This is 8.6 times the pressure at IVC, 10 times the pressure at IVO, and more than 17 times the pressure at EVC. No wonder this is our dominant wave tuning event.

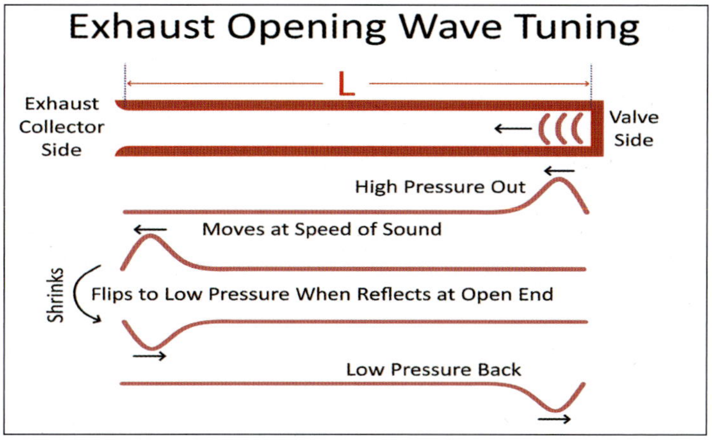

Exhaust Opening Wave Tuning

L

Exhaust Collector Side

Valve Side

High Pressure Out

Moves at Speed of Sound

Shrinks

Flips to Low Pressure When Reflects at Open End

Low Pressure Back

Image 7-4: Getting this shark-fin image of a pressure wave in your mind will change the way you approach camshafts and header systems. The EVO sets the timing of this fin, and the exhaust opening rate in the low- to mid-lift region sets the leading-edge shape. In most bracket-race classes, we use a softer EVO design that is less sensitive to small changes in header length and collector design. In Sprint Car applications, we use a fast EVO that is extremely sensitive to small changes in the header system.

I cannot count the number of hours that Jack Burns and I have discussed shaping this wave form and using it to its full potential, especially regarding the exhaust opening, headers, and collectors. Waves are interesting because when they hit a wall, they bounce back with the same sign, but they flip when they encounter any opening.

Hence, as the high-pressure wave from EVO that easily outruns the mass flow makes it to the opening at the header collector or a step, it is reflected as a flipped and less-intense low-pressure wave. Our job is to set the header lengths so the low-pressure wave returns at the right time to both increased exhaust flow as the piston approaches peak velocity on the way up (around 70 degrees BTDC) and lowers the chamber pressure as the intake valve opens through overlap.

If this is done properly, the pressure in the chamber and exhaust port will be lower than the intake port pressure as the intake valve opens. It is amazing that an engine running at high speed can have flow from the intake port into the chamber some 30- to 50-plus degrees before TDC while the piston races up toward TDC. Also, consider how much more time

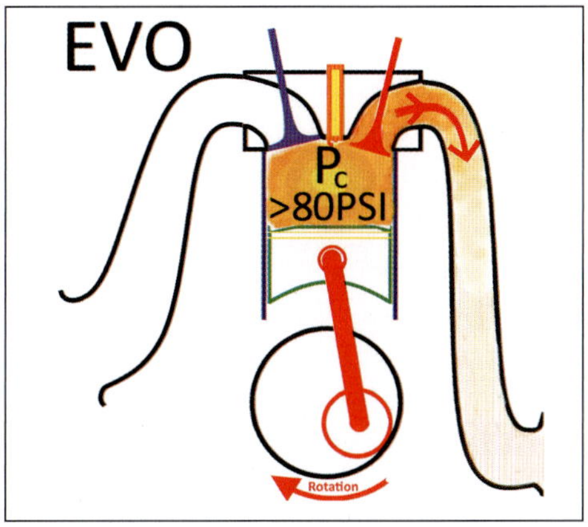

EVO

P_c

>80PSI

Rotation

Image 7-3: Have you ever been driving and had a tire blowout? The pop is rather awesome, even with only 25 to 40 psi of air in the tire. Comparatively, the exhaust opens a chamber at 80 to 150-plus psi. The energy released creates a serious pop. Picture this pressure wave going through the header pipe at the speed of sound toward the collector.

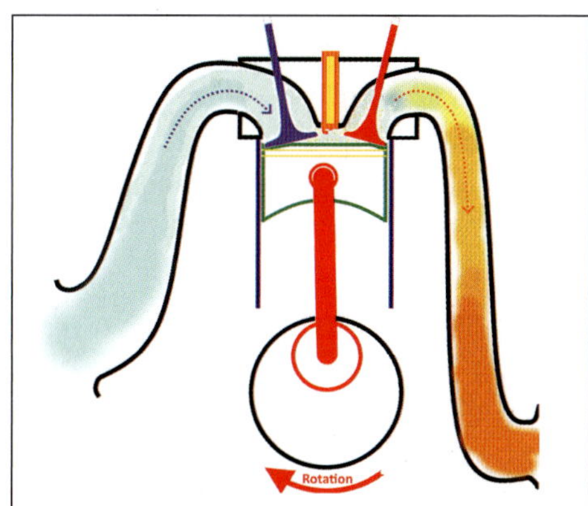

Image 7-5: If the exhaust wave retuned at the correct time, pressure in the exhaust bowl region should have been low enough to draw the chamber down below 1 bar of atmospheric pressure (ATM) at IVO. For about 30-plus degrees, as the piston is still rising, air is being drawn into the low-pressure chamber from the high pressure in the intake bowl.

Image 7-6: Fuel pooled under the carburetors, and there were serious issues as fuel fell out of suspension down these runners on the long track. However, this is cool! (Photo Courtesy Walt Felix)

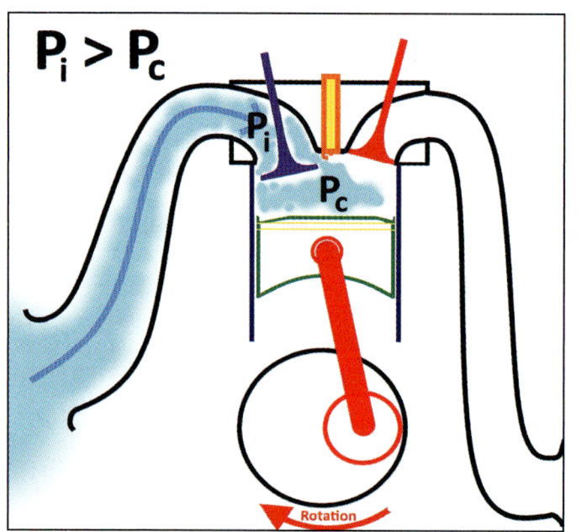

Image 7-7: With a strong signal possible from IVO all the way to 70 degrees ATDC, the intake wave is more like an ocean swell than a shark fin. This can be good, as there should also be a long positive reflection.

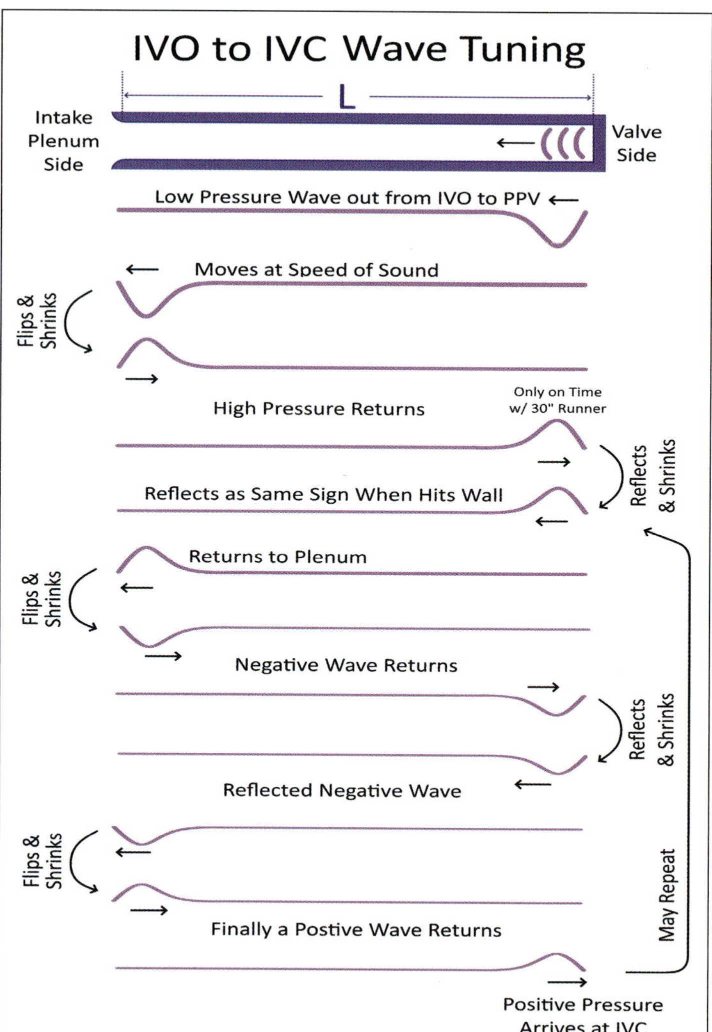

Image 7-8: When we think about the intake and trying to mimic exhaust-wave tuning, that would use the negative wave from the filling and catch the reflected positive wave at IVC (as shown in this diagram). Packaging that first reflection is a bear, so we generally target the third or fifth (or higher) at low RPM.

this gives the intake port to fill the cylinder at high RPM. Using wave tuning, intake flow is started well before TDC instead of waiting until peak piston velocity around 70 degrees after TDC. This allows us to open the IVO much earlier than without wave tuning. In fact, most unrestricted race engines are more limited by piston-to-valve constraints in the combustion chamber than otherwise opening the intake too soon in their operating range.

Tuning the header length correctly for both the desired RPM and EVO so that the first reflected negative wave peak will arrive near the overlap region (between IVO and EVC) is the first key to wave tuning. Not only does the EVO point matter, but the shape of the exhaust opening ramp can also drastically alter the shape of the resulting positive pressure wave.

In many Sprint Car applications, an exhaust profile that opens the exhaust valve as fast as possible is used. This results in a longer power stroke (more low-end torque) but also creates a very sharp pressure wave. This sharp wave requires more care and tuning with the header lengths. In a typical Sprint Car engine shop, there are several headers and different collector configurations to try with each camshaft and track combination.

However, in most Sportsman drag-race applications, smoother exhaust profiles are used. These hurt the low-speed torque far less than one might imagine, and the softer exhaust opening creates a more rounded pressure wave in the header. This waveform may not tune as sharply at any one RPM, but it makes the engine far less sensitive to small changes of the header or collector. Not only does the waveform change the header sensitivity, but it also changes the tone of the exhaust note.

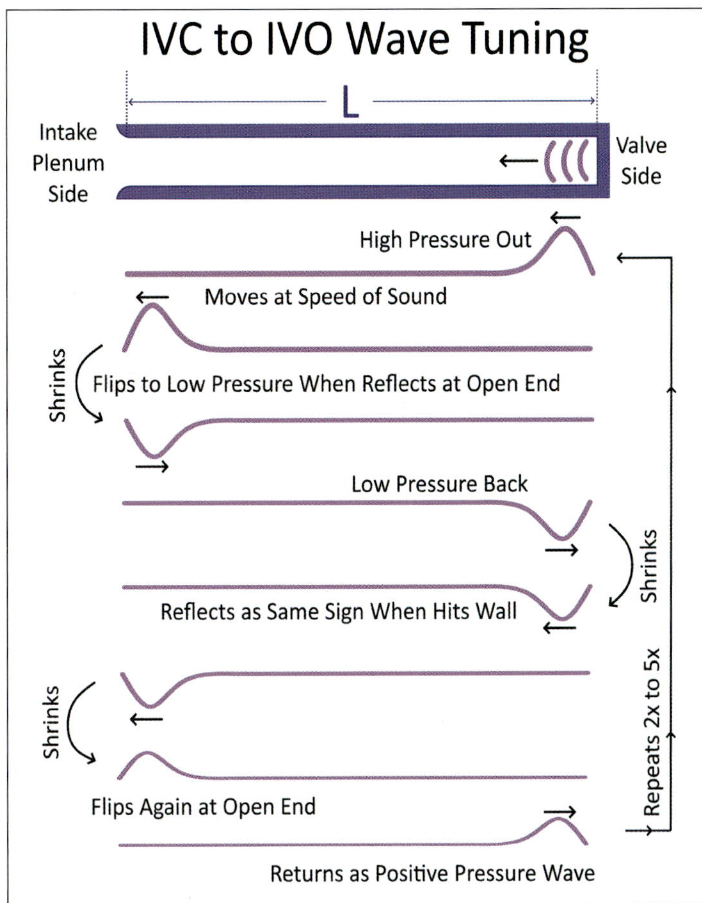

Image 7-9: The stronger intake wave is from IVC all the way back around to IVO. As the intake closes, there can be a rather strong signal from either the piston rising or the onrushing air slamming into the closing intake valve. This is nothing like the 80 psi at EVO (8 psi is common). I enjoy thinking about wave tuning providing more boost at IVC than many street forced-induction systems. Wave tuning can help boosted engines too. The extra pressure at IVC bouncing back and forth is the target in this diagram. The goal is to time it to arrive as a positive pressure wave at IVO to help push the intake charge inside while the header creates negative chamber pressure.

Optimizing Intake Port Length

The biggest difference in intake tuning and exhaust tuning is that there really are no good ways to use the primary reflected wave on the intake. Chrysler's Ramchargers group worked on this in the 1950s and made a production primary-wave intake for the 1960–1964 cross-ram 383 and 413 intake manifolds. These had 30-plus-inch primary lengths that placed the carburetors over the opposite wheel. With all of this length, the fuel fell out of suspension and caused numerous issues.

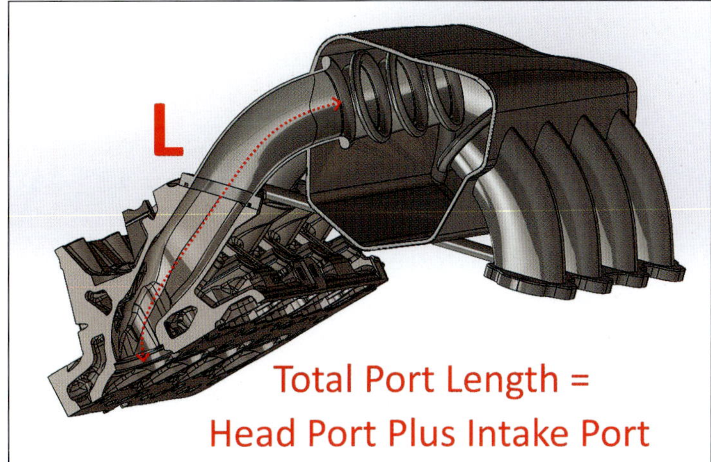

Image 7-10: When we discuss intake runner length, remember that we are really discussing from the backside of the intake valve to the runner entry. You may have a head that incorporates a long or short section of this total port, but the air should not care which part it is inside along its path.

It was difficult to make a runner that long that was not restrictive. Holley made the Sky-Ram as a joke, but crazy taper would need to be added to keep it from being flow restrictive on the port walls. Typically, instead of the primary reflection, intake systems operate on orders or multiple reflections of the reflective wave.

This gives the intake designer some choices on design. Even at the same RPM, you may see a circle-track system that is longer, designed for the second reflection, whereas a drag-race system might be short to be optimized around the third reflection. This can be confusing for some engine builders, as there will be an intermediate length that is perfectly wrong for that same RPM with a negative wave that arrives when you want a positive wave.

When an engine properly uses wave tuning, the camshaft events work in conjunction with well-sized and proper-length runners, which often results in 110 to 120 percent VE. I'm not really trying to push you toward Dynomation 6 or any other engine modeling software, but these platforms are the best way to visualize what's going on inside the runners.

There are two wave tuning opportunities with the intake runner. The first is to use the negative pressure wave from the exhaust along with the negative pressure dip from the piston dropping after TDC. Together, these create a long negative wave that reflects as a positive wave. Because of packaging, we generally catch the

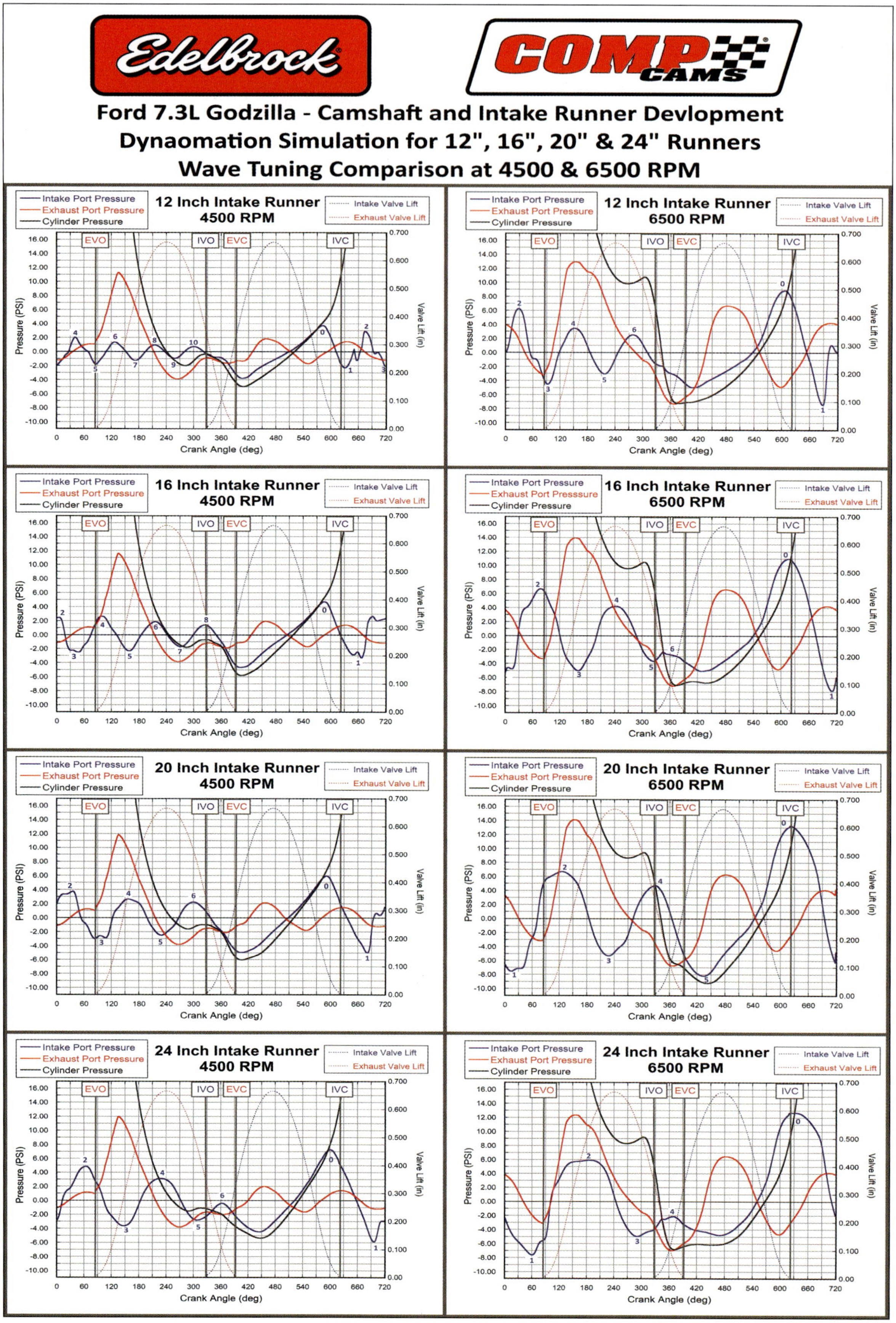

Ford 7.3L Godzilla - Camshaft and Intake Runner Devlopment
Dynaomation Simulation for 12", 16", 20" & 24" Runners
Wave Tuning Comparison at 4500 & 6500 RPM

12 Inch Intake Runner 4500 RPM

12 Inch Intake Runner 6500 RPM

16 Inch Intake Runner 4500 RPM

16 Inch Intake Runner 6500 RPM

20 Inch Intake Runner 4500 RPM

20 Inch Intake Runner 6500 RPM

24 Inch Intake Runner 4500 RPM

24 Inch Intake Runner 6500 RPM

Image 7-11: Jeff Krangnes and I spent hours looking at these intake simulations and comparing them to our dyno test with different runner lengths. We ran several cams on the dyno with different intake designs too. Here is the 4,500 and 6,500, as that was in the region of peak torque and peak power with what I believe will be a popular camshaft. This engine rewards us when we catch one of those blue wave peaks arriving between IVO and TDC in the model and the real world.

second, third, or fourth positive wave, as we cannot make a reasonable runner long enough to catch the first.

The second reflection is stronger than the third because some energy is lost at each reflection. If the positive wave is timed correctly, it is common to see 4- to 16-plus-psi pressure above ambient behind the valve near intake closing in racing applications. This combination of the reflected high-pressure wave and the momentum of the entering air work together like boost to continue filling the cylinder as the captured volume shrinks as the piston rises to allow the following: 1) more filling, 2) a later IVC, and 3) higher cylinder pressure at IVC than possible without optimized wave tuning.

Regardless of which order is caught or missed at IVC as the piston rises and the intake valve shuts, there is always a positive pressure spike in the intake bowl as the intake closes. The length of the intake is set so that this positive wave can be reflected and used at IVO.

Unlike the other wave-tuning examples where we used the inverse reflection (in the IVC to IVO case), we want to use the positive pressure from IVC at IVO, so we try to catch the even number reflections instead of the odd. Going back to the Dynomation 6 simulation, we recently made a good model of our Ford Godzilla test engine. After running a few prototype intakes and camshafts, we experimentally found a length that was extremely good in the 3,000- to 7,000-rpm window.

Image 7-12: A few years ago, FAST introduced various intake runner length options for the LSXR intake. Selecting the best runner length for your application is not only dependent on the RPM but the cam timing is also very important. This intake provides a wide range of lengths, so I run the blue runners in my road-race engine. Looking back at the Image 7-11, you can see why you want to optimize the length for your camshaft and RPM range.

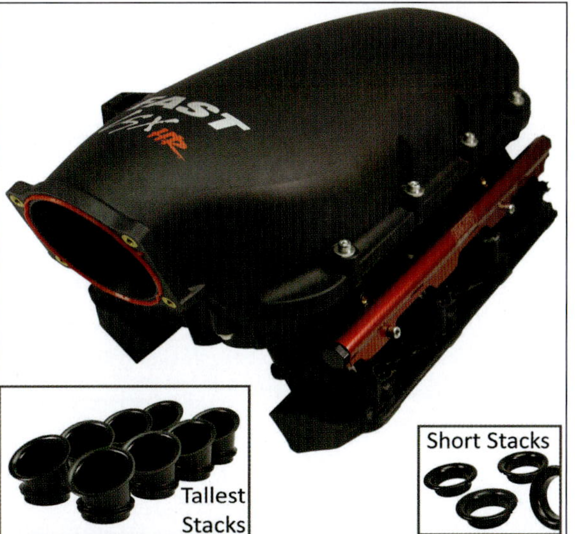

Image 7-13: The FAST LSXR intake has most of the runner length made into the base, but very much like what you might see for a Sprint Car or IMSA DP intake, we incorporated three stack or bell-mouth attachment lengths that fit under the lid. This allows the engine builder to tune the intake around the camshaft and engine speed, but most street applications benefit from the longest ones on the lower left.

Image 7-14: Note the different stacks and camshafts on the bench while we tested the early LSXHR intake manifold. These parts 100 percent work together or don't work at all.

Going back to Dynomation, we plugged in the camshaft and ran a sweep of intake runners with steps from 12 to 24 inches in 250-rpm increments.

From these simulations, shown in Image 7-11, the exhaust-bowl pressure (P_x) is plotted in red, combustion-chamber pressure (P_c) is in black, and intake-bowl pressure (P_i) is in blue with the test valve lift curves at both 4,500 and 6,500 rpm. This is shown for 4-inch-runner-length steps. There is a lot of information in this graph, but pay the most attention to the intake pressure wave that starts at IVC and reflects all the way around to the next IVO.

Note that certain lengths produce 3 to 5 psi positive pressure in the intake bowl at IVO. We already discussed using wave tuning to push more air in on the closing side, but this is at the opening. Using this wave boost with the negative pressure in the exhaust from that reflected

Image 7-15: Some people get sick of all the LS swaps, but swapping a Gen III into almost any car or truck is awesome from a performance and durability standpoint. Unfortunately, the early truck intakes are ugly, and they are very restrictive. The later ones are not much better looking. Going to an RHS short-runner sheet-metal intake makes the engine look better, but you need a different intake closing point. Otherwise, the low-end torque drops like a rock. RHS introduced these cam, intake, and throttle-body kits that bring even the very low-RPM torque back above stock while adding more than 100 hp above the stock LM7. The cam and intake need to be developed together.

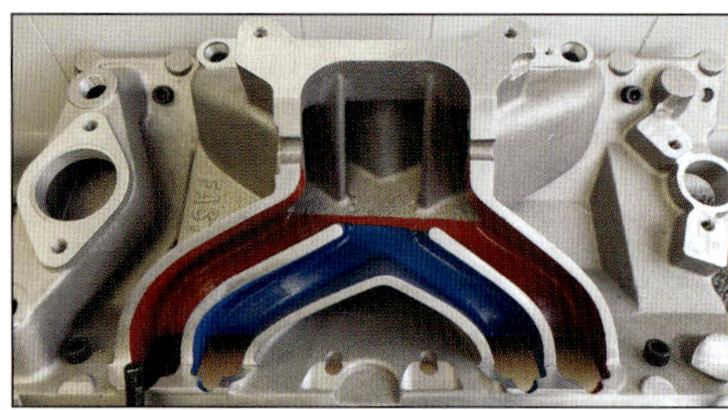

Image 7-16: Here, we see how much longer the outer cylinder runners are (red) and how much shorter the inner cylinder runners are (blue). We expect that both lengths run best with uniquely optimized camshaft events. There is sometimes a benefit to having different runner lengths in race applications that restrict peak torque and peak power (balance of performance). By tuning each cylinder to a unique torque curve shape (some tuning earlier and some later), the total can be extremely flat.

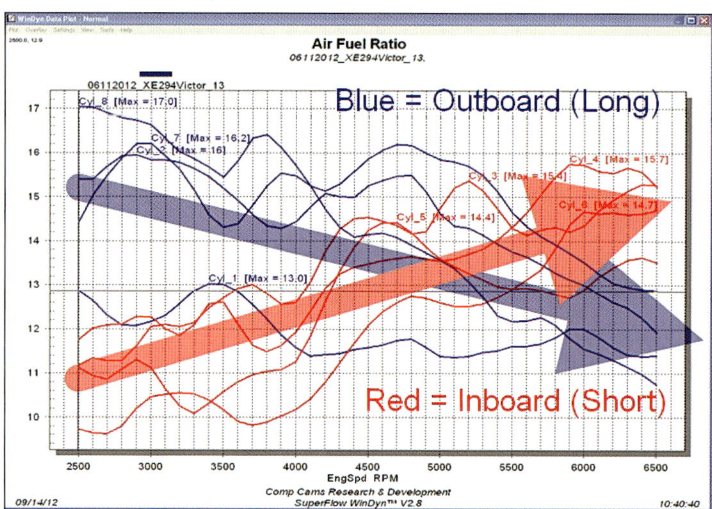

Image 7-17: With different runner lengths, you need to alter the fuel and spark for each configuration. Running two different runner lengths with the same cam timing tends to rob air to the cylinders that are working best, but the heavier fuel does not always follow. Hence, with a carburetor, throttle-body EFI, or port EFI, we see the long runners lean at low RPM and rich at high RPM with most single 4-barrel-style intakes. On this carburetor test, Cylinder 1 has some sort of identity crisis and is fat everywhere.

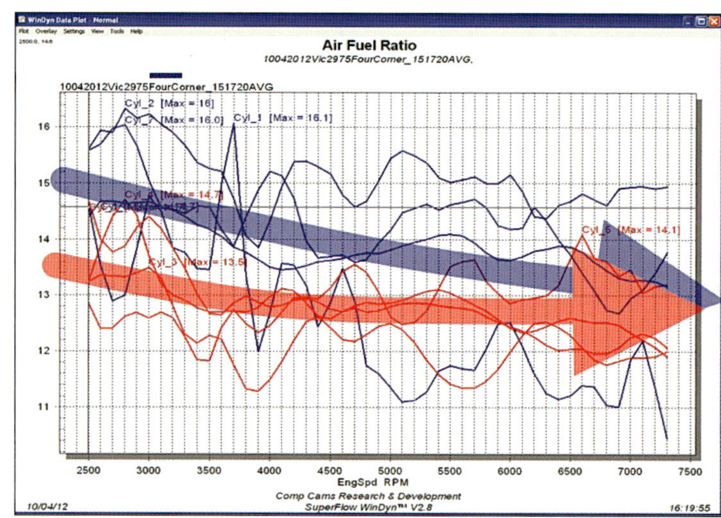

Image 7-18: By tweaking the cam specs to equal air demand, we have made the inboard and outboard cylinders closely match air demand throughout the dyno pull. This is typically worth about 5 to 10 hp, as you can run all the cylinders closer to their optimum air-fuel ratio without running a few dangerously lean.

Images 7-19 and 7-20: On the Eagle and Apache Hemi engines, Dodge added a flapper valve in the intake that opens at a certain RPM and drastically shortens the length traveled for the reflected wave. This results in a very long runner at low RPM and a rather short one at high RPM. Compared to something like the aluminum intake introduced on the SRT 6.1L, this intake design is almost 15 ft-lbs low and plus 15 hp at very high RPM. The only better active intakes have a belt drive up front.

wave, we create the pressure differential required to start a fresh charge into the chamber well before the ideal Otto cycle is possible.

A Systems Approach to Wave Tuning

Wave tuning started by using the tremendous exhaust energy at EVO to initiate pressure waves. Then, the intake and exhaust systems were allowed to communicate and phase together during overlap. Using this tuning is exactly why today's naturally aspirated (NA) unrestricted race engines fill 10 to 20 percent better than the ideal case. Unfortunately, one component in the system is often believed to be independent of the others. You cannot properly design an intake runner without knowing the valve timing, and you need to have a pretty good idea of header configuration.

Unequal-Length Intake Runners

Most single-carburetor V-8 intakes have at least two runner lengths, often more than 2 inches different in length. This is most easily seen in the section view of a single plane, but there is a larger difference in the outer versus inner cylinders on most dual-plane designs.

Knowing this difference, the normal technique for pre-EFI NASCAR engines is to close the intake valve approximately 2 to 4 degrees later for the longer-runner outer cylinders. Moving the EVO a bit earlier on those cylinders helps equal out the air demand per cylinder throughout the RPM range to result in more consistent air-fuel ratios from cylinder to cylinder.

Another option is to change the length of the runners. The engineers at Dodge did a great job with a rather simple system to allow the Eagle and Apache Hemi intakes to act long at low speed and short at high speed. Nick Smithburg constructed a more attractive variable-length system for the *Engine Masters* competition. The best way to make a naturally aspirated engine tune across a wide RPM range is with an adjustable intake runner.

Image 7-21: This is Nick Smithburg's 2017 **Engine Masters** ***competition entry with the variable stack lengths that move up or down with stepper motor control. What an awesome modern build of a classic Hemi.***

MOVING VALVE EVENTS

Now that we have covered what is going on at each valve event, based on both the filling and emptying and wave tuning points of view, we will focus on how to move these events. The tools covered in this chapter are some of the most useful ideas to offer any professional engine builder. We start with the basics and then move to how to test any engine on our dyno as we dial in toward the best possible camshaft.

Standard Optimization Techniques

When developing a new line of camshafts or starting with a new engine, have a matrix of similar camshafts to test each valve event independently. This approach sometimes requires a benchtop full of camshafts and is the best practice for professional race teams. However, before you spend a week on the dyno swapping cams, a few simple tests will help you quickly and inexpensively optimize valve timing.

Advancing a Camshaft

Every four-stroke engine wants to tell you where to put the valve timing. You can spend a fortune on textbooks, modeling software, classes, and advice and never get as far as if you asked your engine what it likes.

With so many adjustable timing sets and quick-access options available on the dyno or in testing, your first approach is to advance and retard your camshaft. To do this, you need to know how much piston-to-valve clearance is available. With an optimized piston and chamber, there probably will not be much room. However, if you have even a little room to move the camshaft, always start with this approach.

When you advance a camshaft, all four timing events move. If we take an example camshaft that has a 115-degree LSA with 1 degree of advance and move it to 5 degrees of advance, the intake lobe centerline moves from 114 to 110 degrees after TDC, and the exhaust centerline moves from 116 to 120 degrees before TDC (as shown in Image 8-6).

This four-degree advance moves all four events 4 degrees earlier. We already looked closely at PV diagrams to see how this four-degree earlier EVO helps reduce exhaust-pumping losses at higher RPM at the expense of a shorter power stroke and less torque low. However, the four-degree earlier IVC is more important and will help the low-RPM performance because of the earlier closed door.

Images 8-1 and 8-2: Sometimes asking your engine where it wants the cam is just a few keystrokes away. Today, many engines come with computer-controlled phaser systems, such as this L92 unit. You typically want to run a limiter in a performance application because swinging a cam with intake and exhaust lobes attached will always rob clearance from one side or the other, and about 20 crank degrees of adjustability is needed instead of the 50 to 62 that is found in stock phasers.

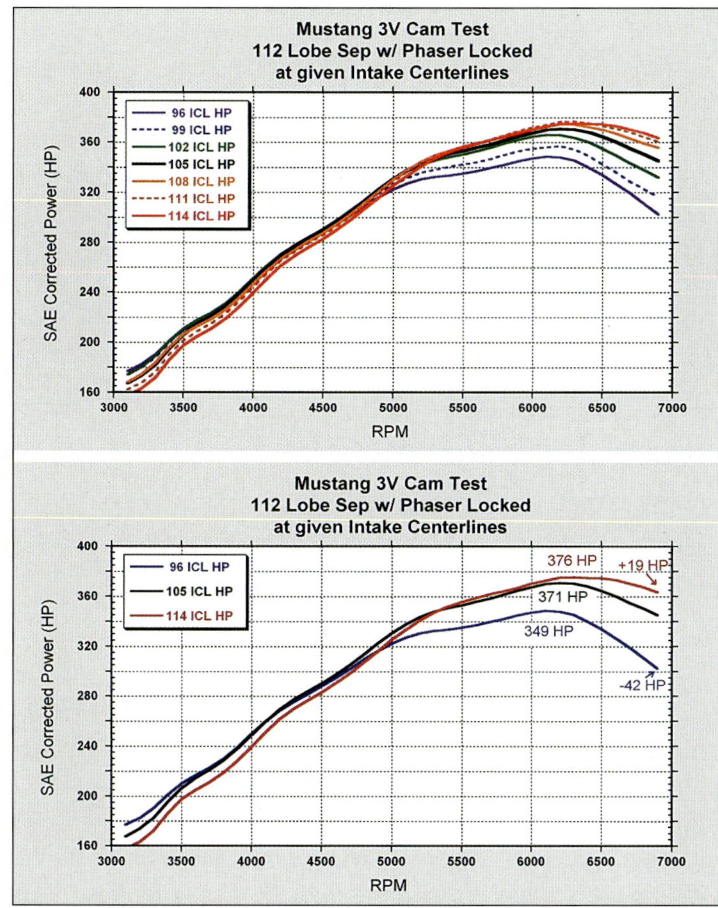

Image 8-3: Letting the phaser chase the intake closing point and intake wave on this 3V Ford modular engine picked up the low-end torque about 15 ft-lbs and the high-end power 19 hp (compared to the best overall fixed-cam position). I can't imagine why anyone would want to eliminate the variable-cam systems on a street engine. The bottom graph is just the top graph uncluttered. When tuning a phaser system on the dyno, we run a fixed-step test and then map the phaser for the best position at each RPM using something like the top graph.

Image 8-5: There are numerous offset crank keys and bushing kits, timing sets, easy access covers, and belt drives on the market today. One important note is that the pin never drives the camshaft. A single 7/16-inch x 20 bolt at 80 ft-lbs torque provides over 10,000 pounds of clamping force. The 3/8-inch x 24 bolts at 45 ft-lbs provide 6,900 pounds of clamping force each. When you see a failed dowel pin, it was the clamping that failed, not the pin. You can remove the pin altogether to degree the camshaft if you properly tighten the drive bolts.

Likewise, shutting the intake door to the chamber earlier will hurt at high RPM because there is more charge momentum and less time to fill the chamber. With the added 4 degrees of advance, the overlap triangle is shifted toward the exhaust side with the intake opening 4 degrees earlier and the exhaust closing 4 degrees later. This tends to push more exhaust into the intake tract at low RPM but can let the cylinder fill

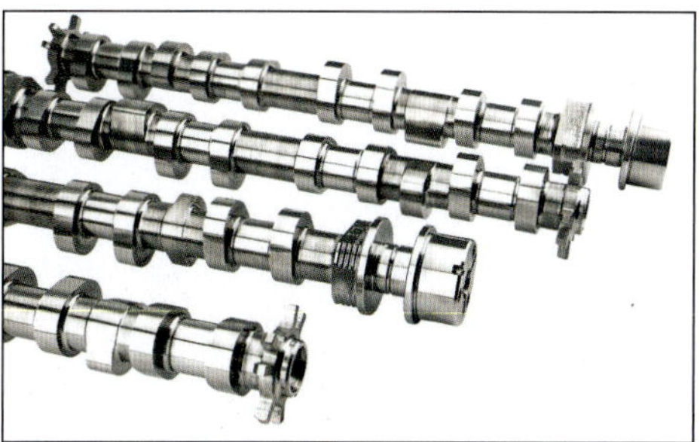

Image 8-4: With the 3V, the exhaust often moves the wrong direction, as we saw how an earlier EVO helps at high RPM. The Ford Coyote eliminated this issue by giving separate control of the intake and exhaust camshafts. In the latest form, with either the GT350 or 2018-and-newer heads, the Coyote is a truly world-class performance platform.

better at near peak torque, as there is going to be more intake valve lift at 70 ATDC with the advanced intake opening.

What we ask the engine when we advance and retard the camshaft is not, "What is perfect?" but, "Which direction should I head?" and, "How sensitive are you?"

The downside of trying to optimize a combination by advancing or retarding the camshaft is that all four events are moved. It might love one change, hate another, and have mixed sensitivity to the other two events. In this case, the engine might not appear very sensitive, but vast improvements can be made if you ask better questions.

Changing the Lash

Moving from advance to lash helps ask a more specific question, but it is only available in solid adjustment applications. Sorry, hydraulics. As shown in Image 8-7, even going from 0.016-inch lash to 0.024-inch lash does not move the valve events as much as our four-degree advance swing. In fact, every 0.004-inch lash is only one degree per side at 0.050-inch valve lift.

However, what you gain from lash is an ability to ask follow-up questions to what the engine told you when the camshaft was advanced or retarded. For instance, if you advanced the camshaft on the dyno and it did not fall off much up top, take that advanced position and try a modified lash loop. Generally, a lash loop starts on the intake side.

After running the suggested lash, first try 0.004 inch tighter on the

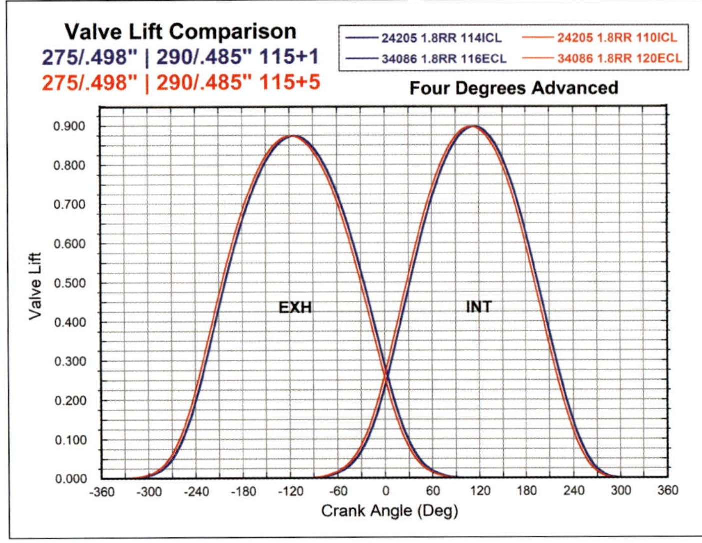

Image 8-6: *If you advance a camshaft and the valve events are almost optimized, the dyno curve should look like you stuck a pin in the torque curve somewhere between peak torque and peak power and pivoted the torque curve a few degrees about that pin. If you lose more or less than with a pivot at either end, something, most likely EVO, was off. On a few occasions, I have seen the exhaust opening so far off that as we advanced a camshaft, the power increased past peak. In a case like this, the original IVC is typically too early for the RPM and the EVO was much too late.*

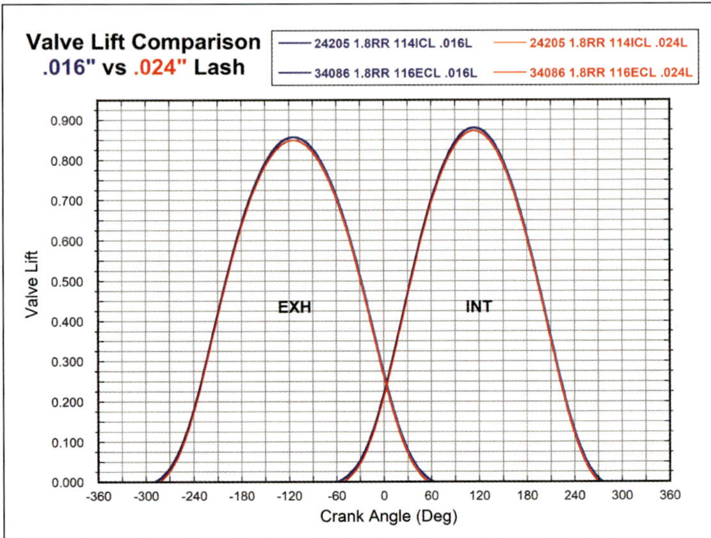

Image 8-7: *These lash changes will be more difficult to interpret than advance and retard. Along with the timing points, you are always changing the dynamics of the valve motion when you change lash. In fact, you might need to reduce your maximum engine speed with the looser lash test. Be aware that exhaust lash will change the high-pressure exhaust wave shape that initiates wave tuning. Even with those limitations, valve lash loops are a great tool to provide a good direction on your next camshaft grind and confirm what you believe what the advance and retard test might have been saying.*

Lash Effect on *Valve* Durations

24205 (MMO 275/.498" Tappet)

Lash	0.016"	0.020"	0.024"	Approximate Change Per 0.004" Lash
Dur @ .010"	318	314	310	4 Deg
Dur @ .050"	287	285	283	2 Deg
Dur @ .200"	232	231	230	1 Deg
Dur @ .400"	183	182	181	1 Deg

Image 8-8: *Even 0.004-inch lash can make a 4-degree change at the lash point, but this change acts more like the 2-degree change at 0.050 inch because there is very little mass flow at low lift. However, it makes everything quicker low and everything that is relatively fatter high, which can be misleading if you try to separate how the engine responds to events versus the curve shape. Although, it is the easiest and quickest change to make at the track or on the dyno as Jeff Smith demonstrates.*

intake. Then, try 0.004 inch looser on the intake if tighter was worse in the desired range. With those results, use the best intake setting and try 0.004-inch-tighter exhaust followed by 0.004-inch-looser exhaust.

For the case where the advanced setting was better when it was high, change the loop to start with 0.004-inch tighter on the exhaust because the engine already hinted that it might like an earlier EVO. After that, try a looser intake next to see if it is off.

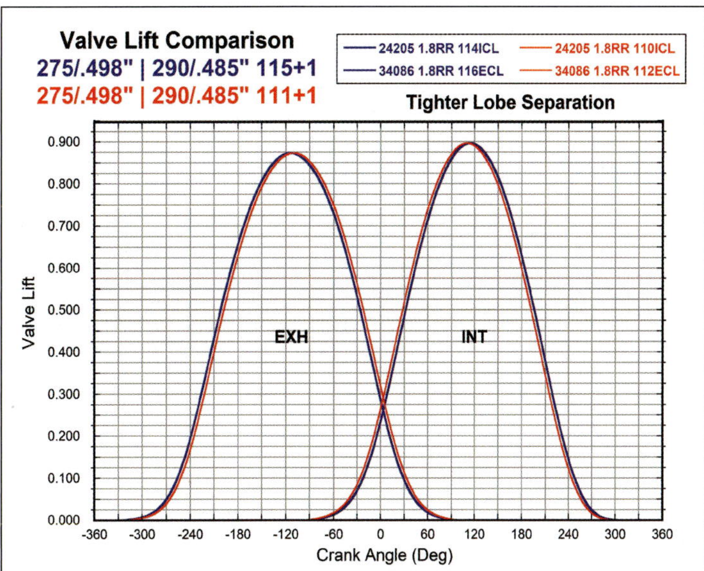

Image 8-10: The negative aspect of only changing the LSA is that we really don't have any idea which of those multiple changes the engine responded to most strongly. If we have already run the baseline cam advanced and retarded and run a lash loop, perhaps we can do the same test matrix on the tighter LSA version and gain more clarity about which events are most sensitive.

Changing the Lobe Separation

I do not generally recommend the next two changes, but they are extremely common. Before I show you what I recommend, I want to show what I don't recommend so that you can see why these changes often lead people astray.

In Image 8-10, we have the same baseline camshaft with a 115-degree LSA versus a 111-degree LSA, both with 1 degree advance. Like advance, this moves all four valve events. The earlier IVC is the dominant event to bring both peak torque and peak power to a lower RPM. The next most important event is EVO, and here it is later, which should increase performance from peak torque down at a cost of higher speed power. With the tighter LSA, there is increased overlap. If the engine has clearance, this helps improve wave tuning to make it stronger in the optimized region, especially if the engine is not flow restricted on the intake or exhaust.

For these reasons, we see why people say that tight-LSA camshafts are peakier. The increased overlap will have some cost at very low RPM because of reversion outside of the tuned window, not to mention some detriment to low-speed vacuum and throttle response. However, there is more of the lope sound with added overlap that I like.

Most race engines are so well tuned with their intake and header lengths that they will always respond positively to increased overlap with more airflow (improved VE). What keeps lobe separations wider on unrestricted race engines is typically piston-to-valve clearance.

Dean Harvey (who handled most Pro Stock accounts at Comp from the late 1990s through 2021) and I used to ask Pro Stock engine builders to set up one test engine with deeper valve pockets so that we could run cam advance sweeps. Whenever we did this, the engine pointed us to more duration and tighter LSA. However, even though the airflow was higher with increased overlap, the baseline engines with less relief and a more compact combustion chamber need less timing and ran better upstairs. The development engine with the larger, tighter cam and deep pockets didn't burn the fuel as well.

The problem with deep pockets is they require ugly domes to get back lost compression. For most applications, you cannot achieve the compression needed with deep reliefs without making the piston and chamber ugly, thereby hurting BSFC and combustion efficiency more than airflow and VE were helped with the increased overlap.

I wish there was a good way around this, but at some point, you need to limit your overlap. This may be because of either mechanical limits or idle manner and low-RPM response. Because of these limits, lobe separation becomes not a target for performance but a result of other limitations as you optimize your EVO and IVC around a given overlap target.

Changing Duration

After lash and lobe separation, you probably know exactly where I am headed with changes in duration. The intake or exhaust can be changed independently of the other when grinding a new camshaft, but let's first look at the graph of an

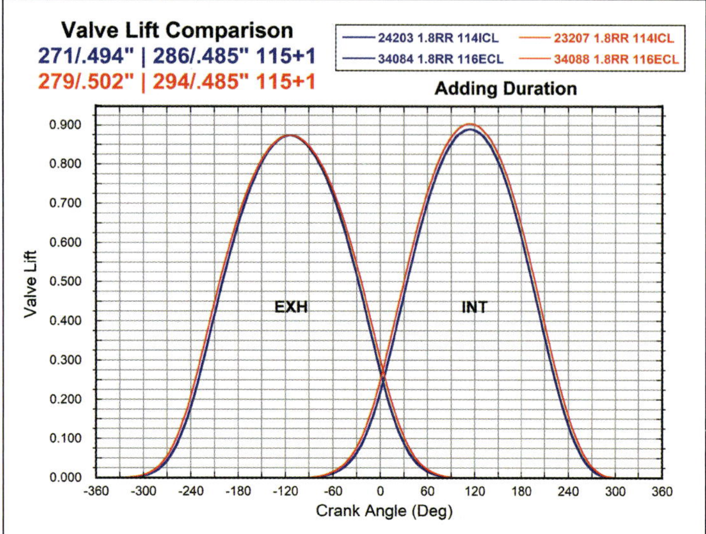

Image 8-11:* *Eight degrees seems like a huge change. However, this moves each valve timing event exactly the same distance as we achieved when we advanced the camshaft 4 degrees. In fact, the two opening events (EVO and IVO) of the plus-8-degree larger duration camshaft are in the same places they were for the baseline camshaft in the advanced position. The two closings also moved 4 degrees in the opposite direction from when we advanced the camshaft.

8-degree step on both sides with the same lobe separation and advance in Image 8-11.

The reason we typically see this 8-degree change in duration make a larger difference on the dyno than a 4-degree advance change is because the area under the curve has been significantly changed as well as the valve events. With more duration, each port is given more time in the high-lift and high-flow regions to fill or empty the cylinder, so the engine responds to both the events, and the increased flow potential duration is increased.

While we are on duration, most competition race engines tend to run slightly less duration than the maximum power created over the intended operating range. This certainly holds true in applications that see throttle changes (road race and circle track come most quickly to mind, but this is the case in foot-brake drag cars as well) as less overlap, a slightly late EVO, and slightly early IVC all work together to increase part-throttle performance and increase port velocities. Hence, if a 4-degree-smaller camshaft is very close on the dyno to a 4-degree-larger grind, you generally have happier drivers with the smaller camshaft.

Improved Optimization Techniques

If we want to optimize all four valve timing events, we need to learn how to specify camshaft changes that move only one event at a time. The first reaction for most is that they could never afford to make one change at a time.

However, if you have already tested various advance and lash settings, you probably have a very good idea about the questions to ask next. Knowing that IVC is the most important event, we may have that dialed in quite well from our initial testing. Because overlap is likely dictated by other factors, that may already be well set as well.

We will go through how to test each event independently, but I will start at EVO because it is the event I typically isolate first. After optimizing EVO independently, go back to see how IVC responds. Then, play with IVO and EVC if there is space, time, money, and vacuum to spare.

Moving Exhaust Opening

If you have never moved one valve timing event at a time, the changes required seem a bit intimidating. To make this easier, tables are provided in this chapter with the camshaft changes required for each 4-degree adjustment. Looking at Image 8-12, to advance the EVO 4 degrees, the exhaust duration must

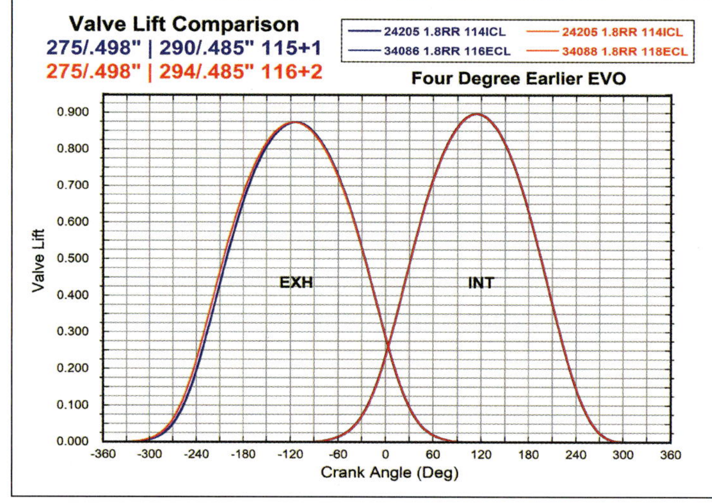

Image 8-12: It is very difficult to guess or model exactly how this will cumulatively change the power curve, as there is a tremendous pressure and temperature gradient at EVO. However, instead of guessing, it is easy to use this technique and ask the engine how it responds to the independent early EVO.

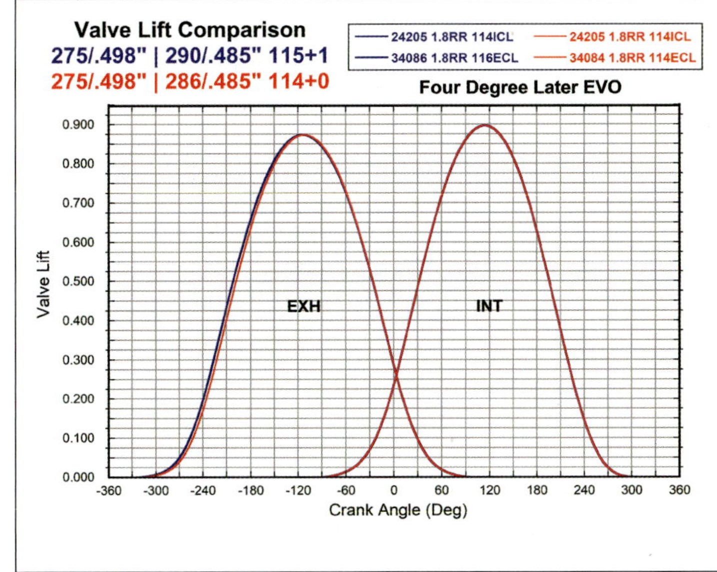

Image 8-13: When looking at this 4-degree-later EVO, we need to understand that any engine is extremely numb to whether the exhaust valve reaches peak lift at 116 or 114 degrees BTDC. However, your engine will be very responsive to how the valve opening is delayed by 4 degrees in that 300 to 180 degrees BTDC region. Pay attention to events over LSA and centerlines.

increase 4 degrees and both the lobe separation and advance must increase 1 degree. This leaves the intake centerline at the same angle while the exhaust centerline is moved out 2 degrees.

By moving the ECL out 2 degrees and increasing the duration 4 degrees, the opening side is moved out a full 4 degrees while the closing side falls in at the same location. Because the intake lobe and centerline remain unchanged, this new combination isolates as a single-valve timing event (as shown in Image 8-13).

Thinking about the PV diagram example, we know exactly how the earlier EVO will hurt the top loop at high RPM but reduce the bottom pumping loop area at higher RPM. Also consider how this earlier EVO will alter wave tuning.

Because cylinder pressure decreases during the power stroke, opening the exhaust earlier will always result in more energy in the positive pressure wave that heads down the header tubes after EVO. This earlier opening will alter when the primary negative reflection arrives back at the exhaust valve and chamber earlier. Together, this means a stronger wave will arrive back earlier in the exhausts stroke or overlap region for most of the tuned RPM range.

Likewise, we can go 4 degrees smaller on exhaust duration along with -1 LSA and +1 advance and independently move the exhaust opening 4 degrees later. This creates the equal

Advancing Exhaust Opening
Moving the EVO 4 Degrees Earlier

Characteristic	Change
Intake Duration	Same
Exhaust Duration	+4 Degrees
Lobe Separation	+1 Degree
Advance	+1 Degree
Intake Centerline	Same
Exhaust Centerline	+2 Degrees

Delaying Exhaust Opening
Moving the EVO 4 Degrees Later

Characteristic	Change
Intake Duration	Same
Exhaust Duration	-4 Degrees
Lobe Separation	-1 Degree
Advance	-1 Degree
Intake Centerline	Same
Exhaust Centerline	-2 Degrees

Image 8-14: Think of this as a cheat sheet to change just EVO. If you want to move it just 2 degrees, move it half as much.

Advancing Intake Closing
Moving the IVC 4 Degrees Earlier

Characteristic	Change
Intake Duration	-4 Degrees
Exhaust Duration	Same
Lobe Separation	-1 Degree
Advance	+1 Degree
Intake Centerline	-2 Degrees
Exhaust Centerline	Same

Delaying Intake Closing
Moving the IVC 4 Degrees Later

Characteristic	Change
Intake Duration	+4 Degrees
Exhaust Duration	Same
Lobe Separation	+1 Degree
Advance	-1 Degree
Intake Centerline	+2 Degrees
Exhaust Centerline	Same

Image 8-15: Like the previous chart with EVO, this makes the same 4-degree changes in IVC. I am more likely to divide these numbers by 2 and move the IVC by only 2 degrees.

but opposite effects of everything listed above. If the engine really does not like the earlier EVO move, there is a good chance it will like the opposite direction of a later EVO.

Camshafts with Weird Specifications

At some point, almost everyone has looked at someone's camshaft specs for a specific example (perhaps a 2-barrel carbureted circle-track or *Engine Masters* competition engine) and thought, "Those are weird!" If the engine is successful, there is an extremely high likelihood the methods we have outlined have been used. The engine builder likely advanced and retarded a baseline camshaft on the dyno, played with lash, and ordered a new camshaft that moved the valve event(s) in the direction that worked best.

When you start going down this road, trust that the engine never reads a specification card. I have designed enough asymmetric lobes to know that every engine is numb to exactly where peak lift occurs. Cylinder head port flow is flat for the last 0.050 to 0.100 inch of valve lift, so peak lift can be moved by several degrees in that lift range without changing the profile much lower in the lift curve. By tweaking profile nose symmetry, I have made two camshafts at 102 LSA and 112 LSA that were indistinguishable from each other on the dyno.

Put aside any preconceived notion about what lobe separation or duration is needed for a given application or engine characteristic. Using this approach, you might wind up with a 102 LSA camshaft in a 106 ICL. You also might move out to a 124 LSA in at 120 ICL. If you get stuck thinking the engine responds directly to LSA or duration, you lose the ability to optimize each event.

However, if you ask your engine good questions about the valve events it likes, pay careful attention to its response and follow where it leads to open a new path to move toward extraordinary performance.

Moving Intake Closing

As discussed earlier, you probably had a good idea of where the optimal intake closing should be after advancing or retarding the baseline camshaft and running a lash loop. However, now that the exhaust opening is optimized, the wave tuning may be stronger, and it is wise to verify the best intake closing point.

You could go either direction on IVC first, but you should have some idea either from running a lash loop on the intake or retesting +/-2 advance with the optimized exhaust camshaft. If an earlier intake closing is believed to have more potential, a camshaft can be ground with -4 degrees at 0.050 inch on the intake, the same exhaust as ran best, -1 LSA and +1 advance. This moves the intake centerline in 2 degrees and intake closing 4 degrees earlier while leaving the same exhaust centerline and events (as shown in Image 8-16). The opposite changes can be made with duration, LSA, and advance

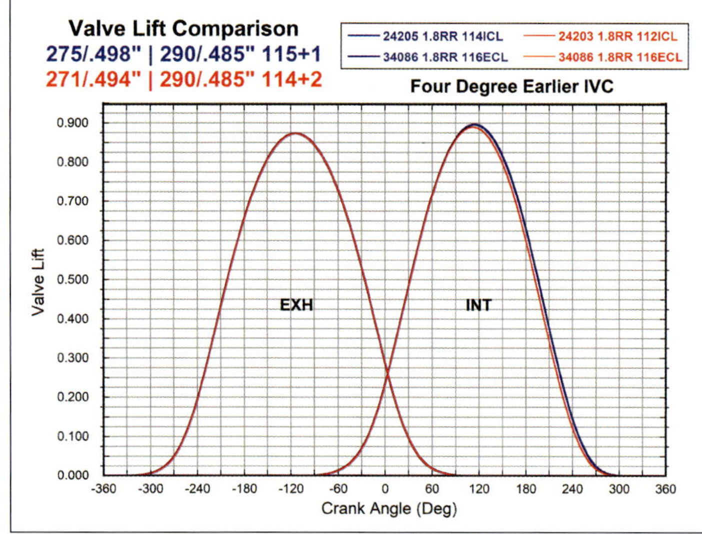

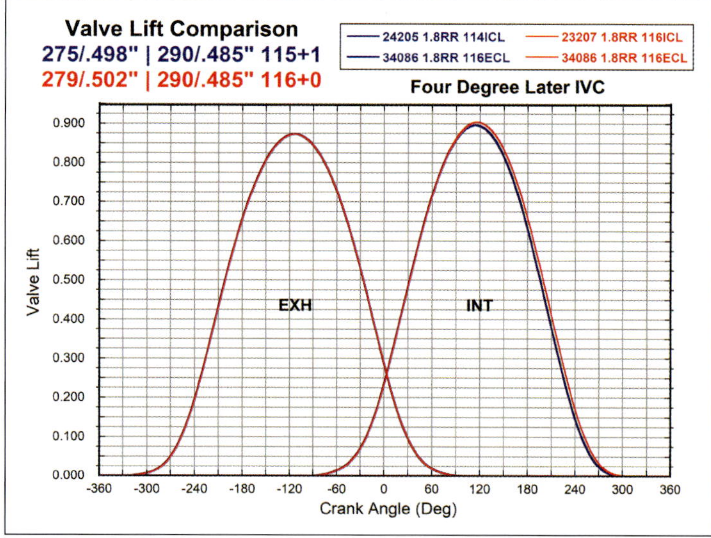

Images 8-16 and 8-17: Intake valve closing is the most important event. We have a good idea of where it wants to be from advancing and retarding the camshaft. Hence, I started with EVO before IVC. Then, I typically go back with an optimized EVO and test an earlier or later IVC with the new EVO. Why? From wave tuning, we know our new EVO has changed the wave tuning, so there is a good chance that the engine wants a slightly different IVC.

Advancing Intake Opening Moving the IVO 4 Degrees Earlier	
Characteristic	Change
Intake Duration	+4 Degrees
Exhaust Duration	Same
Lobe Separation	-1 Degree
Advance	+1 Degree
Intake Centerline	-2 Degrees
Exhaust Centerline	Same

Delaying Intake Opening Moving the IVO 4 Degrees Later	
Characteristic	Change
Intake Duration	-4 Degrees
Exhaust Duration	Same
Lobe Separation	+1 Degree
Advance	-1 Degree
Intake Centerline	+2 Degrees
Exhaust Centerline	Same

Image 8-18: This is a simple chart for moving IVO.

to move the IVC 4 degrees later (as shown in Image 8-17).

The specs can be moved half as much (2 duration, 0.5 LSA and advance) and move the IVC by 2 degrees. Some cam companies do not like half-degree specs, but we don't have any trouble with that at Comp. I do not recommend 2-degree changes on the exhaust side, but sometimes it is helpful when you are close on the intake closing.

Moving IVO and EVC (Overlap)

Playing with the overlap triangle is not as sensitive as the outside events and brings up other concerns. When we play with IVO or EVC in a NASCAR or Pro Stock–type application, it tends to require a different piston. When the intake valve is less than 0.080 inch from the piston at 10 ATDC, the reduced volume between the two increases the signal to the port. Too much of a gap dampens that signal. When the IVO is moved (as shown in Image 8-18), please think about piston-to-valve clearance, compression, and idle vacuum.

Typically, the valve will be moving about 0.005 inch per crank degree in this region for race applications. Hence, the 4-degree earlier IVO is going to reduce intake piston-to-valve clearance by about 0.020 inch, and the 4-degree later IVO increases clearance by 0.020 inch (as shown in Images 8-19 and 8-20).

In Image 8-21, the changes required to move the exhaust valve closing are shown. Running very tight piston-to-valve clearance on the exhaust is far more dangerous due to a very hot valve being chased by a piston. A cool intake chasing a piston might rub some carbon off without issues. Not only is tight piston-to-valve clearance more dangerous on the exhaust side but it is also less beneficial. There are none of the unexplainable gains when you run under 0.080 inch like

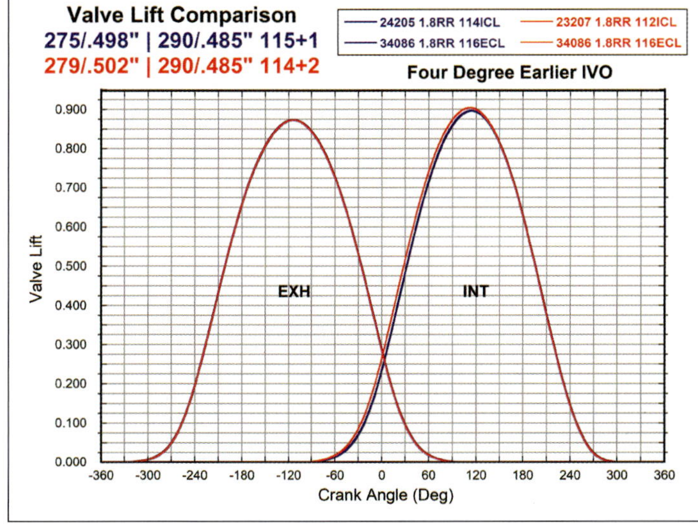

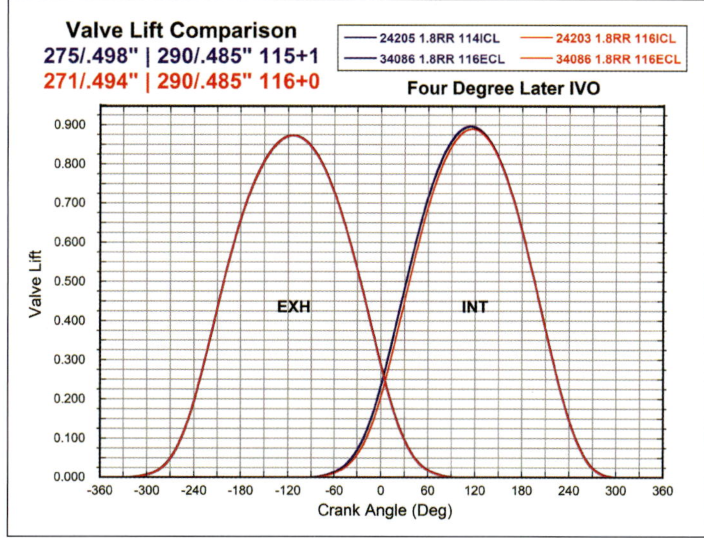

Images 8-19 and 8-20: Note in these graphs how moving IVO is going to change the wave tuning for the intake runner for both the IVO to IVC and IVC back around to IVO cases. These are small changes but need to be considered. Also, note that the idle vacuum and part-throttle response at low RPM (before the header exhaust wave is retuned at the correct time) are reduced as overlap increases.

Advancing Exhaust Closing Moving the EVC 4 Degrees Earlier	
Characteristic	Change
Intake Duration	Same
Exhaust Duration	-4 Degrees
Lobe Separation	+1 Degree
Advance	+1 Degree
Intake Centerline	Same
Exhaust Centerline	+2 Degrees

Delaying Exhaust Closing Moving the EVC 4 Degrees Later	
Characteristic	Change
Intake Duration	Same
Exhaust Duration	+4 Degrees
Lobe Separation	-1 Degree
Advance	-1 Degree
Intake Centerline	Same
Exhaust Centerline	-2 Degrees

***Image 8-21:** All four charts look very similar, but each moves a single different event.*

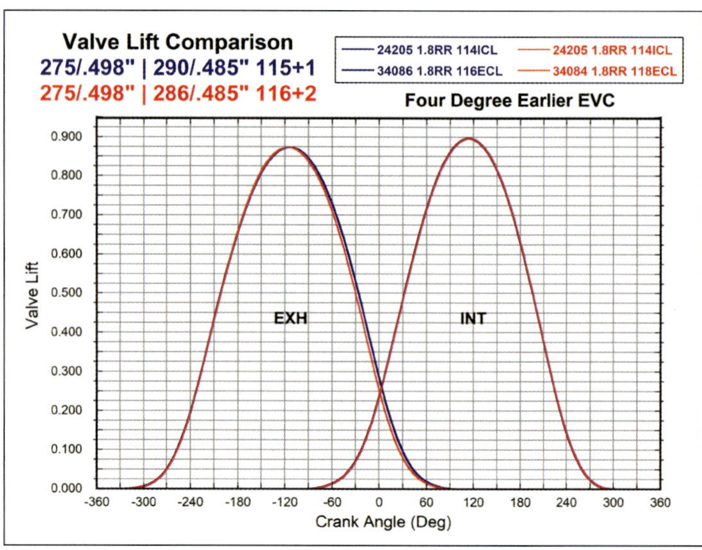

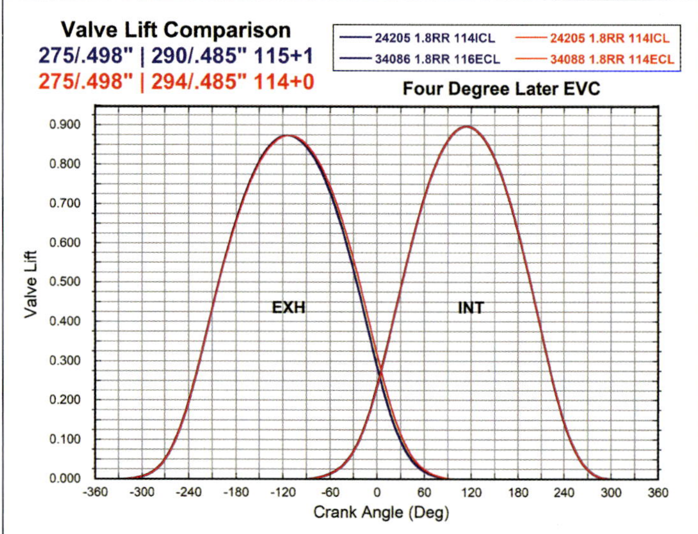

***Images 8-22 and 8-23:** We use changes in EVC to optimize the communication and mixing in many applications. This can be very important for drawing the inlet charge where the system is tuned, but a reduction in overlap can help eliminate torque curve holes in other applications. How engines respond to EVO in terms of preignition is often strange as well. Diluted mixture is less prone, but a hotter mixture is more prone to detonate.*

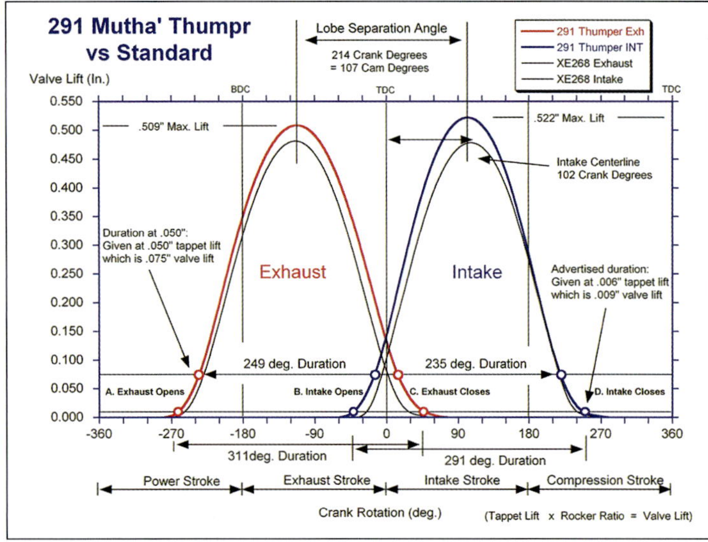

***Image 8-24:** It seems odd to end this chapter by showing a camshaft designed around sound, but the Thumper series was developed by individually optimizing events to do several jobs well (including that sound), while not worrying about the resulting specs, which seemed somewhat outlandish at the time.*

you might see on the intake. Wailing and gnashing of teeth happen when the piston knocks the head off an exhaust valve. The graph of a 4-degree earlier and later EVC is in Images 8-22 and 8-23.

Valve Event Optimization Reminder

When you start moving events, try to forget everything you know about what durations, lobe separation, and advance specifications are supposed to be best for your application. If you weigh yourself down thinking, "That can't be right," you will trick yourself into not believing good data.

Camshaft and Cylinder Head Selection

Most engine builds begin with the base engine short-block. You may be constrained by rules, strong emotions for a platform, or your budget. However, for our performance goals, I recommend that any build (with or without platform constraints) should begin with our thoughts focused on the cylinder head selection.

If I told you the camshaft was more important than the cylinder head, that would be a lie. Cylinder head flow is even more important than displacement in a naturally aspirated engine. Even though flow-bench data does not do a good job at replicating the pulsed flow of a running engine, it provides a good approximation of the minimum intake port cross-section between the port entry and combustion chamber. Flow data can't tell how much power will be made, but it can give you a good approximation for the maximum power that can possibly be made.

Scan the QR code below to see Jon Kaase's video that shows air and fuel pulsing through a racing engine.

Images 9-1 and 9-2: Two small-block Chevy engines are on the same Comp/Edelbrock dyno, but one makes about 200 hp more than the other. The solid-roller camshaft and dry-sump system certainly help, but the raised-port 18-degree-style race heads are the biggest difference. Without the increased flow, the engine on the right would still be better, but the heads allow the higher RPM and increased airflow and provide the foundation that allows everything else to work.

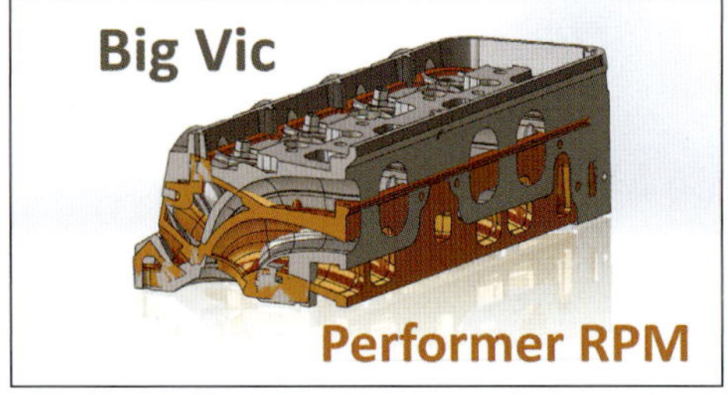

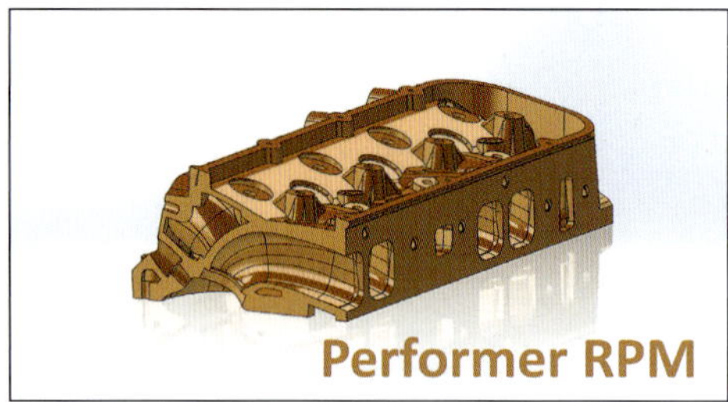

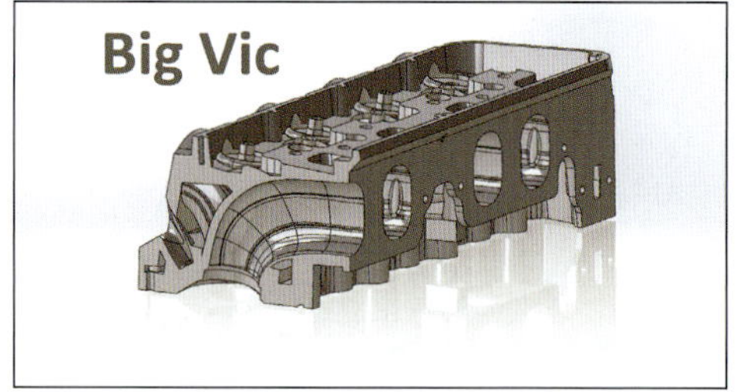

***Images 9-3, 9-4, and 9-5:** There is so much more to flow than just cross-section and flow-bench data. The big-block Chevy Edelbrock Performer RPM head is excellent for a stock-port-height head. However, the Big Vic brings the port higher and requires a different intake manifold but straightens out the bend. Regardless of what the flow bench says, that straight path is a huge improvement and will result in better filling. Also, it will want an earlier IVC at the same RPM.*

Cylinder head flow data is generally given in cubic feet per minute (CFM) and rated at 28 inches of water column pressure drop inside the chamber at various valve lifts. I recommend John Baechtel's *Performance Automotive Engine Math* and Harold Bettes and Bill Hancock's *Dyno Testing and Tuning* books (both from CarTech) for even more details on flow measurement and how it relates to horsepower. There are probably 10,000 ways to improve the head on a flow bench under constant flow that does nothing for power when the flow is anything but steady.

If the maximum intake flow in CFM at the highest achieved valve lift is examined, the following maximum naturally aspirated gasoline power limits are typically accurate. On the street, where you are limited on compression and overlap and wave tuning because of idle and low-RPM transient response or throttle tip-in, a great V-8 engine can approach 2 hp/cfm. Note that I said nothing about displacement. With a 250-cfm small-block Chevy head and a 480-hp goal (1.9 hp/cfm), it is far easier to achieve that on a 383 than a 350, and easier on a 350 than a 327 with this same cylinder head, compression, and bore. However, the reason is because you are typically limited on street builds by a minimum idle vacuum for power brakes or not stalling when going into gear.

Not only will the longer stroke have more rotational inertia or flywheel effect but it also draws more air at 800 rpm, thereby creating more vacuum even with the same camshaft. This allows us to run both more camshaft duration and overlap for the same RPM on the larger engine to get closer to that 2 hp/cfm target, which will be covered in Chapter 12.

A very good race engine will have more compression, greater piston-to-valve clearance, and have the intake and exhaust runner lengths tuned for the intended RPM with very little concern for performance outside a perhaps 2,500-rpm window while on the track. If a race engine idles at 1,800 rpm and stalls if you try to take it easy in the pits, no one cares.

A larger emphasis on wave tuning over idle stability moves our horsepower/CFM target up into the 2.1 to 2.4 range. Road-race engines tend to be a bit lower because they tune through a wider RPM window and are more focused on endurance. Drag-race engines can be higher because they stay at higher lift near that peak flow longer, mostly because they run springs that allow that (just not over as many cycles as needed for higher-endurance applications). Good circle-track engines fall somewhere between road race and drag race.

Almost any good race engine with 330-cfm heads will be in the 700- to 800-hp range. Again, note these targets only work if you are not restricted. Throw a 500 cfm 2-barrel on that 750-hp engine, and it is back below 500 hp. Also, it cannot have forced induction, N_2O, nitro, or any highly oxygenated fuels. Use the naturally aspirated targets with all of these as a reference, but then factor in either manifold pressure or how it brings more oxygen to the chamber.

I personally find NHRA Super Stock engines fascinating. These engines are limited to a certain-sized cc intake runner, so they are effectively limited on maximum intake port cross-section. With this limit and almost endless rubbing on parts and optimizing their packages, these engine builders routinely achieve performance in the 2.5 to 2.7 hp/cfm range. To do this, every part works together to maximize performance over a tight 1,500-rpm range.

As for the absolute best horsepower/CFM we see in American V-8 racing, it is with the NHRA Pro Stock engines. They may be down a bit today with both the mandated throttle body and snorkel that acts a bit like a large restrictor plate, and the 10,500-rpm limit forced them to focus on a slightly lower RPM than where peak power is required. However, they are very close to 3 hp/cfm.

For those who think this just applies to 2V engines with eight cylinders, you can divide any of these estimation factors by 2 for 4 cylinders or multiply by 0.75 for 6-cylinders. If you look at a good 600-cc sport bike cylinder head, it might flow 115 to 125 cfm on the intake.

From the factory, these have rather performance-oriented camshafts, intake systems, and headers, so that should fall into our 2 hp/cfm range for a V-8 that equals 1 hp/cfm for an inline 4. If you look up power for these bikes, seeing that the best factory bikes are right around 115 to 125 hp should be no surprise.

Exhaust to Intake Flow Percentages and Flow Curve Shapes

Before we leave flow-bench data behind for good, let's cover exhaust flow and flow curve shapes. The intake to exhaust flow percentage is generally used by people selecting camshafts to determine where to start when choosing how much exhaust duration should be run relative to intake durations for maximum performance.

The best rule of thumb I know is that a cylinder head with an exhaust flow of approximately 85 percent of intake runs best naturally aspirated very close to the same duration on intake and exhaust. The old-school folks will say this flow percentage works with a straight-pattern camshaft. Today, a different lobe series is normally used on the intake than exhaust, even if they are the same general duration.

Maximum E/I Flow%	Typical Exh "Split"
100%	-15
95%	-10
90%	-5
85%	0
80%	5
75%	10
70%	15
65%	20
60%	25
55%	30
50%	35

Image 9-6: Please do not use this exclusively to determine exhaust duration splits. Experiment with EVO and EVC as was described in Chapter 8. However, this is useful for getting started. If you want to fill in the curve at low RPM, go with a later EVO. If you need the engine to carry better, go with a later EVO. This is handy for trying the first grind on any new combination.

Most performance two-valve cylinder heads have less than an 85-percent balance, which makes sense because we have a huge pressure differential when the exhaust valve is opened. This makes mass flow much easier on the exhaust side than intake side, where we deal with dramatically smaller pressure differences between the intake plenum and combustion chamber.

The larger intake valve and more optimized valve location are to be expected. As you drop to 80-percent E/I or maximum exhaust flow divided by maximum intake flow, the engine tends to perform best with a split pattern with four to six degrees more exhaust than intake duration. Going to the more typical 75-percent E/I range, camshafts often perform best with 8 to 12 degrees added to the exhaust side.

Cylinder Head Configuration

Pent roof heads have been mentioned a few times regarding cylinder head configuration, so I will define the four common configurations in motorsports today and elaborate a bit on how they differ in respect to camshafts.

Wedge Heads

These include any cylinder heads with all the valves inline and at a common angle. These include factory-style small-block and LS/Gen III Chevy, small-block Ford, small-block Chrysler, big-block Chrysler (383s and 440s), and most Pontiac, Oldsmobile, Buick, and Cadillac engines.

These are the most common in that they are the least expensive to manufacture. Having all the guides and seats machined in one setup

Image 9-7: With this cast-iron, 23-degree small-block Chevy head, GM was concerned with cost and weight. Making the port twisted helped keep the head lighter and cheaper. Unfortunately, that makes it difficult to direct air to the chamber. People are pretty good at doing bowl work to get the most out of these, even with not-so-great geometry.

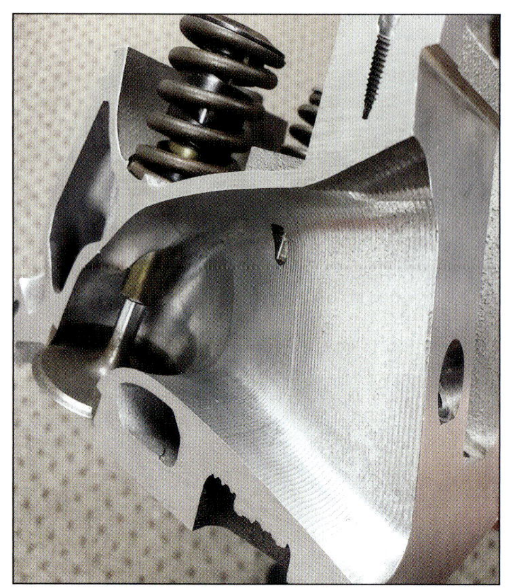

Image 9-8: In comparison to the earlier small-block, this ported LS1 head looks like a dream. With aluminum, the mass is not much of a penalty, and that line-of-sight flow reduces the intake stroke pumping losses. Maybe corporate-average fuel-economy standards help hot rodders in an unintentional way.

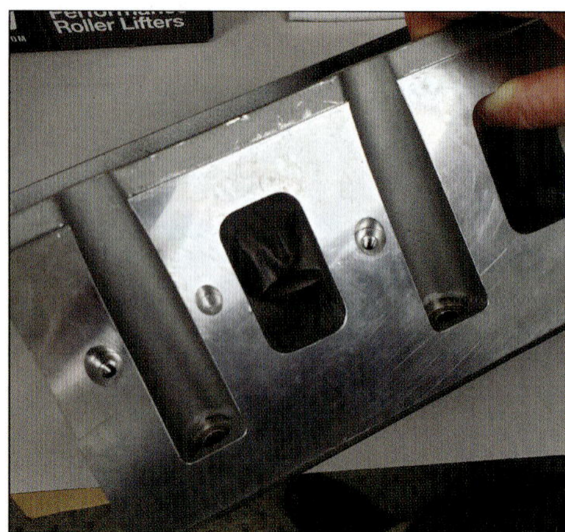

Image 9-9: Maybe the best of the modern Wedge heads, the LS7 port is raised from the LS1 and LS3 and uses offset rockers to clear the pushrods (like the LS3) with a wider port than the LS1. As more sophisticated OEM cylinder head manufacturing equipment became common, factory performance cylinder head designs rotated the valves in the crank axis plane in a canted or splayed arrangement.

Image 9-10: When the big-block Chevy came on the scene, all of the weird (for that time) valve angles and pushrod angles resulted in it being nicknamed the "Porcupine" engine.

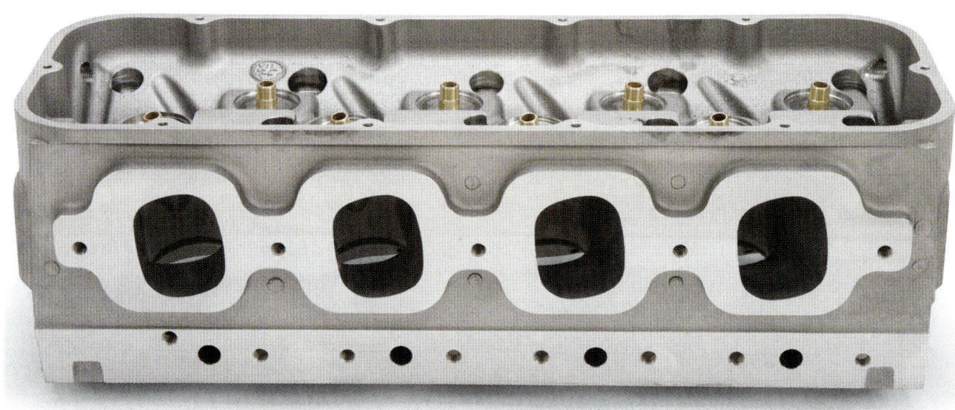

Image 9-11: When you are not restrained by a single 4-barrel carburetor or stock port location, a big-block Chevy can make better power with a symmetrical-port head. This requires a different camshaft lobe layout, but note that the valve angles are still canted in a similar arrangement.

makes this the most economical choice for any OEM. In the aftermarket, some gains can be found by tweaking the valve angles. However, the expense and complications on the valvetrain often make staying with the Wedge configuration the best bang for your buck.

From the camshaft point of view, Wedge heads tend to flow a little less than the others on the flow bench and on the engine and require more duration for the same RPM. However, the valves also never interfere with one another with no valve-to-valve collision issues as overlap increases, and the flow from the intake never has an easy path to shortcut out the open exhaust valve. Both point toward commonly running more overlap on Wedge heads than with the other cylinder head configurations.

Splayed and Canted Valve Heads

There are 100 different configurations that can be called canted valve. Basically, these are like Wedge heads above but have the valves tilted so the heads move toward the bore center with lift. They typically have the exhaust valve rotated back at a flatter angle to the deck to better flow out the exhaust. These heads are used on the big-block Chevy, SB2, R07, and GM splayed valve, newer LT1 and LT4, Ford Cleveland, Ford 460, Yates, FR9, RYR45, Dodge R5 and R6, and basically all modern NASCAR engines.

These angle tweaks can be so slight they behave almost exactly like a Wedge head, or so drastic they act far more like a Hemi head. In general, these heads all respond to lift more favorably than a Wedge

Images 9-12 and 9-13: Canted valves are not solely for a race head. This smaller-port Ford 460 head is excellent for towing. The valve arrangement results in more volume closer to the spark plug, so this same style is used with the new GM Gen V (LT) small-block engines and the Ford 7.3L Godzilla engine. However, if you open up the cross-section, even a stock-port-location Ford 460 head will flow plenty of air for racing.

Image 9-15: All later Hemi heads tend to flow extremely well. Their limits are due to items such as limited compression ratio without huge domes, difficult combustion efficiency, and the valve-to-valve interference or overlap shortcutting issues.

Image 9-14: Regarding the 7.3L Ford Godzilla engine, note the straight shot to the valve with the stock port location. This engine needs very few changes to produce about 600 hp. I can't wait for everything that will happen with this platform in the years to come.

Image 9-16: With the valve stood up and two plugs, the Gen III Dodge Hemi might have the best combustion of any of that era of V-8. I find that a testament to the designers, especially for a layout that was always seen as limited by combustion efficiency.

Image 9-17: This is the intake port on my old pickup truck's Hemi. This Eagle head with CNC port work by Dave Weber at Modern Muscle Extreme really moves the truck well.

head. The reason is the intake valve head moves closer toward the cylinder center as lift increases to reduce the shrouding from the cylinder bore.

Because of the improved flow, they tend to require less duration for a given displacement and RPM. As the exhaust angle is flattened out, you have to be more careful with overlap. With the canted angle, it is already easier for the intake charge to shortcut across the chamber and out the exhaust valve. The more you rotate the exhaust valve angle and placement, the easier it is for your intake charge to access this path.

Hemi Heads

A true hemispherical chamber, like the original early Dodge engines or the BMW flat-four motorcycle engine, are almost a full half-sphere with very steep valve angles. You can imagine how easy it is for intake airflow to skip the chamber altogether by heading directly from the intake port across the short bridge and out the exhaust port during overlap.

Be very aware of valve-to-valve interference on some Hemi layouts as many will collide before they both reach 0.200-inch lift. Fortunately, this valve-to-valve clearance is easy to check with the heads off the engine with a dial indicator on both valves of one cylinder along with a couple of very light checking springs.

More modern Hemi-style designs have the valves stand up considerably, and the chamber is more carefully shaped for optimum combustion than a simple hemisphere. Most have the valves nearly perpendicular to the head axis, unlike the parallel valve arrangement of a Wedge head. The Pro Stock Hemi designs are a combination of a Hemi and a canted valve head.

Because the exhaust valve on all Hemi-style heads faces the correct direction for improved exhaust flow, the exhaust side should always flow better and, therefore, the exhaust opening can be later. The interference and robbing leads to less overlap or an earlier exhaust closing. It does not take a ton of math to quickly realize the later exhaust opening and earlier exhaust closing means a Hemi-style head generally runs less exhaust duration than a similar Wedge or canted valve head. Most of this will follow the improved flow, but perhaps you want to cheat the Wedge exhaust big from our chart and cheat the Hemi small. With some attention to detail in the chamber, Hemi heads can be extremely impressive.

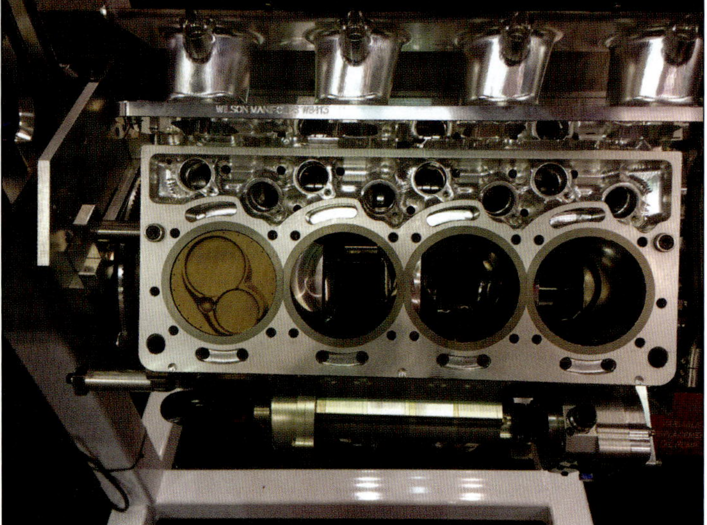

Images 9-18 and 9-19: Dan Jesel's Equal 8 is a great example of a twisted Hemi that is more Hemi than Wedge influenced. It is optimized for both flow and combustion without regard to how it should look.

Pent Roof Heads

Almost every four-valve gasoline engine uses some form of a Pent Roof, or penta, combustion chamber. The intakes are at one angle like a small wedge, the exhaust is at another angle like another smaller wedge, the spark plug generally is in the middle, and there are two wall angles and two quench pads.

For our purposes, treat all Pent Roof 4V heads like they are four-valve Hemi heads. There are steep-angled Pent Roofs that act like the earlier Hemi heads, and the modern Pent Roof heads are flatter and more like the modern Hemi two-valve heads. For a given bore size, the Pent Roof flows more air due to the increased valve area, so they act like really good Hemi heads.

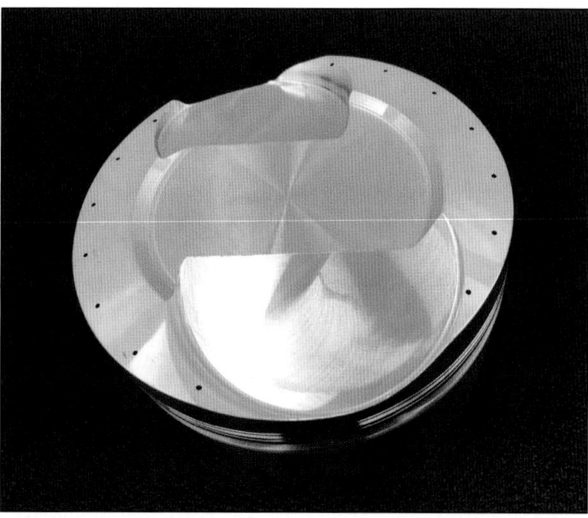

Image 9-20: Jon Kaase's 828-ci Ford Hemi Mountain Motor piston does away with the notion that all Hemi race pistons are required to have deep valve reliefs and a bad chamber. Jon moved everything around from the original configuration, but the long stroke and low rod-to-stroke ratio ensure that this piston moves away from TDC so rapidly that the valve has plenty of room. When an engine's stroke is greater than the bore, a Hemi arrangement always seems better than any two-valve Wedge derivative (canted or otherwise).

The Combustion Chamber

For years when we selected the camshaft, we tried to get the engine builders to buy a set of test pistons with extra-deep valve pockets to allow us to try different camshafts and move the camshaft advanced and retarded on the dyno, often along with a lash loop, to see how the engine responded. As combustion chambers became smaller, the piston domes constantly became smaller.

We saw timing advance for peak power decrease, probably because they didn't realize the piston top is just as important to the real chamber as the recess in the cylinder head. It may seem intuitive today, but a 15:1 piston with deeper reliefs and a larger dome sticking up into the head creates a much less efferent chamber than a 15:1 piston with very shallow reliefs, yet less dome. Going over the hills and through the woods might be fine for a Christmas trip to Grandma's, but the flame front in a combustion chamber performs much better and is far more efferent with a straight path.

CFM per Cubic Inch

We started the discussion on cylinder heads and camshaft by stating that horsepower per CFM is more of a limit than horsepower per cubic inch. Now, let's think about CFM per cubic inch. One of the most surprising things to me early in my career was playing with the same 18-degree-style race heads on a few different small-block Chevy blocks. With a very short stroke (2.75 inches), we need very little duration to peak past 9,500 rpm in a Comp Eliminator engine. It was very difficult to get any compression into that engine, and the rod-to-stroke ratio was far too long (piston camped at TDC), so the lobe separation had to be a bit wider. We might have been 15 to 20 degrees shorter at 0.050-inch duration than the same engine with a 3.5-inch stroke.

There's similar feedback in all cases. Take a 455 Pontiac Super Stock application. These need around 280 duration at 0.050 inch to peak at 6,500 to 6,800 rpm, but that head must fight to make 250 cfm on the intake with the stock volume. If we take a similar displacement engine with a 350-cfm head, say a 4.100-inch stroke LS7, it can peak at the same RPM with perhaps 20 to 30 degrees less duration. When we have heads on any V-8 that flow almost 1 cfm per cubic inch, they can peak above 7,000 rpm with very short durations, perhaps under 230 at 0.050 inch.

In any application, especially when working on an engine where you don't have a ton of experience running, using the CFM per cubic inch comparison is extremely useful. If a 300-ci engine has a 250-cfm head (0.83 cfm/ci) and a 400-ci engine has 333 cfm, along with the same general rod-to-stroke ratio and runner lengths, both will need similar cam timing. This has to be scaled for the number of cylinders, as a 2 cfm per ci on a 4-cylinder equals 1.5 cfm per cubic inch on a 6-cylinder, and 1 hp per cfm on an 8-cylinder.

Other Engine Considerations

While cylinder heads need to be our first concern when selecting a camshaft for a given application and operating range, it is only the beginning. In this chapter, we dive into the other common considerations that will alter our valve-timing and lobe-profile decisions.

Image 10-1: This rotating assembly provides bore-to-stroke and rod-to-stroke ratios. Looking at parts while we talk and think about them is quite useful.

Bore-to-Stroke Ratios

Early in my career, I spent a good deal of time looking at bore-to-stroke ratios and believed I found a good way to move valve timing events based on this relationship. However, with higher-flowing cylinder heads, it seems that the real driver is far more related to either CFM per cubic inch or rod-to-stroke than actual bore-to-stroke ratios. Perhaps you want to glance at max piston speeds, but when Vance and Hines ran their 160-ci V-Twin four-valve Pro Stock motorcycle engine, those values grew so high that they stopped calculating max velocity and just looked at the piston wear and life.

The cam specifications required totally fell into a logical range for that flow per cylinder displacement, even with the very long stroke. The same was true for Jon Kaase's 4V Ford modular engine that won *Engine Masters*. The bore on both of these examples, as well as any 800-plus-ci Mountain Motor, is quite a bit smaller than the stroke, but the cam specs fall right in line with where they would with a larger bore and shorter stroke if the cylinder head flow was the same.

The reason people tend to run larger camshafts with longer strokes and sub-1:1 bore-to-stroke ratios are as follows:

1) The smaller bore requires either smaller valves or shrouds larger valves, which results in less flow. Less flow per cubic inch requires more duration for the same engine.
2) The piston drops away from TDC more quickly with a longer stroke, especially if the rod-to-stroke ratio drops, to allow more piston-to-valve clearance. This allows more room for overlap and a stronger pressure drop early in the intake stroke, both of which can result in increased intake tract momentum and allow a later intake closing.
3) Longer stroke engines have more inertia in their rotating assemblies, which makes idle misfire and loss of vacuum less of an issue in street applications.
4) Smaller bore engines have less distance for the flame travel and generally better combustion efficiency. A pure spherical combustion chamber offers the quickest

Image 10-2: As we discussed on rocker arms, mass and MOI don't have to trend together. With a longer stroke, even a lightweight crankshaft can have significant inertia.

Image 10-3: This is a camshaft out of a Champ Car World Series (CART) engine. These V-8 engines were developed from the ground up around tight space constraints and limited displacement. By the end of the CART series, these engines operated as high as 17,000 rpm (or maybe a bit higher).

possible combustion. Larger bore-to-stroke ratios make the chamber a more pancake shape.

5) A longer stroke is always going to give a bit more lever arm during the power stroke, which helps with torque at lower RPM. A shorter rod-to-stroke ratio helps with the geometry at peak pressure a bit too. One of the main reasons to have an early intake and later exhaust opening is to achieve a given torque goal at lower RPM. A long stroke always makes this easier and allows you to focus the cam specs more on peak power.

There is a good reason why people say that there is no replacement for displacement. Most of the five reasons the duration tends to grow as the bore-to-stroke ratio drops is more about the stroke increasing than the bore shrinking.

It is interesting to think about the combustion efficiency part. Most of the engines that won the *Engine Masters* competition were very close to 1:1 on bore to stroke. That is related to numbers four and five above. If you follow either NHRA Competition Eliminator or land speed classes closely, you will notice that in the sub-270-ci classes, V-6 engines tend to significantly out-perform short-stroke V-8 engines.

I have tried to help many customers and amazing engine builders, such as Keith Dorton, with very short-stroke domestic V-8 OHV engines. Between the limited piston-to-valve clearance, low piston velocities, high RPM, and the early intake closing needed, these might be the most challenging engines to operate near their potential. You can do a rather good job at small displacement with a clean-sheet V-8 engine design like one of the 2002 TRD RV-8F competition engines from 2002, but nothing fits very well, as the stroke drops below about 2.7 inches in a typical domestic small-block configuration.

Rod-to-Stroke Ratios

While bore-to-stroke effects are mostly secondary (something else is the primary driver), rod-to-stroke ratios directly change both the piston motion and force vectors on the crank. Going back to the 1990s, long-rod engines (1.8:1+ rod to stroke) were extremely popular. The

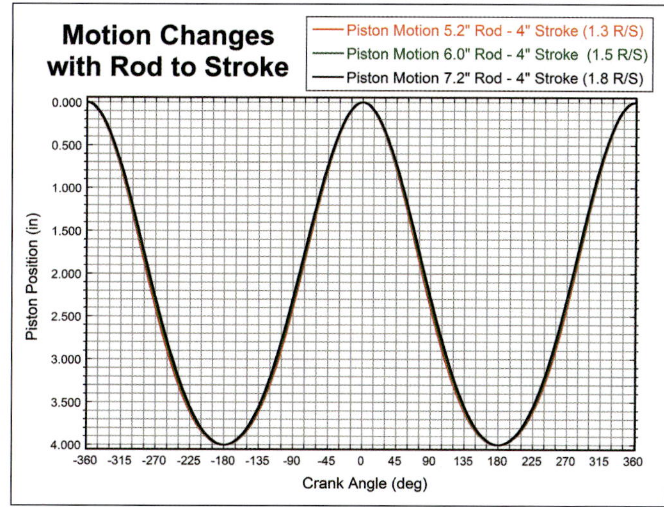

Image 10-4: It is difficult to see small changes in rod-to-stroke ratios on the typical 720-degree plots, but going from 1.3:1 to 1.5:1 to 1.8:1 helps. The black curve is the piston motion with a very long 1.8:1 ratio. This ratio is normally seen on short-stroke applications, but I have the motion for a 4-inch stroke and a 7.200-inch rod. The longer the rod-to-stroke ratio, the more the piston motion looks like a sine wave (symmetric at top and bottom). The green is a typical 1.5:1 rod-to-stroke ratio (6-inch rod, 4-inch stroke) and the red is a 1.3:1 ratio (5.2-inch rod, 4-inch stroke).

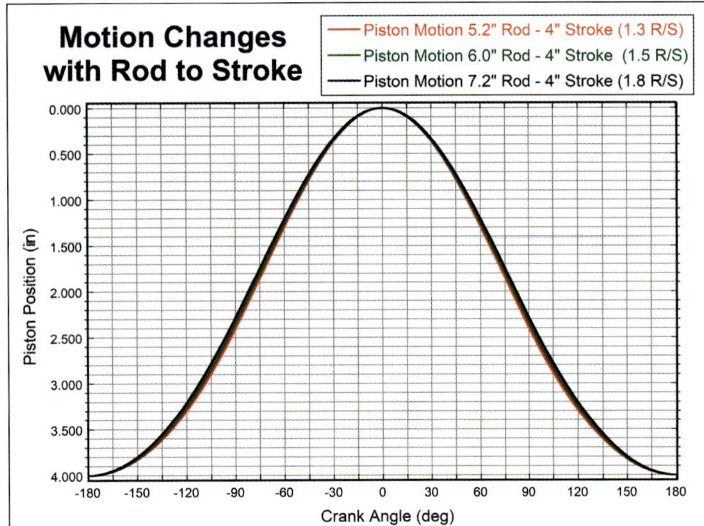

Image 10-5: Scaling this down for one trip from BDC to TDC and back to BDC, we see how the red line pulls away from TDC much more rapidly, then camps at BDC. This gives the exhaust more time to get out one trip to BDC and allows the intake charge more time to get onboard the next trip. One negative result is more side wear on the piston, and the other is that pistons seal best and are lightest with the pin as high as possible without getting into the oil ring. Hence, a short deck is required to really take advantage of a short rod.

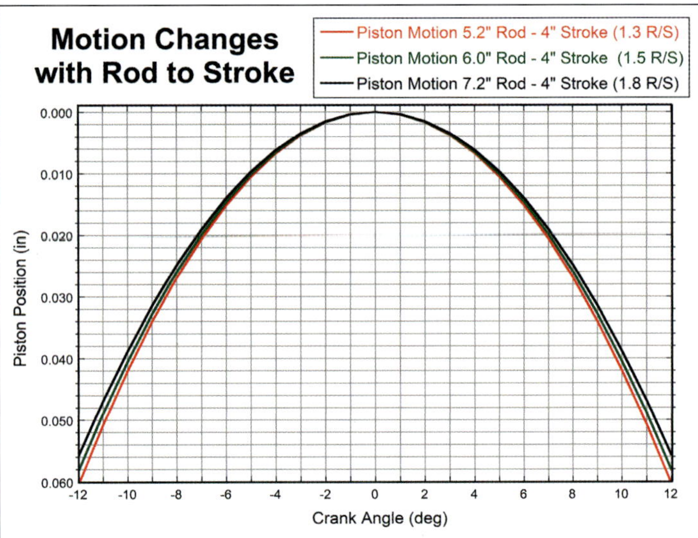

Image 10-6: Zooming in to the top of the motion, we see how slowly the long rod gets out of the valve's way, yet how much more quickly the red curve drops. This creates more swept volume sooner to both increase the max and early draw on the inlet port. I began my career as a long-rod fan, but today I lean more toward minimal deck height and short(ish) rods. However, I don't mind if anyone disagrees.

first idea was the piston would sideload less and improve ring seal. The second attribute people mentioned was the piston stayed close to TDC for more degrees to allow more complete combustion before the volume increased during the power stroke.

Neither of these is wrong. When you have a very long rod-to-stroke ratio, the piston motion is more like a sine wave, symmetric about TDC and BDC of piston motion, and there is less sideloading of the piston. However, my assumption is most of the benefits seen were from moving the pin farther up in the piston.

Going the opposite direction, as the rod-to-stroke ratio decreases, the piston spends more and more time near BDC, and peak velocity becomes higher and moves earlier in the downstroke. This provides both more time to fill after peak piston velocity and a stronger low pressure signal in the intake stroke. Shortly after the long-rod craze went through circle-track classes, a short-deck trend went through NHRA Pro Stock.

Much of the thought of this approach had to do with shortening the intake runners, but it also led to a short rod-to-stroke ratio. Even at very high engine speeds, any friction from the side loading and reduced combustion efficiency from the less piston time near TDC was more than offset by the increased signal and better cylinder filling with the shorter rod-to-stroke ratio. Certainly, the lighter rotating assembly and shorter runners to a common plenum under carburetors helped as well.

From a cam selection point of view, keep in mind that long rod-to-stroke ratios give us less room for overlap without big reliefs or interference issues. The shorter rods provide extra signal (and longer) before the piston begins rising quickly to allow for a slightly later intake closing. In general, we can get by with a larger duration camshaft with a short rod. However, we never want to recommend a lower pin height to achieve the short rod to stroke as it hurts the piston and combustion efficiency more than the faster piston motion early, and camping out at BDC helps the airflow.

Know there is something to be said about Ford's practice of using the short 8.2-inch deck on the 3-inch stroke 302 and a taller 9.5-inch deck on the 351 Windsor over Chevrolet's practice of using the same 9-inch small-block deck regardless of stroke. When building a clean-sheet race engine, set up the crank and piston first, then setting up the deck just

Image 10-7: This new Edelbrock VRS-4150 utilizes 16 air bleeds and more circuits like you might have seen on a Pro Stock carburetor yet in a standard square bore arrangement. Regardless of the increased tunability, all carburetors react primarily to airflow. Hence, we may want more overlap to increase VE around peak torque in applications that are always on and off the throttle, such as circle-track racing, even if we incur a BSFC penalty.

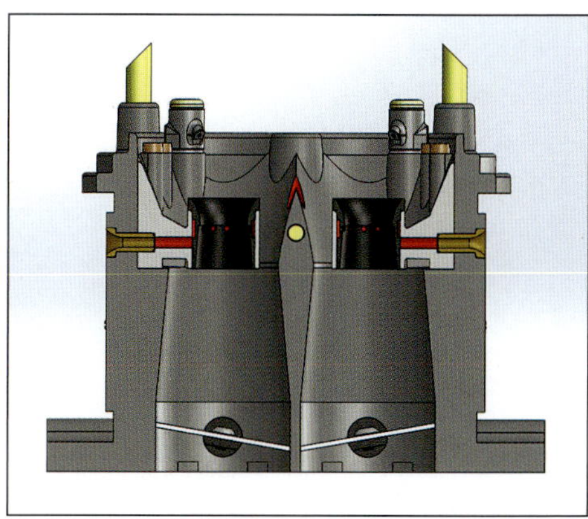

Images 10-8 and 10-9: Note in this cross-section how the bores are Venturi shaped. Adding the booster further reduces the minimal area and greatly increases signal to the fuel, but does so with some pressure drop into the intake manifold. Typically, we see about 1 to 2 inches of vacuum needed to provide excellent signal. However, this is a 3- to 7-percent loss of pressure, so we start with about a 15-hp penalty to EFI on a 500-hp engine. Even with a loss of pressure, the increased atomization and improved distribution of a carburetor tends to make up that 15 hp above most EFI systems.

high enough for the piston skirt to clear the counterweights is as good of a practice if the rod to stroke is reasonable.

EFI versus Carbureted

As you select a camshaft, I highly recommend your first consideration is always getting the most possible air into the chamber at IVC. Everything else should be someone else's problem. However, there are some interesting considerations with carburetors and various EFI systems to at least consider. You will almost always see carbureted race classes run tighter LSA camshafts than an almost identical class with EFI. Knowing how events are related to centerlines, we can quickly see these engines appear to like more overlap, a later EVO, and an earlier IVC.

Overlap

Let's address overlap first. If an engine likes more overlap, especially when it has to give up some compression with race gas to get it, it is trying to tell you that VE (total airflow) has become more important that BSFC (totally efficiency). This makes sense with carbureted applications, especially in classes like road race or circle track where throttle changes are frequent and response is paramount. The carburetor responds mostly to airflow and not throttle changes. Carburetors have a squirter pump to add fuel during throttle input and help, but they really need airflow to atomize fuel and work.

Adding some overlap with a carburetor, even if it compromises the chamber shape, will let the header

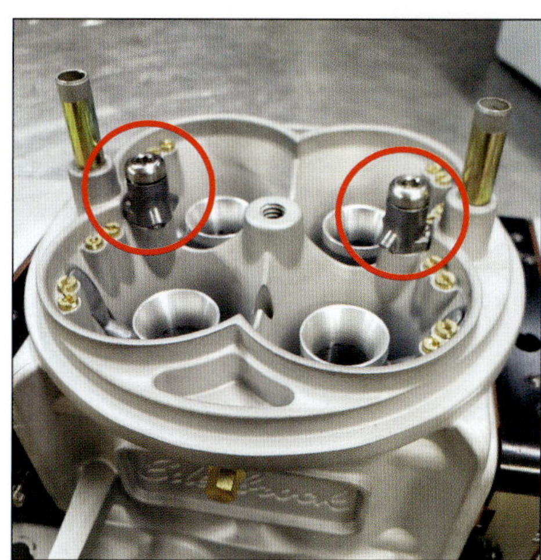

Image 10-10: These are the squirter nozzles that are used to give the engine the required shot of fuel as the throttles are opened before the airflow speed draws fuel with the air. Getting that shot correct for each application is often what sets the great carburetor tuners apart from the pack.

Image 10-11: There is no real reason that a throttle-body EFI system could not outperform a carburetor. It does not need any pressure drop to draw fuel, but a fast air column certainly helps keep the fuel in suspension. (Photo Courtesy Hunter Pauloski)

signal pull harder on the carburetor and improve responsiveness around peak torque where the header is typically tuned.

We can get this same airflow increase around peak torque with more overlap on EFI systems, but they certainly do not need the signal to supply fuel. In these systems, assuming you have a good tuner, you can properly balance the VE (airflow) concerns with the BSCF

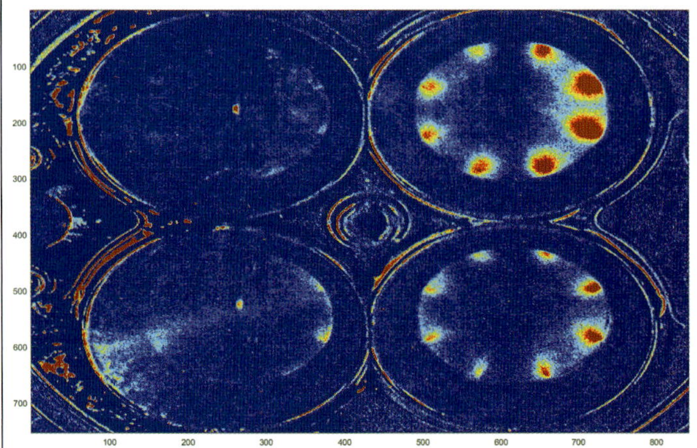

Image 10-12: My son, Conner Godbold, is almost finished with his Doctor of Philosophy (PhD) degree from Georgia Tech, but he stopped by to do some math on Hunter Pauloski's pictures. Conner wrote a method to take out the background and measure the intensity change, pixel by pixel, on fuel flow. The closer we can get to a light-blue haze, the better.

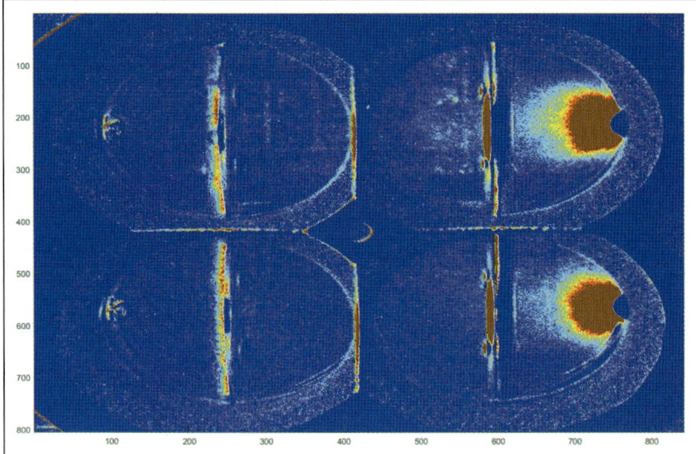

Image 10-14: Unfortunately, the shot injector firing at low speeds makes timing the injection difficult to achieve uniformity that is comparable to a carburetor.

Image 10-13: The first FAST EZ EFI had a single pin target in each throttle bore. The fuel is targeted to hit that at high speed and break up into small particles.

Image 10-15: In the FAST EZ EFI 2.0, we went to eight injectors and had very good distribution by hitting the pins high in a mixing bowl below the blades. The problem with this approach is that you need the same number of expensive injectors as are needed with a port-injection system.

(efficiency) optimization. Most EFI tuners have a much easier time at lower speeds with a little less overlap. Older OEM systems are extremely sensitive to too much overlap, but modern aftermarket systems are much less sensitive.

Carbureted systems need to keep the fuel in suspension in the air column the entire way to the chamber. These wet-flow systems tend to be shorter on overall length. These shorter runners lead to earlier IVC, which falls right in line with how a tighter LSA changes IVC.

In truth, we would rather not think about the fueling system when choosing the camshaft. Attention should be placed on filling the cylinder and balancing EVO between increased power out and reduced pumping losses. Nevertheless, it's also important to understand why we tend to add overlap with a carburetor and reduce it with EFI. It all comes down to signal versus efficiency, with some thought to idle stability and tuning.

Image 10-16: Going with a port-injection system such as this, you get rid of the pressure drop of a carburetor and the distribution problems of a less expensive throttle-body-injection system. You do not get all of the 15 hp back because fuel evaporation from the carburetor fuel mist cools the charge going down the runner.

Image 10-17: After going to a port-injection system, the throttle-body and runner configurations open completely. Wet flow is difficult because you must keep fuel in suspension. Dry flow does not give you evaporative cooling, but you don't have to worry about those pools of fuel like we talked about with the cross ram. The ProFlow4 EFI system that controls these last two systems is flexible enough to run with any camshaft that you can run carbureted.

Octane and Other Fuel Considerations

Much as with the fueling system, all fuels perform similarly in terms of airflow and cylinder filling. However, performance can be improved with a few tweaks based on the fuel used. Going from something like pump gas to a standard race fuel, there are only small changes to consider. In fact, if the piston, gasket, and chamber cannot be altered, there may be no change at all. Race gas may burn slower, especially at low compression, so low-compression engines run on race gas create very high temperatures in the exhaust system.

When NASCAR went to a 9:1 rule in some lower classes, drivers experienced blisters on their feet from the hot exhaust gases. If there is available oxygen, fuel will react and release heat. That heat energy goes one of three places. It will perform work on the crank, heat the water, or make its way out the exhaust. Optimizing the ignition timing is the main way to keep more for the crank with a slower reacting fuel, but a later exhaust opening can certainly help reduce the energy in the exhaust.

For 99 percent of naturally aspirated race gas applications, aim for a very high compression ratio (>14:1). This makes the overlap region extremely important, especially in shorter stroke applications. Recently, from the cam side, we have used slightly slower opening designs (Comp Cams low shock) to give more overlap time when we cannot fit more lift at 10 ATDC. Likewise, a softer closing exhaust can add time even within very limited lift at 10 BTDC.

We always wind up working closely with the piston and chamber designers in professional race engines. I wish the camshaft was the most important factor, but adding one to two percent to VE with more overlap while reducing combustion efficiency by three to five percent with a slower chamber is going to be a net loss.

Alcohol, Methanol, and Oxygenated Fuels

As we move from race gas to alcohol, methanol, and oxygenated fuels, we have three main attributes to consider. The first is the fuel brings some oxygen with it to the dance. The second is that the fuel flow is much greater and will displace room for air downstream in the ports after it is introduced. Third, we must consider the fuels will be difficult to keep either suspended in droplets or vaporized so they will properly combust.

Most oxygenated fuels are not that much different from normal gasoline, so these considerations are not as important. If the port acts smaller, due to the added fuel volume, perhaps a couple of degrees later IVC will be enough to compensate for the added velocity and momentum in the port.

These fuels tend to be more forgiving at a richer lambda value than gasoline. As it goes past lambda 0.8 on normal or race gasoline, performance tends to suffer greatly. With these fuels, richer is not nearly as detrimental, especially with added ignition timing. Because these require so much fuel to reach lambda 0.8 and can run with even more, we must be aware of the heat in the chamber to vaporize the fuel. Compression ratio is the first and best tool used to add heat.

QND HYDRAULIC ROLLERS

The QND series is based off the popular LXL series profiles but are optimized to be used in smaller journal applications including standard (1.868") Small Block Chevy engines with lower (1.5:1 to 1.65:1) rocker ratios. These lobes have a softer closing ramp than the Xtreme Energy series and are a great choice for either marine or industrial applications where lift is important as well as low seat erosion over time and low valve noise. Also a great choice for the exhaust lobe in any application.

CAMSHAFT TYPE	LOBE NUMBER	RATED DURATION	DURATION IN DEGREES		LOBE LIFT	TAPPET LIFT @ TDC		THEORETICAL VALVE LIFT @ "0" Lash ROCKER ARM RATIO		
			@ .050	@ .200		106°	110°	1.5	1.6	1.7
QND	13354	266	211	133	.365	.049	.038	.548	.584	.621
Rated Duration @	13355	270	215	137	.365	.054	.034	.548	.584	.621
.006" Tappet Lift	13356	274	219	141	.365	.061	.049	.548	.584	.621
Journal = S,B,F,R...	13357	278	223	145	.365	.067	.055	.548	.584	.621
MI 28.0 (13.5/14.5)	13358	282	227	148	.365	.074	.061	.548	.584	.621
	13366	306	251	171	.375	.119	.103	.563	.600	.638
	13353	322	267	186	.383	.150	.134	.575	.613	.651

Image 10-18: The QND series was initially developed for oil well generators that run off any gases that arise with the oil. Because these are low-speed lobes, the soft-closing section can be at low lift. There are lower pushrod loads and not as much deflection at low speeds. This design family flairs out the closing ramp to set the valves down quite easily.

Forced induction is a great tool as well. From the camshaft point of view, a later EVO can be used to keep more heat in the chamber and not go out the exhaust. This may hurt the performance past peak power due to exhaust pumping losses, but in general the best methanol and alcohol engines will have both a later IVC and EVO than a similar gasoline engine. You can get there by retarding the camshaft, but to get the maximum compression, you want less overlap and a bit later IVO just for room. The EVO tends to move more like three to eight degrees later compared to the one to three degree changes we see with IVC. For best performance, a new cam is the best choice if making this fuel change.

Propane and Natural Gas

If you solely look at airflow, you wouldn't change the valve timing with these fuels, but there are a few considerations to be made. The biggest concern is valve-seat erosion with these fuels, and other fuels provide more lubrication than propane and natural gas. Chamber heat can be tweaked some with exhaust valve opening.

However, the fuel itself pulls less heat out of the exhaust valve during overlap. Hence, valve-seat erosion is the primary camshaft focus with these fuels. The normal approach is to utilize profiles with slower valve closing rates for the same service interval. This becomes extremely evident in industrial applications but must be considered, even in drag racing. If you can run some sort of "dual fuel," it will help with both erosion and heat rejection. Otherwise, simply rely on the engine's water-cooling system and try to help with slower valve closing rates and perhaps an earlier EVO.

Nitromethane

From a camshaft point of view, nitromethane certainly has the volume considerations of methanol, but once it is running, you don't have to worry about heat in the chamber. For naturally aspirated nitro applications like the N/A Nitro engines in NHRA

***Image 10-19:** Even at 14,000 hp, the physics of Top Fuel is no different than it is for other engines. We are still trying to time IVC to capture maximum charge mass, and overlap is dictated by valve-to-valve and piston-to-valve limits. The most unique challenge is the pressure at EVO. The energy here certainly stands out in this Friday-night qualifying pass by my friend Clay Millican.*

***Image 10-20:** I forgot what we told Clay Millican to get the cam back that he used to win his first race on Father's Day at Bristol in 2017. However, before I had it polished, something caught my eye. I thought I saw a dip in the exhaust-opening ramps, but they seemed both deep and high up the ramp. Instead of guessing, I ran an Adcole report. I just about fell out of my chair when I studied the next graph (Image 10-21).*

Top Alcohol Dragster, compression ratio is a major consideration, and intake closing may need to be altered depending on weather considerations to get the heat in the chamber needed for proper combustion.

The main consideration with nitromethane is opening the exhaust valve. Peak cylinder pressures in NHRA Top Fuel are lower than in Pro Mod classes. However, nitro burns more slowly and releases heat and maintains high pressures well past 90 degrees of crank rotation.

This does amazing things for powering the vehicle and produces some awesome flames, but it also means the exhaust valve no longer opens against 5 to 10 bar—more like 50 bar. People are often surprised at how late the EVO is on a Top Fuel engine. The crazy part is when we try to open it earlier, it simply does not open. Failed lifters, broken rockers, cams with troughs in the opening flank, failed pushrods, and even failed rocker stands occur when we try to open the exhaust valve too soon.

We now run different opening ramps on Top Fuel exhaust lobes after we examined an exhaust lobe failure on one of Clay Millican's Top Fuel cams. With Top Fuel, a Spintron cannot help on the exhaust side as nitro burns quite slowly and results in high cylinder pressure at exhaust valve opening. There are no good Top Fuel dynos, so you are required to learn on the track.

When we check camshafts on our Adcole gauges, it plots an error plot. One time when I looked at a cam to see if the wear was too much to regrind, something on that plot caught my eye. I don't know if you have ever been on a golf course after pros have played through, but it happened to me when I was young. I had what I thought was a very good drive and second shot, only to step over divots from the pro's second shots as I was about to take my third. That was exactly how I felt looking at Image 10-21. On all eight exhaust lobes, there was a 0.005-inch divot that was 20-plus degrees after the exhaust valves were supposed to open.

Suddenly, my cam design thoughts changed to the GPS voice saying "recalculating." The exhaust was not opening where we expected. I had an opening ramp that was not half as long as it needed to be when the engine was truly loaded. By changing the exhaust opening ramp, we were not only able to reduce failures, more than doubling the cam life, but Clay also set several ET records with the new design.

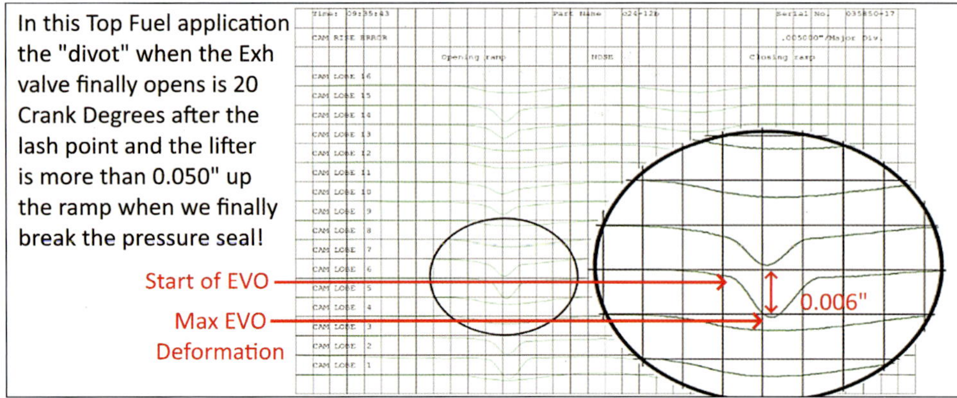

Image 10-21: In addition to all the normal sheets, we have the option to print an error report that is a line that shows how far the measured data is from design every degree. The 0.005-inch dip at the cam on all the exhaust lobes was surprising. Where that dip occurred was shocking. The valve was trying to open for 10-plus cam degrees or 20-plus crank degrees before breaking the chamber seal. Looking closely at this data changed my approach to all fuel exhaust profiles that helped Clay set a few national ET records along the way.

Modern Performance Diesel Engines

Valve timing in diesel applications does not change much from other applications, but you have to be aware that cylinder pressure is now the driver of combustion and not spark. The intake closing point is even more important at low RPM. Valve-to-piston clearance is always tight and critical to account for properly. If you reduce compression with valve reliefs or delay the IVC with a larger camshaft, more boost will be required for good combustion.

Otherwise, cylinder pressure will be lower at the injection point and reduce the combustion efficiency. Charge motion is also critical on earlier diesel applications. With today's high-pressure fuel systems, there is likely enough energy in the injected stream to ignore swirl and tumble in the cylinder and chamber. It is not as important as it was in earlier diesel engines. However, there is still significant carryover of high-swirl port and chamber designs.

As valve lift gets higher in either a 4V or 2V head, tumble becomes an effective mixing solution. This is equally true in gasoline engines but could be valuable in race diesel applications. Swirl reduces flow, especially in 4V applications, where tumble does not have the same negative influence.

Variable Advance, Centerline, Duration, and/or Lift Systems

We discussed this in detail with the valve event chapters, but variable timing points open up the world of possibilities for maximizing performance over a wider RPM range, but you do have to be careful. If the system can mechanically put the valve and piston in the same location at the same time, it will. They don't have to be together for more than a millisecond before that spells doom for your engine.

On the positive side, advancing the IVC at low RPM can be worth 5 percent or more (15-plus ft-lbs on 300 ft-lbs) over the best low to high compromise closing point. The same holds true at high RPM as well, with 5-percent more power at or past peak with IVC retarded. Applications like the L92 and L99 6.2L GM Engines, 5.7L Eagle and 6.4L Apache Hemi, and Ford 5.0L Coyote run remarkably well with even moderately sized camshafts over a wide range of engine speeds with the camshaft and phaser tables optimized. Dual phaser systems, like the Coyote, have the advantage of moving the exhaust in the appropriate direction while chasing the intake port pressure wave for best IVC at each RPM. However, the single phaser GM and Hemi systems are almost as effective, even when moving the EVO in the wrong direction for the target engine speed. This is because IVC is far more critical for best performance. EVO is always a bit of give and take with a too-early EVO that hurts the power stroke but reduces the exhaust pumping losses.

To run the proper-sized camshafts through a peak low-end torque to peak high-end power sweep, we need about 15 to 20 crank degrees swing. Most phaser systems are primarily used to throttle the engine without creating manifold vacuum, so they will have 50 degrees or more swing. To get the full effective sweep for power with minimal valve-to-piston limitations, Comp Cams recommends phaser limiters with all performance GM and Dodge variable valve timing (VVT) camshafts.

When tuning the phaser tables on any VVT engine, the best approach is to start with the intake or single camshaft at full advance. If you have intake and exhaust control, keep the exhaust at a reasonable fixed position while sweeping the intake camshaft (114 or the main stock location works well). Run the dyno (engine or chassis) test first at full advance and then move it back in four crank degrees (two cam) steps until it stops gaining power at high RPM. Once you have four to six test sweeps, you can quickly see what settings are best at each RPM. Then, make a phaser table curve to extrapolate the best position in between.

Once you have the intake camshaft phaser table for the Coyote or other independent exhaust versus intake systems, test the exhaust four advanced and then four retarded. Look at the results to decide whether you want to try either advanced or retarded. Using those steps, pick what worked best at each RPM and make a smooth curve of the best exhaust like the best intake table. With the exhaust properly positioned, try the intake curve shifted a little forward or back to see if the shape needs to change a bit with the rephased EVO to alter the pressure wave on the intake.

Variable valve timing and lift electronic control (VTEC) systems are similar, but instead of positioning, the duration and lift can be changed. This makes for some pretty awesome race designs if you allow the smaller (primary and secondary) profiles to grow considerably from the mileage grind used in the OEM application. A smaller camshaft for peak torque and a larger camshaft for peak power should be every race engine builder's dream. Tune carefully and be extremely careful with piston-to-valve clearance.

Both VVT and VTEC systems really shine when looking over a 4,000-plus-rpm range. However, for racing, we typically operate at full throttle over a much narrower band. VVT systems can be sensitive to high spring loads and oil aeration.

Because you have to set up the valve piston valve reliefs for the tightest centerlines and maximum possible valve lift near TDC, much of what you might gain on VE is easily lost to lost compression and efficiency in competition engines. Because of the clearance and control issues in race engines, these systems are not typically used in racing. Where both VVT and all variable valve motion systems excel is in street performance applications where they allow the engine to perform extremely well at from below 2,800 rpm all the way past 6,800 rpm.

Image 10-22: Diesel engines can be helped with increased intake flow and lower exhaust temperatures by changing the camshaft, but we must be laser focused on piston-to-valve clearance in all but competition engines. Even then, you may damage combustion efficiency more than you help VE with too deep of reliefs.

Variable Displacement Systems

While I question why anyone would remove a VVT system on a street performance build, it is easy to understand why DOD Delete kits are popular in the performance aftermarket. For decades, the concept of an engine that runs on four cylinders under part throttle cruising but smoothy transitions to eight as more power is requested (throttle pedal depressed) has been coveted. When Delphi developed the lifters that could be activated (locked) or deactivated (unlocked) by switching an oil feed, both Dodge and GM were able to build tons of trucks with large V-8 engines while still appeasing the CAFÉ gods. For hot rodders everywhere, we have been given a near endless supply of great V-8 engines that can be found throughout junkyards near and far, and many of our daily driver pickups perform better than they would have otherwise.

The negative of these systems is they require very slow lash take-up ramps on the switching lifter profiles, as these are normally open hydraulic systems. If you run profiles for the switching lifters on standard lifters, the cylinder bleeds pressure with those long ramps.

Likewise, if you use a switching lifter on a profile developed for standard lifters, you will have considerable noise and short intervals before either the lifter or valve seats are damaged. The complexity of the switching lifters leads to many valid concerns. For the OEM designers, they could not resist the +1 to +2 MPG this system provides on the highway. However, for performance engine builders, it is far better to plug these passages and run conventional lifters and profiles developed for maximum performance.

Image 10-23: Warning: If you run a camshaft optimized for large amounts of nitrous and send it down the drag strip without the bottle open, prepare to be disappointed. The torque that you traded at lower engine speeds with an early EVO is going to make your launch and shift recovery rather awful. Also, you need real atmosphere in the chamber with the nitrous for controlled combustion.

Power Adders

Many people treat all power adders roughly the same, but the way each changes cylinder filling, pressures, and performance varies considerably, so let's look at each separately.

Nitrous Oxide

Nitrous camshafts may be the most misunderstood parts in the aftermarket. If you occasionally run nitrous, and the added power is less than 25 percent of the total power (100 hp added to a 400-hp engine), there is almost no benefit to changing the camshaft. Nitrous typically adds fuel and the N_2O to the port, so you might assume it would be a little like alcohol and requires later IVC.

However, it greatly cools the intake charge as nitrous boils and enters the air stream at nearly -130° F. When we measure the air ingested into an engine with a dyno air hat, the overall airflow changes very little with those small (25 percent) nitrous additions. However, as the nitrous flow increases, you can pressurize the runners and plenum to create a noticeable decrease in the outside air ingested.

If the intake runner gas dynamics are not what we need to change on the camshaft with nitrous, why run a nitrous camshaft? Is it just a gimmick? The truth is most of what we are doing with nitrous camshafts is tailoring the nitrous assisted torque curve around available traction. In naturally aspirated applications, giving up 20 ft-lbs at peak torque for 5 hp at peak power typically is a very bad trade.

However, when you introduce nitrous and fuel in the port, you basically add that much horsepower at every RPM.

Think about the torque increase when a 200-hp nitrous shot is activated at 2,500 rpm. Because torque = horsepower x (5,252/RPM), that 5,252/2,500 means you are doubling the torque at 2,500 rpm or adding over 400 ft-lbs on top of the initial torque.

Considering that much cylinder pressure added at low RPM is more likely to push the crank out of the block than effectively accelerate a vehicle, many people use a limit switch so nitrous cannot be activated below a given low limit, such as 4,000 rpm. While this helps, you will still add more torque at 5,000 rpm than 6,500 rpm. For applications that often or always run nitrous, change the valve timing to flatten out this highly skewed torque curve.

The easiest change is to open the exhaust significantly earlier and close the intake slightly later than for the same application without nitrous. If you have more available torque at low RPM than can be effectively used, trading 100-plus ft-lbs at low RPM (which only creates wheel stands or smoking rubber) for anything you can get to the ground at high RPM is a great trade. Hence, the EVO is moved 10, 20, or 40 degrees earlier in drag-race cars running multiple large nitrous kits. Whenever you look down a drag-race exhaust lobe list and see profiles that are 320 to 340-plus at 0.050-inch tappet lift, you can be almost certain they are for nitrous applications.

There is more mass in the combustion chamber that needs to exit with added nitrous. Hence, the earlier exhaust opening not only flattens the torque curve low, but it also reduces the increased exhaust pumping losses at higher RPM for that added mass. Running a larger exhaust valve, port, and header tube is a better way to reduce pumping losses, but the earlier EVO helps when there's an additional 50 percent or more mass to remove.

In general, except some softening of the combustion chamber and the early EVO, make sure you make as much power possible without the nitrous. This allows a larger shot without unstable combustion. If you add more nitrous horsepower than you make with naturally aspirated horsepower (say a 1,200 shot on an 1,100-hp engine), invest in Alcoa stock as you are going to go through pistons like a Top Fuel team. The more air your engine ingests without the nitrous, the more nitrous it can safely run.

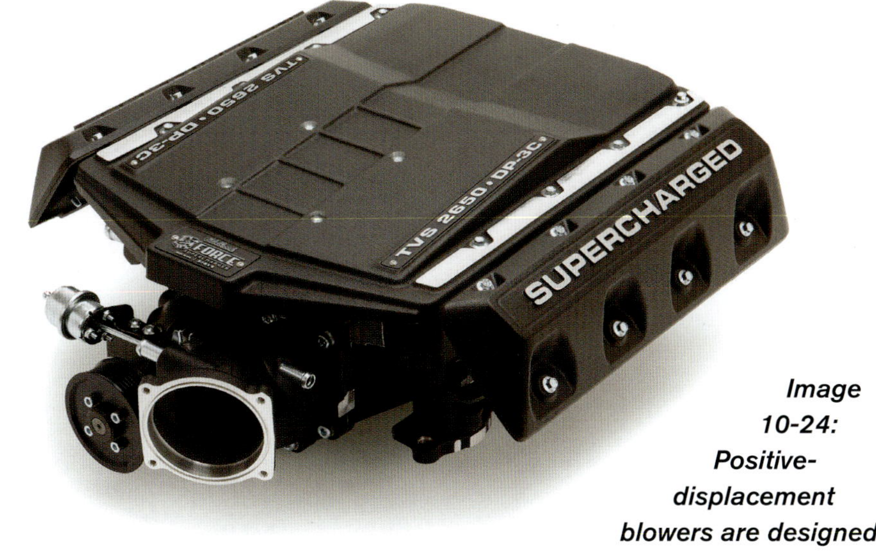

Image 10-24: Positive-displacement blowers are designed to move a certain volume of air from one side to the other each revolution. They are often rated by the displaced volume per revolution. The mass moved is relative to the pressure and temperature fed, so a free-flowing entry is critical, and efficiency will play a key role. Engineered systems, such as this unit from Edelbrock, often have an intercooler built into the blower, and they fit under production hoods.

Positive-Displacement Blowers/Superchargers

Unlike the nitrous application above, a positive-displacement blower (straight roots, lobe, or screw) fundamentally changes the inlet pressure and moves the flow at intake valve opening from being nudged by wave tuning to driven by the blower pressure. Wave tuning with the intake can help a bit in these applications, but with blowers, it is more fine tuning than critical for performance.

Thinking about IVO, with any positive-displacement blower when it is not intentionally bypassed, there will be significant flow into the chamber as soon as the intake opens. Because of the early flow, timing the IVO and sizing overlap is going to be very different from the considerations for naturally aspirated applications.

The general first step is to ask if there is a compressor map available. They are extremely useful because it helps estimate the power potential of the blower using the 10-times rule of thumb between the airflow in pounds per minute and horsepower potential. If a compressor (positive-displacement blower, centrifugal blower, or turbo)

Limited Blower Camshaft Valve Timing

INPUT		Intake		Exhaust	
Duration @ .050":		248.00		274.00	
Offset @ .050":		0.00		0.00	
Cam is ground with Lobe Separation of:				119	
and Advance of:				1	
OUTPUT					
Valve Timing @ .050" Tappet Lift:		Opening		Closing	
	Intake	**6.00**	BTDC	**62.00**	ABDC
	Exhaust	**77.00**	BBDC	**17.00**	ATDC
These specs are with cam installed at:			**118**	Intake Center Line	
			120	Exhaust Center Line	

Large Blower Camshaft Valve Timing

INPUT		Intake		Exhaust	
Duration @ .050":		264.00		274.00	
Offset @ .050":		0.00		0.00	
Cam is ground with Lobe Separation of:				115	
and Advance of:				5	
OUTPUT					
Valve Timing @ .050" Tappet Lift:		Opening		Closing	
	Intake	**22.00**	BTDC	**62.00**	ABDC
	Exhaust	**77.00**	BBDC	**17.00**	ATDC
These specs are with cam installed at:			**110**	Intake Center Line	
			120	Exhaust Center Line	

Image 10-25: With the large blower, the intake may open 16 degrees earlier. You might wonder why someone would ever waste that much air. It is not actually wasted. Cross-flow can drop the manifold pressure into a range where the blower is more efficient and also give the incoming charge added velocity and momentum to better fill the chamber once the exhaust valve closes, like a running start. This overlap also cleans and cools the chamber.

can flow 150 pounds of air each minute at the target pressure ratio (boost) and RPM, the power potential estimate is 1,500 hp. You can subtract 10 percent for the drive power on a blower or add 5 percent for methanol due to the oxygen in the fuel, but this quick look gives us some idea of the flow potential, much like the CFM of a cylinder head.

Once you know the compressor flow, consider the horsepower target for the application. If we have a 1,500-hp-capable compressor and only need 1,000 hp to be competitive, then allowing 500 hp worth of air and fuel to bypass the chamber during overlap can be accepted without concern. Here, added overlap gives the intake charge time to build speed, and this compressor can replenish the air that took the shortcut.

However, if you have a blower than can only flow 125 lbs/min and you need to make 1,100-plus hp (think NHRA Factory Shootout), you have to be extremely careful with overlap. The earlier intake opening can still help increase flow, but there's a limited air supply, so this blower behaves more like a restrictor plate–type engine. In these, we see much later intake openings and slightly earlier exhaust closings. The cam specs might be more like 248/274 at 0.050 inch on 119+ LSA with a small blower at high RPM compared to 260/274 at 115 LSA with a larger blower with all other things equal.

The reason these smaller blowers are often run at such high engine speeds in competition is the blower speed is often physically limited by rule with pulley sizes. If so, the only way to run the blower faster is to spin the crank faster. To allow the engine to operate at those increased speeds, the profiles must be stable, and the exhaust opening must be early enough to not create exhaust pumping losses at high speeds, so consider an earlier EVO too. Stability might be the most important aspect of any forced induction valvetrain system.

For naturally aspirated applications, there's natural difficulty with driving an engine too far into valvetrain distress without significant power loss. Because some forced induction systems are so effective at moving air, they often take it well past the point of stability. You are still likely to be down 100, 200, or more hp, but with a 1,200-plus-hp engine, it might not be noticeable enough to lift.

Bower camshafts are often tuned to shape the torque curve, just like with nitrous applications. Older roots blowers are known to produce amazing torque at low RPM. On these, we often intentionally add duration to soften the lower-RPM torque. The response will be excellent due to the positive displacement air feed, but we will choose to give up some lower end that was impossible to use to gain power at higher RPM, which is easier to get to the pavement.

One common mistake with all forced induction applications is an assumption that intake port speeds are higher. The opposite is true. Forced induction adds density, so the peak mass flow is higher but not at peak velocity. Because of the pressure differential at intake opening, the cylinder starts to fill earlier, more efficiently, and more completely than the same engine without a blower.

The intake closing may still be delayed, but that is because we are trying to reduce torque early and help it carry at higher RPM. As far at the crank angle where air stops filling the cylinder and is pushed back into the intake runner, that happens slightly earlier in any blower application. If we decide on the same or later IVC with a blower as NA, it is for torque curve shaping and moving the best tuned range to higher RPM.

Centrifugal Superchargers

The major difference between positive-displacement blowers and centrifugal superchargers is the end of the power curve. The most modern centrifugal race superchargers spin fast enough so there is very little to almost no boost delay from when the vehicle launches until the boost is in the desired range. However, street systems require the engine to climb past peak torque before it begins building proper boost for best performance.

From the camshaft point of view, we need to tailor the torque curve with the valve timing points. The first step is always going to be choosing profiles, valve springs, and a system that is stable in the desired RPM range. Then, we select the intake closing with more attention to low RPM than high to be certain we get a great launch and/or throttle response for this centrifugal system. If there is a stable valvetrain and the exhaust opening is early enough not to create severe exhaust pumping losses at high RPM, the centrifugal compressor will provide all the air needed at high RPM.

The exhaust opening is very similar between the positive-displacement and centrifugal blower system. When positive-displacement blowers use a later EVO, it is typically because the camshaft was designed to run at a

Image 10-26: Exactly as we discussed with the blowers, the compressor side of any turbo has a map that describes the pressure ratio (boost), airflow, shaft speed, and the input power required. This turbo was sized for a max-effort street 5.3L engine, so both the compressor and the exhaust side (turbine) became limiting above 1,100 hp when run on a 427 LS above 7,500 rpm. How big a turbo is will have everything to do with the RPM and displacement of the engine processing the air and fuel.

lower RPM. Both systems are similar on overlap with the same considerations of compressor map to power goals. The biggest differences are in street applications, especially with factory EFI systems. Positive displacement systems always dampen the negative aspects of overlap. The rotors slap the reflected wave back and reduce misfire. Because centrifugal systems are farther upstream and do almost nothing at idle, the overlap and vacuum targets are very close to naturally aspirated to work well with the control system.

A great way of thinking about centrifugal blowers is that they are basically naturally aspirated engines until you spin the centrifugal blower fast enough to build boost. At that point, the blower becomes the airflow driver, and the piston engine can be viewed almost as a processor. If you select the camshaft to get the engine and blower into the happy speed as quickly as possible and do not choke the system with too late of an exhaust opening, you will have one very fast package.

Turbo Systems

If you are building a turbo system, the two most important pieces of information needed to properly select the camshaft are:

1) Boost to backpressure ratios through the operating range
2) Airflow the turbo can support (as shown on the compressor map)

Turbocharged engines with the similar boost to backpressure (0.8 to 1.5:1) follow the same guidelines as naturally aspirated applications with one vast difference. My friend John Bewley describes these as NA engines somewhere deep in Jupiter. Looking back, we changed IVC depending on CFM per cubic inch. The better the head, the earlier the IVC for the same RPM. Instead of a 350-ci engine with a 300-cfm cylinder head, what if we had a 350-ci engine with a 600-cfm cylinder head? With a similar boost

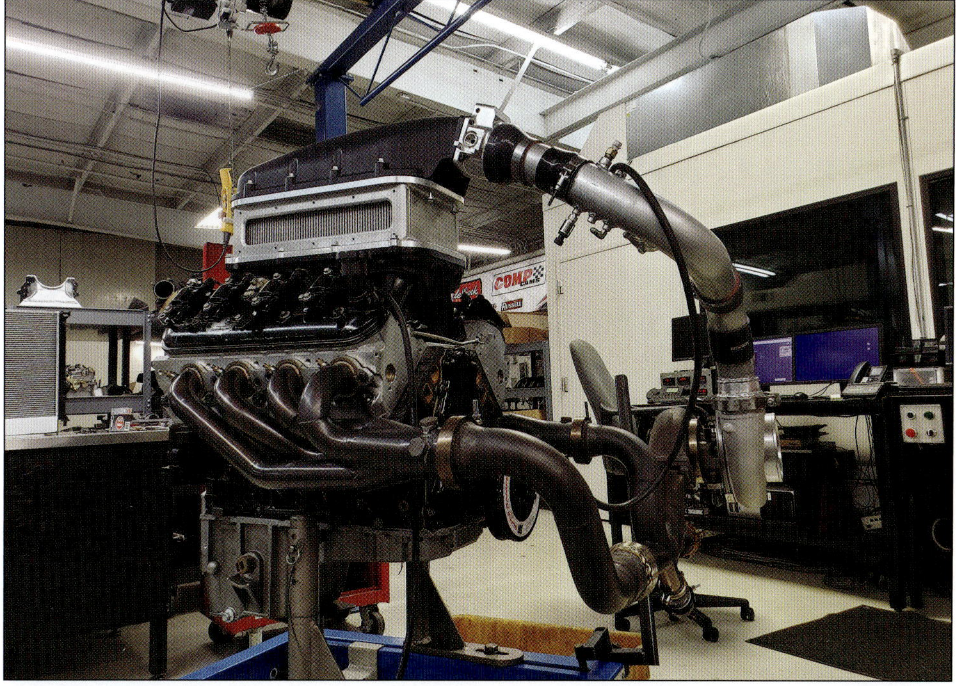

Image 10-27: Going with a shorter header to catch a reflected wave instead of the primary at IVO is a good decision with a turbo system because it puts the turbine closer to the exhaust valve and allows less energy to dissipate. However, we will benefit for using intake runner lengths the same that we would at the same RPM in naturally aspirated applications at the same engine speed and overlap. If we put very short runners on this engine, the midrange power suffers.

to backpressure, that is almost exactly how a turbo engine will perform. That is why you see so many 5.3L Gen III (LS) engines that make awesome power at 7,200 rpm with cams in the low 220s at 0.050 inch.

Why small cams work so well at high RPM in turbo applications has everything to do with air density. When we run engine simulations of turbo engines, we see an increased density along with decreased port velocity. Unless boost is greater than backpressure, it doesn't start filling as soon as the valve opens. However, all the naturally aspirated wave tuning tricks will work exactly the same in turbocharged as NA applications. Most people do not take the time to tune header lengths and intake port lengths for the desired RPM, but doing so is certainly beneficial, especially if you want to take full advantage of overlap.

Overlap is extremely beneficial in a well-developed turbocharged application. Not only can wave tuning and overlap allow the intake port to flow the right direction while the piston is still rising, but it can also help build boost and launch the car at lower RPM. Even systems that reach 2:1 backpressure to boost at high RPM tend to be less than 1:1 at low RPM. When that is the case, the overlap region provides a shot of air and fuel through to the collector from each cylinder overlap cycle. This charge is ignited by the other exhaust gases and acts like an afterburner to help power the turbine side of the turbo. This drives the turbo to higher RPM sooner and helps turbo drag cars off the line and turbo rally cars out of the corner.

However, if you have 3:1-plus backpressure to boost and use overlap to your advantage, you will be very disappointed. When the intake manifold is removed, it will look like someone had a campfire in the intake ports. At IVO, the exhaust gases and carbon are pushed back up the inlet track until the exhaust valve closes and the piston drops to create the pressure drop required to fill the cylinder. Applications like this benefit from shorter and smaller overlap triangles. Some overlap is needed to allow the intake to be sufficiently open at 70 degrees after TDC when the piston velocity is highest, but these systems are the ones that lead to the belief that all turbo systems should have 120-plus LSA and shorter exhaust than intake duration. Going back to the 2300 Ford in the Mustang SVO, the stock turbine (exhaust side) was very restrictive, so closing the exhaust early is required to fill the cylinder. While amazing advancements have been made on the compressor side of turbo systems, the ones that have changed the camshaft selection the most have been on the exhaust turbine (hot) side.

If we move our attention from a 1980s Pinto engine to a modern Pro Mod application, the specs will move from 218/212 at 0.050-inch valve lift with a 120-plus LSA to something more like 266/290 at 0.050-inch tappet lift on about a 118 LSA. In the modern Pro Mod, the backpressure is very close to the boost, and the intake and exhaust ports are well tuned. The cam is probably 20 degrees shorter duration on the intake and maybe 10 to 15 degrees shorter on the exhaust than on the same engine at the same RPM without the turbo.

Overlap is more limited by two factors in these applications. The first limit is piston-to-valve clearance. However, if the compressor inlet is unlimited, the best cam is likely larger and more like a 115 LSA. Just as with blowers, turbo-application engine builders must be aware of the compressor map limits to power capability and use that information to make decisions on how much overlap can be run without letting too much of the intake charge pass through during overlap. Pro Mod lets more through than it would for peak power alone, as the biggest challenge compared to the blower and nitrous cars in the first 330 feet. The added overlap hurts with lost air mass over the last half track, but it is beneficial early in the run and provides extra energy to the turbine side to build boost.

Taking those durations and centerlines, look at the events and consider how they compare to the same engine in NA trim. That 266/290 118 inches at 116 gives the flowing timing:

	Opening		Closing	
Intake	17.00	BTDC	69.00	ABDC
Exhaust	85.00	BBDC	25.00	ATDC

Compared to an NA 288/306 118 plus 2 events:

	Opening		Closing	
Intake	28.00	BTDC	80.00	ABDC
Exhaust	93.00	BBDC	33.00	ATDC

***Image 10-28:** While this Edelbrock turbo system for the Ford EcoBoost 3.5L engine uses compressor and turbine sides that are much larger than stock, this still-compact unit increases responsiveness required for both towing and low-speed fun. When dealing with limited-size turbos, be aware of overlap at high speed. Being able to move all four camshafts helps.*

We've explained what the less overlap (IVO + EVC) of 42 versus 61 degrees has to do with the airflow limit. Also, the IVC of 69 versus 80 has to do with the slower intake port velocity and better fill with a denser charge. What about EVO? If we delayed the EVO to 85 degrees, the Pro Mod has more difficulty from exhaust pumping losses at very high RPM.

With the added power, the exhaust is opened with 10-bar-plus cylinder pressure (140-plus psi). The exhaust system average pressure might be in the 4-bar range, but we hope to use the wave tuning to drop that to maybe plus 2 bar at EVO. Just like with an NA application, opening the exhaust earlier reduces exhaust pumping losses by giving the exhaust mass more time to exit the chamber.

One nice feature of turbo engines is that while the crank still powers the compressor through the turbine, the exhaust pumping losses as the piston rises toward TDC are used for something instead of being a pure loss. In an NA application, nothing good comes from exhaust pumping. In a turbo application, think of the pumping losses like a blower belt. The work lost pushing the exhaust out is also work done driving the turbine. I'm not saying that what was bad is now good, but some loss in the PV loop is needed to drive the turbine side. Still, there is never a free lunch with EVO as it helps somewhere and hurts somewhere else.

If you look at Comp Cams shelf grinds for Turbo LS applications, note the street grind designed to work with full exhaust has less exhaust duration and overlap than the more street/strip camshaft. If the turbo is your only muffler that dumps out through a 4-inch-plus bullhorn, there will be less backpressure and the added exhaust duration and overlap are used effectively. However, setting up for higher backpressure is of very little loss on the street.

The late EVO makes the engine more responsive low with a longer effective power stroke, and the turbo feeds it through the mid- to high range. It might be down 25 to 50 hp high, but that's not horrible on an 800-hp street car. Honestly, you probably shred tires through first and second if you go full boost on the street, and by third gear up that extra 50 hp barely changes the floor of the jailhouse if you get caught.

The added responsiveness low can honestly be more fun than the added power high of the more

GM LS Turbo 4.8L & 5.3L

	APPLICATIONS/CAMSHAFTS	VALVE SETTING IN.	VALVE SETTING EX.	RPM OPERATING RANGE	CAM ONLY PART #	DURATION ADVERTISED IN.	DURATION ADVERTISED EX.	DURATION @ .050" IN.	DURATION @ .050" EX.	VALVE LIFT w/ 1.7 ROCKER IN.	VALVE LIFT w/ 1.7 ROCKER EX.	LOBE SEP. ANGLE
Street	**HYDRAULIC ROLLER** – Perfect choice for 4.8L & 5.3L "cam only" turbo engines w/ unknown back pressure. 7400 RPM stability with CK & MK Kits.	Hyd.	Hyd.	2300-7400	**54-330-11**	278	280	223	225	.598	.600	115
Race	**HYDRAULIC ROLLER** – Perfect choice for 5.3L with upgraded, lower back pressure turbo systems. 7400 RPM stability with CK & MK Kits.	Hyd.	Hyd.	2500-7400	**54-332-11**	286	292	231	237	.605	.610	115
								+8	+12			

***Image 10-29:** When there is a restrictive exhaust or turbine, reduce overlap and select the EVO and IVC for a lower RPM before the system is choked. Just going to a less-restrictive turbo system allows us to add 10 degrees of overlap, a 4-degree-later IVC, and a 6-degree-earlier EVO.*

race-oriented cam specs, so miss to the small duration side on street grinds. However, on a well-prepared drag strip with slicks and a race suspension, 900 hp is better than 800 hp, so get your backpressure under control and go with the race specs.

Compound or Multiple Power Adders

When Forrest Gump talked about some things going together like peas and carrots, I am sure he was thinking about turbos and nitrous. The right turbo is always a size or two smaller than the one that makes the most power, otherwise it is lazy to spool and build boost. However, even the slightest sniff of nitrous adds all that low-end mass flow, along with amazing thermal energy in the exhaust, to almost magically kick the turbine side. It only takes a small shot (like 100 hp on a 400-hp NA application) to get a larger turbo going off the line, so there is little reason to turn it off once the engine makes 800 hp with the boost. You get the benefit of the larger turbo and use far less nitrous than with a nitrous-only application.

For the camshaft, simply move the exhaust opening a little earlier and know that you don't require as much work from the crank to drive the turbine at lower engine speeds. The only three negatives of the combined approach are the cost of dual systems, the pain of occasionally filling bottles, and the lack of appreciation from most sanctioning bodies of the dual-power-added approach.

Image 10-30: When the whole building is rocking from a day's worth of 1,000-plus-hp dyno pulls as intercoolers and camshafts are tested, the marketing department takes photos and video. Nolan Smith (pictured), Trent Goodwin, and Roman Greene have been a huge help with many of the images throughout this book.

The second-best dual-power-adder approach is a big turbo(s) filling a smallish blower. Take the 2003 Ford Cobra with the OEM 1.8L factory supercharger. If you add a large turbo or pair upstream, the added mass flow of the blower at low RPM gives the turbo a kick low. Likewise, the blower moves far more total mass when fed by two-plus atmospheres of pressurized air. Looking at the typical compressor map for the blower, multiply the mass flow by the atmospheres fed. Hence, what was a 650-hp blower is a 1,300-hp blower when fed a cool 15 psi after a turbo and intercooler. Without the intercooler, there's still a significant improvement over stock.

Tractor-pull diesel classes (Super Stock) are the only common applications where I have dealt with staged turbos. The biggest benefit of this approach is the lower backpressure to boost over a single system. There are significant complexity, cost, and weight concerns to this approach, but you have to be a little mad at your money to compete in this class. This is the class that forced me to rethink valve-spring seat loads for all boosted applications.

When someone runs 90-plus psi on a 3-plus-inch OD valve, there are 600-plus pounds on the backside of that intake valve (7 square inches times 90 psi). When I asked Dave Bamber how much seat load he ran, he told me about 80 to 100 pounds. How do you close a valve with 100 pounds when you have 600 pounds pushing on one side? Well, that is pretty easy if you have 650 pounds pushing on the other side.

Valve-Spring Selection with Boost

The common fallacy with almost all boosted spring calculations is from someone not looking at the pressure on both sides of the valve at each event. At IVC, you never want to close the valve until the pressure is greater in the chamber than the port. Otherwise, you limit flow into the chamber. Up until peak power, you are likely closing the valve too late and well after the pressures were equalized. That is why advancing the cam helps at lower speed.

Past peak power you may be closing a bit early. For this reason, I do often recommend about 10- to 20-plus percent more seat load on boosted applications. The range has more to do with how well they optimized their cam timing than any boost to valve area calculation. Those calculations came into popularity during the early days of the sports compact racing after the first *Fast and Furious* movie was released. People added turbos to otherwise factory engines with factory camshafts and revved them well past where the IVC or cam profile was optimized. Because of those two factors, the gorilla springs worked. You can sometimes do two wrong things and luck into something that works, then believe you were right in your reasoning.

Back to staged turbo systems. When you select the camshafts for staged turbo systems, it is basically a hybrid combination of what to do for a very good turbo system and what is best with a good blower. There will always be more pressure in the inlet port than exhaust, so flow begins as soon as the intake cracks like a blower. Also, the power to drive comes from the exhaust stroke, not directly from the crank snout, so that is like a normal turbo.

A large centrifugal supercharger might benefit from a sniff of nitrous, especially if not driven at high speeds at lower RPM. Most other combinations do not seem as beneficial. Staged blowers tend to add a whole lot of a headache for less benefit. Parallel blowers are really the same as a single blower and allow a smaller blower to act twice as large. Positive displacement blowers plus nitrous are a recipe to blow the crank out at low RPM. This might make for a fun experiment with a very strong diesel, at least to know if the crank comes out first or the block splits in two. Cam-wise, just go big to try and reshape the doubly skewed torque curve flatter.

As an overview for all power adders, and maybe all engines, you are setting timing points based on two major factors. The first is pressure across the valve at IVC. The second is shaping the torque curve to best match the application, which is far less realized yet extremely important for best performance. You may hear that every cam is a turbo cam or every camshaft is a blower camshaft. While that is true enough from one point of view, it by no means guarantees that every camshaft is a good turbo or blower camshaft for a given application.

Thermal Management

There are many non-intuitive things we can do with camshafts. We mentioned this a bit with fuels but it should have its own section to dive in just a bit deeper. On most air-cooled engines, and especially air-cooled Harley V-Twins, we add considerable overlap for fuel cooling. Most air-cooled engines run well rich of stoichiometry, and the added fuel during overlap is used to draw heat from the piston top and exhaust valve. If we were to set overlap only based on peak power, they would not sound as cool, nor would they run as cool (pun intended).

EVO plays a huge part into where heat will flow. The longer the exhaust valve is shut, the more goes into the head, cylinder, and eventually water in water-cooled applications. The earlier the exhaust opens, the larger slice of the Chapter 4 (Image 4-9) energy pie goes into the exhaust. By playing with both EVO and ignition timing, more energy can be moved into the exhaust stream. We talked about how most good engines share heat as one-third to the crank, one-third to the water, and one-third out the exhaust. Delaying the ignition timing and moving the exhaust opening earlier, both move the energy from the engine cooling and into the exhaust gases.

In liquid fueled applications, by increasing overlap and opening the exhaust earlier, we can reduce the cooling requirements of the radiator. However, EGTs will increase. If we need to reduce EGTs, or collector temps in endurance turbocharged applications, the opposite approach can be taken. Delaying EVO, reducing overlap, and adding a bit more timing can all lead to lower exhaust and under-hood temperatures.

VALVETRAIN SELECTION

I am guilty of saving the hardest questions for last. Once you know what type of camshaft you are going to run and are getting closer on the general specs, you need to select the best lobe families for the job at hand. The easy button is to call someone at the camshaft company to ask for help and grind the camshaft. I assume that you want to be more involved, so we will go through what I would ask.

Camshaft Type

The first thing to determine is what type of lifter will be run and if it is an OHC engine. Then, breaking it down to a hydraulic flat tappet, solid flat tappet, hydraulic roller, or solid roller is a great step.

Over the next decade, flat-tappet camshafts will likely grow significantly in price. Their nose radius limits the lift for a given duration, like a triangle with a rounded nose shown in Images 2-46 and 2-47 in Chapter 2, so you likely will not be able to run the lift to the desired range. The tappet profile velocity is quite limited before a flat-tappet lobe goes off the edge of the lifter, so in general, you will be down on area with any flat design compared to a roller.

Lastly, even in the OEM world, flat-tappet failures were so awful in the 1980s that both GM and Ford spent well over $100 extra on hundreds of thousands of pickups each year. Take a minute to think about what forced those companies to spend between $30 and $100 million each year to go to a roller camshaft. It was not for performance, as early rollers had the same tappet and valve motion—nor was it for emissions or mileage. What forced them to make that investment was warranty

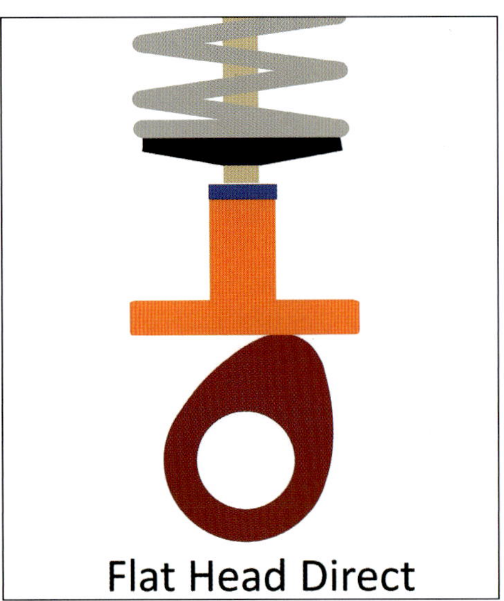

Image 11-1: When dealing with a flathead layout, tappet motion is valve motion. With a flat-faced direct-acting tappet, the lobe can be constructed by adding tappet lift to the base-circle radius and weeping on a surface grinder like we discussed with the theory of envelopes in Chapter 1. The cam is maroon, the tappet is orange, the lash adjustment is blue, the valve is taupe, and the spring is gray.

Image 11-2: These cams were cut from tappet data on a surface grinder. The process left 360 facets, but they are polished until a nice model lobe is made. These were then used to make the Berco master. The roller-cam model required more math and time as you had to go up and down at each angle for the concave sides.

Image 11-3: In the rooms above engineering, we have filing cabinets full of our original models. Each of these took dozens of hours of design and manufacturing time before the master was made and the first camshaft was ground. We have digital data on all these now, and the CNC grinders don't need a physical representation of the lobe to copy, so these have been relegated to being very cool conversation pieces.

Image 11-4: It looks almost as straight-forward in a Briggs & Stratton 5 hp as it did in Image 11-1, but here is how the valvetrain lays out in respect to the rest of the engine. I thank Sheldon Gecker Jr. for having this engine sliced up when he worked in our Go Parts division.

Image 11-5: These photos of Keith and Jeff Dorton's land-speed racing flathead Ford show the OEM-style flat-faced flathead next to the Jesel roller lifter for this same application. The Dorton flathead land-speed builds are awesome. Compared to a typical pushrod and rocker layout, a flathead should be amazingly stiff, but Ford left out a cam bearing that I wish it had kept. While the Briggs & Stratton requires setting the lash by filing the tappet, a flathead Ford uses screw adjusters that can be accessed from the valley of the V. (Photo Courtesy Jeff Honeycutt)

Image 11-6: Note the adjusters in the valley of this Ford flathead. Imagine taking off the carburetors and intake, getting down there with a wrench, and regularly adjusting the lash on these engines that were produced by the millions by Ford over the period from 1932 to 1953.

Image 11-7: This should look very familiar, especially if you hold Image 11-1 upside down and imagine the spring swallowed into the lifter. This is the overhead camshaft bucket design. It flowed very soon after the flathead design but is still extremely popular today in almost all types of engines. Just like the flathead, here tappet motion is valve motion and requires no conversions from a cam designer's point of view.

Image 11-8: This is the Vance & Hines Pro Stock bike with a V-rod, 4V V-twin cylinder head and valvetrain that was successful in NHRA from about 2010 until they were required to go back to a 2V layout. The keyed and radius-pad-faced diamond-like carbon (DLC) buckets allow well over 0.750-inch lift. With DLC, this configuration is more like a roller flathead than a conventional flat tappet. (Photo Courtesy Byron Hines)

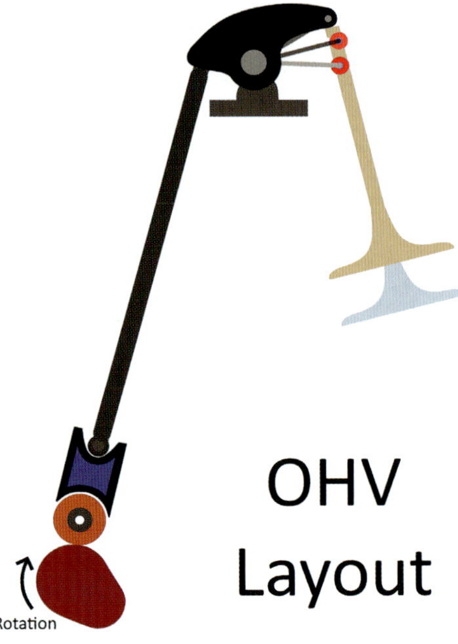

Image 11-9: The OHV layout is certainly the most common layout in American motorsports. While having the disadvantage of being the most difficult layout to make extremely stiff because the pushrods bend, rockers flex, cams bend, and the stands move around, these systems continue to improve every generation. The best OHV systems today are quite impressive, and this configuration allows very compact V engines relative to displacement.

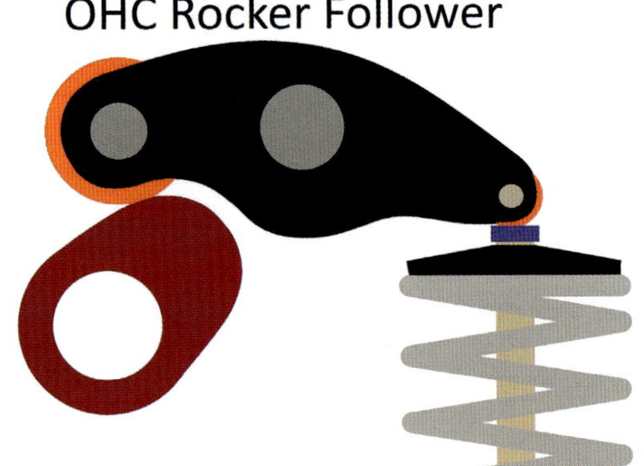

Image 11-11: The OHC rocker follower is reminiscent of the OHV but with the pushrod missing. This layout drops the cam lower in the cylinder head than the direct bucket style and allows one camshaft to operate both intake and exhaust valves in a 2V Hemi or 3V or 4V Pent Roof chamber layout. Because the cam-to-lobe contact moves from the close side next to the trunnion over to the far side, the rocker ratio can vary from less than 1:1 to more than 2:1 through the valve motion. It requires a sophisticated design conversion to create the required profile for a given valve motion design.

Image 11-12: This Honda V-6 cylinder head has been modified to allow access to the roller OHC rocker followers to measure accurately on the coordinate measuring machine (CMM). Note that these are still solid adjustment, which are much lighter than hydraulics with an OHC rocker layout. Also shown is the variable valve timing and lift electronic control (VTEC) system. In this system, the outboard intake rockers control the valve motion at low RPM, and a pin connects all three rockers, so the middle lobe and rocker controls the valve at high RPM. These compact engines have a well-earned reputation for durability, efficiency, and performance over a wide range of engine speeds.

Image 11-13: This compact weed trimmer engine has stamped OHC rocker followers adjusted on studs with a ball pivot riding on a plastic camshaft. I enjoy seeing such a combination of old and new technology.

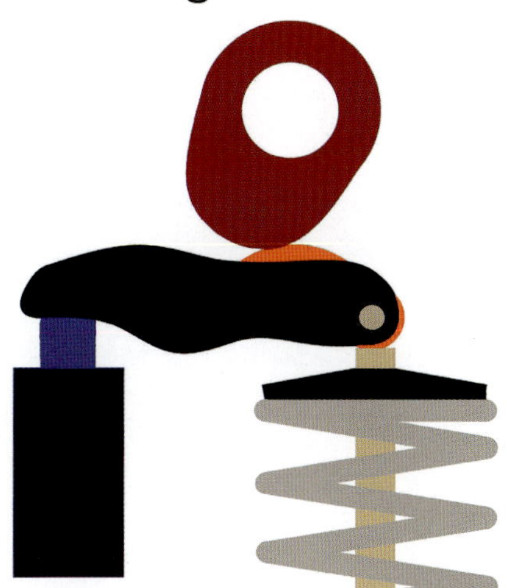

Image 11-14: The OHC rocker body bends at the pivot and both sides add mass, so what if we put the cam and valve on the same side? That is exactly how the OHC finger geometries are created. This is drastically stiffer than the OHC rocker layout with a much lower MOI. Most modern OHC engine designers try to incorporate this layout when possible.

Image 11-15: This is the Leagon's Racing Heads Ford Pinto 2300 mini stock engine. This OHC finger engine has seen sustained success across the dirt-track series. It quite often finds itself running against the OHC rocker Toyota 22RE. These cam lobes always look asymmetric (even if the valve motion is close to symmetric) because of the way the contact point moves toward and away from the valve tip on both sides. (Photo Courtesy Leagon's Racing Heads)

Image 11-16: Note the more-compact roller rockers and valve springs that would be equally at home on a dirt late-model or NASCAR-type engine used by Gary Stanton in the SX11 Midget. Not only is the valvetrain great but the ports and chambers are also awesome.

Image 11-17: Moving to ever lower mass followers, Formula 1 and then Moto GP went to this style of very light OHC finger followers instead of buckets. These are lighter and allow better spring oiling without pressure building up around the valve seals. That design of layout made its way to the production BMW bike, then to this Yamaha R1, and now to the 5.5L Corvette Z06. Note how compact and light this system can be if you are willing to invest serious attention to detail.

Image 11-18: The most common OHC finger layout is a compact roller finger follower. This became popular with the Ford Modular 4.6L and 5.4L V-8 SOHC 2V engines and the DOHC 4V. Then, it was refined for each generation through the current Ford Coyote. Each version is lower mass and higher stiffness. This is a picture of Chris Smith's Aston Martin V12 from Elan, which is closely related to the Ford Duratec V-6. Many Audi systems and the current Lamborghini V10 system are extremely close as well. This design is not as light as the DLC slider, but it is far less expensive.

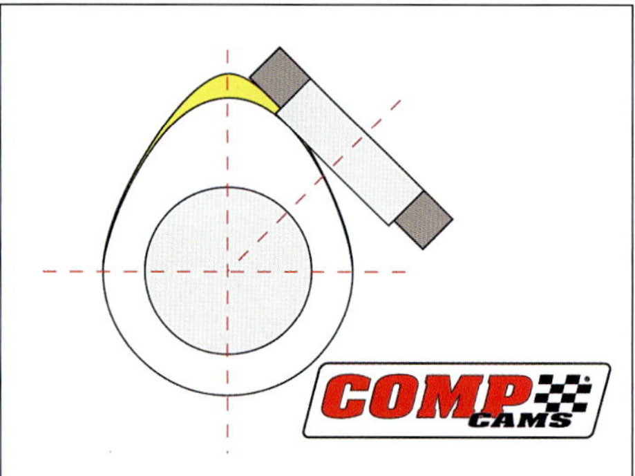

Image 11-19: This white profile uses almost all of the light gray tappet-face diameter. If you tried to run the yellow profile with the light gray tappet, you can see how the contact would go over the edge. However, you can safely run either the yellow or white profiles with the dark gray tappet. Some people believe running a 0.875- or 0.904-inch tappet on an 0.842-inch design results in different motion. As you can see here, it does not change the motion.

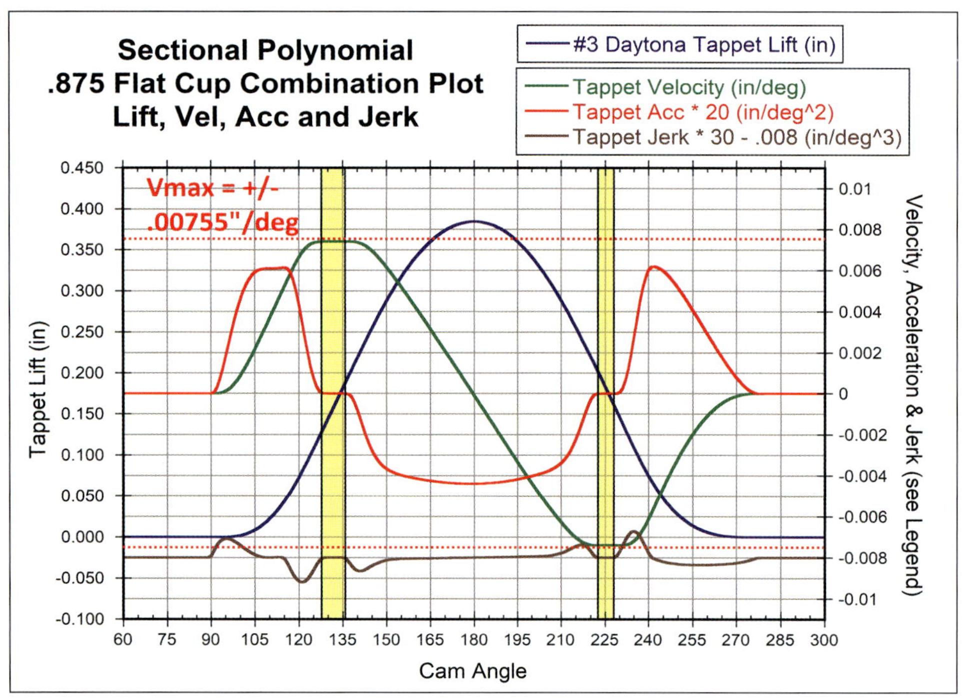

Image 11-20: To see how to maximize area when constrained by a velocity limit, look back at the sectional polynomial NASCAR design. Note the dotted red lines where the tappet contact would go off the edge if exceeded. The yellow regions highlight where we camped at this limit for about 8 cam (16 crank) degrees on the opening side and 6 cam (12 crank) degrees on the closing side. This technique was like playing The Price is Right *on the lifter foot (closest without going over).*

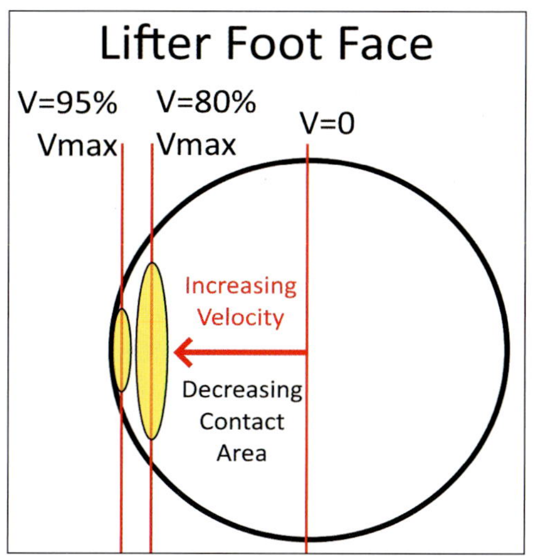

***Image 11-21:** While going over the edge results in immediate failure, it is wise to stay back. The closer that you get to the lifter-face edge, the smaller the region on the lifter foot that will support the total pushrod load in the max velocity region. As you can see, 80 percent of V_{max} results in significantly more contact area than 95 percent. A few physics geeks are thinking that forces should be zero at V_{max}, but that is not the case when surge, separation, and deflection are included.*

Lobe	6587	34327	
Ratio	1.6:1	1.6:1	
Lash	0.012	0.012	
Valve Duration			Increase
0.050	271	273	2
0.200	216	217	1
0.400	150	158	8
0.500	113	123	10
0.600	58	76	+18 or +31%

***Image 11-22:** On* Motor-Trend's Engine Masters *series (Season 7, Episode 111), a small-block Chrysler was tested using a very good 0.940-inch solid flat-tappet camshaft as well as a new Comp low-shock solid-roller grind. The low-shock attributes even allowed the same valve springs to be used. Looking at this chart, with almost 10 percent added to the 0.500-inch valve-lift duration and 31-plus-percent more time above 0.600-inch valve lift, you can see why the new cam added 35 hp.*

issues from failed camshafts. Imagine those problems with light OEM springs, smooth OEM cams, low lifts, large-nose radii, and the high ZDDP oils of that day.

***Image 11-23:** At some point in the future, DLC lifters may become affordable and have far fewer concerns about flat-tappet cam failure and allow stronger steel camshafts and higher spring loads to be used safely. It would still have limited area and most of the same power reduction compared to a roller but would make a flat tappet more attractive than it is currently with iron cams and lifters.*

Now, extrapolate that to the oils of today and higher-lift and quicker camshafts. People who say they never fail flat-tappet camshafts simply don't build enough to see the statistical problems. We have come a long way with surface finish, as well as phosphate dip, but there is always a statistically significant chance of failure with any iron flat-tappet camshaft and lifter up to the point I could never suggest an engine builder go that route unless forced to by rules. If the rules require a flat tappet, then you have to play the cards you were dealt.

Choosing Hydraulic versus Solid

If we have proven that every cam being a turbo cam is faulty logic, we can just as easily disprove that every cam is a solid cam. I design both hydraulic and solid the same, except the hydraulics are designed around 0.006-inch lash versus what typically is a looser target for a solid (sometimes a tight 0.012 to 0.015 inch and sometimes 0.025-plus inch). Many people believe the solid cams are quicker or higher acceleration. In general, the acceleration is determined by the target RPM. Because most hydraulic-roller profiles are optimized for sub-6,500 rpm, and most solid-roller profiles are designed to run above 7,500 rpm, hydraulic-roller profiles tend to be quicker than the average solid-roller profile.

As more lobe families have been introduced, the newer solid-roller profiles are in every way better than a hydraulic design used with a solid lifter. The biggest issue with the solid lifter on a hydraulic profile is getting close to the 0.006-inch target hot lash. If you have an aluminum block, it is basically impossible. With an iron block and head, it can be done if you don't have any valve-seat erosion. With an iron block and aluminum head, it falls in that "almost possible" range.

What can get you in trouble with very tight lash is a little seat erosion and a cold morning. One year at the

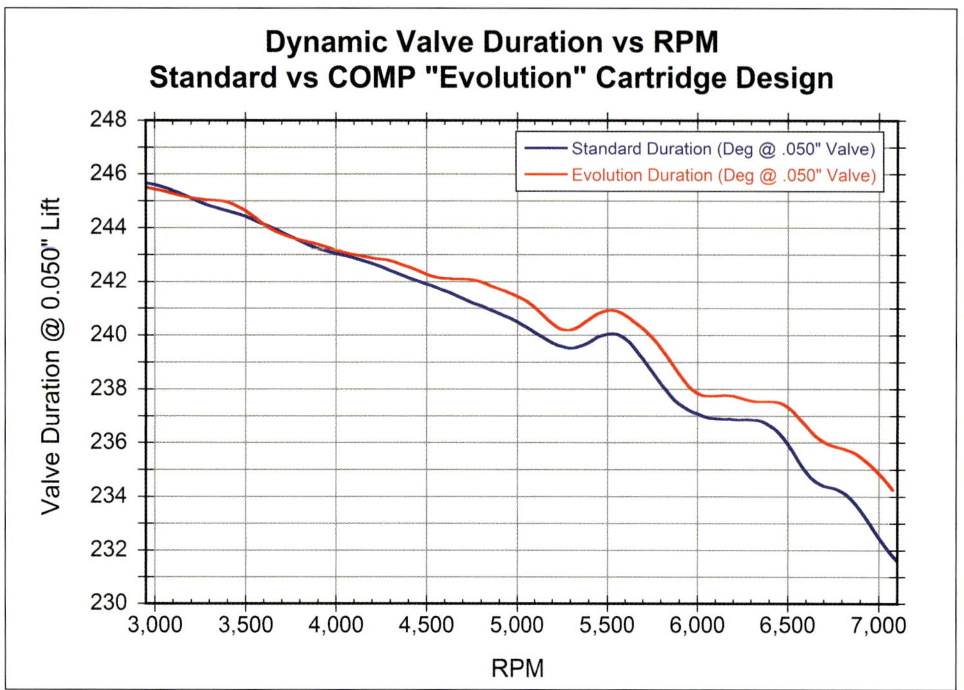

Image 11-24: Here, the measured duration at 0.050-inch valve lift changes with RPM between two hydraulic lifters on the Spintron. We wish this slope was uphill, but deflection in the rest of the system always results in losses with engine speed and resulting loads. The new Comp Cams evolution lifter is stiffer than a traditional design.

24 Hours of Daytona race, when I was enamored with very tight lash, IMSA red flagged the race for rain. A cold front came through while the cars, without heaters, sat. When the engines restarted, there was 0 lash or cracked valves on many engines.

As the drivers put heat in the engines too quickly, several engines failed from the exhaust gases that acted like a plasma torch around the seat. I probably got a few engine builders fired that day and fell out of love with very tight lash just as quickly as I had fallen in love with the idea. Remember, the exhaust valve heats up and grows before the head and block. An engine can start with 0.001-inch lash, then tighten up to under 0. My rule of thumb is to always run at least 0.004-inch cold lash, and I prefer 0.006 inch on the exhaust.

To pick between a solid and a hydraulic, we must decide if stiffness or ease of maintenance is more important. Stiffness is a big deal because every camshaft has variable duration. The problem is that they start big when they need to be small. As loads rise with RPM, they become smaller when you want them to get bigger. When we plot RPM versus duration with a hydraulic, the drop is always greater than with a solid. While that is a disadvantage, setting lash with most low-mass rocker arms can be difficult. Our XD-A pushrods help, but even that can add four hours to setting lash.

While hydraulic systems can never be as stiff as a solid system, we have gotten much closer with the Comp Cams new Evolution cartridge lifter. The cartridge moves the sealing surface from the body, so deflection under high side loading is far less. We also greatly increased the wall thickness for less bore distortion under higher pressures and moved the cartridge higher in the hydraulic body, where there is less distortion. Together with new manufacturing technologies that improve surface finish and part geometry, these greatly reduce the compromise of a hydraulic-roller lifter compared to a solid-roller design.

The most common questions I hear regarding hydraulic-roller lifters are about how much RPM they can allow and how much spring load can be used. On the RPM side, we designed systems that operated above 9,000 rpm with OEM-style hydraulic-roller lifters before the Evolution lifter was available. We had hundreds of 9,000-plus-rpm dyno pulls on a 6L LS with stock LS3 valves that we built for intake manifold testing.

Before NHRA allowed solid lifters in the Stock Eliminator classes, we had several lobe families and hundreds of profiles that commonly went over 8,000 rpm in competition. Because the lift rule is measured with 0 lash, this is one place where you want a sub-0.006-inch lash design on a solid where possible. Many of the engine builders use the same profiles on their solid lifters as they ran with hydraulics, but now a new generation of low-shock tight-lash solids is growing in popularity.

Basically, there is no hard-and-fast rule for how high the RPM can be with a hydraulic roller. If we wanted to make a 10,000-rpm hydraulic-roller LS tomorrow, I'm confident we would nail it on the first or second attempt. The lobe profile, system stiffness, and valve spring must be optimized for that job, but

Images 11-25 and 11-26: The XD-A is a patented shim-adjustable pushrod that we developed to make setting lash much easier on non-adjustable valvetrain systems, such as the LS, while stiffening the pushrod and without adding rocker mass. I made this prototype pushrod and shims on a lathe from hardened material and added some heat, but the results are awesome and stay under 0.010-inch bounce until almost 10,000 rpm.

COMP Cams Valve Train Dynamics Testing

Dynamics Testing 5

Lobe:	23792R	Valve	Stock LS7
Lobe Lift (in)	.389	Mass (gms)	N/A
Tappet	96956	Valve Spring	7230
Pushrod	XD-A	Installed Height (in)	1.891
Diameter (in)	7/16 & 5/16	Installed Load (lbs)	-
Length (in)	~8.100	Open Height (in)	1.211
Wall Thickness (in)	.105	Open Load (lbs)	-
Mass (gms)	N/A	Rate (lbs/in)	519
Rocker Arm	Stock Body w/ Bushing	Coil Bind Height (in)	1.129
Ratio		Distance To Coil Bind (in)	.082
Retainer	1774	Lash (in)	.010
Mass (gms)	N/A	Valve Lift (in)	.680
Locks/Lash Cap	Stock		
Mass (gms)	N/A		

Static Lift (in): .680
Max Laser Lift (in): 0.6918

Max Laser Bounce (in): 0.0245
Max Engine Speed (rpm): 10078.3

Test Objective:
Determin limit speed with LS7 Bushed Shaft

Notes:
10,000 RPM, limit speed not yet reached.

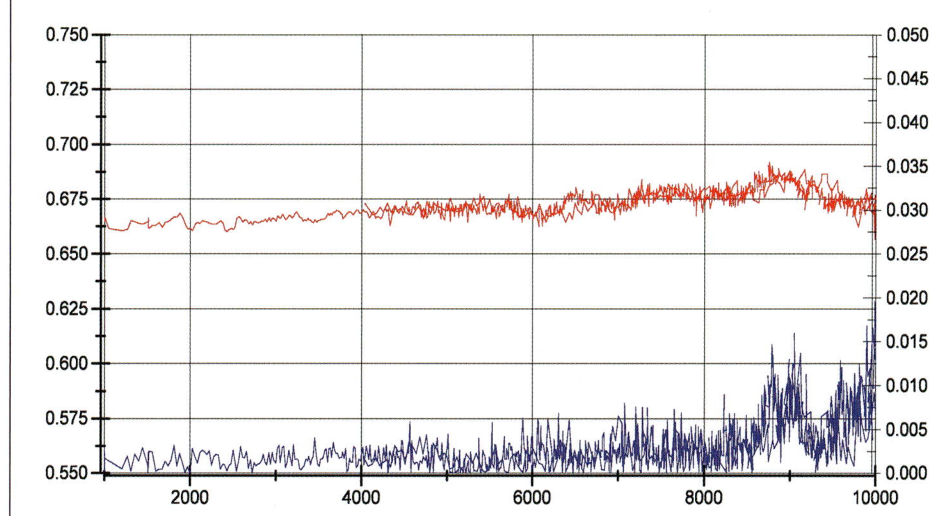

there is no free lunch. The smoother profile will reduce responsiveness and torque at lower RPM, so you don't want to build an 8,000-rpm package for a 6,500-rpm application.

RPM Head Space

My term for the RPM difference in the maximum RPM in operation compared to the RPM where the valvetrain goes out of control is "head space." For most systems, you want about 500 to 1,000 rpm between where it will operate and where it goes bonkers. For marine applications where the prop goes out of the water with some frequency, you will want 1,000 to 1,500 rpm to let the drivetrain unwind and the engine free rev. The same goes for road race applications with non-professional drivers. A missed downshift or time on an ignition-cut rev limiter both require significant head space to avoid disaster.

With any hydraulic lifter, you need more head space than with a solid because the lifter is slower to recover if it goes out of control. The hydraulic control piston inside can either collapse down and result in very high effective lash, or get to the top and hold the valve open in what people used to call pump up. Either condition requires time at lower

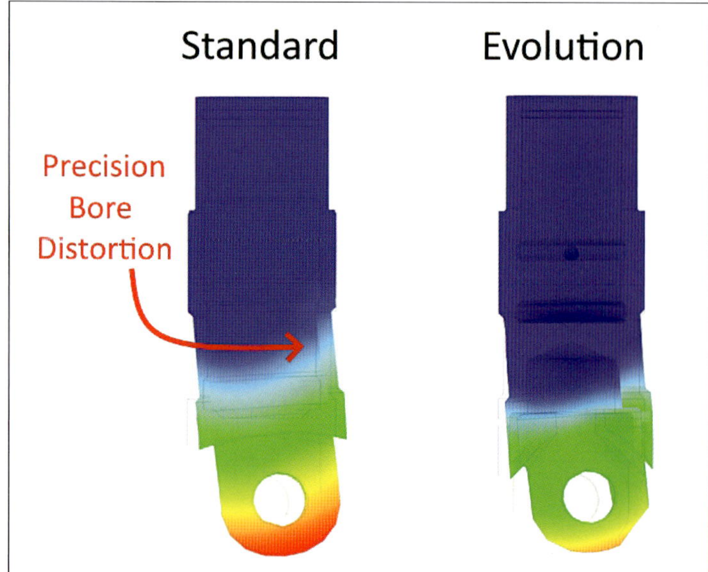

Image 11-27: Hydraulic-roller and solid-roller cam forces try to push the wheel over and up. This leads to considerable distortion of the lower region of the hydraulic bore of a conventional lifter. With the smaller cartridge, we move the hydraulic system up and into a thicker region with very little distortion. Then, we add a second containment system that is equally robust to hold the increased internal pressures.

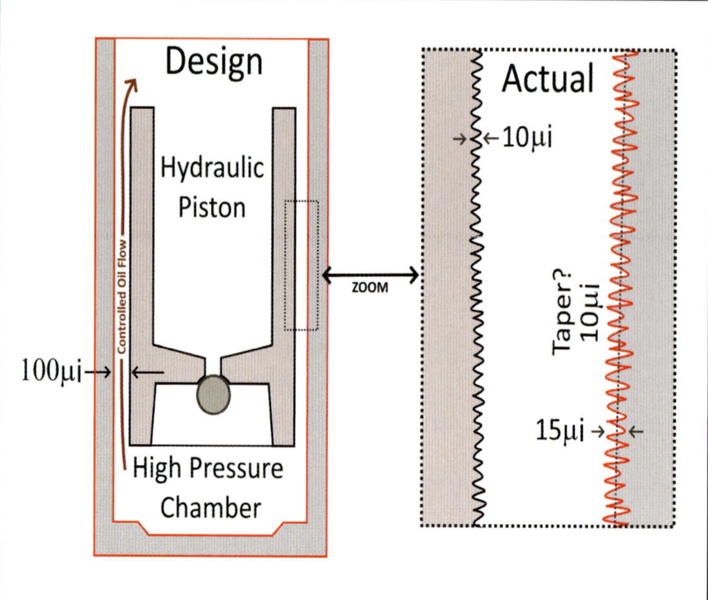

Image 11-28: This sketch shows the controlled flow path that sets the hydraulic stiffness of a hydraulic lifter. The better finish and improved geometrical control of the cartridge design allows more-precise oil control, and less distortion adds further performance enhancements over the conventional layout.

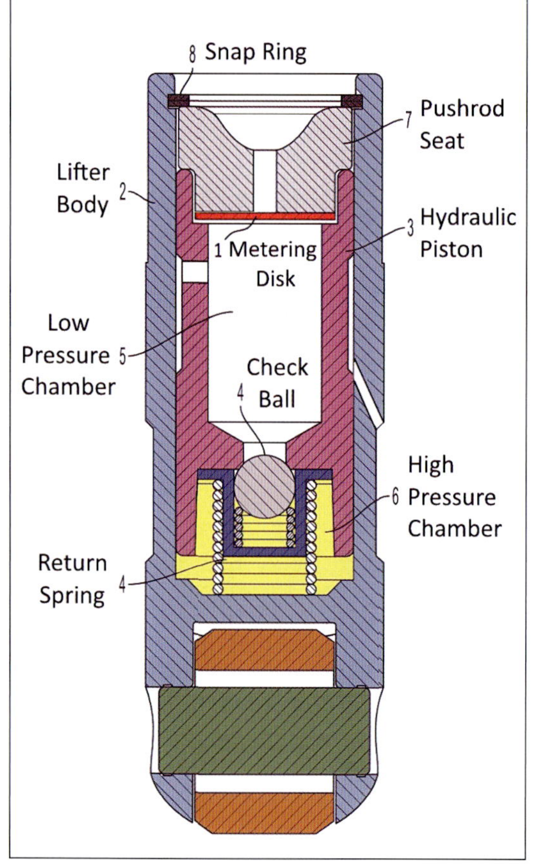

Image 11-29: A book could easily be based on this image alone. Instead, just note that the hydraulic piston (3) and check ball (4) work together to seal the higher-pressure chamber (6) to allow this style of lifter to self-adjust. Any aeration in the oil causes the lifter to act soft. Even small changes in diameter or surface condition of the hydraulic piston or the internal bore will change the bleed down and control.

Image 11-30: On the top right is a conventional hydraulic roller with the hydraulic piston beneath. Below those two are the evolution cartridge insert and its smaller hydraulic piston. At first, it is difficult to imagine the same load on the smaller piston. However, thinking of fluids as nearly incompressible, it becomes evident that the smaller system can have great benefits if the containment cartridge is stiff enough not to deflect excessively under higher pressures.

speed for the lifter to resolve, so it is best to leave more room before the system can go haywire. There is nothing similar that happens with a solid. If you go out of control, the spring might remain upset, but a solid lifter forgot it happened unless you damaged a wheel or initiated some other failure. In either case, with a solid there is not a lifter recovery time. You either hurt it or you did not.

Hydraulic-Lifter Valve-Spring Load Limits

Going back to those questions, if RPM is difficult to answer, as it depends on the profile and spring, the spring question is even more difficult. The lifter body gives us our clearest limit. There is never a good reason to think that 650-plus-pound open loads are safe on a 0.700-inch lifter wheel. We know the instantaneous pushrod loads will be over 1,000 pounds during the high acceleration opening and closing ramps at 6,000-plus rpm on almost any hydraulic-roller engine.

Hence, the lifter can withstand quick 1,000-pound hits, but going down the interstate at 2,000 rpm and seeing a 900-plus-pound load (spring open time rocker arm) 1,000 times a minute or 60,000 times an hour seems like cruel and unusual punishment for most hydraulic-roller designs. I am only thinking about the lifter body and not the hydraulic system inside.

If we build a body with the same wheel and axle package as a solid, then what are the negatives of 650-plus-pound open loads? Honestly, bleed down is the only problem. Unlike those quick opening and closing load pulses at high RPM, the valve typically stays 70 percent open for hundreds of degrees. If we double the open load, we will also double the effective lash gained as the hydraulic piston bleeds down. This tends to make hydraulic lifters create more noise and less durability with very high open loads. This is a far more significant issue on the street than in race-only applications because the time loaded is shorter at RPM.

If our open load thoughts are 400 pounds is easy, 500 is fine, 600 is iffy, and 700 pounds is dangerous unless the body and hydraulic system are improved, then what about seat loads? Honestly, I doubt they matter. When the valve is on the seat, what is the pushrod and lifter hydraulic load? At that point, the stem holds all the spring load, so the pushrod only sees the return spring of the hydraulic system plus the oil pressure times the hydraulic piston area. That is the same if you have a 50-pound seat or 500-pound seat.

We already talked about the 1,000-plus-pounds inertial loads the pushrod and lifter will experience as the valve starts to open. The difference in adding 150 or 200 pounds is only 5 percent on the total load. Sometimes those pushrod loads are closer to 2,000 pounds and the lifter is okay. I have a difficult time seeing how seat load is going to be much of an issue on a hydraulic system. We need to watch open loads, but don't overthink the seat loads. They are all zero to the lifter and pushrod once the valve is on the seat.

Oil Temp and Aeriation

One last thing to add to our hydraulic versus solid decision matrix is oil condition. The hotter the oil gets, or the lighter weight oil you run, the faster the hydraulics will bleed down. This adds lash to the system and shrinks your camshaft. The reason very few bracket cars run a hydraulic is how those small oil temp changes alter duration. If you could hold the oil temps totally consistent, there would be little reason not to go hydraulic.

The other oil question mark is aeration. In running engines, millions of tiny air bubbles are always trapped in the oil. Dry-sump tanks do a great job of getting rid of the larger ones, and air separators can take it a step further. Still, hydraulic systems have to squish the air before they can start acting more like a solid. That variable lash take-up as a function of oil aeration is another factor to consider when running a solid or hydraulic. Knowing that my wet-sump road-race car was likely to gulp some air from time to time, I went solid roller.

However, after several failed engine bearing from those gulps, I added both a dry sump system and an oil accumulator. At this point, there is little performance benefit of a solid camshaft over an equally modern hydraulic design (7,500 rpm and 0.670-inch lift).

Hydraulic versus Solid Decision Time

With all we have covered, our decision should be easy. If you are building a professional race engine that will compete on maximum and average power, go with the solid roller. You can run higher lift, higher spring loads, and lose less duration at high RPM. If you are developing a spec race engine, both options could make sense and the hydraulic could be an awesome choice.

The spec engines that Ilmor builds for NASCAR and SRX both employ state-of-the-art hydraulic valvetrain systems. With their ability to meet or exceed the power,

RPM, and durability targets, going solid is just added cost. Likewise, in most boosted applications, it is so easy to make 1,000-plus hp with a hydraulic valvetrain that it does not make sense to swap to solids unless you want more RPM, extremely high lift, or something different than the common approach. However, you could not compete with a modern Pro Mod engine with a hydraulic counterpart.

The only wrong answer is to run a hydraulic when you need extremely high spring loads. If it requires 1,000 pounds of open load to be competitive in a class, skip the hydraulic thoughts. Hydraulic-roller lifters were run by the Vipers in the IMSA and Rolex 24 GTD classes. These required updated profiles and improved lifters, but they were able to compete with solid rollers on equal footing in those restricted classes. The hydraulic has some advantages in that the lash does not change as much with engine temperature. If a crew chief wants to tape up the nose and run over 250°F water temps, the lash change is due to the changing oil viscosity with the hydraulic. If you have an aluminum block and head like the Viper, the solid lash can open up another 0.005 inch with very hot engine conditions.

Every day we see hydraulic systems winning in classes that were solid lifter only. Hydraulic technology continues to develop, and someday soon we may see hydraulics winning events we assumed would always be solid roller only.

Deciding Target Lift

Once we have figured out the lifter, we must decide on the lift target. As air demand per revolution is higher at peak torque than peak power, RPM is not as important to our lift target as many might believe. Two fundamental aspects should determine our target.

Valve Lift to Diameter

If the rules are open, the best way to start targeting lift is to measure your intake valve diameters. If you know the valve-seat configuration and valve diameter, you will have a good target lift estimation. Going back to the 1980s with poorly blended 45-degree seats, 25-percent lift to diameter was considered enough to maximize flow. This makes sense remembering the approximate 2-inch OD valves and sub-0.500-inch-lift cams of that day. As valve jobs improved with multi-angle cutters and better valve designs, a good target lift today for a 45-degree seat is closer to 30 percent of the intake valve diameter to intake valve lift (L/D). For a modern LS3 with a 2.165-inch valve and a good factory 45-degree seat, there is little improvement past 2.165 x 0.3 = 0.650-inch lift.

However, a good cylinder head porter can clean up the bowls, do additional work around the seat, and make the same cylinder head continue to gain well into the 35-percent L/D range or 0.750-inch lift. If the target is set for production 45-degree seats at 30 percent, a race ported 45-degree seat should run 33 percent for endurance and 35 percent in drag race–oriented applications, with most of the difference due to how thick the 45-degree step is on the seat.

As the valve-seat angle is increased past 45 degrees, the low lift flow suffers a bit, but the high lift improves. That low lift flow restriction seems to

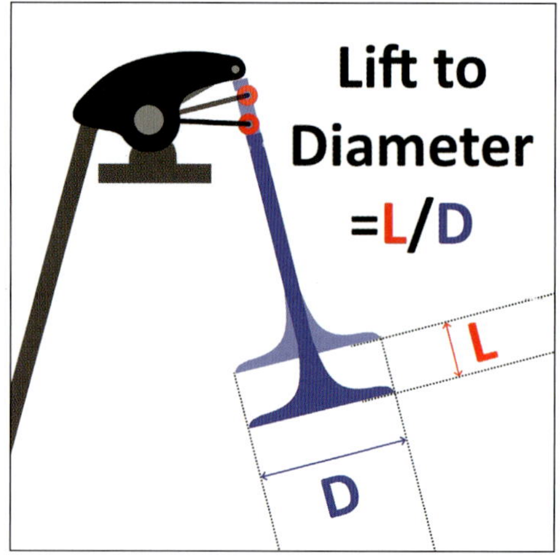

Image 11-31: Look closely at the ratio of the intake valve diameter to intake valve lift (L/D). The old rule of thumb is that 25 percent provides enough curtain area to suffice. As seat angles and ports improved, this moved to 30 percent on the street and 45 percent with steep angles in some race applications. However, L/D greater than 40 percent is probably less advantageous than is commonly known. Looking at flow data with these ratios in mind is another great starting point.

not be an issue on the exhaust, likely because we are sonically choked at low lift at EVO and want signal more than mass flow near EVC. Likewise, in race applications, IVO is about signal, and IVC occurs when the flow has reversed. For racing, that first and last 10 percent of lift might be numb to performance.

For 50-degree seats, we see improvements across the board at 35 percent that continue to 40 percent or even slightly higher lifts, depending on the valve-seat cutter configuration and work done by the cylinder head port designer. In many professional classes, valve-seat angles are 53 degrees or slightly more. In this range, we see measurable improvement going somewhat above 40 percent L/D. NHRA Pro Stock run the highest common L/D values on the intake side with a common target in the 43 to 45 percent range. While I have seen some experimentation with 50-percent L/D targets on the intake side, I am not sure I have ever seen it improve performance in any application. At some point, the valve head is so small compared to the curtain area and flow discharge cone that it is no longer a factor in flow. This commonly occurs well before 50-percent L/D.

If 30-percent street, 33-percent endurance race or street strip, 35-percent drag race, 45 degrees, 38 to 40 percent with 50-plus-degree seats, and 45-percent maximum effort 55-plus-degree seats is our intake target, what about max lift on the exhaust side? The answer is that it does not matter nearly as much. This should make sense considering how the exhaust flows past that valve.

There will always be a huge flow pulse from EVO through BDC as the combustion pressure is redirected to push out the exhaust gases. There will be a second pulse of high flow velocity around 70 degrees before TDC on the exhaust stroke. There, piston velocity is the highest and the chamber volume shrinks rapidly. This creates the second high flow region. However, neither of these regions of highest exhaust mass flow or port speeds is in the region of max lift (100 to 130 degrees before TDC).

To make life easy, many people run the same valve spring on the intake and exhaust side. Because we know that springs like a certain distance to bind and should be set up in a certain range of the designs installed height, the easy button is to run roughly the same exhaust lift as intake lift. Knowing that peak intake flow occurs near peak lift, peak exhaust flow falls away from peak lift results in improved performance if they are opened faster around BDC and the valve is held open higher at 70 degrees BTDC. If you think about the cam flanks as motorcycle ramps, making them steeper tends to make the valve go higher. If we believe steep ramps are good and too much separation between the exhaust lobe and exhaust lifter is bad, as a large gap can and will lead to a hard crash, it makes sense why we would not look too closely at L/D on the exhaust.

Selecting Lift and Profiles around the Valve Spring

I often choose a profile based on the valve spring. A lot of people wrongly assume that running a spring under the designed lift is fine, but that approach is wrong. Many applications have a few good valve-spring options. If you look at NHRA Pro Stock, there are a handful of options available, and perhaps fewer if you look at intake and exhaust separately.

Likewise, engine builders for both Sprint Car and late-model engines have less than a dozen readily available valve springs that can be successfully used for top level competition. While it is rather easy to tweak camshaft profiles or make a one-off version specifically for an application, valve springs are wound on CNC coilers and go through a dozen processing steps. Once you have a valve spring that works well, a successful valve-spring company will want to make tens of thousands of it at a time.

For this reason, while I both design valve springs and have worked with many of the best, the best path is typically to pick a successful valve spring and then optimize the cam profile around that excellent valve spring design. If someone like Chris Osborn were to call me up and say he had a new spring that he thinks will work awesome, I would quickly try to run those on our Spintron and work to develop new profiles to take full advantage of any new design.

Image 11-32: I often have a valve spring in mind as I start designing or selecting a camshaft. Knowing that each spring sets up in a certain height range and needs to be run within a certain distance to bind sets the lift target limits. Then I go back and look at L/D. Both this small 2000s NASCAR restrictor plate spring on the left and dual conical on the right tend to move under my preferred L/D target, but they perform so well dynamically that I often take the lift hit to run a quicker cam profile with a more durable and stable spring.

Fred Astaire and Ginger Rogers (Cam Lobe and Valve Spring)

My wife is a huge fan of old movies. Those were never my first choice, but after enough prodding I have grown to appreciate many, even some of her favorite musicals. Watching with a physics background, I am always interested in how choreographers worked the routines of two dancers together. Fred Astaire was athletically gifted and one of the best dancers of any generation. When he was doing a solo, the choreographer and director let him fly. However, when dancing with Ginger Rogers, who was also a gifted dancer, they had to calm things down a bit and work to maximize the combined visual effect of the pair. I'm not sure we can compare the two because whatever move Fred did, Ginger was supposed to do backward and in high heels. The key was to focus on Ginger's limits under those conditions and optimize Fred's part accordingly.

I've had the awesome privilege of working with many of the best professional race teams in NASCAR. Together we work to find the absolute best valve spring that can be developed for their package. That becomes Ginger. Then, my job is to design the valve motion and resulting cam profile (Fred) that most perfectly matches what Ginger can do for their mileage and cycle target.

Note the director could not just find any female that happened to be a certain height, weight, and strength. If Ginger was injured, they could not run out and grab any roughly 5'5" blonde that weighed about 125 pounds with a vertical leap above the 90th percentile and think she would do. From the NFL combine, we know that does not work for comparing cornerbacks, much less dancers.

That approach does not work for valve springs either.

Valve springs are amazingly simple in many ways. They are wire formed into coils with the ends ground square. They provide the load to control valve motion. As discussed in Chapter 3 (Images 3-37 through 3-39), if the load applied is greater than the effective system mass times the negative valve acceleration, the system stays in control. What makes each design so special is how each coil vibrates and interacts with its neighbors. The coiled spring is basically a compact torsion bar. Each coil has a higher rate and frequency if the free spacing is wider, and a lower rate and frequency if it is tightly spaced. Thicker wire provides higher loads or lower stress but at the cost of lower frequency. The cam profile can be seen like a packet of different tuning forks, each one able to excite the spring if it hits that coil's frequency.

Not only do we have to consider coil frequency, but also coil dampening. With dual springs or single springs with flat wire dampeners, one of the dampening methods is obvious. The friction between coils as they move helps keep the spring from going into resonance. There is a downside because the inside diameter of the spring is where each coil is most highly stressed. Rubbing this surface is not what we think of as a good idea, especially with all the surface conditioning performed on the spring to add compressive stresses.

The other major dampening factor is how the coils interact when they collide. While these collisions can become violent and damaging if a spring goes totally out of control, lighter collisions are extremely beneficial for coil control.

If you ever listen to a Spintron test, especially when limit speed is being investigated, pay close attention to the sounds. You will hear the valve closings, which sound much like the in-car microphone from a NASCAR broadcast. If you listen closely, there is a higher frequency overtone that is mostly due to coil collisions. As the RPM increases, they will get louder, then quieter, several times, and then very loud right before the system goes out of control.

Conical valve springs are interesting because they rely on the coil interaction along with the different natural frequency of each coil to do most of the damping. With a conical round wire, the coil above will move somewhat inside the lower coil the nest as they come together. This can provide amazing dampening. However, this makes setting up the distance to real bind critical with a conical valve spring.

Beehive valve springs fall somewhere in between a conventional and conical spring. They are typically ovate wire that does not nest, but the top two or three coils have very different frequency. However, there are typically two or three coils in the bottom that have nearly the same frequency. When a beehive goes out of control, these bottom coils are generally the ones that were excited.

Looking back at double springs developed in the 1960s, the outer spring was doing 90 percent of the work, and the smaller, inner coil was there as a bit of a helper. Today, the inner and outer springs share the work and have their stresses and frequencies well matched to work as good teammates. Getting these teammates to work well together is why some springs perform so much better than others dynamically, even with similar specs.

When I said there were only a dozen or so spring sets that worked in today's late-model race engines, it is not that there are not hundreds of options with very similar loads, rates, installed heights, and diameters, just like there were lots of 5-foot, 5-inch female dancers in the 1940s.

Likewise, I might be able to tell you what a minimal open load needs to be for a certain profile with a given system mass, rocker ratio, and RPM.

Image 11-33: Always design around the best possible valve spring available. This is a new circle track–focused small-OD dual spring that I am very excited to test.

Image 11-34: This Equal 8 rocker is an excellent design. I care less about rocker ratios if there are large enough journals. Something about 1.9:1 seems to be the best compromise of pushrod angles, stiffness, and MOI. The pushrod side can be very sensitive if the backside is too short, but the stiffness goes down at total rocker length to the third power and MOI goes up. However, I would much rather have a great 2.2:1- or 1.7:1-ratio design than a good 1.9:1-ratio rocker design.

Image 11-35: We gain two important factors when going to a larger-journal roller camshaft. The first is the larger base circle that allows a larger barrel. The larger the main shaft or barrel of the cam, the less it bends when loaded, as was said with system stiffness in Images 2-66 to 2-68. The second benefit is that it allows more tappet acceleration.

However, there are perhaps a hundred valve springs that would not run well, even with the right loads, because they do not work well with the input frequencies from that profile. The reason we need to know so much about the spring selected is because that will help zero in on the correct profile.

Rocker Ratio, Journal Size, and Lifter Wheel

The next series of questions I ask when selecting a profile help me narrow what options are available. We now have a lift target and valve spring in mind. We now need to know the rocker arm ratio (or ratio options) to give us a very good idea of the lobe lift target. We can start to narrow down the selection by the journal size and lifter wheel or foot diameter. Designs for larger journals can be a little softer off the seat and make up for it later. However, a small journal is like launching a car with a low power motor.

If you watch much drag racing and NHRA Stock Eliminator in particular, you know many of those cars need to leave the line violently. Many of the stick cars run a heavy flywheel and rev the engine high to use the stored rotational energy to accelerate off the line. Similarly, with a small journal design, the profiles need to be quicker at very low lift to make up for the limited peak acceleration.

However, many large journal designs run a much more optimized acceleration throughout the curve. If we go back to a drag-race analogy, these are more like a Pro Mod that slips the clutch a ton off the line but grabs more and more as the vehicle accelerates and shoots out like an arrow. The same basic factors are involved with wheel size.

Because of the design compromises of smaller journal designs, I rarely use a small-block Chevy (1.868 inch) journal design when I have 55 mm-(2.165 inch)-or-larger journals. In the Comp Cams lobe catalogs, the roller profiles are generally sectioned off by application and journal size. Once I know the journal and lifter wheel size, I can move to the small journal lobes if required or use the more modern designs for larger journals and lifter wheels when possible.

Journal	Lift	BCR	BCR*2	Min Barrel (BCD-.030)
SBC				
1.868	0.350	0.582	1.164	1.134
1.868	0.375	0.557	1.114	1.084
1.868	0.400	0.532	1.064	1.034
1.868	0.425	0.507	1.014	0.984
1.868	0.450	0.482	0.964	0.934
1.868	0.475	0.457	0.914	0.884
1.868	0.500	0.432	0.864	0.834
1.868	0.525	0.407	0.814	0.784
BBC				
1.948	0.400	0.572	1.144	1.114
1.948	0.425	0.547	1.094	1.064
1.948	0.450	0.522	1.044	1.014
1.948	0.475	0.497	0.994	0.964
1.948	0.500	0.472	0.944	0.914
1.948	0.525	0.447	0.894	0.864
1.948	0.550	0.422	0.844	0.814
SBF				
2.051	0.400	0.6235	1.247	1.217
2.051	0.425	0.5985	1.197	1.167
2.051	0.450	0.5735	1.147	1.117
2.051	0.475	0.5485	1.097	1.067
2.051	0.500	0.5235	1.047	1.017
2.051	0.525	0.4985	0.997	0.967
2.051	0.550	0.4735	0.947	0.917
2.051	0.575	0.4485	0.897	0.867

Journal	Lift	BCR	BCR*2	Min Barrel (BCD-.030)
BBF				
2.125	0.400	0.6605	1.321	1.291
2.125	0.425	0.6355	1.271	1.241
2.125	0.450	0.6105	1.221	1.191
2.125	0.475	0.5855	1.171	1.141
2.125	0.500	0.5605	1.121	1.091
2.125	0.525	0.5355	1.071	1.041
2.125	0.550	0.5105	1.021	0.991
2.125	0.575	0.4855	0.971	0.941
55mm				
2.165	0.425	0.6555	1.311	1.281
2.165	0.450	0.6305	1.261	1.231
2.165	0.475	0.6055	1.211	1.181
2.165	0.500	0.5805	1.161	1.131
2.165	0.525	0.5555	1.111	1.081
2.165	0.550	0.5305	1.061	1.031
2.165	0.575	0.5055	1.011	0.981
2.165	0.600	0.4805	0.961	0.931
60mm				
2.362	0.450	0.729	1.458	1.428
2.362	0.475	0.704	1.408	1.378
2.362	0.500	0.679	1.358	1.328
2.362	0.525	0.654	1.308	1.278
2.362	0.550	0.629	1.258	1.228
2.362	0.575	0.604	1.208	1.178
2.362	0.600	0.579	1.158	1.128
2.362	0.625	0.554	1.108	1.078
2.362	0.650	0.529	1.058	1.028

Image 11-36: I wish every race cam had at least a 1.200-inch barrel (as seen in Image 2-67), but most legacy engines don't have real estate. This chart lets you quickly find the max base circle and barrel size for common-lift journal sizes and lift ranges. It is based on BCR = J ÷ 2 minus lobe lift minus clearance. A chart can be quicker than doing the math.

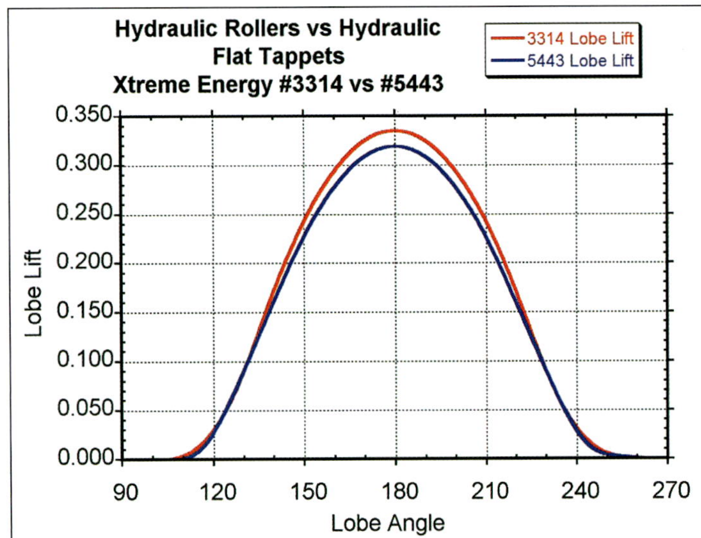

Image 11-37: These two tappet lift profiles are probably the highest sellers for Comp Cams over the past 20 years and represent the most popular flat and roller Xtreme Energy intake designs. Note the quicker seat timing of the blue flat-tappet designs but significantly increased area of the red roller profile.

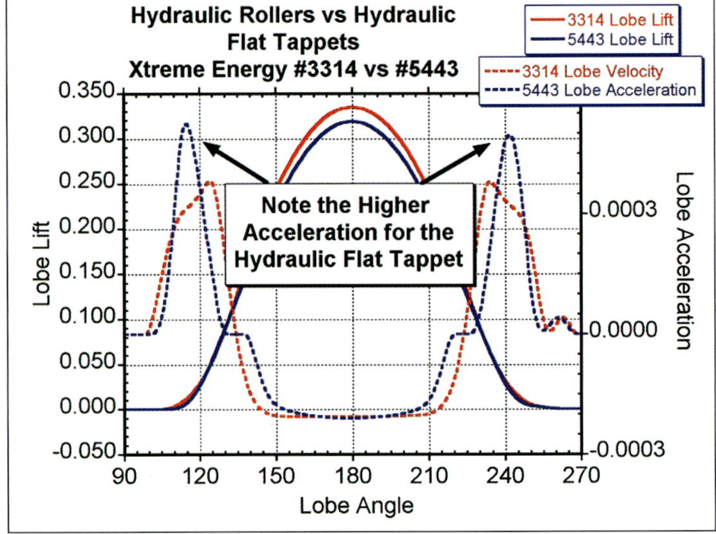

Image 11-38: We see the much higher acceleration of the blue flat-tappet designs and the long constant radius of curvature sections of the red Xtreme Energy hydraulic roller. As great as the XE flat performed, the XE roller was even better because of the added lift and area. Harvey Crane helped me tremendously as I worked up to these designs when I was only 27 years old. Today's new LS designs are far better because we are not as limited with acceleration because of the larger 55-mm versus 1.868-inch journal.

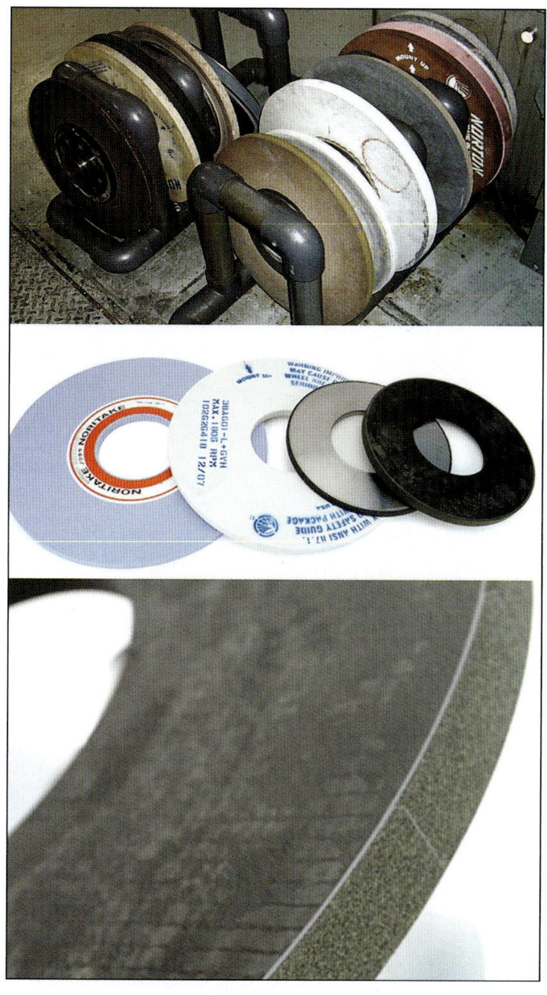

Image 11-39: We grind camshafts with grinding wheels. This wheel must fit into any inverted region with enough room to allow coolant to be forced into the grinding contact region. Over the years, wheels kept getting smaller and better to allow for new designs and better camshafts.

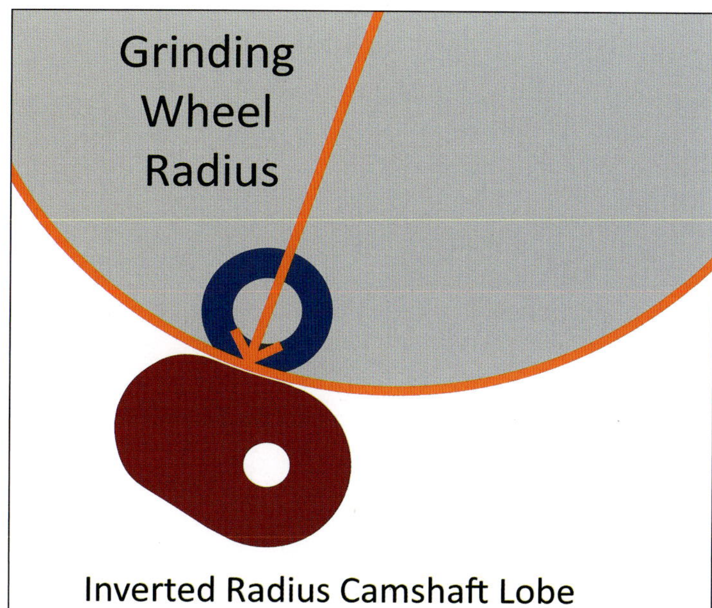

Image 11-40: Seeing where the roller wheel rides (navy blue circle) on the lobe as well as where the grinding wheel must fit (large orange circle) makes the limit far easier to envision. The tight region is difficult to cool, and the increased surface contact area generates increased heat. More heat and less cool is bad! If the cam surface temperature reaches above 350°F during grind, the surface layer will be tempered and hardness is reduced. This soft layer can lead to lifter tracking and early failure.

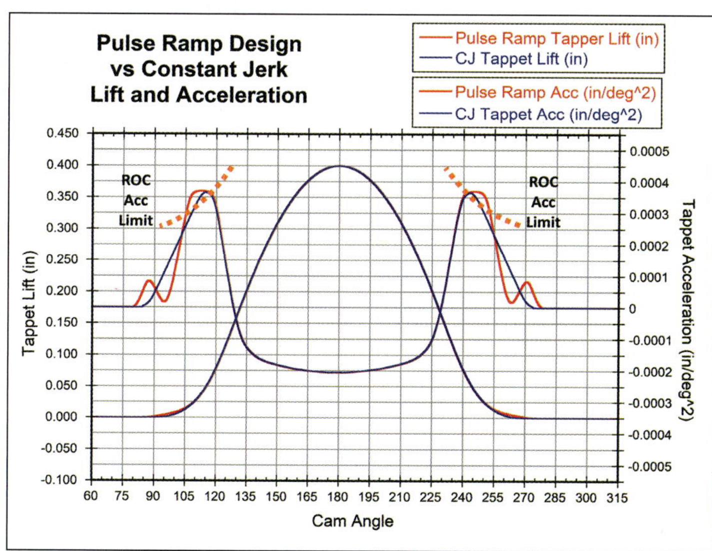

Image 11-41: A constant-jerk cam design with a similar-spec pulsed acceleration cam design is shown in blue. The orange dotted curve represents the radius of the curvature limit. Note that the CJ design does not go as far over, but both need to be redesigned to work under that limit.

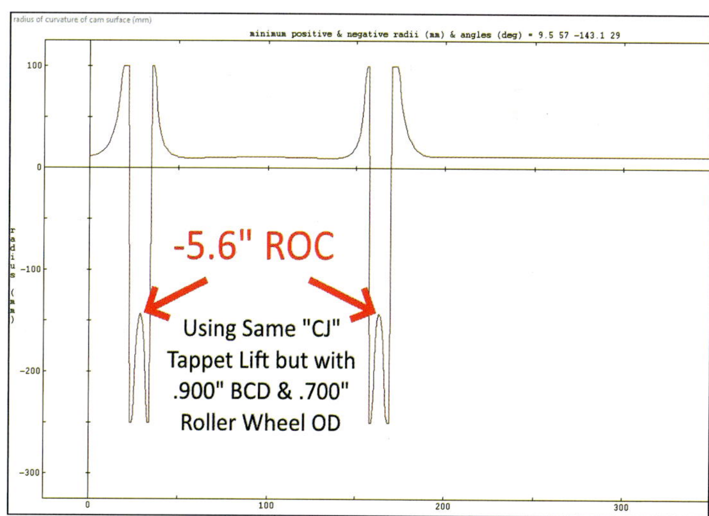

Image 11-42: This is how small the surface radii drop if we try to make the constant-jerk design without modification at a 0.900-inch base circle with a 0.700-inch OD roller wheel. To grind safely at a -5.6-inch radius, we need a 6-inch OD wheel. However, small wheels break down more quickly and tend to grind less accurately. A better solution is a larger base circle and journal.

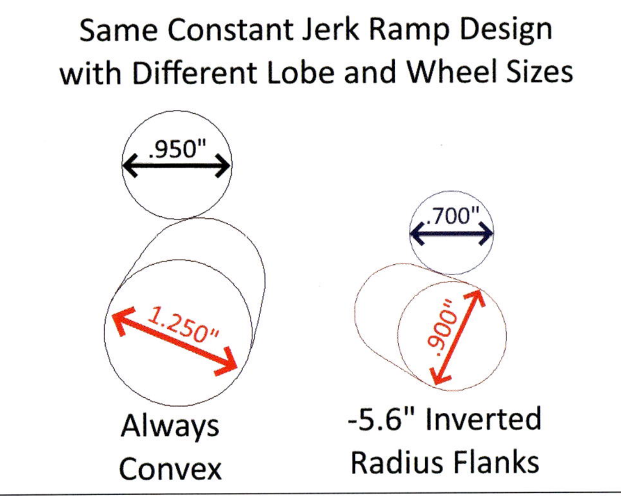

Image 11-43: This shows the same design converted with two different cam and lifter geometries to see how the lobe shape changes in 4stHEAD. Something that is basically impossible to grind with a small lobe and lifter wheel is easy with a larger system. Also, the larger parts have greater stiffness.

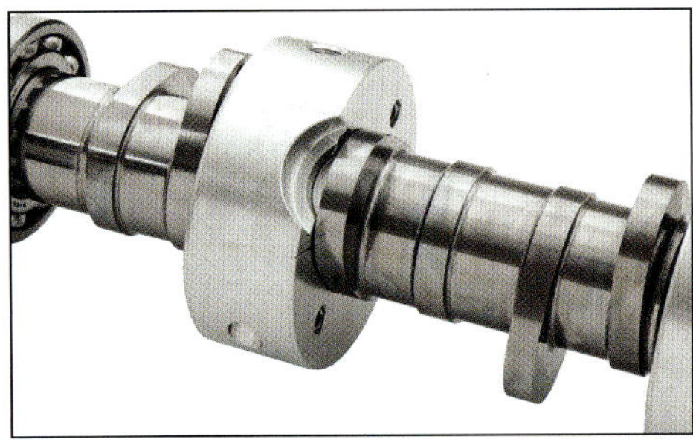

Image 11-44: These Jesel clamshell journals allow the effective journal size to be as large at the cam tunnel in the block. Something must keep the clamshells from spinning, and oil provisions are required, but this is a great way to find a little more room inside a confined space.

Image 11-45: Wheel-guided lifters have been used for the last hundred years. I have seen them on older Harley engines and other applications. However, this has been reintroduced into the domestic V-8 drag-race world recently. My only concern in endurance is slowing down the roller wheel. However, I love the larger wheel.

There may be times when you want an older, small-journal design on a large-journal application, but that is mostly because a certain profile works at this engine speed with a certain valve spring. It is generally better to take advantage of the larger journal with a lobe design that takes advantage of that system.

RPM and Durability Targets

Now that the selection has been narrowed by lift, valve spring, and best profiles, I ask about target RPM range and durability targets. The higher the RPM or longer the durability target, the less aggressive profile should be selected. When the profile is so fast it slaps the valve spring silly, even if is it still in control, it will oscillate rather violently. Then, the valve is closed and the lifter is on the base circle. Each time a coil oscillates from near closed to relaxed, that oscillation counts as a cycle of that coil. The more the spring is highly stressed, the fewer cycles it will last before failure.

Cycle Counts for Various Applications

To put this in perspective, look at the number of spring cycles in various applications. The math to do so is not too difficult. Divide the average RPM by two to get cycles per minute. Divide that by 60 for cycles per second in low endurance applications, or multiply by 60 for cycles per hour in high endurance applications. We see how it plays out for various applications in Image 11-46.

For a Professional Series Drag Race spring, even a few thousand cycles can be more than enough between replacement. However, I have had sprint boat customers in Australia try to use those same valve springs and wonder why some fail in the warmup pond. A valve spring optimized for a handful of seconds at high speed may have such high internal stress that 15 minutes at idle exceeds its design life.

Moving down the list, a high-RPM Bonneville engine might see 30,000 cycles, and a Sportsman drag-race engine is designed for around 100 passes before refresh or just under 100,000 cycles. Moving into the circle-track world, an hour of racing is roughly 250,000 cycles. Different customers and series will have different refresh targets, but a quarter million to maybe 2 million would be normal. That 2 million definitely requires lower stress springs and a smoother profile as it approaches the life target of a NASCAR Cup engine.

Going up in cycles, a 24 Hours of Daytona or Le Mans engine runs closer to 5 million cycles in a race

Pro Stock Type

Cam/Spring Cycles	**3,000**	input
Engine Cycles	6,000	calc
Avg RPM (Racing)	10,000	input
Avg RPS (Racing)	166.7	calc
Racing Sec	36.0	calc
Lap Sec	7	input
# laps	**5**	total

Bonneville

Cam/Spring Cycles	**30,000**	input
Engine Cycles	60,000	calc
Avg RPM (Racing)	9,000	input
Avg RPS (Racing)	150.0	calc
Racing Sec	400.0	calc
Lap Sec	70	input
# laps	**6**	total

Sportsman Drag Race

Cam/Spring Cycles	**100,000**	input
Engine Cycles	200,000	calc
Avg RPM (Racing)	6,500	input
Avg RPS (Racing)	108.3	calc
Racing Sec	1846.2	calc
Lap Sec	13	input
# laps	**142**	total

Sportsman Circle Track

Cam/Spring Cycles	**250,000**	input
Engine Cycles	500,000	calc
Avg RPM (Racing)	8,000	input
Avg RPH (Racing)	480000	calc
Racing Hours	1.0	calc
Lap Sec	15	input
# laps	**250**	total

NASCAR Type

Cam/Spring Cycles	**2,000,000**	input
Engine Cycles	4,000,000	calc
Avg RPM (Racing)	8500	input
Avg RPH (Racing)	510000	calc
Racing Hours	7.8	calc
Lap Sec	40	input
# laps	**706**	total

Daytona / Le Mans 24

Cam/Spring Cycles	**5,000,000**	input
Engine Cycles	10,000,000	calc
Avg RPM (Racing)	6000	input
Avg RPH (Racing)	360000	calc
Racing Hours	27.8	calc
Lap Sec	110	input
# laps	**909**	total

Automotive OEM Level

Cam/Spring Cycles	**200,000,000**	input
Engine Cycles	400,000,000	calc
Avg RPM (Cruising)	2000	input
Avg RPH (Cruising)	120000	calc
Cruising Hours	3333.3	calc
AVG MPH (Cruising)	60	input
Cruising Miles	**200,000**	total

Commercial ORT Level

Cam/Spring Cycles	**1,000,000,000**	input
Engine Cycles	2,000,000,000	calc
Avg RPM (Cruising)	1600	input
Avg RPH (Cruising)	96000	calc
Cruising Hours	20833.3	calc
AVG MPH (Cruising)	60	input
Cruising Miles	**1,250,000**	total

Drag Week Road

Cam/Spring Cycles	**2,000,000**	input
Engine Cycles	4,000,000	calc
Avg RPM (Cruising)	3100	input
Avg RPH (Cruising)	186000	calc
Cruising Hours	21.5	calc
AVG MPH (Cruising)	60	input
Cruising Miles	**1,290**	total

Drag Week Track

Cam/Spring Cycles	**20,000**	input
Engine Cycles	40,000	calc
Avg RPM (Racing)	9,000	input
Avg RPS (Racing)	150.0	calc
Racing Sec	266.7	calc
Lap Sec	8.5	input
# laps	**31**	total

***Image 11-46:** I have been fortunate to work with top teams in almost every form of professional racing. To do each job well, think about the number of cycles in the application. If you treat a 24 Hours of Le Mans valvetrain like you would an NHRA Pro Stock, you might have a great half of a lap, but it is not going to live through that long night. Notice where I must concentrate on Drag Week application, with the high 20,000-rpm race cycles being eclipsed by those 2 million road cycles!*

and practice. That sounds like a lot, but every 10,000 automotive miles on the road is close to 10 million cycles. Yes, 5 million race engine cycles is a lot more stressful than 10 million road engine cycles because of all those extra coil surge oscillations at speed. An OEM valvetrain engineer targets 200-million-plus spring cycles to cover double a factory 100,000 mile warranty.

However, that pales in comparison to the 1-billion-plus cycles required for over the road trucks to go 1-million-plus miles between engine overhauls.

One fun application is the Drag Week style events where street reconfigured drag-race cars drive from event to event to compete for the low average elapsed time. Because of the steep gears and large cams, these vehicles might turn 3,000-plus rpm on the street and see 2 million cycles during roughly 20 hours of drive time. This requires something more like a circle track than professional drag-race spring limit. However, the competitive NA classes see 20,000 cycles in the 9,000-rpm range at high lift. This combination makes these events among my favorites.

Comparing Profile Aggressiveness

One of the best ways to determine aggressiveness has historically been to look at the major intensity (MI). The term was coined by Harvey Crane and is the 0.020-inch duration minus the 0.050-inch duration of a given profile. Every profile in a family should have the same MI. Today, with so many slower opening low-shock designs available, looking at the total MI is not extremely useful. A slow opening can make something far more stable, but the responsiveness and power is far more related to the closing side intensity.

In the Comp Cams lobe listing, in the same region where the journal sizes are listed, the MI is followed by the opening and closing splits. If we compare a 30-degree MI lobe with 15/15 splits to a 33-degree MI lobe with 16.5/16.5 splits, the 33 is far smoother. However, a newer low shock with 18/15 is the same MI as the 33, but very similar in power and responsiveness to the 30 (15/15). Knowing the design is more modern, it may be even friendlier on the valve spring and not set it into resonance than an older 33 (16.5/16.5). Hence, look at both the total MI and the closing split when comparing different families.

After looking at the intensity, the next tell on aggressiveness is the duration at 0.200 inch. If you compare two lobe families with close to the same MI, the one with the larger 0.200-inch duration is more aggressive. If MI is a comparison of the profile acceleration in the low lift region, then 0.200-inch duration tells more about the velocity. An MBW-series lobe #24446 is 33.4 MI with 19.1/14.3 splits, 280 at 0.050 inch, and 206 at 0.200 inch at 0.549-inch lift. This is not as easy on parts as the MMO 24358 that is 33 MAI with 18.4/14.6 splits, 281 at 0.050 inch, and a full 2 degrees shorter (204) at 0.200 inch, even with a higher 0.566-inch lift.

A lobe with higher lift and smaller at 0.200 inch is pointier over the nose. While this has higher peak nose acceleration, this shape tends to match the spring loads available more closely than a profile that is larger at 0.200 inch with lower lift and a flatter or fatter nose.

Optimizing the Camshaft for the Application

As we close out the chapter on components, I realize I have been foolish enough to fall victim to one of the three classic blunders. The first two may have originated in *The Princess Bride* movie from 1987 and involve something about a land war in Asia and Sicilians. The third classic blunder is when someone focuses only on the engine and not the application when developing a camshaft. If the camshaft is like a football coach, it is not enough to know the players on your team. A good football coach needs to understand the game situation (position on the field, down, distance, and score) and something about the opponent's defense to call the right play.

Likewise, to develop a camshaft that calls out the correct valve timing and aggressiveness, we need a detailed understanding of the vehicle, how it is going to be used, and what we want to achieve with the torque curve shape to be successful.

Why Do Cam Guys Ask so Much about My Vehicle?

The absolute best person at camshaft selection I ever watched is my close friend Gordon Holloway. I don't know how many NHRA Wallys and NASCAR trophies correspond to a camshaft he picked in the winning engine, but it is probably in the thousands. For 20-plus years, I ran something by him a couple times every week. In our last ten years, he started bouncing ideas past me too. It was always encouraging if he asked about something other than making a lobe profile faster or smoother.

I remember telling him I liked

a certain spec on a drag-race engine and Gordon responded, "You can't give him that cam, you dummy. It's going in a heavy car with a glide." I was naive enough at the time not to understand, so he took a piece of paper and sketched out the RPM trace to show how the engine sits at the converter stall speed for more than 1 second at launch and drops back to that speed again at the 1-2 shift. Gordon was 100-percent correct, and I learned the beginnings of what will be covered for the remainder of this chapter.

Where Should I Start?

For racing applications, my job with the camshaft is to make as much power as possible when the driver is at full throttle. This focus typically sets my lower and upper boundaries of the RPM range that matter. However, in the real world of racing, points are not scored like the *Engine Masters* competitions that friends Jon Kaase and Tony Bischoff have won so many times. Their engines are run on the dyno over a certain RPM range, and whomever has the largest score of average torque plus average power wins.

Looking more closely at the heavy car with a power glide sitting on the converter for a second or more at launch and then for maybe half that time at the 1-2 shift, let us assume the vehicle has a 3,800-rpm stall converter, shifts at 7,000 rpm, and goes through the lights (finish) at 7,200 rpm.

Gordon explained that even a 50-hp increase from 6,800 to 7,200 will not offset a 15 ft-lbs decrease from 3,500 to 4,500 rpm. In drag racing, every 0.1 second added to the first 60 feet is generally going to add twice as much to the quarter mile times, so you must get the vehicle moving well initially (right off the hit in drag racing terms) to have excellent performance.

Walking through our offices, you may hear someone asking about tire size, gear ratios, and suspension details and might think those questions are asked to make the customer feel good. That's not the case at all. To know how much to concentrate on that hit, we need to know if the customer has traction available without spinning the tires. Something as simple as knowing the gear ratios will help estimate how long the engine will be at the stall speed. The higher the numerical gear ratio, the sooner the RPM rises as the car moves away from the starting line.

Regarding camshafts, the most common mistake I see people make is focusing on how much peak power a combination can make with an optimized camshaft and not enough time thinking about how to shape the torque curve to optimize performance expressly for the given application. Even for race engine builders testing over the full RPM range and considering how long the engine stays inside each RPM window, there is a siren call to glance past the low end and focus on the big numbers. Let's consider a couple of tools to help avoid that trap.

Recording Torque at Lowest Wide-Open Engine Speed

It sounds almost elementary to say this, but if you are building a drag-race, circle-track, or road-race engine, the value of looking at real track data with engine speed and throttle position is under appreciated. When systems like RacePak first became widely used in sportsman racing, I remember working with a Super Stock class customer. He came back to the pits and was amazed how quickly he could analyze the RPM data. He wanted to figure out how much clutch bite needed to come from the springs and from the centrifugal weights, but I was mesmerized looking at the RPM trends at launch.

Initial acceleration is paramount in almost every motorsport event outside of land speed racing. Sometimes we have too much power at low RPM and are bleeding it off to gain traction, so we want to look for the lowest RPM where we have full torque demand, which means full throttle and no power reduction strategies. Look over all the data closely, and even pay attention to restarts in circle track and road racing. If drag racing with an automatic, this RPM is your real stall speed. Regardless, write down that RPM.

Then, circle the torque here in red on every dyno sheet. Do whatever it takes to make that number important to you. There will be times where it may be best to sacrifice 5 ft-lbs to make 20-plus hp at high RPM, but in most applications, losing torque there needs to make you cringe. If you take this to heart, drivers and customers are going to love your engines. If you do this when selecting camshafts, customers are going to love driving engines with your camshafts.

EVO is going to be the biggest player here, as we saw in the PV plots for the 427 simulation. IVC is going to be a close second. If you are going to miss, miss a little late on EVO and a little early on IVC. It might cost you in top speed or a chassis dyno shootout, but it pays dividends on the track for most motorsports and all street applications. However, if you are only racing Bonneville or have a jet boat, the lowest RPM where peak throttle is used will be quite high.

Tip-in or Transient Throttle Response

There is another important attribute to consider. This is often called tip-in response, which probably traces back to the Harley guys that first started talking about how camshafts changed their throttle response characteristics. If you have access to an AVL AC dyno with full controls, you can test this easily. Honestly, that makes torque curve shaping very easy as a professional level AVL system can tell you how each change affects lap times. For most of us, analyzing transient response is not so easy. We have all felt poor response in cars where the engine seemed to almost stumble if floored at too low of an RPM, even when the carburetor was tuned with the right jets, bleeds, and squirters.

There are two good indicators for testing response on a conventional water brake dyno. The first is to look at torque 1,000 rpm below your lowest full-throttle number. If the torque is great a 4,500, the engine is pretty much guaranteed to be responsive at 5,500 rpm. If there is a big hole at 4,500, it may stumble under throttle changes from 5,000 to 5,500.

The other trick is to look at light load vacuum at the tip in speed. Say you want to know how an engine is going to respond to throttle changes from cruising at 3,000 rpm. Test by loading it to what you think is a cruising torque (probably less than 50 ft-lbs) and see how much vacuum the engine pulls. The more vacuum at this light load at this RPM, the quicker the engine will be able to fill the intake with air when the throttle cracks.

Where the low torque number was controlled mostly with EVO and IVC, responsiveness will have a strong correlation with overlap. You want enough overlap to make the red circled number big but not so much that this transient response test is hurt. The easy way around our transient problem is to increase the lowest operating speed. It is amazing how easy it is to make vacuum and torque at 5,000 rpm compared to 2,500 rpm. This is one more reason that increased rear gear ratios are addictive in most race series.

Idle Characteristics on the Street

In addition to transient response, street applications require you to keep an eye on idle vacuum. If you have something like a 1995 Z28 with a factory computer, there may be strong tuning constraints for idle vacuum to avoid lots of grief when tuning. You may also be limited by vacuum brakes or other accessories. Vacuum pop-up headlights where one winks is a personal favorite.

The combustion stumble at idle, where filling, air-fuel, or burn rate differences cause the misfire known as lope, is very subjective. Some people love lope. Some people hate it. Wet marine exhaust, which tends to suck water back into the combustion chamber with more than 1 degree of overlap at 0.050 inch, is another idle vacuum constraint.

There are no great rules that cover all people or applications. Long strokes and heavy rotating assemblies are less sensitive to overlap, but you need to be mindful of the idle vacuum targets for your application. If you don't set a target, like 14 inches at 950 rpm, then it is going to be impossible not to draw more overlap in street applications. Unfortunately, low vacuum results in unhappy customers. I don't particularly like a customer giving me a specific vacuum target, as there are so many things outside my control (ring seal, idle mixture, timing, and chamber efficiency) that play almost as much of a role as overlap. However, I try to set something like a personal bogey with each street design and only compare camshafts with similar idle vacuum instead of focusing on similar duration.

With the Same Engine and Car, Can Driving Style Really Matter?

Personally, I enjoy road racing, especially in high-power cars. If I built a camshaft for myself, one for a very talented driver, and another for a phenomenal driver like Kyle Larson or anyone in that crazy talented league, they would change in some rather surprising ways. Because I tend to be too hard on the throttle out of a corner, running an earlier exhaust opening and later intake closing with a bit more overlap can help me not spin coming out of the corners. This is a crutch to that red circle rule that I use to cover my lack of talent.

However, a phenomenal driver would never let the engine RPM drop as much as I do in the corners and would probably wind up very close to the camshaft I need for my best laps—but for totally opposite reasons even when running 20 seconds a lap faster than me. We can use this torque shaping trick for less experienced drivers in circle track and drag racing. Softening the hit is how some people describe this approach to tuning with valve events around driver needs.

A very good, yet not exceptionally gifted, driver might come out of the same corner 10 mph faster than me but 5 mph slower than Kyle. They have the throttle control to be able to control all the available torque in third, but not the car control to be

Driver	Exit Speed	Gear	RPM
Billy	78	3	4200
Joe Good	88	3	4800
Gifted Driver	93	2	6600

Image 11-47: When looking at exit speed and gearing for a moderate-speed road-race corner, there can be more than a 2,000-rpm difference between a professional and a novice driver coming out of the same corner in the same car. Next-level camshaft development includes both the car and driver as well as the engine configuration.

Rear Ratio	3.23	3.23	3.23	3.23	Rear Ratio
Tire Radius (in)	12.35	12.35	12.35	12.35	Tire Radius (in)
Gear	1	2	3	4	Gear
Ratio	2.43	1.61	1.23	1.00	Ratio
Engine Speed	Speed	Speed	Speed	Speed	Engine Speed
1700	15.9	24.0	31.4	38.7	1700
2000	18.7	28.3	37.0	45.5	2000
2300	21.5	32.5	42.5	52.3	2300
2600	24.3	36.7	48.1	59.2	2600
2800	26.2	39.6	51.8	63.7	2800
3000	28.1	42.4	55.5	68.3	3000
3200	30.0	45.2	59.2	72.8	3200
3400	31.8	48.0	62.9	77.4	3400
3600	33.7	50.9	66.6	81.9	3600
3800	35.6	53.7	70.3	86.5	3800
4000	37.4	56.5	74.0	91.0	4000
4200	39.3	59.3	77.7	95.6	4200
4400	41.2	62.2	81.4	100.1	4400
4600	43.1	65.0	85.1	104.7	4600
4800	44.9	67.8	88.8	109.2	4800
5000	46.8	70.7	92.5	113.8	5000
5200	48.7	73.5	96.2	118.3	5200
5400	50.6	76.3	99.9	122.9	5400
5600	52.4	79.1	103.6	127.4	5600
5800	54.3	82.0	107.3	132.0	5800
6000	56.2	84.8	111.0	136.5	6000
6200	58.0	87.6	114.7	141.1	6200
6400	59.9	90.4	118.4	145.6	6400
6600	61.8	93.3	122.1	150.2	6600
6800	63.7	96.1	125.8	154.7	6800
7000	65.5	98.9	129.5	159.3	7000
7200	67.4	101.7	133.2	163.8	7200
7400	69.3	104.6	136.9	168.4	7400
7600	71.2	107.4	140.6	172.9	7600
7800	73.0	110.2	144.3	177.5	7800
8000	74.9	113.0	148.0	182.0	8000

Image 11-48: I use gearing charts such as this in road-race applications. Race teams look at these to determine their best gearing combinations. I use them to think about how we need to tailor the torque curve. They can also show me where another 500-rpm limit speed will come in very handy.

faster shifting all the way back to second and running through the gears with too much stuff going on behind the wheel. Where you put the red circle is different for all three drivers.

A chart of exit speed mph, gear, and RPM might look something like Image 11-47. For the good driver, the only reason they do not want that extra 33-percent wheel torque of second gear is all the shifting required takes away the concentration of the racing line. They are faster not shifting as much as the gifted driver but also need the added 5 to 15 percent given in the 4,000 to 5,500 zone with a later exhaust opening and earlier intake closing. Sure, that will take away a few percent from 7,000 to 8,000 rpm, but he is only there at the end of the long straights, which will have better lap times and set up passes more easily with more grunt coming off the corners at lower RPM.

The gifted driver is not even thinking about shifts. They blip the throttle as the engine approaches the red line and their right hand executes the shift almost like an involuntary response. That 4,000 to 5,500 rpm zone will only be seen when in the pits or during the victory lap. Giving more in the 6,500 to 8,000 zone is paramount for the best lap times.

Image 11-48 is the gearing map for my LS-powered BMW and shows how I look at gearing choices and torque mapping the camshaft around the driver. The blue cells are the no-go (or try not to go) when racing region. The green cells are the 6,600-rpm shift recovery points for short shifts to the next gear.

In short, while your main focus is the engine, you need to spend almost as much time picking the camshaft around the customer and application.

Camshaft Selection Examples

As we look at the following three examples, note how we use all the techniques described. These examples are more street oriented than some of the race topics covered, but other than idle vacuum, there is very little that fundamentally changes about how intake closing and exhaust opening are moved to shape the torque curve. I have great data with dozens of cams through these three applications, and it is evident how extremely sensitive each is as we change profiles and angles.

Small-Block Chevy Crate Upgrades: 350 versus 383

One of the quickest, easiest, and best ways to upgrade any crate engine has always been to optimize the camshaft around your personal goals. However, Edelbrock has tried to get ahead of this for its customers through new testing to see what the best all-around performance grind might be for general applications.

The most difficult part of general use cam selection is targeting idle vacuum. If the bar is set too low, the engine may stall when put in gear or when an accessory (such as air conditioning or power steering) pulls power from the crank. Add a vacuum brake booster or something with vacuum-powered headlights, and not enough vacuum will cause heartache and complaints. However, if not enough overlap is incorporated, then both peak power and torque are severely penalized, and the engine sounds rather anemic.

The first step toward better valvetrain packages was to test several new lobe series on the Spintron with current valve weights and a selection of valve springs. This was interesting because we found something a little surprising. The shorter-duration-camshaft profiles tend to be more stable with a quicker, higher opening and closing acceleration lobe profile, whereas the larger duration camshafts are more stable with a smoother design. This had everything to do with the frequency of the valve spring and the distance between maximum opening and closing velocity. The quicker camshaft simply gave the shorter duration system more time to turn around, whereas the slower design was even more stable when the durations increased.

With the new lobe designs and proven valvetrain packages determined, we tested a selection of camshafts, including the following three designs noted by the intake duration at 0.006-inch tappet lift, the intake lobe series, and the lobe separation (as shown in Image 12-2). The smallest 272MGZ111 (in blue) has by far the least overlap. This was designed to be very high in vacuum in a 350, be very stable to 6,500-plus rpm, and increase power above most current crate offerings.

Then, we went up to the mid-sized 290LDS113, which is like what we want in our own hot rods, to see how much performance improved and vacuum dropped with a larger cam and more overlap.

Finally, we went to a more-expensive valvetrain system with a better spring for more lift and ran the largest, 296MGZ113, in a 383 version of the engine with a larger-port cylinder head.

We quickly noticed two things on the dyno. First, the 350 liked the cams more advanced than the 383, which was not terribly surprising as the shorter-stroke version has a bit more difficulty building chamber pressure before IVC. The second was something we should have known but often fail to consider. Zooming

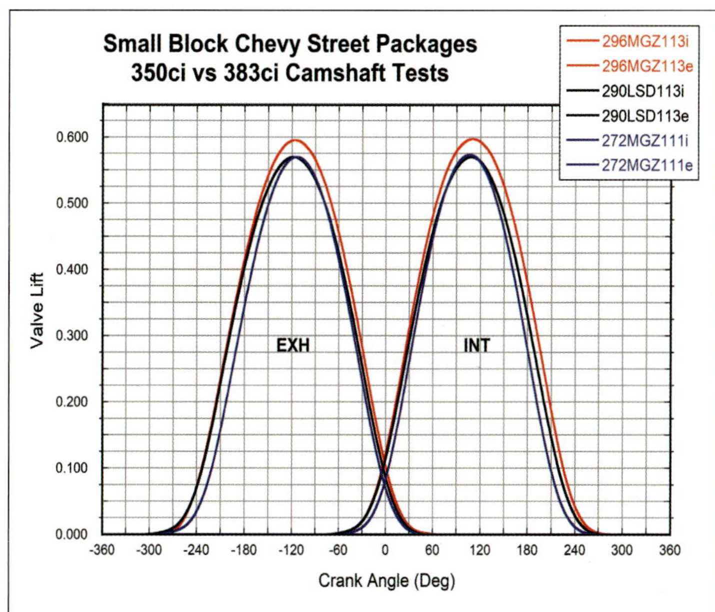

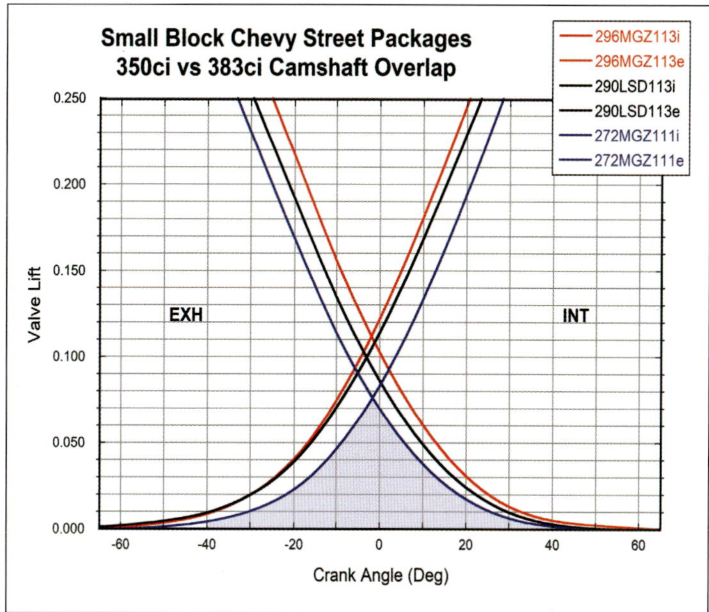

Images 12-2 and 12-3: Comparing all the different camshafts we tested with the small-block Chevy crate engine, the lift with the 383-ci design jumps out, but that has more to do with a higher-quality spring than the displacement. However, focusing on the overlap and idle vacuum is the biggest challenge of this exercise.

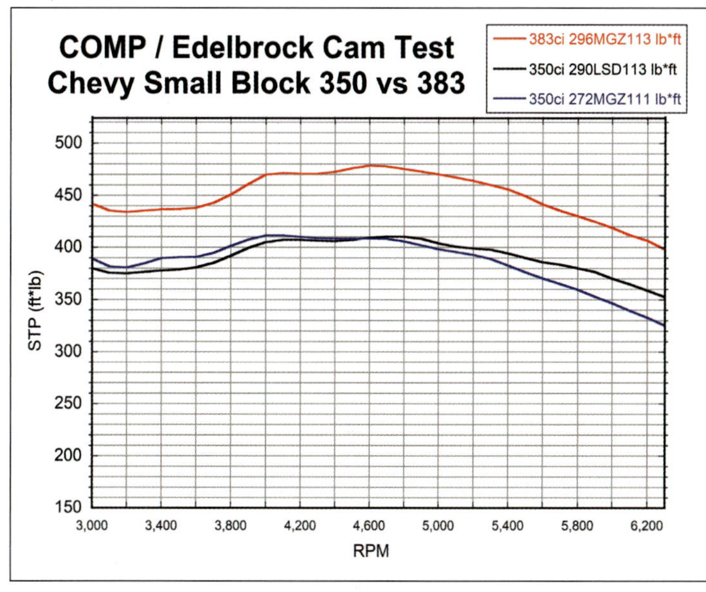

Image 12-4: There are several factors, including stroke, rod to stroke, and a better spring that all work in our favor with these 383-ci builds. Having more vacuum even with more overlap and a larger camshaft is great. Plus, 50 ft-lbs at 3,000 rpm is awesome.

in on the overlap in Image 12-3, the shaded blue overlap triangle of the smallest grind is much smaller than the black, and the red overlap triangle is larger than both of them.

We underestimated how difficult it was going to be to make our idle vacuum targets with the 350, yet these same targets are extremely easy with the 383. You might believe the 27 ci going from 3.48- to 3.75-inch stroke would slightly improve vacuum, but the differences due to stroke, rod to stroke, compression, and other factors makes a tremendous difference. The 350 with the

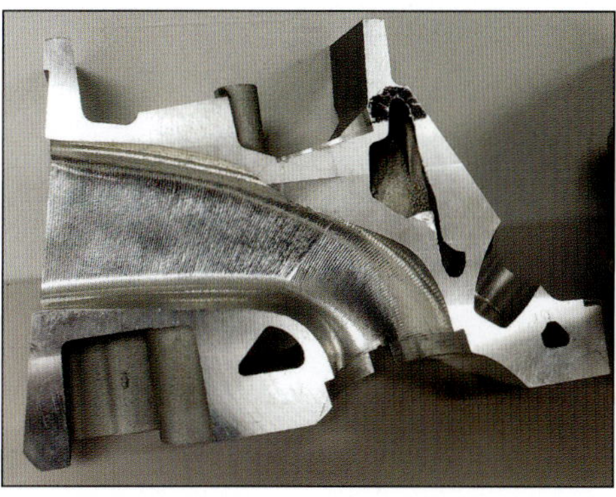

Images 12-5 and 12-6: This is a 23-degree, stock-port-height Chevy head. I can see a little of the intake valve head, and the bowl work makes these far better than stock heads. I wish the port floor was raised an inch or more, which would straighten out the flow path more like this CNC-ported aftermarket LS3.

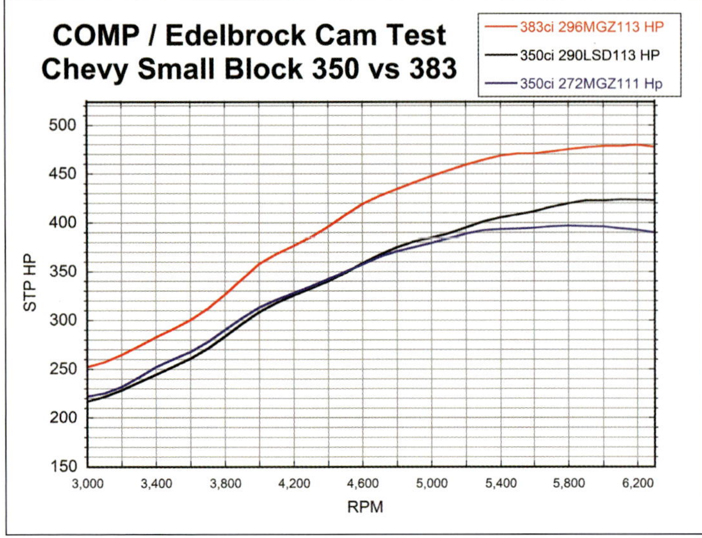

Image 12-7: The black 350 power curve does not achieve the vacuum target, so we really crank the wind up when comparing the red 383 line to the blue 350. We might get closer to the black with some work, but the 383 almost makes this too easy.

black 290 grind was lower than our target vacuum, where the 383 with the red 296 grind breezed past our target and pulled as much as the 350 with the small 272 grind.

The torque improvements with the longer stroke were impressive (shown in Image 12-4). These 23-degree engines with the restrictive port, by modern standards, beg for duration. Between the two 350-ci camshafts, the difference in low-RPM torque was only around 10 ft-lbs. You almost always want to make that trade with the same peak torque between cams and 20 to 25 ft-lbs added at high RPM. The only reason not to go with the black grind is idle torque.

After working on the RHS 502 LS a decade or so ago, I should have remembered it took me three tries to add enough duration for the 4.600-inch stroke, yet it still idled like a kitten. Likewise, the street versions of Sonny's big engines generally have camshaft durations that make a Pro Stock engine builder jealous yet pull great vacuum at idle. Basically, stroke plus rotational inertia will cure a world of street manner ills.

By adding the duration to feed the 23-degree head's limited port and enough overlap to let the wave tuning do its magic, the power improvement of the 383 over the 350 is shown in Image 12-7. Regardless if you see this graph as an 80-plus-hp increase with the same vacuum or a 50-plus-hp increase with similar overlap, it is a great improvement all around.

COMP Cams Valve Train Dynamics Testing

23740S Intake Lobe Testing - 8000 RPM 1

Lobe:	23740S	Valve	2.020
Lobe Lift (in)	.405	Mass (gms)	-
Tappet	96818	Valve Spring	26526
Pushrod	Trend	Installed Height (in)	1.794
Diameter (in)	5/16	Installed Load (lbs)	-
Length (in)	8.000	Open Height (in)	1.118
Wall Thickness (in)	.105	Open Load (lbs)	-
Mass (gms)	-	Rate (lbs/in)	497
Rocker Arm	1817	Coil Bind Height (in)	1.046
Ratio	1.7	Distance To Coil Bind (in)	.072
Retainer	1777	Lash (in)	.013
Mass (gms)	-	Valve Lift (in)	.676
Locks/Lash Cap	648		
Mass (gms)	-		

Static Lift (in): .676
Max Laser Lift (in): 0.7509

Max Laser Bounce (in): 0.0356
Max Engine Speed (rpm): 8045.2

Test Objective:
Determine Limit Speed
Intake Lobe 23740S

Notes:
Limit Speed Found, 8000RPM. This is due to valve loft, not valve bounce. The intake valve begins critical lofting near 7700 RPM. By 8000 RPM, the valve is lofting to nearly .750 inches, at which point the spring is coil bound.

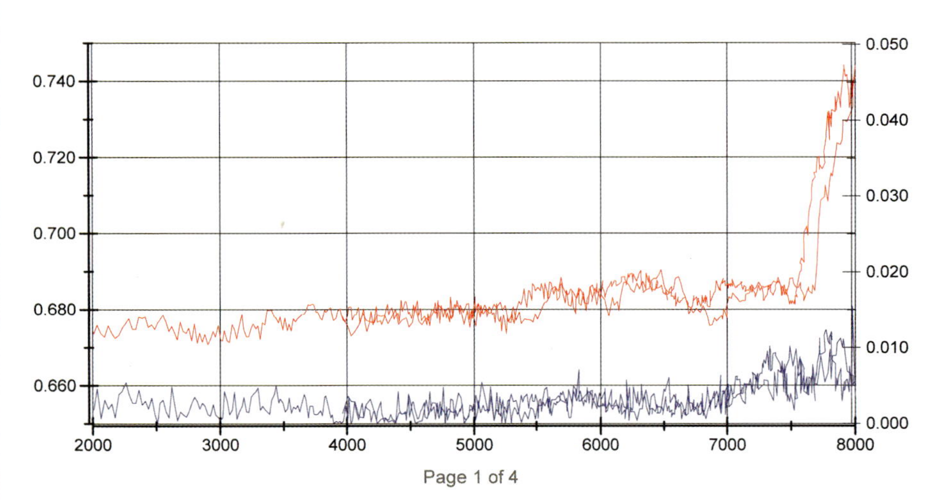

Image 12-8: Even a rather fast solid-roller profile can achieve 7,500-rpm stability. If you are willing to put up with a little more maintenance, setup time, and a slight tick, this is a great option.

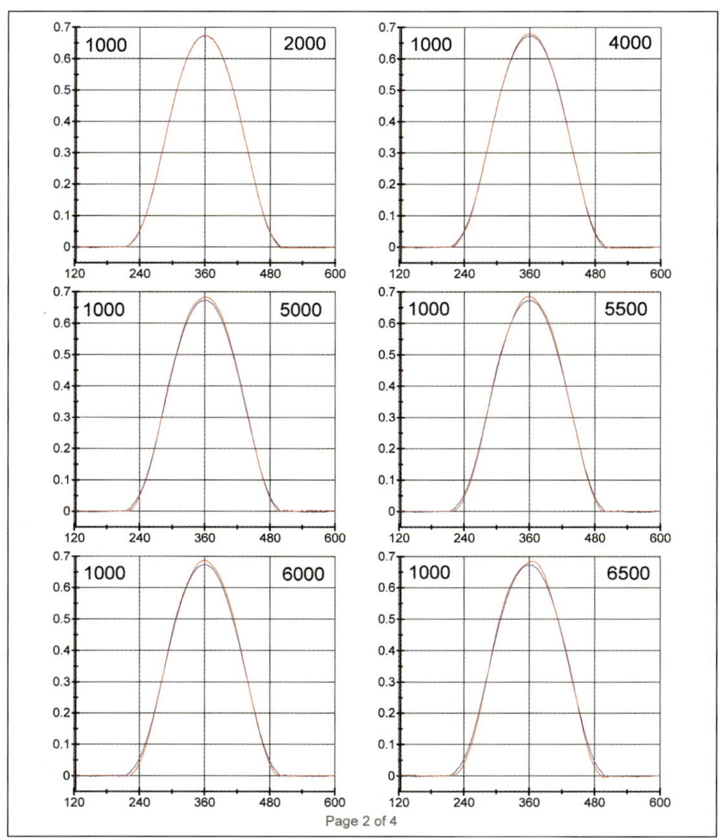

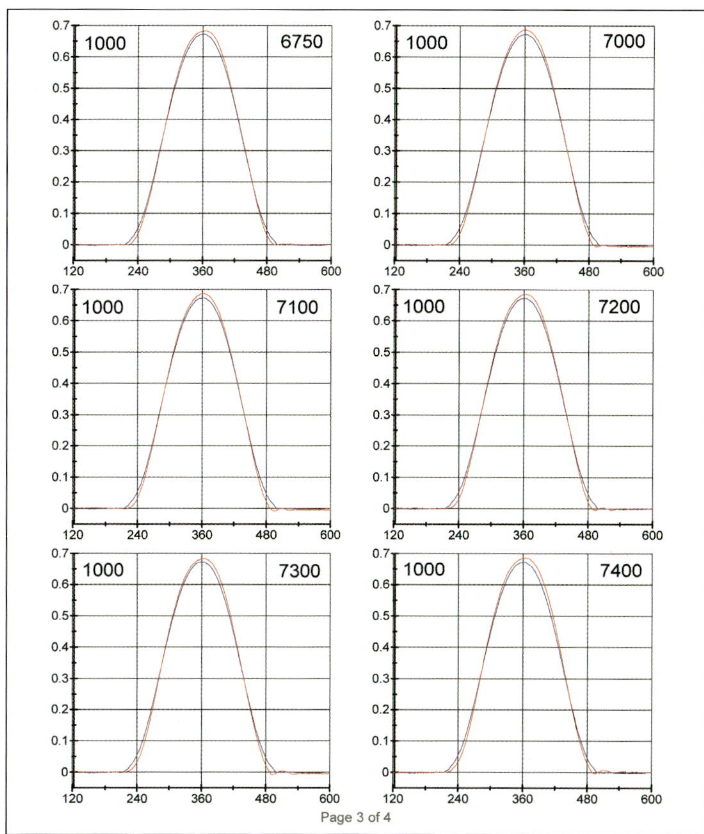

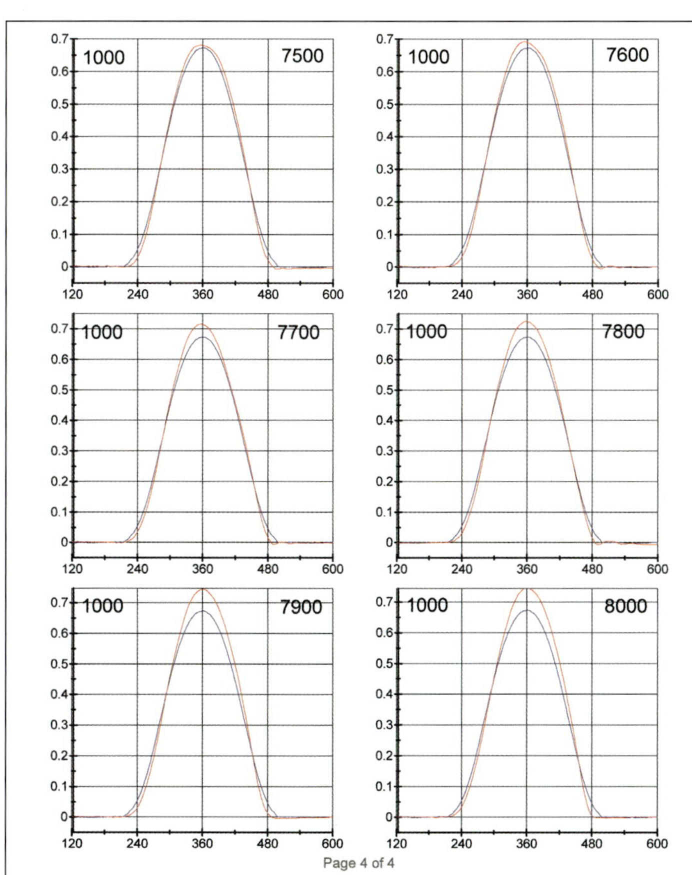

Images 12-9, 12-10, and 12-11: When looking over a Spintron report, look at the dynamic path over the nose. Sometimes there is loft and a bit of a crash that does not show up in bounce. Even the slight crash at 7,500 is not very bad, but you don't want to try to live at higher speed.

Early in my career, I was not impressed with stroker engines because I knew the port cross-section set the airflow and power limits. However, when you think about street applications where you are more vacuum limited instead of displacement limited (as is common in racing), the 383 is an amazing value proposition for performance. Looking back at that torque curve, no one will argue that 50 ft-lbs gained through the middle doesn't feel awesome!

Street versus Racing

I am sure someone noticed the specific output (horsepower/ci and torque/ci) is better on the 383 than 350, so why not always go that direction in racing? To answer, we must understand that idle vacuum and a limited maximum RPM both favor the 383. If you take away those constraints, you see more 4.155-inch-bore

COMP Cams

```
PART #: 12-000-11                    SN#:660244-21
ENGINE: CAMSHAFT, CS SPECIAL ROLLER        PART #: 12-000-11

GRIND#: Camshaft, 33768S/24150S SR 112.00 + 4.00
SPC INSTR 1:
SPC INSTR 2:
SPC INSTR 3:
                              INTAKE       EXHAUST
VALVE ADJUSTMENT              .016         .018
GROSS VALVE LIFT              .622         .607
DURATION @
 .020  TAPPET LIFT            276          283
VALVE TIMING        OPEN              CLOSE
@  .050      INT:   15      BTDC      51      ABDC
             EXH:   62      BBDC      10      ATDC
THESE SPECS ARE FOR CAM INSTALLED
@ 108.0   INTAKE CENTER LINE
                              INTAKE       EXHAUST
DURATION @ .050               245.00       252.00
LOBE LIFT                     .4150        .4050
LOBE SEPARATION               112.00
```

Image 12-12: This grind was the largest cam that fit Jamison's less-constrained 383. By blueprinting all the piston-to-valve and coil-bind specifications (as was covered in Chapter 2), he picked up about 30 hp over something with less lift and less overlap.

Image 12-13: There is absolutely nothing that required added vacuum on this Willis, so we took the gloves off on the build.

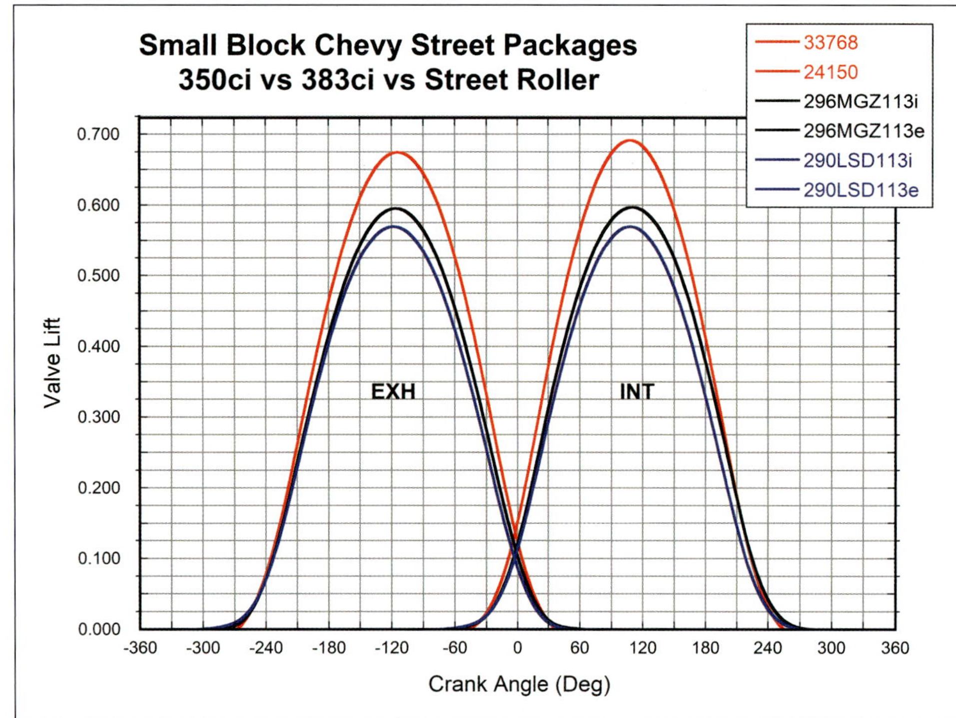

Image 12-14: Jamison's solid-roller, low-shock camshaft is shown here in red versus the 383 hydraulic-roller grind in black and the 350 hydraulic-roller grind in blue. The lash on the solid roller is shown but with no deflection on the hydraulic rollers, so they probably are not as close in a running engine.

and 3.48-inch-stroke combinations than 4.030-inch-bore with 3.75-inch-stroke race engines because the increased bore unshrouds the valves and allows higher airflow. However, for increased idle vacuum, the long-stroke combination is king.

How About More Power in a Street Small-Block Chevy?

One of our testing engineers finished this test and wanted to build something a little more race-like but still somewhat street friendly for his Willis. We had done some Spintron work with Chris Potter on a great 1.7:1, low-shock, solid-roller package a few years ago, so we redid it one step larger with all the overlap that would fit for Jamison's cam.

In the 1946 Willys Overland Wagon, there are no vacuum accessories to consider. He was happy with it sounding a little angry and being somewhat temperamental below 3,000 rpm. An overlay of this grind to the more friendly, general-use grinds is shown in Image 12-14. It is difficult to compare a solid-lifter camshaft that has a very precise lash point to the hydraulic designs where the lash varies with the hydraulic bleed down, loads, oil viscosity, temperature, and a host of other variables.

With that in mind, you can see how closely the low-lift timing of this aggressive camshaft matches the other grinds. The extra compression of this build helps the low end, but it was built with a short-runner, single-plane Edelbrock Victor EFI system. Larger-port heads really don't like low RPM as much as the performer RPM intakes of the other engines. That said, the torque shown in Image 12-16 is extremely nice if you do not try a 2,500-rpm pull. The power in Image 12-17 embarrasses most lightly modified LS1s, even if the standard port height means this small-block Chevy head has a dog-leg turn that would impress Arnold Palmer.

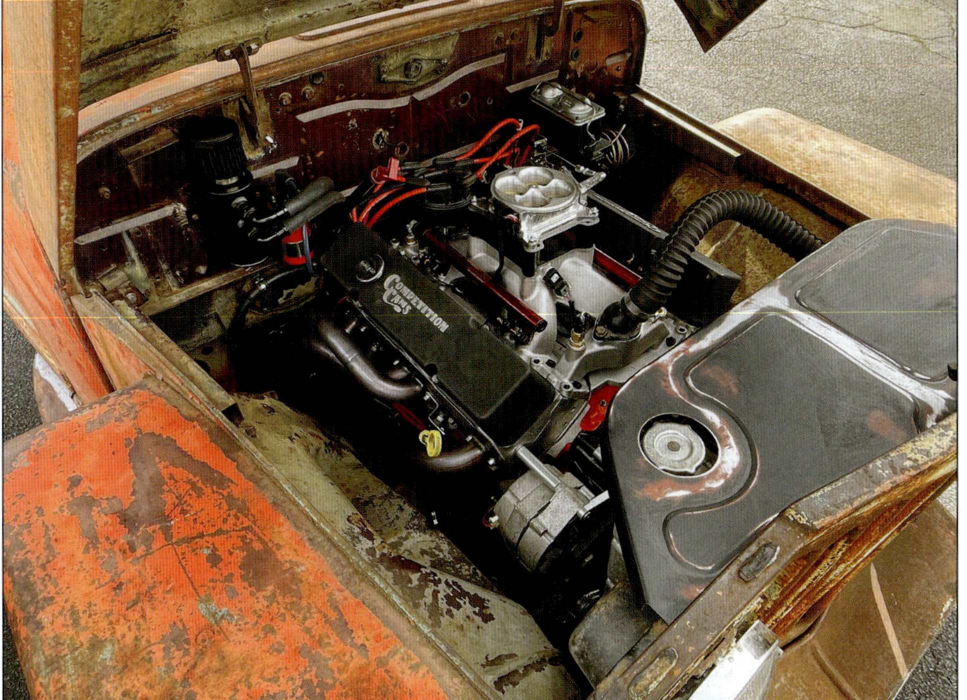

Image 12-15: This solid-roller engine looks great with the single-plane intake and EFI system. Jamison had to do some work on the headers. Someone might already have that platform in an LS swap, but we could not find one for a small-block Chevy.

The small-block Chevy certainly has its place at the high-performance table, but it takes some hits on either manners or performance compared to a more modern port-layout engine. Keep in mind that the camshaft is the coach or conductor for your engine. It does not make power by itself, but it can be optimized to help increase displacement (more air demand) and/or increase air supply (better heads and intake) to reach their full potential. Also, some coaches are better than others.

GM 5.3L LM7 Cams: C10 Pickup to Circle-Track and Drift

You might think the LM7 cam selection is almost identical to the small-block Chevy. In some ways you are right, but there are two major differences. First, the LM7 has

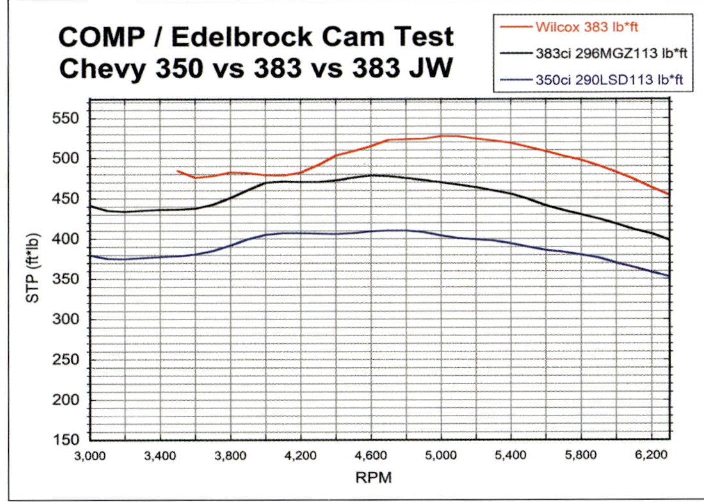

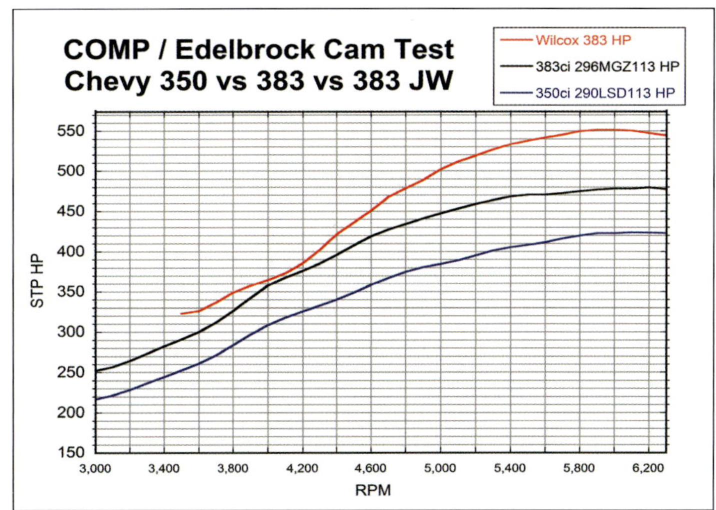

Images 12-16 and 12-17: Here are the torque and horsepower comparisons that show what Jamison got for his hard work: better heads and not caring about vacuum or sub-3500 wide-open throttle performance. Almost 50 ft-lbs peak to peak is great, and 70-plus hp is even better.

Image 12-18: This poor 5.3L spent months getting abused on our dyno and never missed a beat.

a much better cylinder head. There is almost 25 fewer cubic inches and 50 cfm better head flow, so the CFM per cubic inch is moving in a great direction. This means the intake can be closed 10 degrees earlier and peak at the same RPM. The second major difference is the EFI system. You can get much better runner lengths with EFI, but the factory computer is much easier to tune if the overlap is kept under control.

EFI Thumpr Grinds

It is important to determine if someone is more concerned with sound or performance. It may seem like an odd question, but the losses for focusing on sound are only in the 10–20 ft-lbs torque in the 2,500- to 3,500-rpm range and almost nothing at high RPM. Most of the changes are in EVO and overlap that were discussed earlier. If sound is important, and it is going into a truck or heavy vehicle, start by looking at the 54-700-11, 54-701-11, 54-702-11, and 54-703-11 EFI Thumpr grinds.

Because the 54-702-11 and 54-703-11 are basically the same except for lift, we will focus on the 700, 701, and 703 versus the factory LM7 (as shown in Image 12-22). These camshafts all have similar overlap that is dramatically more than a stock GM LM7 5.3 truck camshaft.

Images 12-19 and 12-20: The first step is to grind everything we want to test. Then, we line them up on the table outside the dyno cell to wait their turn on the pump.

Image 12-21: This 54-700-11 camshaft was designed for awesome sound. Individually, someone must decide if 10 ft-lbs low is a worthwhile trade for the exhaust note. We only have a given amount of energy available in the cylinder, and it can either be used to push the piston or push out exhaust.

This reduces the idle vacuum to create some of the misfire that creates some of the lope sound. The lift around TDC fits well with the factory piston-to-valve clearance limits (as shown in Image 12-23).

A torque comparison that uses a mostly stock 5.3L, dyno headers, and trailblazer intake is shown in Image 12-24. The two smaller Thumpr grinds are above stock torque throughout the test range. The SuperFlow water brake limits us from going below 2,500 rpm. By 3,000 rpm, the Thumpr grinds are up 15–25 ft-lbs over the

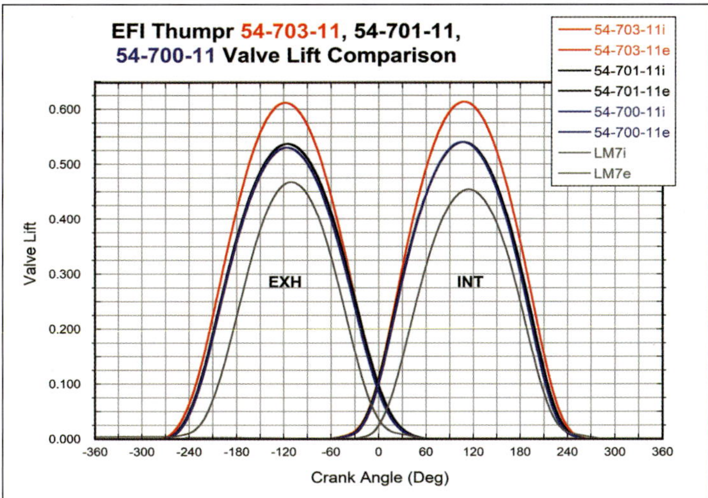

Image 12-22: We tested both more and less overlap when developing the Thumpr grinds, but this amount creates enough overlap to produce the vacuum needed to tune the factory computer. These are friendly in parking-lot traffic and manageable with all factory accessories at a reasonable idle speed around 900 rpm.

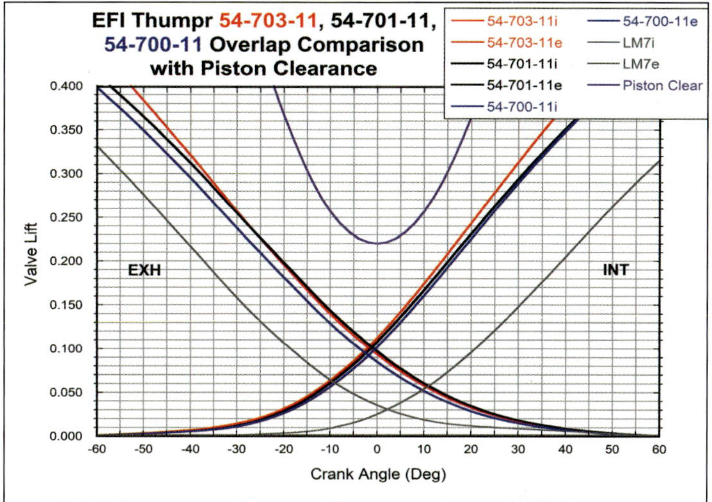

Image 12-23: Some cam companies do not pay close enough attention to piston-to-valve clearance. When I look at piston-to-valve clearance for shelf grinds, I consider all tolerances stacked up to be certain that these part numbers will not only fit our test engine, but also any engine a customer would build with a stock long-block.

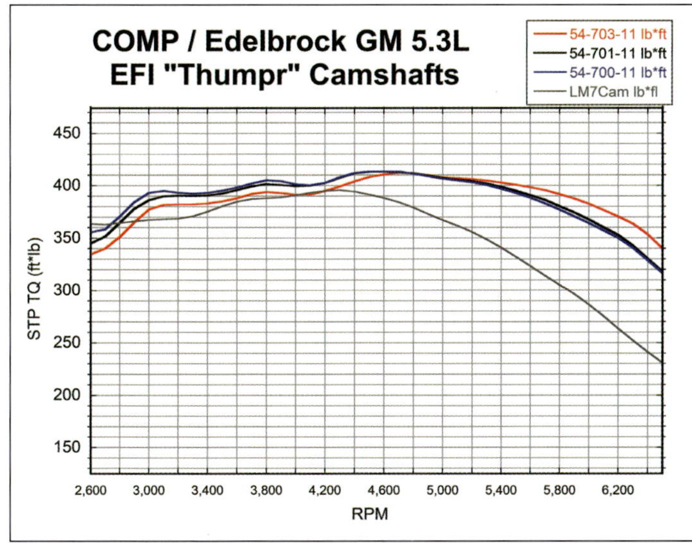

Image 12-24: If we were to put a pin through the torque curve at 4,800 rpm, these Thumpr grinds would almost pivot at that spot. The red 54-703-11 might be a little higher and lower at the extremes because of the higher lift. We really don't fall below stock torque anywhere, even when targeting sound.

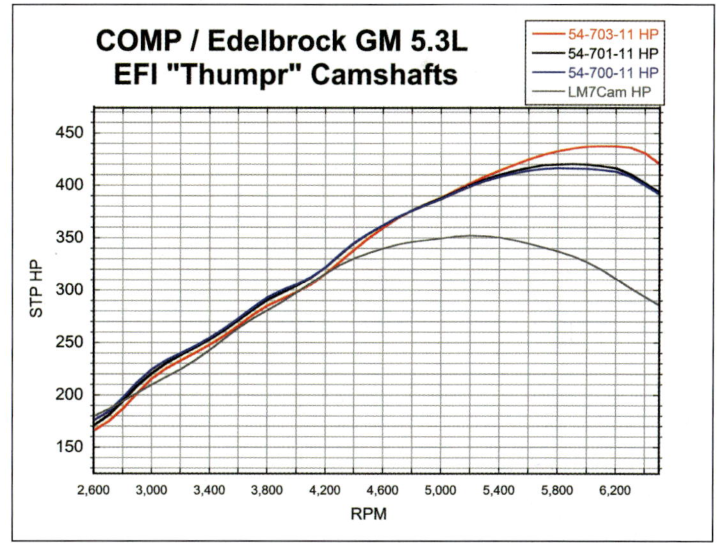

Image 12-25: Increasing power from about 350 hp stock to 415 hp or almost 440 hp makes this Thumpr series an excellent choice for any cam-only upgraded 5.3L application. This is especially true if you want to sell a vehicle or love the sound of a racy engine.

stock LM7 camshaft, which is something noticeable as soon as you floor a pickup with a factory converter.

Looking at power in Image 12-25, the Thumpr grinds are all up almost 40 hp at the stock 5,200-rpm peak then take off with a 100 to 125 hp increase over stock at 6,200 rpm. The peak-to-peak differences are around 65 to 85 hp. These grinds sound awesome with the slow and early EVO creating a deep, strong sound without any tin-drum pop. The overlap increases idle misfire to a

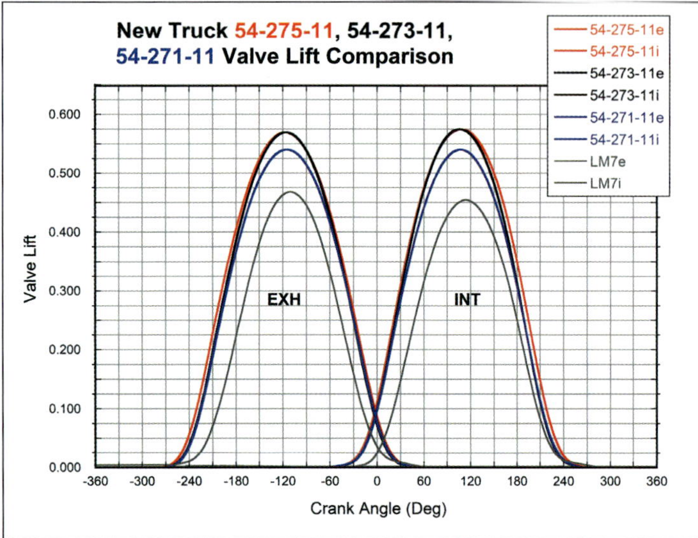

Image 12-26: The Thumpr series is great for most customers, but if your taste is more like mine, increased low- to mid-range bite is preferable over the Thumpr's cool bark. There really is no wrong answer, so let your own goals lead your decisions.

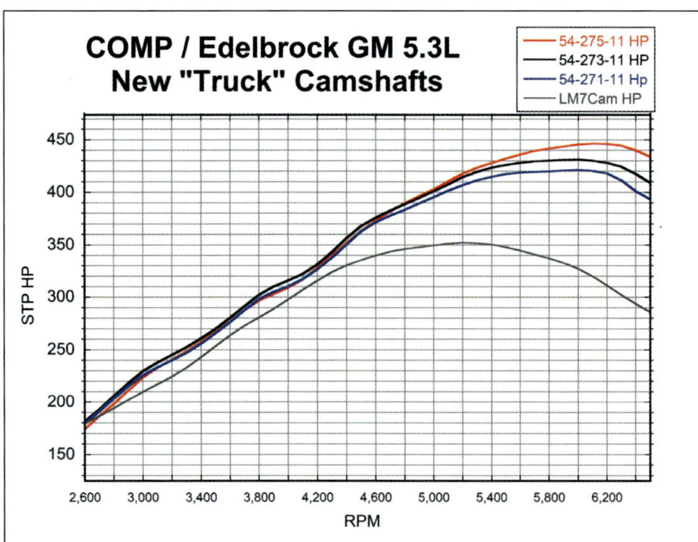

Image 12-28: The added torque of the 54-273-11 represents 15 hp basically for free if swapped to the inexpensive 26906 valve spring kit. However, if you don't need every bit of that low-end torque, there is another 25 hp available at 6,500 rpm with the 54-275-11.

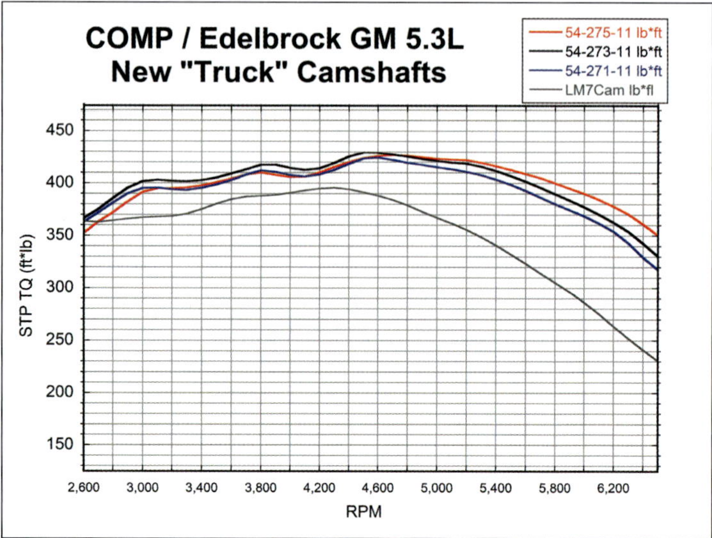

Image 12-27: The 54-271-11 is optimized to run dependably on any stock GM Gen III valve spring. The 54-273-11 has almost the same seat timing, but note how both the quicker ramp designs and 0.035-inch additional lift of the 54-273-11 results in approximately 10 ft-lbs from 3,000 all the way to 6,500-plus rpm. Optimizing the lobe for the spring is not just a tool for the track. It works in any application.

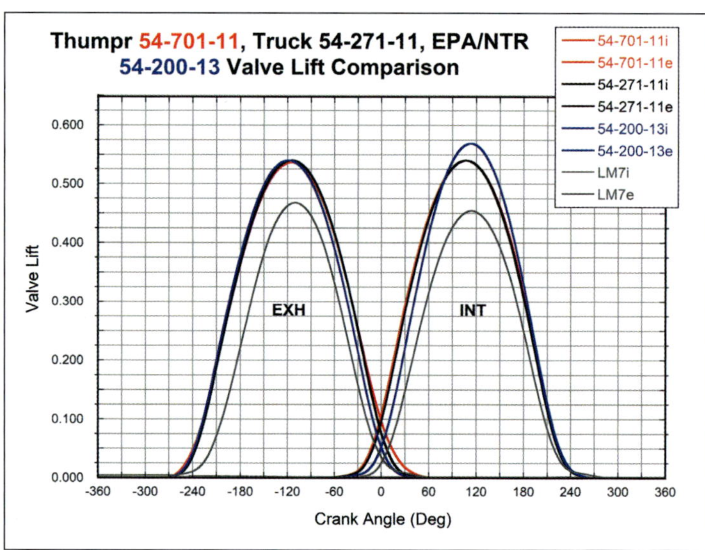

Image 12-29: This graph shows the lower-lift truck camshaft in black, the medium-lift Thumpr in red, and the 54-200-13 LS3 California Air Resources Board (CARB)–certified cam in blue. The LS3 springs allow 0.575-inch lift so it cannot be run in a 5.3L without a slight spring upgrade (GM Blue or Comp 26906).

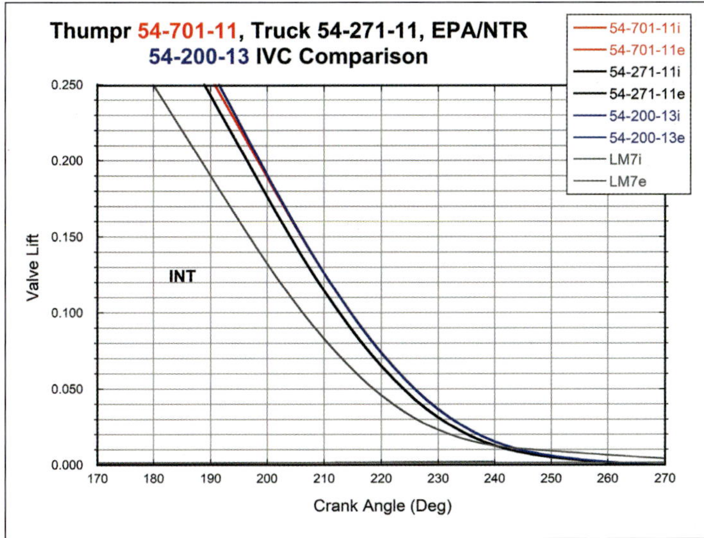

Image 12-30: Because all three grinds are developed to run in the same RPM range, we should not be surprised how the closing points almost directly overlay one another. The truck grind is the earliest because it focuses more on low-speed torque.

very popular range without making the EFI system difficult to tune. The IVC range for these cams is perfect for most vehicle weights, gear ratios, and transmission options.

New Truck Grinds

As great as the EFI Thumpr cams run in a 5.3L pickup, could we do better? If you want to impress your buddies, sell a truck quick, or have something that sounds racy while being totally comfortable every day, the Thumpr cams are for you. However, if you are more interested in low- to mid-range torque and response than the idle sound, we can tweak the overlap a bit and delay the exhaust opening to use wave tuning for more filling than sound.

Image 12-26 shows the three new truck grinds compared to the factory LM7 grind. The blue 54-271-11 has lower lift to work with any factory GM Gen III valve spring. The black 54-273-11 has basically the same specs with the lift optimized around the new Comp 26906 spring kit. This 0.575-inch range is right at our performance 30-percent L/D (lift to intake valve diameter) target for 45-degree seats and allows the use of an inexpensive and extremely durable spring kit.

For larger engines, lighter vehicles, or anyone more focused on top-end power, there is the 54-275-11 grind in red. With a touch more overlap, an earlier EVO, and a later IVC, this moves everything higher in the RPM range.

Image 12-27 shows the torque curves for these three grinds. The

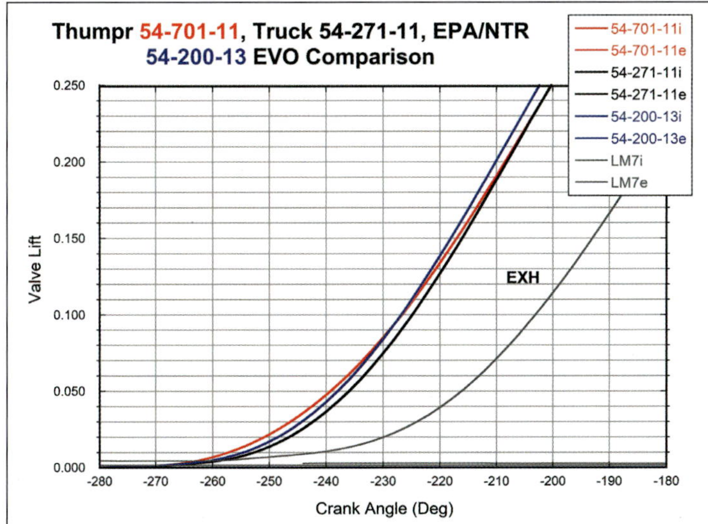

Image 12-31: The differences are far greater on the EVO side. You can see how the slow opening of the Thumpr exhaust is shaped to create a particular sound. Race cars have both pop and blat overtones. The timing and speed help create both in the Thumpr. The truck grind has a later and much faster opening that creates a different exhaust wave shark-fin shape.

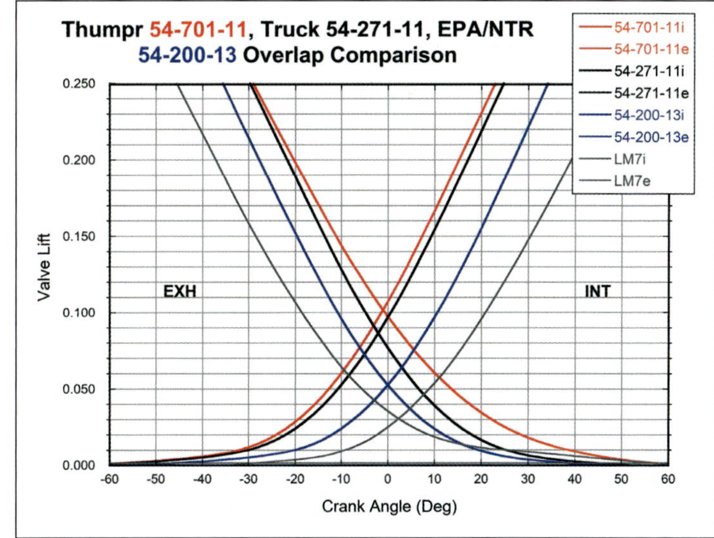

Image 12-32: In the overlap region, the 54-200-13 CARB grind must be smaller to pass the CARB/EPA bag test. More overlap greatly helps the midrange but fails our test. The 54-271-11 has great overlap for an idle rumble but is more optimized for great peak torque. The 54-701-11 has the slowest and most overlap.

Image 12-33: This is the torque curve (not the wave) on the 54-271-11. The fast EVO creates a powerful tuning effect that helps the intake at 3,000, 3,800, and 4,600 rpm. However, even in the valleys, we are better than the small overlap 54-200-11.

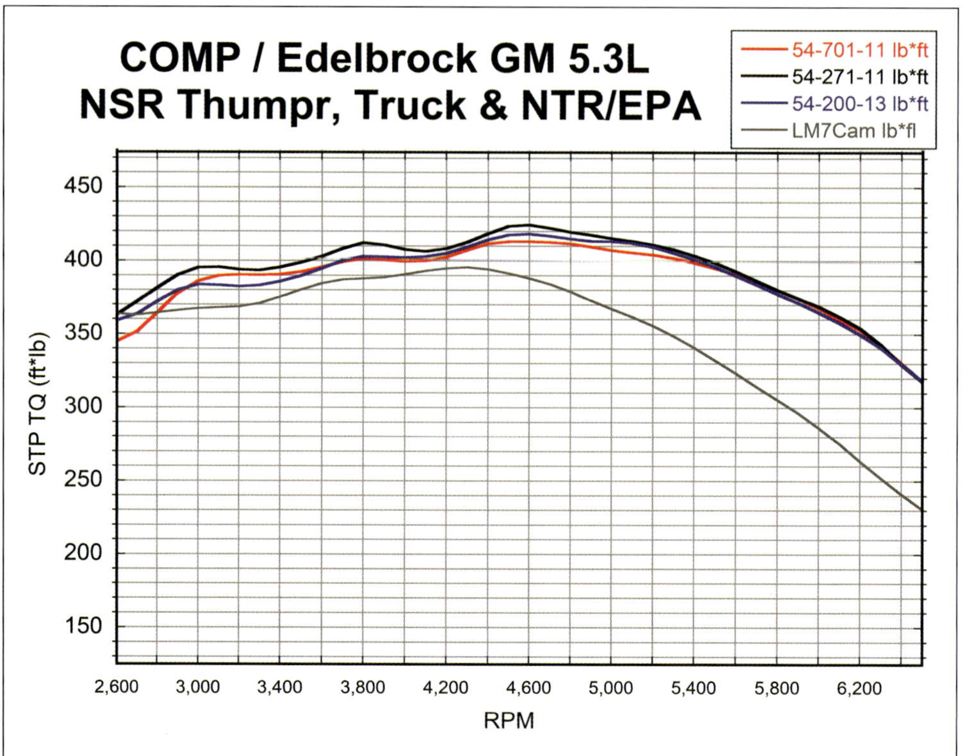

0.575-inch versus 0.541-inch lift is worth about 5 ft-lbs across the board. Hence, if you are swapping springs, I recommend the 54-273-11 over the 54-271-11. However, a 0.575-inch lift requires a spring change. Comparing the 54-275-11 to 54-273-11, there's the normal -15 ft-lbs down low from the earlier EVO and later IVC of the 275, but it's 20-plus ft-lbs at 6,500 rpm because of those same valve timing changes.

One thing of great interest is the Trailblazer intake has long runners with very little taper. With the faster EVO of these truck grinds, we get stronger wave tuning. The places where this tunes, especially at 3,000, 3,800, and 4,600 rpm, all show a 10 to 20 ft-lb bump that was much less apparent in the slower opening Thumpr grinds. We see this same effect whenever a faster exhaust opening is incorporated in race applications. If the intake runners are more curved, of unequal length, or have more taper, the waves are less pronounced.

Looking at power in Image 12-28, it's obvious how attractive that extra torque is from the 54-275-11 when horsepower is calculated. The other cams are nice, but we are now flirting with 450 hp from a 353-hp baseline with the factory camshaft looking at peak-to-peak power. The reduced overlap and later EVO does not result in the race sounds from this truck cam like with the Thumpr, but it still has a noticeable lope if the idle is set

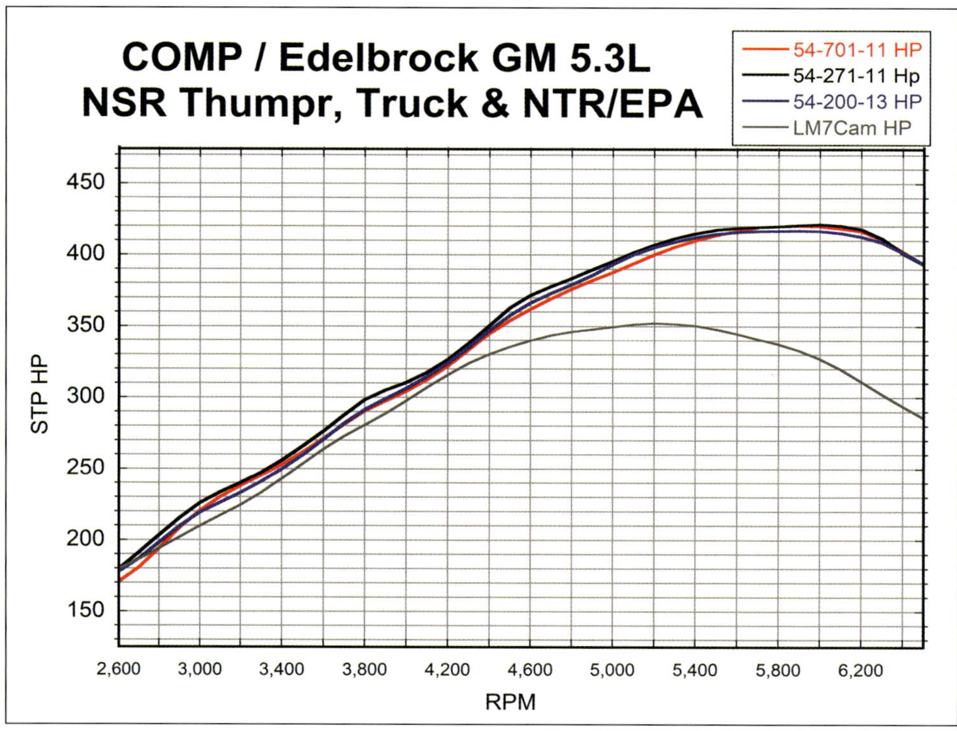

Image 12-34: As for peak power, these three camshafts virtually overlay. You don't give up power by going with the emissions-certified grind, but you do give up torque and sound. We drove our test Suburban with the 54-200-13 and evolution lifters to PRI and back last year. When you get on the throttle, around 4,000 to 4,500 rpm, you expect the engine to lay over because it sounds so stock, but it just takes off and puts a smile on almost anyone's face.

low. It's more of a nod from racers than something your grandmother would not ride in to go to church. All three of the truck grinds have a deep and strong exhaust note, but here it is a subtle and nice byproduct rather than the intended design.

Thumpr versus Truck versus CARB/EPA Grinds

We have a very good Environmental Protection Agency (EPA)/California Air Resources Board (CARB)–certified camshaft grind we run in the 5.3L to compare different overlap triangles of the 54-200-13 (CARB/EPA), 54-271-11 (truck), and 54-701-11 (Thumpr) (as shown in Image 12-29). The EPA grind has the highest lift, as it was developed around the 26906, LS6, and LS3 valve springs, whereas the other two started with the factory truck spring.

What first jumps out to me is that all these cams were designed for the same basic cylinder head and RPM, so the IVCs lay almost over one another. With this, we expect peak torque and power to occur at almost the same RPM for all three.

Moving to EVO, the slower EVO of the Thumpr in red is used for the excellent sound through a more rounded exhaust pulse waveform.

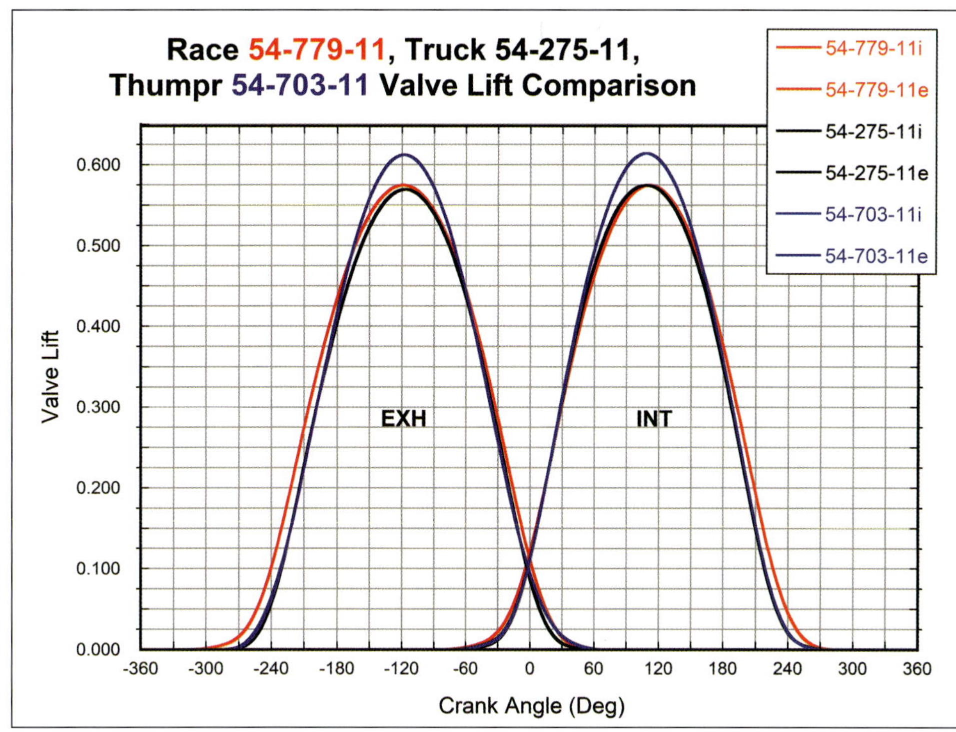

Image 12-35: We are adding the 54-799-11 drift camshaft to the mix. It is developed for budget 5.3L to 6.0L builds for circle-track racing, drag racing, or drifting. The idea was to have something that would run to 7,500-plus rpm with the 26906 valve-spring kit. We have that with the larger "truck" cam in black and high lift (26918 spring) Thumpr in blue. You can see how much less valve velocity the higher-RPM race cam requires with less slope.

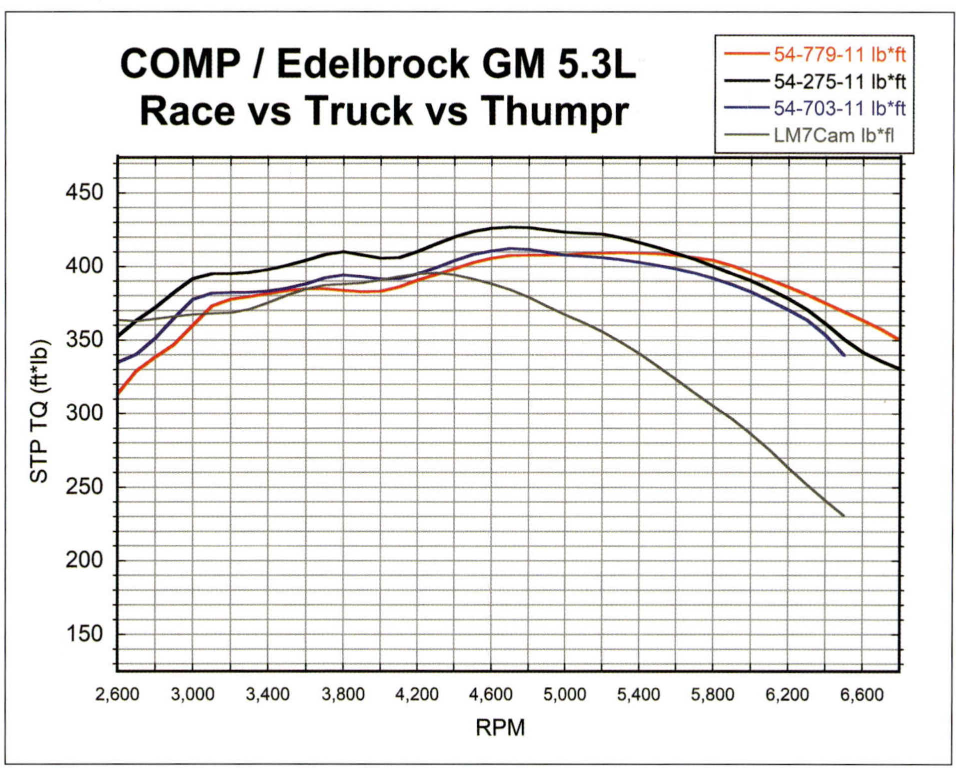

Image 12-36: The truck camshaft murders the other two in the low- to mid-range. The race grind looks rather anemic to 5,000 rpm, but when you put more gear to it, the torque at the tire is best. The Thumpr sounds awesome and is not awful on torque. Note how the faster exhaust opening of the truck cam results in stronger wave tuning, as seen at 3,100, 3,800, and 4,800 rpm. All of the design techniques that were mentioned for race engines work just as well in street applications.

The EPA cam opens next and is far quicker than the Thumpr but is similar in shape to the latest EVO truck grind. However, none open as slowly or as late as the factory LM7 camshaft, which had some runout.

Image 12-32 shows the overlap is the clearest difference in the three grinds. The CARB/EPA grind must keep overlap small to pass the first bag test for startup hydrocarbon emissions. There is perhaps 50 percent more area than the stock 5.3L, but it actually closes the exhaust sooner than the factory camshaft. Moving to the 54-271-11, we see another 0.030-inch lift where the overlap triangle peaks a few degrees before TDC. This shape provides a nice, sharp window for the exhaust and intake to communicate as we saw with the torque curve waves.

Finally, this overlap comparison shows the Thumpr in red with the far slower exhaust closing adding another 0.015- to 0.020-inch exhaust lift from TDC to almost 40 degrees after TDC, along with the slower EVO. This long, slow overlap triangle gives the strong overlap sound people love.

Moving to the torque comparison for the camshafts in Image 12-33, you may be shocked these basically overlay from 5,500 to 6,500 rpm. The reduced overlap of the 54-200-13 definitely shows up from 2,600 to 4,600 rpm versus the greater overlap 54-271-11 truck grind.

I love the great sound of the Thumpr for many applications, but it does cost you about 10 ft-lbs from 3,000 to 5,000 rpm.

With the horsepower comparison in Image 12-34, you see the CARB/EPA cam is not as good as the other two, but it is close and can drop into a 5.3L without any tuning required if the engine is non-AFM. We run

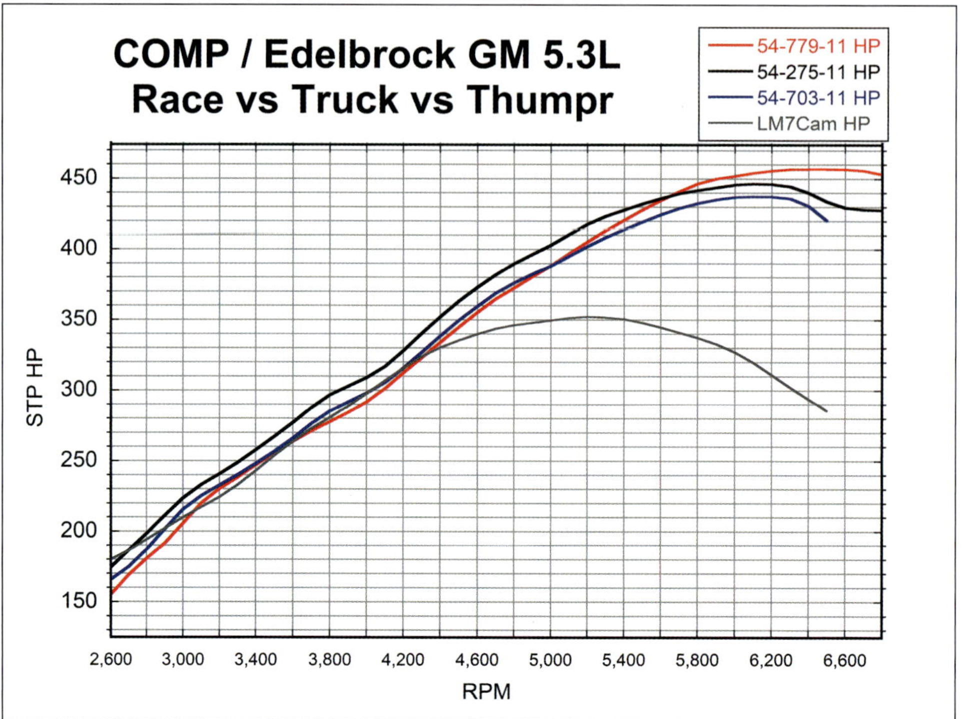

Image 12-37: Power-wise, use the 54-779-11 for high RPM. It can live between 5,000 and 7,500 its whole life as happily as anywhere. The 54-275-11 can run 6,800-plus rpm but prefers to live under 6,500 rpm. These two cams kind of make the 54-703-11 look a little sad, even with 435 hp. There are no bad choices, as each does its job extremely well.

Image 12-38: Thanks to Cody Williams (pictured) for all of the 5.3L testing, Dave Henninger for his time in research and development, and Chris Potter for supporting this extensive 5.3L test matrix. We learned a great deal and have awesome data.

this camshaft in our long-term test Suburban with a DOD delete kit with no other tune. I rode in this vehicle from PRI with our Edelbrock CCO, product development VP, and engineering head of testing, and it is awesome. It sounds and acts almost stock until you hit that 4,500-rpm point where the graphs diverge from stock. I promise that you look for places to put your foot into the floorboard of this Suburban. You cannot go wrong with any of these three camshafts.

The red 54-701-11 sounds best, the black 54-271-11 has the best grunt in the middle, and the 54-701-11 makes a drag racer smile at the cruise-in. Any of these will make anyone extremely happy 95 percent of the time, but each does its intended job just a little better than the other two. There is nothing magic as to why. Each event does exactly what it should do to the curve. The faster or slower rates also do exactly what they should do to the curves.

Taking the 5.3L Racing!

Going one step further, let's take the biggest truck and Thumpr grind and overlay it to our 7,500-plus-rpm 54-779-11 race grind in Image 12-35. This was made for 5.7L–6.2L drift and circle-track applications, but it still works great in a 5.3L with minimal configuration changes. The blue Thumper grind has the lift increase optimized for the 26918 valve spring. The 26906 is such a great value that we configured the later 54-779-11 and 54-275-11 around the 0.575-inch spring. The race cam has more overlap before TDC than even the Thumpr, but in this case, it is a race grind and not just something that sounds like a race grind. Note the 54-779-11 is considerably softer at low lifts with a drastically earlier EVO and IVC. When we want to go 7,500-plus rpm with a steel valve and a light spring on a hydraulic roller, the profile asks less of the spring, or Fred must be easier on Ginger.

With the torque comparison in Image 12-36, it shows a 20 to 30 ft-lb penalty to run the race cam in the 2,600 to 4,200 rpm range. We make that up with gear in a drift car. A 20-percent increase in safe RPM means swapping 3.5x gears for 4.2x gears, which gives a 20-percent increase in rear wheel torque at the same speed. That 10-percent penalty at the flywheel is a 10-percent gain with more gear at the tire, and a good drift-car or circle-track driver should never be below 4,500 rpm anyway. This cam is awful in a daily driver and does not sound any better than those smaller Thumpr grinds, but you will worry about launching rods out of the block before you ever consider valvetrain issues, which is perfect for a budget race build. The horsepower in Image 12-37 shows the added 25 hp at 6,800 rpm of the race grind. The 54-275-11 truck grind is optimized to do almost everything below 6,400 rpm. The 54-779-11 race grind cleared its throat at 5,400 rpm and is ready to really sing past 7,500 rpm.

There really is not a bad camshaft in this mix. Every one of these

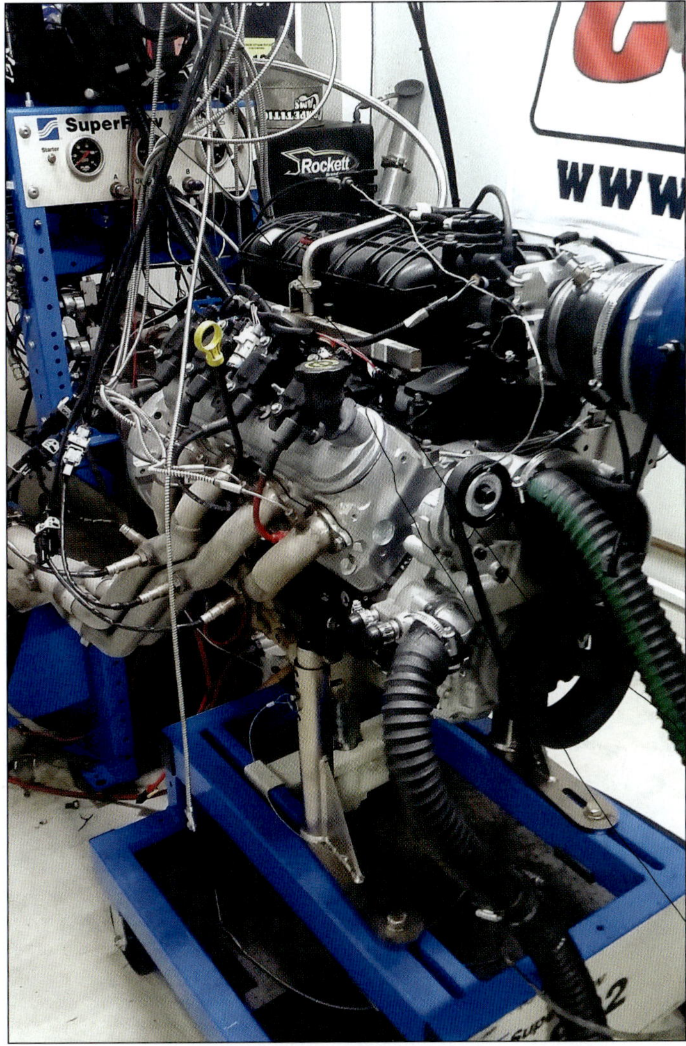

***Image 12-39:** Things look the same on the outside, but this 5.3L might be hiding a trick or two inside.*

Image 12-40: This is a lightweight LS core made for Le Mans racing.

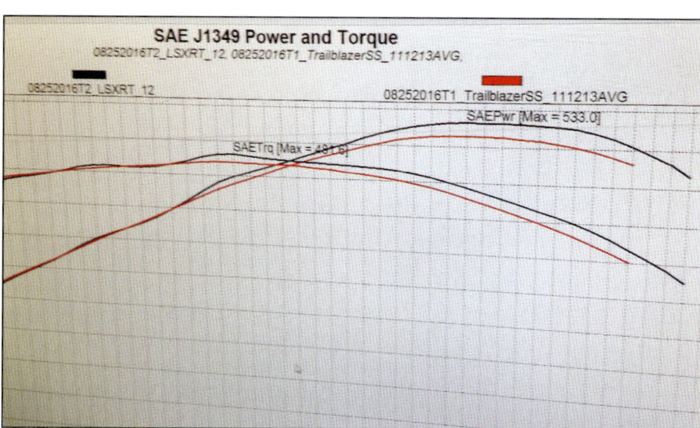

Image 12-41: I can neither confirm nor deny this dyno curve had anything to do with the ChumpCar build. However, I can confirm that all the cam tricks from the 383 work the same on a Gen III 383 (almost down to the same horsepower gains).

Image 12-42: Matt Moran started to believe that German engineers did not build a 1994 BMW to fit a 2000 GM Gen III V-8.

Image 12-43: No one gets out of the "GMW" without a serious smile, except when it comes back on the wrecker.

was chosen because it does something extraordinarily well. However, you always want to choose a camshaft optimized for your goals. Every camshaft was run on the Edelbrock dyno with the same 5.3L engine with zero other changes. There is no bad choice among these for the engine. We are trying to provide the perfect camshaft to achieve your personal application and desires.

Some might wonder what would happen if we played some of the same small-block Chevy tricks with the 5.3L. Something general is to run a 4.00-inch versus the standard 3.78-inch stroke, increase the bore to 3.900 inches versus the standard 3.780 inches (most iron blocks have thick enough cylinder walls), run CNC ported, and swap in a similar solid-roller grind to what we saw in Chapter 11, perhaps with a lightweight LS core made for Le Mans racing (as shown in Image 12-40). If the air demand, displacement, and air supply were increased with the headwork and reoptimized the valvetrain, the resulting power curve might look like Image 12-41. If the engine was forced unwillingly into a E36 BMW, it might create some awesome smiles at the track.

6.4L Hemi: Blower and Cam Packages

If you want to make a list of the least informed statements common in the performance world, here's your number-one submission: "Camshaft doesn't matter in forced induction engines. Just run stock."

Just because someone says a camshaft is a blower or turbo camshaft does not guarantee the lobe profiles and valve events are optimized for those applications. Engines don't

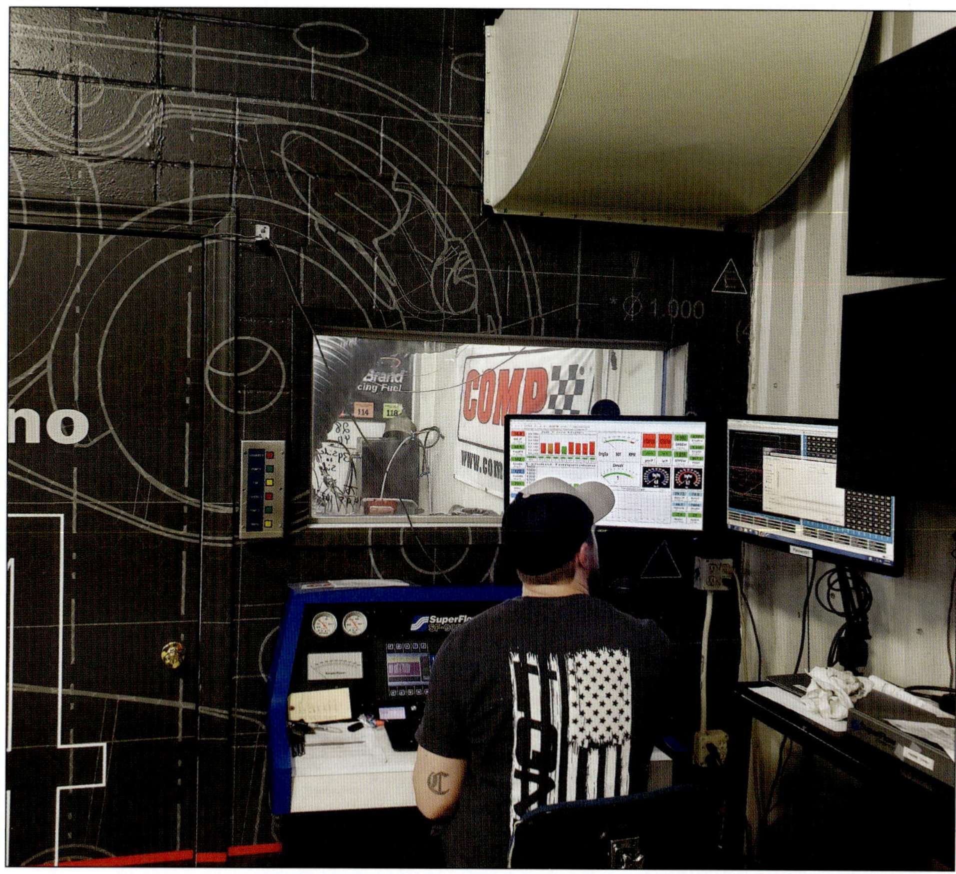

Image 12-44: Cody seems to prefer big-power blown-Hemi testing over swapping cams a dozen times during the GM 5.3L tests. I don't really blame him. The most amazing thing about these pulls was how normal they seemed. A Gen III Hemi with a blower is a little louder at wide-open throttle than without, but the engine does not act dramatic in any way. Then, you look at the power curve and almost fall out of your chair.

Image 12-45: This is the master cam and valvetrain kit for the 6.4L Hemi with a blower. There is far more that went into this combination than clever marketing and guesswork. Each system was tested and retested with various pulleys and fuels on the dyno.

Image 12-46: We could not wait to see what the Comp cams would do for the Edelbrock blowers on our dyno.

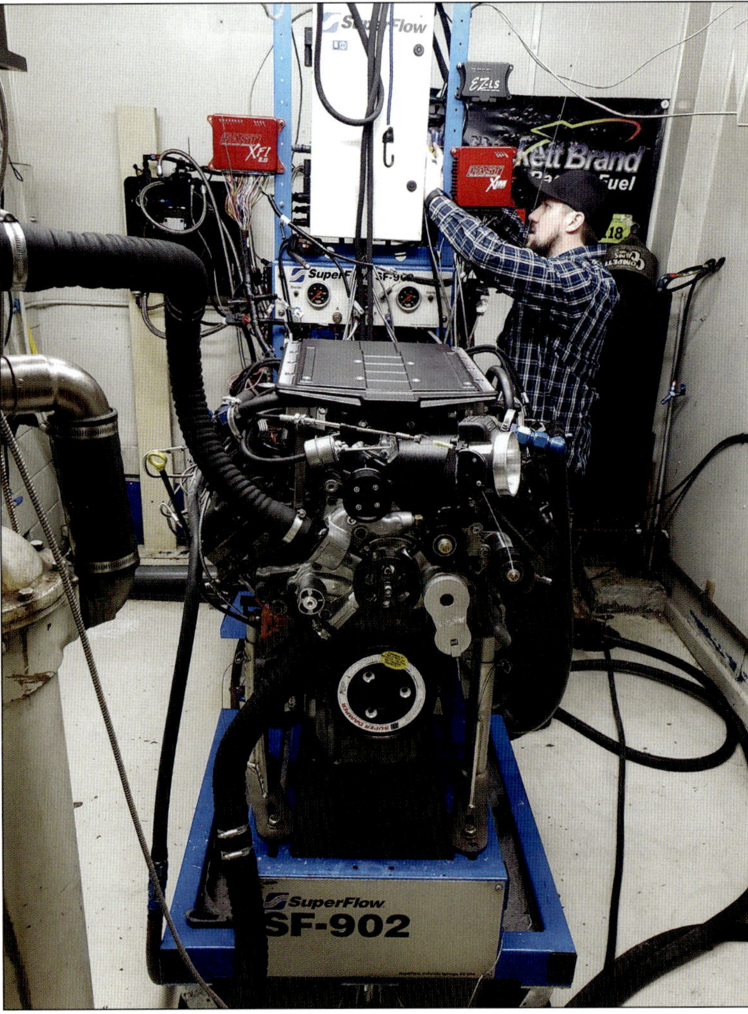

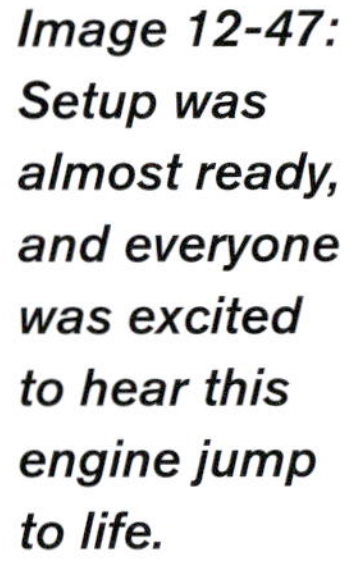

Image 12-47: Setup was almost ready, and everyone was excited to hear this engine jump to life.

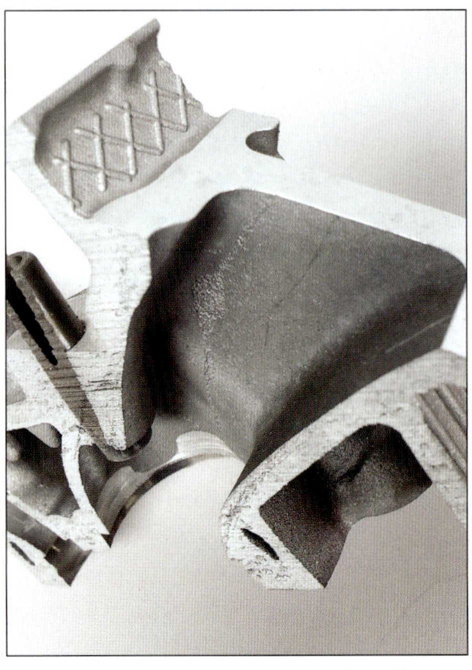

Image 12-48: The straight shot down the port and into the chamber with the latest-generation Hemi head is screaming to be force fed.

read marketing materials. You may find someone's turbo grind that runs best NA or some NA grind that works best with a blower.

My general approach is to start by focusing on engine speed. Typically, we need to migrate to smoother lobes with forced induction as these systems increase the maximum system airflow capacity. The increased density will result in a significant improvement in mass flow without necessarily higher port velocities when under pressure. Additionally, as the power levels increase, there will be higher remaining cylinder pressures when opening the exhaust valve, which requires a smoother exhaust opening profile.

After stability is considered, we optimize valve timing for the pressures experienced across each valve in the region around each opening and closing event. We discussed changing the overlap slightly between turbo camshafts for low backpressure versus high backpressure applications as well as between small and large blowers for the power goals. Each event needs to be carefully considered. I promise that if you could swap the cam specs among NHRA Pro Mod Blower, Pro Mod Turbo, and Pro Mod Nitrous engines, none of the three would be able to qualify with either of the other's camshaft.

A great example to show how dramatically a forced induction engine can respond to the right camshaft change is the 6.4L Dodge Hemi with the Edelbrock 2650 Supercharger. The Hemi head is probably an even straighter shot down the port to the valve than the LS. This nice twin plug chamber configuration loves to have more air forced inside. Hemi engines and Superchargers are a match made in performance heaven.

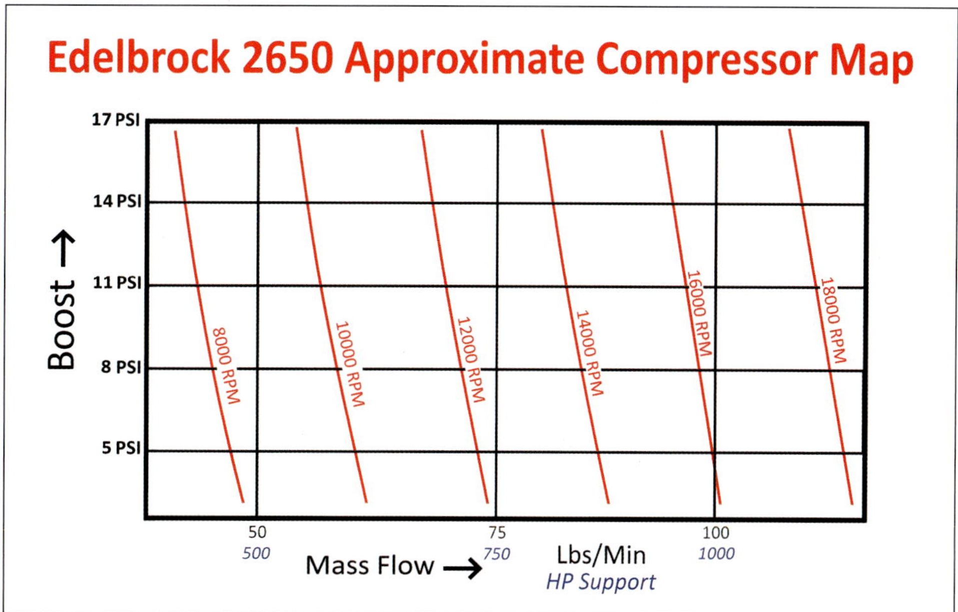

Image 12-49: Whenever possible, use a compressor map as a guide for forced-induction camshaft selection. Looking at this, we know the blower needs to be spinning more than 16,000 rpm to support 1,000 hp. This system should make 800-plus hp without much effort, and 1,200 hp will be very challenging.

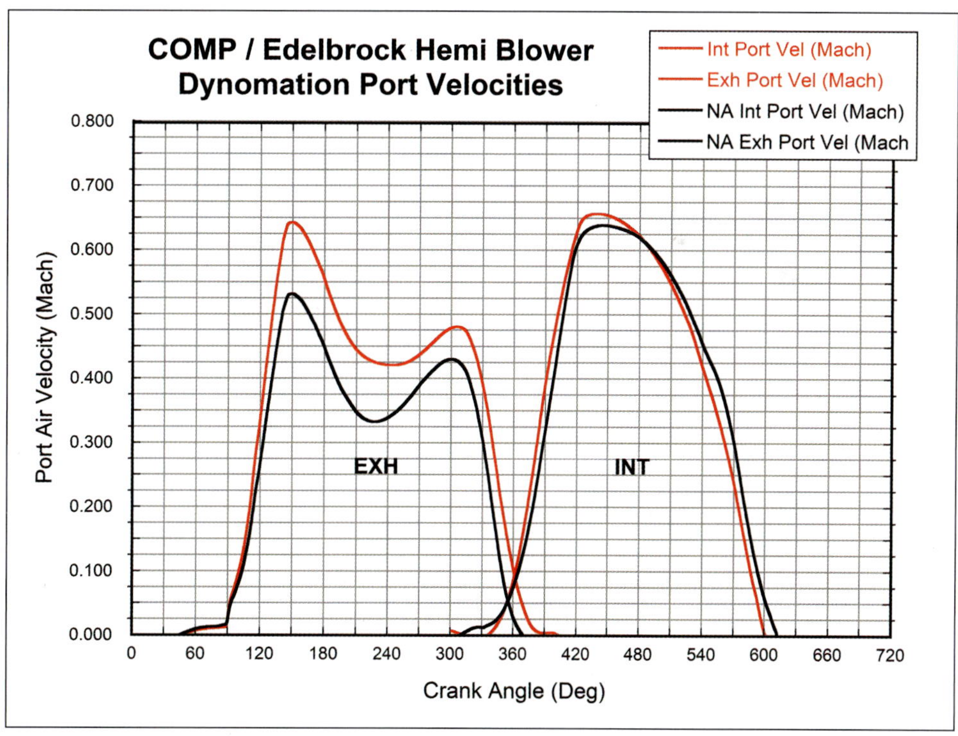

Image 12-50: We have mentioned forced induction port velocities, but here is the simulation of our 6.4L with and without boost if the same intake was used. Note how the intake port velocity jumps up early because the blower supplies plenty of encouragement but is lower on the closing side. On the exhaust side, we increased port velocity because of the additional mass. Fortunately, the Hemi has a great exhaust port.

Tailoring the Cam Design for this Supercharger

When looking at the compressor map for the Edelbrock 2650 Supercharger, it quickly becomes apparent it really likes to spin. There is an almost linear relationship between supercharger RPM and mass flow. Eventually, the internal inertial forces cause the rotors to expand and eat the case if it moves too far off the right end of this chart (Image 12-49). Regardless of the pulley you choose, from a very conservative 3.5-inch top pulley or the moonshot 2.625-inch pulley, the total airflow will keep increasing with RPM to set an important design constraint. It is difficult for customers to shift gears when the power climbs, which leaves us three options.

The first camshaft design technique to help this engine peak closer to 6,500 than 8,500 rpm and promote safer shift points is to delay the exhaust opening to choke the engine with exhaust-pumping losses at high speed. Thinking back to the first PV graphs, this means timing EVO so the bottom loop increases and turns the power curve downward at some reasonable RPM. This is the same technique we covered with the 427LS example with the early versus late EVO in a naturally aspirated application but applied to a boosted system. The effect is the same, but the onset is earlier when we double the power without increasing the exit door size (exhaust port).

To show this, I modeled the 6.4L with the blower in Dynomation 6, which allowed us to look behind the curtain at some engine characteristics that are difficult to measure. The simulated port velocities are shown in Image 12-50. Note the much higher exhaust port velocities even with a 3.25-inch top pulley and under 10 psi of boost pressure at 7,000 rpm. The exit door did not change, but now there is 785-plus hp instead of about 550 hp worth of exhaust mass to get out of the cylinder. I say 785-plus because there might be almost 100 hp of blower adsorption, along with additional exhaust pumping losses in this condition.

Unfortunately, the late EVO technique tends to reduce peak power, and the corresponding low-RPM torque improvement typically only shreds tires in supercharged applications.

I hate to think about the most common technique to make power roll past 6,500, but it needs to be mentioned. If very quick lobe designs are used, they are going to go out of control at an even earlier RPM with the blower, especially on the exhaust side. A valvetrain system that has some bounce at 6,500 without a blower will have more with the blower.

The cylinder-pressure log P versus log V simulation diagram for this engine with and without the blower using the same intake manifold is shown in Image 12-51. Note the 135 psi (9.2 bar) that the exhaust valve must push against, even with only a 3.2-inch pulley. With the 1.65-inch-diameter exhaust valve, this equates to almost 290 pounds to overcome, which increases the valvetrain deflection and effective opening lash.

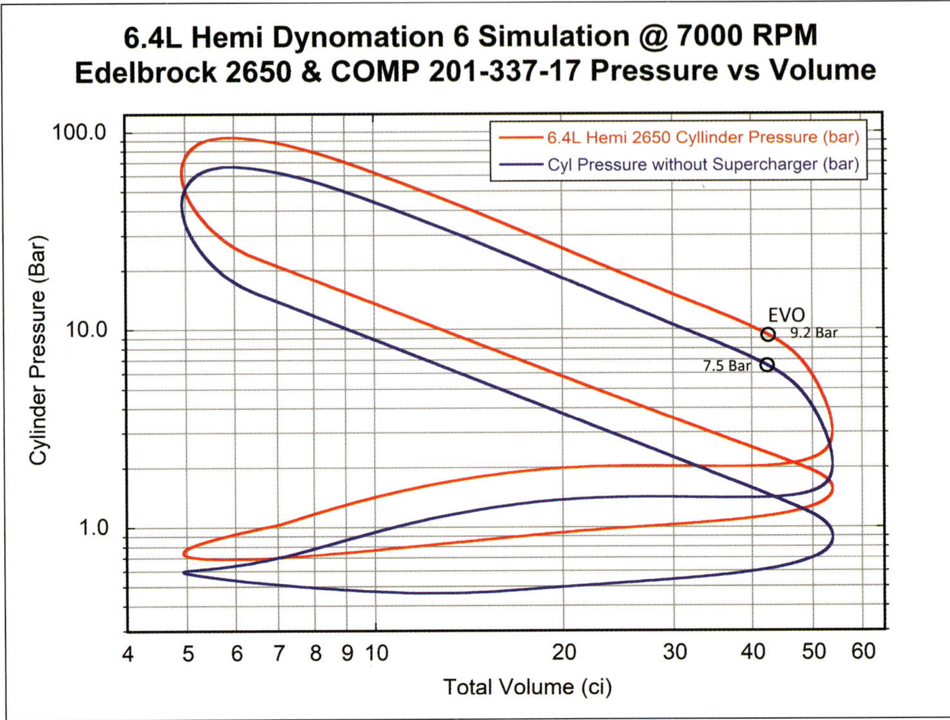

Image 12-51: I love looking at PV loops, simulated or real. We see here why a smoother exhaust profile is required. There is going to be more pressure against the exhaust valve face in the cylinder at EVO and very little pressure increase on the back side with a good header. Notice how the loops shift upward.

Image 12-52: The Hemi camshafts look great after our MSE superfinishing process.

The intake dynamics are generally not much worse as the pressure across the intake valve at IVO helps, and the pressure difference between the chamber and intake port at IVC should be close to zero if the valve closes at the correct angle. However, with greater power, added crank torsional vibration from firing will make its way through the timing system to the camshaft.

If the valvetrain system dynamics are not smooth, valve bounce will limit high-RPM power and force the curve to change directions. The

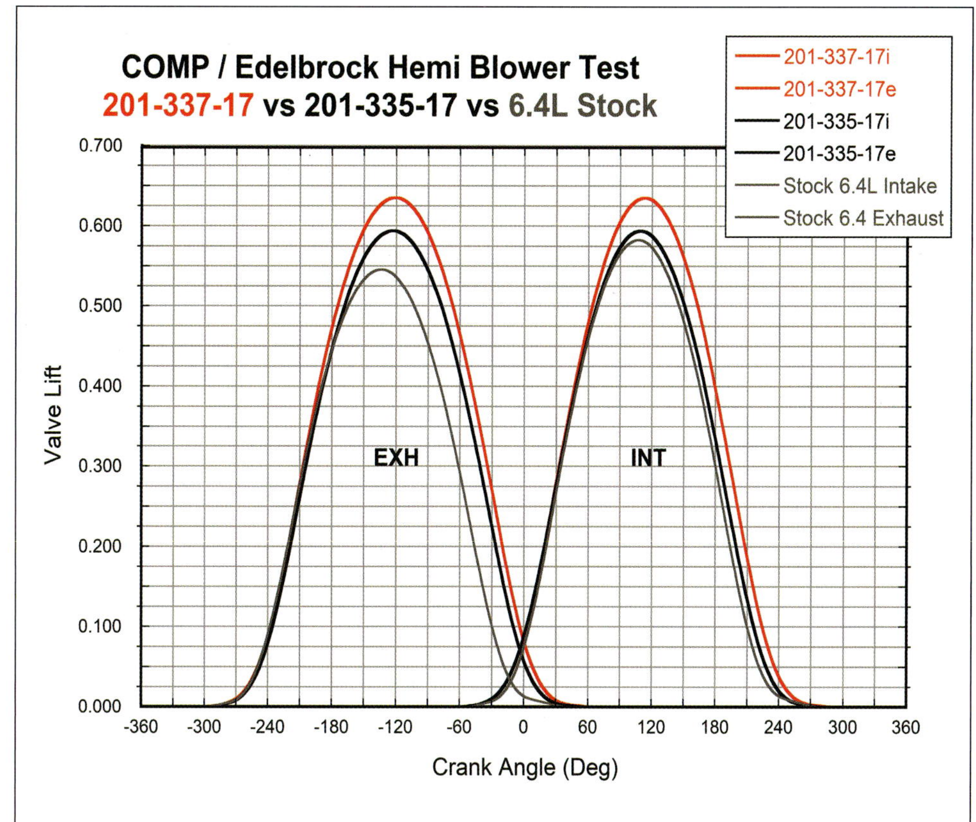

Image 12-53: This plot shows exactly what we are doing with valve timing on these blower grinds. We would love to open the intake valve even sooner, but there is a piston with a very small relief in the way. The 201-335-17 is optimized for a limiter, so we must be careful on the EVC. The 201-337-17 is better with the cam locked and can have a later EVC. IVC changes exactly like you would think based on RPM targets.

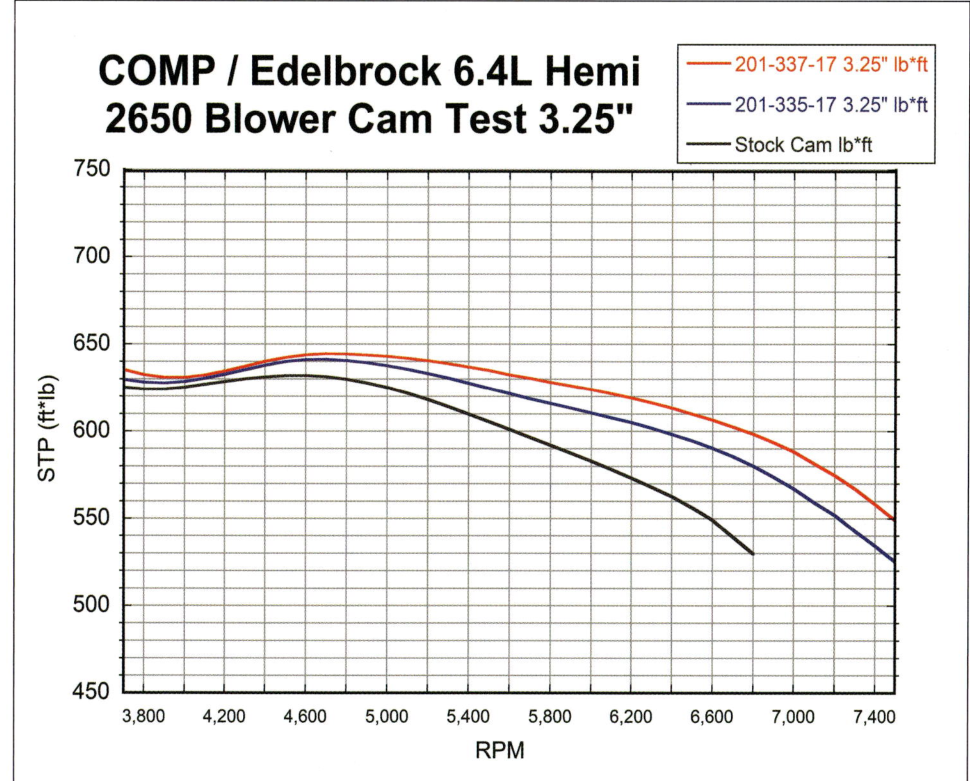

Image 12-54: The engine has increased torque everywhere over stock, with the biggest changes at high RPM.

resulting sounds might encourage the driver to shift or lift. However, this is the worst possible choice as bad dynamics will always lead to early engine failure.

The decision not to seriously limit the RPM much with EVO and not at all with bad dynamics means the only good solution is to develop a package that will run safely at high RPM. That is exactly what we did with the Comp 201-335-17 and 201-337-17 cam kits. The overlay of the 201-335-17 (black) and 201-337-17 (red) to the stock 6.4L Apache camshaft (gray) is shown in Image 12-53.

The factory Apache camshaft is one of the best factory performance cams around, but to get the increased exhaust flow out of the exhaust, it needs to open a bit earlier and close much later, as seen from the HBC-5 exhaust port velocity. To avoid exhaust piston-to-valve clearance issues with the later EVC, we specify running a VVT phaser limiter with the 201-335-17 and a phaser lock with the 201-337-17. The limiter reduces the sweep to 10 cam degrees max retard (20 crank) instead of the 25-plus degrees from the factory, while the lock fixes the camshaft in place, which is a very good spot for the larger 201-337-17.

On the intake, the factory piston clearance limit does not leave much room to move intake opening, which can be seen by the small difference among all three cams at 10 ATDC. This VVT system parks the camshaft at full advance, so we only limit how far it retards with a limiter or lock. However, this does not limit either max lift or the intake closing point.

The 201-335-17 is developed around our beehive 26918 spring package, and the higher-lift 201-337-17 is optimized for the higher lift, load, and rate 7230 conical spring kit. Other than the lift and exhaust closing, the biggest difference between the 335 and 337 grinds is the intake closing point. Knowing that the 337 is probably not going to swing back with the phaser at high RPM, we moved the IVC to where we want for peak power around 7,000 rpm. The blower does such a great job filling at low RPM that we do not lose downstairs with the larger camshaft (as shown in torque curves for the three cams with a 3.25-inch pulley at full advance in Image 12-54). I don't know why the bigger cam is a bit better below 4200, but it probably has something to do with more lift or the reduced resistance to flow with a larger cam that moves the boost down to a better sport on the efficiency map.

With any positive displacement supercharger, as the ports or camshaft are improved, the resistance to flow decreases. This results in more flow with less pressure at any RPM. We see that rather clearly with the 3.25-inch pulley on this system in the power curve of Image 12-55. Note the 201-335-17 dropped the boost by about 3.5 psi while the power increased about 65 hp. Going

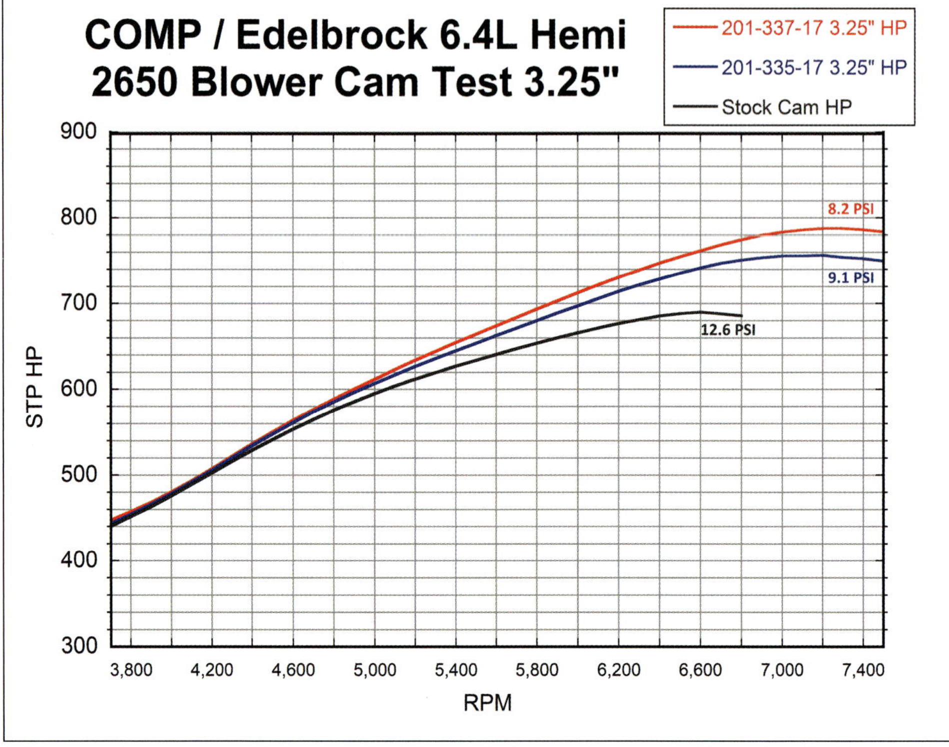

Image 12-55: The larger cam is worth 25-plus hp over the 335 and almost 100 hp over stock with the same pulley and no other changes. The best part is how boost drops with overlap. The big cam has about 30-percent less boost, but boost will trend with the restriction to flow with any positive-displacement blower. This means that it is easier to feed this Hemi with the big blower grind.

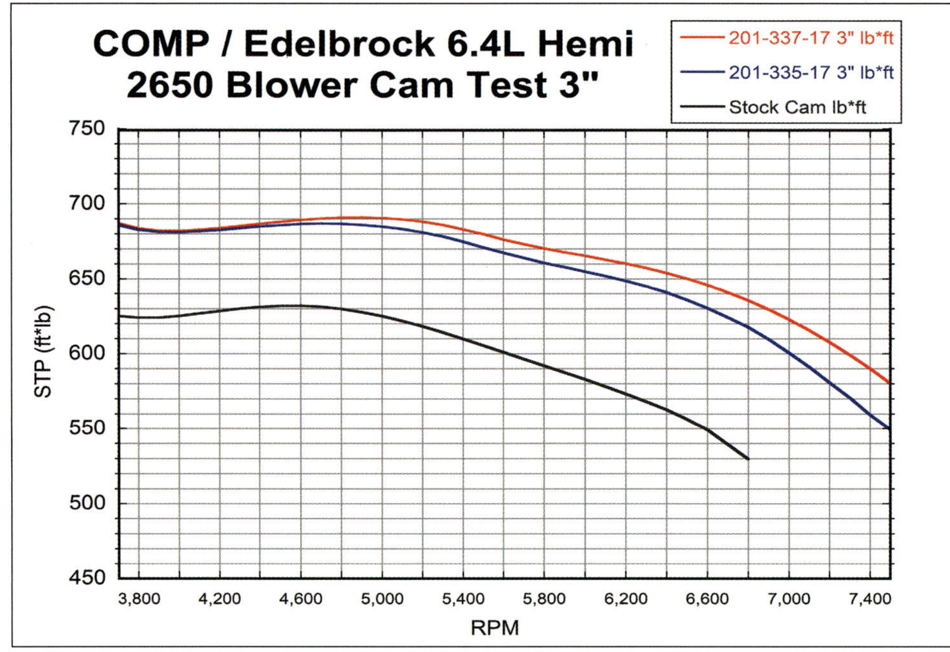

Image 12-56: What if we go to a smaller pulley to get closer to the OEM-cam 12-plus psi of boost? You are going to be shocked, but this Hemi likes a smaller pulley.

to the 201-337-17, the boost drops nearly another PSI and the power increases another 30 hp.

When we drop the pulley size down to 3 inches with the blower cams to bring the boost back up closer to where we were with the 3.25 inch and stock cam, we still see the same trends with the torque curve shapes but shifted upward. The power in Image 12-57 shows the larger 337 grind is now over 830 hp with less than 10 psi of boost, or 140-plus hp above the stock camshaft with 3 psi less maximum boost. I hope this helps you start to see boost more as the restriction to flow that the compressor must overcome instead of the magical secret to power.

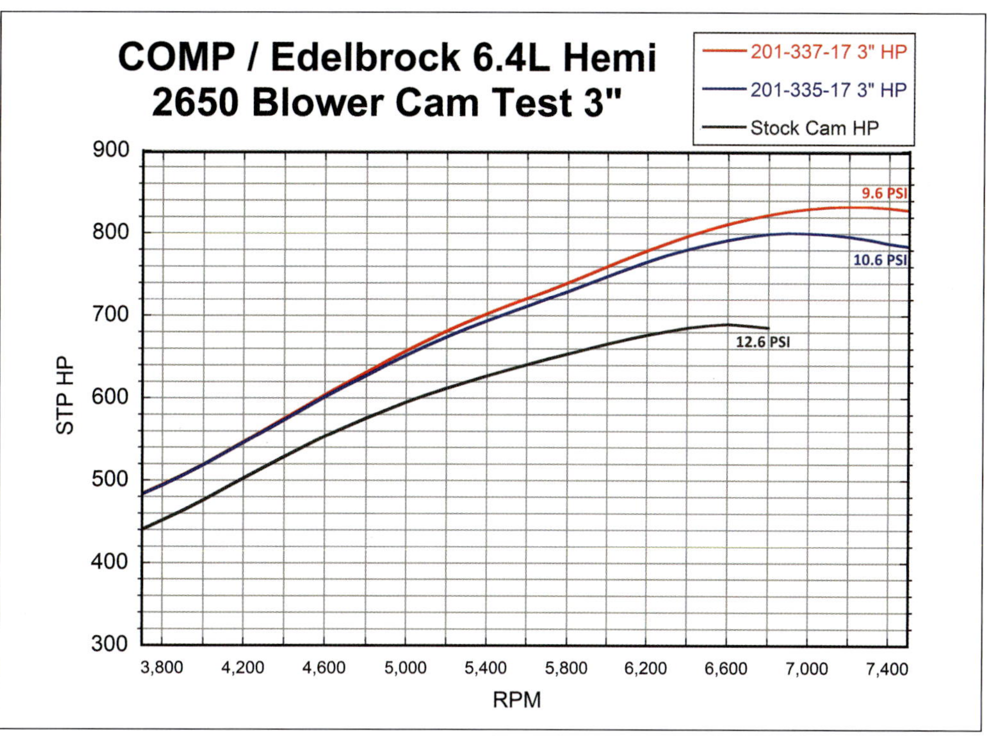

Image 12-57: We still are not near the original 12.6 psi, but we are up 140 hp with 3 psi fewer of boost.

Party Pulley Test

Before you start to think our engineering team is so mature that we would not throw the smallest available pulley on this blower along with race-blend E85 and big injectors, look at what this same engine did with a 2.625-inch top pulley (7.48-inch bottom) in Image 12-58. We ran out of fuel pump and blower speed before 7,200 rpm, but the valvetrain is amazingly stable, and that was absolutely the least dramatic 1,000-plus-hp dyno pull anyone could imagine. Regardless of the 800- or 1,000-hp setup, this 6.4L Hemi ran beautifully upstairs. Until you looked at the fuel flow and saw the power numbers, you would have thought this was a rather mild setup. You can run these in a daily driver on pump gas with the larger pulley.

What a great time to be a gearhead!

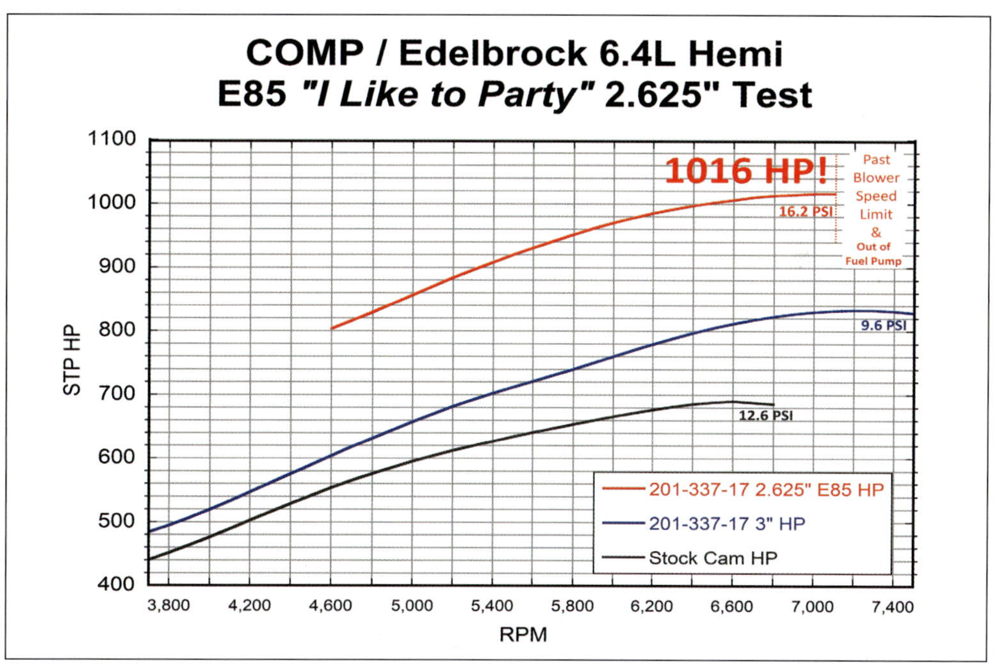

Image 12-58: That 3-inch pulley was awesome, but we were running out of time to get back to 12.6 psi of boost. However, we had a 2.625-inch pulley. It's time to switch to E85 and see how much power this engine, blower, and camshaft can put to the water brake with the party pulley. By 7,200 rpm, we were out of fuel flow, and the blower was at or past the maximum speed limit. However, we had broken into the four-digit power world with a very mild 6.4L camshaft and blower combination.

Glossary	
AFR	Air to fuel ratio
ATDC	After top dead center
BBDC	Before bottom dead center
BDC	Bottom dead center
BMEP	Brake mean effective pressure
BSFC	Brake-specific fuel consumption
BTDC	Before top dead center
CMM	Coordinate measuring machine
DOHC	Dual overhead camshaft
DLC	Diamond-like carbon
E/I	Exhaust to intake ratio
ECL	Exhaust centerline
ECU	Electronic control unit
EFI	Electronic fuel injection
EGT	Exhaust gas temperature
EOC	End of combustion
EVC	Exhaust valve closing
EVO	Exhaust valve opening
FEA	Finite element analysis
ICL	Intake centerline
IMEP	Indicated mean effective pressure
IPW	Injector pulse width
IVC	Intake valve closing
IVO	Intake valve opening
L/D	Lift to intake valve diameter
LSA	Lobe-separation angle
MSE	Mean squared error
MOI	Moment of inertia
OHC	Overhead camshaft
OHV	Overhead valve
PV	Pressure volume
SOC	Start of combustion
SOHC	Single overhead camshaft
TDC	Top dead center
VE	Volumetric efficiency
VTEC	Variable valve timing and lift electronic control
VVT	Variable valve timing